Texas vs. California

Texas vs. California

A History of Their Struggle for the Future of America

KENNETH P. MILLER

OXFORD
UNIVERSITY PRESS

OXFORD
UNIVERSITY PRESS

Oxford University Press is a department of the University of Oxford. It furthers
the University's objective of excellence in research, scholarship, and education
by publishing worldwide. Oxford is a registered trade mark of Oxford University
Press in the UK and certain other countries.

Published in the United States of America by Oxford University Press
198 Madison Avenue, New York, NY 10016, United States of America.

Library of Congress Cataloging-in-Publication Data
Names: Miller, Kenneth P. (Political scientist), author.
Title: Texas vs. California : a history of their struggle for the future of
America / [Kenneth P. Miller].
Description: New York, NY : Oxford University Press, [2020] |
Includes bibliographical references and index.
Identifiers: LCCN 2020006848 (print) | LCCN 2020006849 (ebook) |
ISBN 9780190077365 (hardback) | ISBN 9780190077372 (paperback) |
ISBN 9780190077396 (epub) | ISBN 9780190077402 (online)
Subjects: LCSH: Political culture—United States. |
Right and left (Political science)—United States. | Polarization (Social sciences)—United States. |
Comparative government. | Texas—Politics and government. |
California—Politics and government.
Classification: LCC JK4816 .M55 2007 (print) | LCC JK4816 (ebook) |
DDC 306.20973—dc23
LC record available at https://lccn.loc.gov/2020006848
LC ebook record available at https://lccn.loc.gov/2020006849

1 3 5 7 9 8 6 4 2

Paperback printed by LSC Communications, United States of America
Hardback printed by Bridgeport National Bindery, Inc., United States of America

To Kimberly June Miller,
who introduced me to Texas,
and
to Jenna June Miller,
a new Californian

Contents

Preface

I did not plan to write a preface for this book. Authors often use a preface to introduce readers to their book's themes or to place those themes in context. When considering whether to include one here, I knew that many readers already would be familiar with the partisan division between red and blue America and the rivalry between Texas and California. I thought we could dive in without any introduction.

But as I was finishing this manuscript in early 2020, the Coronavirus Disease 2019 (COVID-19) pandemic spread across the globe and reached the United States, carrying with it a grim threat to public health and to normal social and economic life.

Governors and local officials across the country sought to contain the virus by ordering people to stay home and businesses to close their doors. As everyday activities ground to a halt, markets tumbled and millions lost their jobs. To prevent a further collapse, the federal government sent trillions of dollars of relief to businesses, individuals, and state and local governments. As part of the shutdown, officials postponed elections and curtailed civil liberties.

It was unclear how long the health emergency would last, how far the economy would fall, how much the federal money would help, and how effectively the political system would adapt. Under almost any scenario, the pandemic's damage would be felt for years to come.

The weight of these events convinced me I should say a few words about how the themes in these pages speak to our new, uncertain future.

This book argues that understanding our past helps us see more clearly both our current situation and that which lies ahead. With this perspective, the book follows Texas and California from their origins to the present to explore how they have emerged as leaders of red and blue America, developed contrasting policy agendas, and competed within the federal system. The analysis culminates in the first two decades of the twenty-first century, when the nation more fully polarized and the two states honed their competing policy models.

During these years, and especially after the Great Recession of 2007–2009, both Texas and California flourished. As the book describes, they pursued radically different priorities and struggled with varying challenges, but both could boast successes, including growing economies and budget surpluses.

The Great Disruption of 2020 has closed that chapter. By abruptly halting the nation's longest-running economic expansion, the virus has forced Texas and

California—like all states—to adjust to deeply diminished circumstances. Both models now will undergo a severe stress test. How will each respond as demands for public services surge while tax revenues crater? What will their key industries do to recover from financial collapse? How will voters react to the crisis? And, finally, will the familiar pre-2020 features of American politics—the partisan polarization, red-blue state divide, and Texas-California rivalry—survive this disruption?

Previous crises offer contrasting analogies. In the early 1930s, the Great Depression instigated a massive political realignment that made Democrats the nation's majority party and ushered in fundamental policy changes. By comparison, however, the Great Recession of 2007–2009 helped elect Barack Obama to the White House, but had little lasting effect on the nation's partisan balance or policy direction.

In truth, the crisis of 2020 has no clear precedent. Although this disruption will undoubtedly change American society in many ways, at this writing no one can be certain whether it will fundamentally alter the nation's political or policy orientation.

Many have expressed hope that living through this emergency will cause Americans to "reset" and break free from their entrenched polarization. This book makes the case that we should all approach our differences with greater appreciation and respect for those on the other side, and I certainly hope this experience will spur more of us to do so. But it is probably unrealistic to expect that the pandemic will produce a new national consensus. It is more likely that the profound economic, cultural, and political differences discussed in this book will shape the national debate about how to move forward from this crisis. Similarly, we can expect Texas and California to continue to offer competing visions as they—and the nation as a whole—navigate the uncharted territory ahead.

In that sense, this entire book is a preface to the story of what comes next in the struggle for the nation's future.

K.P.M.
Claremont, California, May 2020

Acknowledgments

A confluence of life experiences inspired me to write this book. I am a native Californian, part of the fifth generation of my family to live in the Golden State. My ancestors were drawn to California by its world-class climate, natural beauty, and boundless opportunities; like they, I developed an abiding love for this special place. I also was drawn to its politics. I worked for a time in the state capitol and, later, made California politics my academic specialization.

My interest in Texas came later. About a decade ago, I met an extraordinary native Texan named Kimberly. When she and I married, I joined a family with deep roots in the Lone Star State. Her parents and entire family welcomed me with open arms and treated me like an honorary Texan. At the time, the rivalry between Texas and California was heating up. As I spent time in both states, I was struck by their similarities as well as their profound differences. The ideas for this book began to take form.

I already knew California well, but I needed to learn more about Texas. In 2017–2018, my college gave me a sabbatical leave, and Kim and I moved to Dallas for a year. I immersed myself in the state's history, culture, politics, and policy through extensive reading, travel, interviews, informal conversations, and close observation. I even tried to master the two-step. The more I learned about Texas, the deeper my appreciation grew. By the end of the year, I was confident I could write an informed comparison of the rivals.

Many people and institutions helped me along the way. I am grateful to them all.

Claremont McKenna College deserves many thanks. This remarkable college has long nurtured my academic career and its Rose Institute of State and Local Government provided crucial support for this book. I am especially indebted to my Rose Institute colleagues, Andy Busch, Bipasa Nadon, and Marionette Moore, for their friendship and practical help—especially for compensating for my absence during my year away.

During my Texas sabbatical, the John Goodwin Tower Center at Southern Methodist University welcomed me as a visiting fellow. Harold Stanley, Jim Hollifield, Luisa del Rosal, and Ray Rafidi created an excellent environment (including Harold's office) in which to work. Meanwhile, the Smith Richardson Foundation, through Senior Program Officer Mark Steinmeyer, offered timely funding and advice during the early stages of the project.

Several Claremont students did stellar work as research assistants. Special thanks to Wesley Whitaker, Adam Yang, Sophia Helland, Bruno Youn, Ben McAnally, Shivani Pandya, and Maya Ghosh. In addition, many people generously offered their time to answer my questions or read various drafts. Edward Miller, Mac Taylor, Tony Quinn, Deborah Gonzalez, Tony Gonzalez, Clark Lee, Dan Walters, Ben Key, Tom Luce, Ray Hunt, Hunter Hunt, Victor Liu, Alexandra Suich Bass, George Seay, Joe Straus, Daniel Hodge, Kathy Uradnik, Joe Bessette, Eric Helland, Jack Pitney, Shanna Rose, Andy Busch, Bob Klitgaard, Annalisa Zox-Weaver, and the anonymous reviewers for Oxford University Press were most helpful. All of them made the book better—of course, I alone am responsible for any errors of fact or interpretation.

Dave McBride, senior editor at Oxford University Press, also deserves much credit. Beginning with our first conversation, Dave expressed unwavering enthusiasm for the project, and he expertly guided the book through the review process to publication.

As noted earlier, my family in both California and Texas made this book possible. My parents, grandparents, and extended family in California instilled in me a love for the Golden State, and my relatives by marriage helped me understand the wonderful complexities of Texas. All of them have inspired me to explain in a faithful way the rivals' distinctive qualities. I am most indebted, by far, to Kim, who helped give life to this book at every stage from its inspiration to completion, through countless conversations and skilled edits. Most of all, when we welcomed a beautiful daughter into our family in the summer of 2019, she helped ensure that this big change in our lives wouldn't prevent me from finishing this work.

Finally, I want to give thanks for the two "siblings" that are the subject of this book, Texas and California. I am grateful for my relationship with these two amazing states, and for the chance to explore their compelling rivalry.

PART I
PATHS TO POLARIZATION

1

Sibling Rivals

For years, Americans have engaged in a struggle over the nation's identity and future direction. As the major parties have taken opposing social and economic positions, most conservatives have sided with the Republican Party and progressives with the Democrats. Over time, this sorting has followed familiar geographic patterns. On political maps, coastal and urban areas look more and more like sapphires surrounded by a rural, interior, crimson sea. Large blocs of states have become solidly right or left, Republican or Democrat, red or blue.[1]

Much has been written about this national polarization, one of the defining political developments of our day. This book offers a new perspective on the conflict by focusing on two of the leading protagonists—the states of Texas and California. These states provide an intriguing way to understand the nation's divisions, because they are, one might say, close siblings that became rivals. Siblings? Yes—because their similarities run so deep.[2] Texas and California have common origins, Sunbelt and borderlands geography, large and diverse populations, powerful economies, and even a history of overlapping political preferences. Yet, toward the end of the twentieth century, they moved in opposite directions and became locked in an ideological battle. California shifted left and embraced progressive Democratic politics while Texas moved right and pursued an aggressive Republican agenda. From opposite sides of the political divide, both transformed their ideologies into policy. As Texas advanced a conservative program of lean government, low taxes, light regulations, low labor costs, heavy development of natural resources, and traditional social policies, California promoted progressive goals on taxes, health care, labor relations, immigrant rights, the environment, social issues, and more. The two states also fought for their competing visions within the federal system. During the Obama years, Texas led red state opposition to progressive federal policies; the day after Donald Trump's election, California spearheaded the resistance to the new administration.

Elected officials in both states stoked the rivalry. Former Texas governor Rick Perry took special delight in the competition. He regularly skewered California's progressive policies and made repeated trips to the Golden State to lure its businesses to Texas. In one advertisement directed at California's business owners, he made a broad appeal: "Building a business is tough," he drawled, "but I hear building a business in California is next to impossible!" He said Texas offered a "zero state income tax, low overall tax burden, sensible regulations, and

Texas vs. California. Kenneth P. Miller, Oxford University Press (2020). © Oxford University Press.
DOI: 10.1093/oso/9780190077402.001.0001.

a fair legal system," which were "just the things to get your business moving—so come to Texas!"[3] Perry's successor, Greg Abbott, advanced the attack, denouncing the Golden State's social and economic policies and warning Texas against a creeping "California-ization." At a gathering of conservative activists, Abbott proclaimed:

> Here is the deal. Texas is the leader of the national movement for capitalism. California leads the race in the United States of America toward socialism. Californians generally think that government should run every detailed nuance of your life, all the way down to dictating what kind of straw you should drink from, and by God, it better not be a drink from Chick-fil-A. . . . California inevitably is going to fail with the policies it is pursuing.[4]

California's leaders responded by asserting their state's superiority. Former governor Jerry Brown called the anti-California rhetoric "another sorry example of the current state of Republican solipsism. The irony is that when they attack California, they attack the very engine of America's prosperity and leadership."[5] During his campaign for governor, Brown's successor, Gavin Newsom, agreed: "In so many ways, the world is looking to us. I wouldn't want to be anyplace else. Eat your heart out, Texas! California is a special place."[6]

The spirited Texas-California rivalry has captured the public imagination, and many politicians, journalists, and pundits have weighed in on the comparative merits of the two sides. Much of the commentary has been polemical, reflecting our era's polarized discourse.

This book seeks to treat the subject in a more open and balanced way, proposing answers to such questions as: What factors caused Texas and California to polarize—especially in light of their many apparent similarities? What have been the practical consequences of their polarization? How have the two states translated their contrasting ideologies into policy? What are the trade-offs of their respective approaches? How have they competed for dominance within the federal system? And, finally, what can be said about the future of these states and their competing visions—both for themselves and for the nation?

If for no other reason, the sheer size and power of the two states give these questions weight. By the mid-1990s, California and Texas ranked, respectively, first and second in state population. For most of American history, New York could boast that it was the nation's most populous state, but California (in 1962) and Texas (in 1994) passed it by.[7] By 2020, California's population had reached approximately forty million, or twice New York's twenty million. Meanwhile, Texas was adding population faster than any other state (far faster than California) and was approaching thirty million in 2020, putting it on pace to challenge California for the title later in the century. By 2020, seven of the nation's eleven largest cities were located either in Texas or California—that is, in order, Los Angeles, Houston, San Antonio, San Diego, Dallas, San Jose, and Austin—and one-fifth of all Americans resided in one of these two states.[8]

The two states had also become the nation's largest economic powers. Although New York retained great economic influence, California and Texas possessed the nation's leading economies as measured by state gross domestic product (GDP). If either state were an independent nation, its economy would rank in the top ten in the world. As of 2019, California's economy ranked fifth, trailing only the United States, China, Japan, and Germany, and ahead of India, the United Kingdom and France; Texas was ninth, behind Italy, but leading Brazil, Canada, and the Russian Federation.[9] The two states' large populations and economies also translated into political clout. Their congressional delegations wielded broad influence, and candidates from the two states frequently vied for the presidency, winning no fewer than eight times between 1964 and 2004. Although New York, Florida, and Illinois could also claim to be "mega-states," California and Texas had risen to the top tier.

Siblings

While these measures highlight the stakes of the Texas-California rivalry, other features of their sibling relationship add intrigue to the story. The resemblances are quite striking. Both Texas and California began their careers as provinces of Spain and Mexico; both were settled by westward-moving Americans during the period of Manifest Destiny; and both won statehood within a five-year span (Texas in 1845; California in 1850). Both have vast land masses (after Alaska, the second and third largest in the nation), yet are highly urbanized. Both states are located on the borderlands of Mexico and the American Sunbelt. Both have abundant natural resources. Both have attracted waves of immigrants from other states and abroad. And, on several measures, the two states have similar demographics. For years, Hispanics have made up a nearly identical, rising share of the population of both states—according to Census Bureau estimates, in 2019 they constituted 39.6 percent of the population in Texas and 39.3 percent in California. Likewise, both California and Texas ranked high on measures of population diversity. As of 2019, the "non-white" share of the population was 63.2 percent in California and 58.5 percent in Texas, making them two of only five majority-minority states.[10]

Moreover, before this age of polarization, the siblings politically overlapped. Surprisingly, Texas and California voted for the same ticket in thirteen of sixteen presidential elections between 1928 and 1988—six times for Democrats and seven times for Republicans.[11] Those results show that for years many citizens of both states voted in a bipartisan way. In Texas, this often meant voting for the Republican candidate for president and for Democrats in down-ballot races; ticket-splitting was common in California, as well. Back then, electoral politics in both states were more centrist, less ideological, and more closely aligned with each other than they are today.

Texas and California also used to share the center of the road on policy issues. Before Texas shifted to the right, its conservatism had a pragmatic streak. During the Great Depression, for example, the Lone Star State embraced several elements of the New Deal; and, from the 1960s through the 1980s, it was willing to increase taxes several times to meet rising spending obligations. Moreover, during the 1990s, Texas was friendly to immigrants who were not lawfully in the country, and as late as 2001 it adopted the Texas DREAM Act, which authorized in-state tuition and financial aid for undocumented immigrant students.[12] Similarly, before moving left, California maintained a balance of progressive and conservative policy choices. For example, the state was long known for assessing relatively high taxes, but in the 1970s it ushered in the national "taxpayer revolt." And, as late as the 1990s, California adopted a string of conservative policies that included the so-called Three-Strikes-and-You're-Out criminal sentencing law, restrictions on benefits for undocumented immigrants, and a prohibition on race-and gender-based affirmative action.[13]

Rivals

Turn-of-the-millennium partisan sorting caused both states to move from two-party competition to one-party dominance. For its part, California became a leader of the nation's progressive Democratic politics. In 1992, the state broke from its long tradition of supporting Republican presidential candidates and voted for the Democratic nominee, Bill Clinton. From that point forward, California consistently backed Democrats for president, with the margin widening over time. By 2016, the gap was so great that Hillary Clinton outpolled Donald Trump by nearly 4.3 million votes—the largest one-state raw popular vote margin in the history of American presidential elections.[14]

Expanding on their success in presidential contests, California Democrats incrementally established broader control over the state's politics. First, in 1992, they locked down the state's two U.S. Senate seats. In that "Year of the Woman," voters sent Democrats Dianne Feinstein and Barbara Boxer to the Senate, and no California Republican has won election to that body ever since. By the end of the 1990s, Democrats were consistently winning statewide offices, with the two-term governorship of Republican Arnold Schwarzenegger (2003–2011) as the main exception. When the "Governator" left office, Democrats established near-total hegemony over the state, increasing their popular vote margins in statewide elections and their seat totals in state legislative and congressional races.

In the 2018 election, California Democrats nearly ran the table. That year, they won a U.S. Senate seat, the governorship, all other statewide elected offices, super-majorities in both houses of the state legislature, and a stunning forty-five of fifty-three U.S. House seats, flipping six districts in some of the state's last remaining Republican areas. Republicans fielded no competitive candidate in most state-wide races and in many districts. Under the state's "top-two" primary system, the general election campaigns for many offices featured no Republican candidate at all, but rather a competition between two Democrats.[15] Arnold Schwarzenegger, the last Republican governor, complained in 2007 that the California Republican Party was "dying at the box office"; after the 2018 elections, others declared that the California GOP was officially dead.[16] Democrats had established near-total one-party control over the Golden State.

Meanwhile, near the turn of the millennium, Republicans gained the upper hand in Texas. The Texas GOP had endured one-party Democratic rule for much of the nineteenth and twentieth centuries. It showed its first signs of life in pres-idential contests. Dwight D. Eisenhower's victories in Texas in the 1950s dem-onstrated that Republicans could compete for the state's electoral votes, and the party's presidential candidates consistently did so, albeit often in losing causes, through the 1960s and 1970s. Texans narrowly supported Democrat Jimmy Carter for president in 1976, but voted for Ronald Reagan in 1980, and thus began an unbroken record of support for Republican presidential candidates, which would become one of the nation's longest such streaks (Figure 1.1).[17]

Republicans eventually dominated other elections in the state. Starting in 1993, they established long-term control over both of the state's U.S. Senate seats, and in 1994, when Republican George W. Bush defeated Democratic governor Ann Richards, they gained a firm grip on that office. Within the next decade, Republicans achieved a monopoly over statewide offices, winning all of them in 1998 and for decades thereafter. Finally, Republicans gained control of the state senate in 1996, the state house of representatives in 2002, and, after a mid-decade redistricting, a majority of the state's seats in the U.S. House of Representatives in 2004—thereby creating a political hegemony that would last for years.[18]

As Republicans asserted power, the Texas Democratic Party organization began to atrophy. Yet, Republicans never established complete one-party dom-inance because Democrats maintained a substantial presence in the state's major cities and along the border with Mexico. In 2018, energized by the U.S. Senate campaign of Congressman Beto O'Rourke and by opposition to President Trump, Democrats increased their vote in these areas, while also making inroads in some formerly Republican territory, especially the suburbs of the state's major cities. But even though Democrats picked up several victories in legislative races

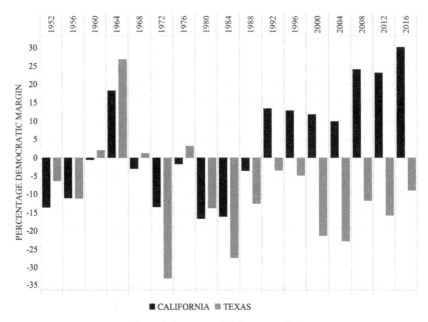

Figure 1.1. Vote in presidential elections, California and Texas, 1952–2016
Source: American Presidency Project

that year, they still failed to crack the GOP's overall control of Texas politics.[19] For the time being, Texas remained predominantly Republican and emphatically conservative.

Policy Rivals

It is easy to associate partisan polarization with policy gridlock because we are used to seeing the connection between the two in Washington, D.C. For decades, Republicans and Democrats have been evenly matched at the national level and have generally divided control over the federal government. Under those conditions, partisan polarization can cause policy gridlock because each side is able to thwart the other's ambitions, thus stalling the policy process. On the other hand, if one party is able to gain a decisive edge, polarization can actually facilitate policymaking. When one party controls all branches of government and maintains internal agreement, it can more easily assert its will. This dynamic now prevails in most states. By 2020, in more than two-thirds of state capitals, one party had gained control of the governor's office and both houses of the legislature—an achievement known as a "trifecta."[20] In those circumstances, the majority party has the opportunity to pursue policies that are consistent with its ideological preferences. Republicans first achieved a trifecta in Texas in the 2002 election; Democrats in California did so in the election of 2010. At that point, the dominant party in each state could implement its policy model without minority party interference.

In Texas, Republicans began carrying out an ambitious conservative agenda. They held the line on taxes, even in times of tight budgets; restricted the ability of local governments to raise taxes; rejected federal funding for Medicaid expansion and unemployment insurance (on the grounds that receiving federal money would obligate Texas to increase its own spending); enacted more stringent abortion regulations; cut funding for family planning services (partly to defund abortion providers); expanded the rights of gun owners, including the ability to "open carry"; provided new incentives for the development of oil and gas reserves; stepped up opposition to illegal immigration (in part by prohibiting local governments from declaring themselves sanctuary cities); and moved to preempt other progressive policy enactments by the state's local governments.

Conversely, as Democrats consolidated power in California, they pursued an ambitious, progressive agenda. They increased income tax rates on top earners to the highest levels in the nation (approved by voters in 2012 and 2016); raised the state minimum wage to $15 per hour (scheduled to take full effect in 2023); expanded other requirements on employers; established the nation's strictest standards to combat climate change; mandated the conversion of the state's power system to renewable energy sources; expanded health care coverage; provided a range of rights and benefits for undocumented immigrants (including establishing California as a sanctuary state); reduced sentences for criminal offenders; increased access to abortion; expanded LGBT rights; established new restrictions on gun ownership; and legalized recreational use of marijuana.

One could view these stark differences between the Texas and California policy models as the flowering of a healthy policy pluralism within the federal system. And, indeed, the two states' radically contrasting policy agendas seemed to represent U.S. Supreme Court justice Louis Brandeis's famous vision of a federal system in which "a single courageous State may, if its citizens choose, serve as a laboratory; and try novel social and economic experiments without risk to the rest of the country."[21] In the era of polarization, both Texas and California were "laboratories" conducting Brandeisian policy experiments. Texas was testing the limits of a conservative, low-tax, low-cost, business-friendly system of state government at a time when citizens increasingly expected an expanding menu of public services. And California was seeing how far it could go in establishing a high-tax, high-regulation, high-cost government in a federal system where people, businesses, and capital are mobile and can always exit to other states. By engaging in these experiments, Texas and California were providing a service to the rest of the nation by presenting evidence of the costs, benefits, and trade-offs of their radically different policy approaches.

On the other hand, the rivals could not—or, at least, did not—confine their experiments to the boundaries of their own states. Because they exist within a larger federal system, states lack full autonomy to implement their policy visions. State-level policies can be altered or even completely disrupted by other forces within that system, including federal prohibitions or mandates. One can easily see, for example, that Texas's commitment to low spending and low taxes could be disrupted at any time by a federal mandate that it increase its spending on health care programs; or that   California's desire to protect undocumented immigrants could be countered by more aggressive federal immigration policies.

As a consequence, both Texas and California believe they cannot afford to remain isolated in their laboratories; instead, they have strong incentives to control federal policy in a way that protects their models—even if that means interfering with their rival's preferred approach. In recent years, both states have joined blocs of like-minded states in efforts to control federal policy through federal litigation and other means. The battles between the red and blue state blocs for control of federal policy have been most intense in areas where their models are essentially incompatible. Under these circumstances, the laboratories could no longer remain as benign as Brandeis envisioned, but rather became war rooms for the competing sides.

The competition between these rivals raises the larger question of the long-term viability of each model. The nation's polarization persists because a strong case can be made for both the conservative and the progressive approaches to governance. Both sides possess strengths as well as weaknesses, and both present a wide range of trade-offs. It is hazardous to predict how the competition will resolve over the long run; nonetheless, a close study of the experience of the two states can help us assess the prospects for their models.

Plan of the Book

This book is organized around three central questions. Part I asks: Why did Texas and California divide despite their many similarities? In a series of chapters, this part compares the states' respective origins, demographics, economies, and cultures, and then provides accounts of their partisan polarization. Part II asks: How have the rivals transformed their competing visions into policy? This section of the book describes the operation of the governing coalitions in the two states and examines how they have approached five contentious policy areas—tax, labor, energy and environment, poverty, and social issues. Finally, Part III asks: What does the future hold for this rivalry? This concluding section offers broad assessments of each side's strengths, vulnerabilities, and future prospects.

In his "House Divided" speech of 1858, Abraham Lincoln famously said, "If we could first know where we are, and whither we are tending, we could better judge what to do, and how to do it."[22] At the time Lincoln spoke, the nation was more deeply divided than at any time before or since. In the early twenty-first century, the nation has entered a new era of sectional and ideological conflict and once again is seeking to answer the pressing questions of "what to do, and how to do it." This book offers no easy answers to these questions, but provides a distinctive perspective on our choices by looking in a new way at "where we are, and whither we are tending." Texas and California helped lead the nation into the era of polarization. Closely examining their rivalry—their political differences, their competing policy choices, and their possible trajectories—will help us understand where we may go from here.

2

Origins

In seeking to understand why Texas and California have become rivals, how much weight should we give to their origins? In *Democracy in America*, Alexis de Tocqueville argued that early experiences explain much. "The whole man is there, if one may put it so, in the cradle," Tocqueville wrote. "Something analogous happens with nations. Peoples always bear some marks of their origin. Circumstances of birth and growth affect all the rest of their careers."[1] If Tocqueville was right, origins matter greatly, and to understand the character of the two states, we would do well to consider their early formation.

California and Texas shared many circumstances of birth and growth. Both were remote colonial possessions of Spain and Mexico; both became targets of American westward expansion; and both gained statehood in the short span between 1845 and 1850.

On the other hand, from the first days of American settlement, the two states developed differently. Almost all the Americans who occupied Texas came from the South and brought with them southern culture, mores, economic models, and worldviews. These southern migrants, who became known as "Texians," mounted a revolution against Mexico, sustained an independent republic, and, critically, sided with their southern neighbors upon achieving statehood. By contrast, both before and after the California gold rush, a more diverse mix of people migrated to faraway California and established a cosmopolitan society on the Pacific Coast. Although its settlers included southerners, California was more aligned with New England and the rest of the North in matters of culture, economics, and politics, and it cast its lot with the North during the secession crisis. These circumstances set Texas and California on paths that ultimately led them to become the leaders of red and blue America. This chapter explores these origins.

Spanish and Mexican Ancestry

Texas and California share Hispanic ancestry—both were Spanish and Mexican before they became American. Spain laid claim to Texas in 1519 and to California in 1542, and, after a long delay, started settling Texas in the 1690s (with a permanent presence in 1716) and California in 1769.[2] In doing so, Spain asserted

Texas vs. California. Kenneth P. Miller, Oxford University Press (2020). © Oxford University Press.
DOI: 10.1093/oso/9780190077402.001.0001.

sovereignty over lands that for millennia had been home to indigenous peoples. In both Texas and California, the Spanish colonizers used their standard playbook: they established Catholic missions to convert the native population (nearly forty missions in Texas and twenty-one in California); built military fortresses called *presidios*; developed civilian towns known as *pueblos*; and awarded private land grants to create *ranchos*. The strategy ultimately failed. Too few priests, soldiers, and settlers occupied these territories to develop and defend them from hostile forces. In Texas, the Spanish faced persistent attacks from Native American tribes and were forced to abandon many missions and other settlements. In California, conditions were less violent, but the Spanish population remained similarly sparse. Historians estimate that, in 1820, Spanish Texans, or *Tejanos*, numbered as few as three thousand, mostly near San Antonio and Goliad, while only a few thousand Spanish Californians, or *Californios*, occupied the string of missions, presidios, pueblos, and ranchos along the Pacific Coast.[3]

When Mexico gained independence from Spain in 1821, the new government failed to secure these possessions. Under Mexican administration, Texas and California remained underpopulated, underdeveloped, poorly defended, and vulnerable to attack. The greatest threat came from Mexico's restive continental neighbor, the United States. Indeed, within just a few years, Americans would occupy and seize these lands.

The U.S. conquest of Mexico's northern frontier was probably inevitable, given the Americans' superior forces and voracious hunger for western lands. In 1803, the Louisiana Purchase extended the U.S. presence into the heart of the continent and opened vast territories to American settlers. By 1820, Americans were surging into Louisiana and Arkansas, and from there could easily cross the Sabine or Red Rivers into East Texas. Getting to the Pacific Coast was far more difficult, requiring months of travel either overland or by ocean voyage, but it, too, beckoned. Few Americans had entered Texas or California, but they were at the doors and would soon burst through.

American Conquest of Texas

Because Texas was closer, its conquest came first. In the last years of Spanish sovereignty, a small number of Americans crossed into Texas and squatted along the Red River and outside Nacogdoches.[4] Others, known as "filibusters," entered Texas between 1819 and 1821, with the aim of leading an insurrection against Spanish rule. Spanish troops thwarted those efforts, but Americans soon pursued a more effective plan by negotiating agreements to establish settlements.

In late 1820, the Spanish governor in San Antonio granted Moses Austin approval to bring American immigrants to Texas, with an initial quota of three hundred families. The government offered settlers large parcels of land at cheap prices and, for a time, tax-free—provided they accept the Catholic faith, pledge an oath of allegiance to Spain, forswear allegiance to any other country, and possess and maintain the land. Moses Austin soon died, but his son, Stephen F. Austin, stepped in and established a colony in East Texas between the Colorado and Brazos Rivers. After sovereignty shifted to Mexico in 1821, the younger Austin won approval to settle even more American immigrants.[5]

In ten years, Austin brought more than 1,500 families from the United States to Texas, making him Texas's most important American colonizer and earning him the title "The Father of Texas." But Austin was not alone—other "empresarios" secured colonization agreements from the Mexican government and provided additional Americans access to Texas lands. These settlers of the 1820s became "the heart of Anglo-Texas."[6] Critically, despite Mexican opposition, many of the Americans brought slaves with them, introducing to Texas chattel slavery and a slave-based agricultural economy.[7]

Why would Spanish and Mexican authorities invite Americans to establish colonies in Texas? Put simply, they had no good options. They knew Mexico's unsettled borderlands were vulnerable to attack, but they could not persuade enough Mexicans to move there. Instead, they hoped that the American settlers would form a protective buffer for Mexico, and, further, would Hispanicize— that is, renounce their loyalty to the United States, become citizens of their new country, and adopt Spanish language, culture, and religion. But of course this strategy ran the risk of hastening an American takeover. Writing in the 1830s, Tocqueville warned that "the inhabitants of the United States are perpetually migrating to Texas, where they purchase land; and although they conform to the laws of the country, they are gradually founding the empire of their own language and their own manners. The province of Texas is still part of the Mexican dominions, but it will soon contain no Mexicans; the same thing has occurred whenever the Anglo-Americans have come into contact with populations of a different origin."[8]

Indeed, American immigrants showed far less interest in becoming Mexican than in seizing economic opportunities while keeping their American way of life. Many were attracted by the prospect of buying land at a discount. Others came to escape debt, foreclosure, and even debtor's prison in the United States.[9] The waves of American settlers quickly brought fresh energy to Texas. As Texas historian T. R. Fehrenbach put it: "In a single decade, these people chopped more wood, cleared more land, broke more soil, raised more crops, had more children, and built more towns than the Spanish had in three hundred years."[10] By 1830, migration had expanded to the point that Americans outnumbered Tejanos. In response, the Mexican government tried to restrict American entry, but, as Tocqueville observed, the American invasion could not be stopped.[11] The flourishing Texians vowed to maintain their autonomy and to oppose Mexican interference in their communities.

In time, tensions between the American settlers and the Mexican government produced the Texas Revolution of 1835–1836. The dramatic events of that struggle—the signing of the Texas Declaration of Independence, the siege of the Alamo, the defeat of Santa Anna at San Jacinto, and the establishment of the Republic—took on legendary status and helped form the identity of future generations of Texans. Of all the states, Texas can claim an origin story closest to the American Revolution. In the same way Americans celebrate the events and heroes of the nation's war for independence, Texans mythologize the Alamo and San Jacinto, and the heroic figures Stephen F. Austin, Sam Houston, Davy Crockett, James Bowie, and William Barret Travis. This vivid history instills in many Texans a sense of identity and pride. Yet, it must be said that Texas's experience as an independent republic was mixed, marked by rapid growth but also by military insecurity, mounting debts, and other troubles. Eventually, in late 1845, Texas set aside its independence and joined the Union as the twenty-eighth state.

American Conquest of California

The American conquest of California took longer, mainly due to the Pacific Coast's greater distance from the rest of the United States. While emigration to Texas was relatively easy, California was almost forbiddingly difficult for Americans to reach during the first half of the nineteenth century. Making the trek across the continent (say, from Missouri) required travel by foot, horseback, or wagon for two thousand miles over the Great Plains, the Rocky Mountains, the Great Basin, and the Sierra Nevada (or to the south, across an unforgiving desert), often through territory occupied by hostile Native American tribes. Moreover, impassible snows blocked most land routes during the winter months. The other option was to make an ocean voyage from the East Coast. The distance from Boston down to Cape Horn and up the Pacific to California was approximately 17,000 miles, one of the longest commercial sea routes in the world. The arduous trip around the Horn often required six months to complete. Those seeking to shorten the voyage could make a land passage across Panama or Nicaragua, but the shortcuts through swamps and jungles presented the risk of yellow fever, cholera, malaria, and other diseases. It is unsurprising, then, that during these years, fewer Americans migrated to California than to Texas.

The earliest American visitors to California came from New England by sea, with the first American ship, the *Otter*, arriving in Monterey in 1796. Twenty years later, in 1816, a Boston carpenter and an African American seaman became California's first American residents when they jumped ship and settled in Monterey. During the 1820s and 1830s, more American vessels set anchor in California. A small number of passengers stayed, including the Massachusetts-born merchant Thomas Larkin, who later became American counsel to Mexican California. In 1826, Jedidiah Smith became the first American to cross the continent to California, leading an expedition of fur trappers through the desert Southwest into Southern California. Smith returned east the following year in the first American crossing of the Sierra Nevada. Soon, other mountain men and trappers, including Kentucky-born Kit Carson, began to enter California, expanding the American presence from New England merchants to rougher characters from places like Kentucky, the Carolinas, Tennessee, and Missouri.[12]

Many early American visitors considered the *Californios* unworthy of a land with such boundless potential, and they dreamed of a future in which the United States controlled the province.[13] In 1835, for example, a young Harvard student named Richard Henry Dana Jr. wrote a classic account of his voyage around the Horn and his time in California. In *Two Years before the Mast*, Dana extolled California as "a country embracing four or five hundred miles of seacoast, with several good harbors; with fine forests in the north; the waters filled with fish, and the plains covered with thousands of herds of cattle; blessed with a climate than which there can be no better in the world; free from all manner of diseases, whether epidemic or endemic; and soil from which corn yields from seventy to eighty fold."[14] But this New England visitor also thought the land was sadly mismanaged and underdeveloped under Mexican rule. He imagined that "in the hands of an enterprising people, what a country this might be."[15]

Mexican officials in California were naturally wary of the growing American presence. They tolerated some visitors but arrested others (including Jedidiah Smith) and ordered them to leave. In 1841, Governor Juan Bautista Alvarado granted Swiss immigrant John Augustus Sutter a large tract in the Central Valley on the condition that he reside in California for a year and become a Mexican citizen. Sutter met the requirements and established a settlement around Sutter's Fort in present-day Sacramento. The Mexican authorities vainly hoped that this settlement would provide protection against attacks. In reality, Sutter's Fort became a point of destination for Americans migrating to California, some of whom would later stage a revolt against Mexican rule.[16]

During these years, the American population of California remained small, but the pace of immigration was accelerating and Americans were gaining a critical mass to challenge the Mexican government. In June 1846, a group of American settlers launched an uprising known as the "Bear Flag Revolt." Within days, they arrested a prominent Mexican leader, General Mariano Guadalupe Vallejo, secured the town of Sonoma, and declared California to be an independent republic. They raised the republic's flag, emblazoned with a bear, over the plaza in Sonoma. California's governor, Pio Pico, condemned the rebels, and Mexican forces engaged them in a series of small but lethal skirmishes.

At first, the Bear Flag Revolt seemed to follow the Texas model—a popular uprising against the Mexican government, driven by the hope of independence and, perhaps, U.S. annexation. Instead, the uprising was overtaken by larger events. In July 1846, American forces arrived in Monterey with news that the United States had declared war on Mexico, and the Bear Flaggers quickly pivoted to support the U.S. military effort.[17] The Mexican-American War would soon separate California from Mexico and make possible its rapid transition to statehood.

Mexican-American War

American hunger for western lands precipitated the war. Waving the banner of "Manifest Destiny," President James K. Polk called for annexation of Texas and acquisition of other territories in the West. Mexico loathed the thought of Texas independence but, even more, its annexation by the United States. Tensions between the two countries mounted when Congress approved statehood for Texas in late 1845. In April 1846, American and Mexican troops converged in territory claimed by both Texas and Mexico. A skirmish ensued, resulting in the deaths of American soldiers. President Polk quickly called for war against Mexico, and Congress concurred, issuing a declaration of war on May 13, 1846.[18]

In California, the Mexican-American War involved six months of intermittent military conflict in places such as San Pascual (near San Diego) and San Gabriel (near Los Angeles). In January 1847, Mexican forces surrendered to American captain John C. Frémont in Southern California in what is known as the Capitulation of Cahuenga. The surrender completed the American conquest of California.[19] The broader war with Mexico was largely settled later in the year, when American forces occupied Mexico City. On February 2, 1848, the United States and Mexico formalized the end of hostilities by signing the Treaty of Guadalupe Hidalgo. Through that treaty, Mexico recognized Texas as a U.S. state, agreed to the Rio Grande as the border between Mexico and Texas, and ceded sovereignty over the rest of its northern territories, including Alta California and what would become all or part of the states of Nevada, Utah, Arizona, New Mexico, Colorado, and Wyoming. The territorial cession was approximately 525,000 square miles in all—nearly half of the Mexican nation. Mexico refused to cede Baja California to the United States, however, fearing an American presence on its western, as well as northern, border. In exchange for these vast territories, the United States paid Mexico $15 million and agreed to settle claims by U.S. citizens against the Mexican government.[20]

Although the American conquest of Texas, California, and the rest of the American Southwest was sealed by the war, the history of Spanish and Mexican sovereignty left deep cultural marks on these borderlands. Texas and California quickly integrated into the United States, but they would never fully lose their Hispanic identity—an identity that would powerfully revive in both states in the years to come.

The Rush for Gold

On January 24, 1848—just days before Mexico officially ceded California to the United States—one of John Sutter's men, James Marshall, saw the glint of gold in the American River, not far from Sutter's Sacramento settlement. News of the discovery produced the largest gold rush in history. California quickly transformed from a remote, sparsely populated outpost into what it would long remain—one of the world's most powerful magnets for aspiring newcomers. Wealth-seekers made the arduous journey to California from all corners of the United States, as well as from South America, Europe, and Asia. The gold rush eventually drew more than 300,000 migrants between 1848 and 1854, with most clustering in San Francisco, Sacramento, and the gold fields of the Sierra foothills.

Contemporary observers described the California gold rush in epic terms. In early 1850, Karl Marx and Frederick Engels wrote that the discovery of gold in California promised to change not only the state, but the entire world. They argued that the "torrents" of gold pouring over America and the Pacific Coast of Asia were drawing new people into international trade and commerce in a way that would have lasting, civilizing effects. Moreover, these events were shifting the geographic patterns of world trade. For more than three centuries, all trade from Europe to the Pacific Ocean had been conducted with a "touching, long-suffering patience around the Cape of Good Hope or Cape Horn," and proposals to establish a safe trade route through the Isthmus of Panama had "all had come to grief." But now, merely eighteen months after the discovery of gold in California, "the Yankees have already set about building a railway, a great over-land road and a canal from the Gulf of Mexico, Pacific trade is already concentrating in Panama, and the journey around Cape Horn has become obsolete." The trade capitals of the world had shifted several times through history—from Tyre, Carthage, and Alexandria in antiquity, to Italy in the Middle Ages, and then to England. Now, Marx and Engels argued, the center of international trade would shift to the Americas—to New York, Panama, and San Francisco. Finally, they saw that the gold rush was creating in California a wealthy and diverse new civilization, unique in human history: "A coastline which stretches across thirty degrees of latitude, one of the most beautiful and fertile in the world and hitherto more or less unpopulated, is now being visibly transformed into a rich, civilized land thickly populated by men of all races, from the Yankee to the Chinese, from the Negro to the Indian and Malay, from the Creole and Mestizo to the European."[21]

These developments—the discovery of gold, the surge of population, the concentration of new wealth, the establishment of new trade routes, and the attention of the world—gave California confidence to seek rapid admission to the Union, which it achieved on September 9, 1850. Even more, the gold rush sealed California's belief in its own exceptionalism—the conviction that it is the most favored place on the face of the earth.

Texas's Southern Identity

When Spain and Mexico opened Texas to American immigration, most of the new arrivals came from the Trans-Appalachian South—Louisiana, Alabama, Arkansas, Tennessee, and Missouri—and nearly all settled in the eastern part of Texas. The warm, wet East Texas climate lent itself to a southern agricultural economy dominated by cotton. At the time, cotton was king—the most profitable commodity in the Americas. In Stephen Austin's view, cotton was critical to developing Texas, even though growing it required slaves.[22] The introduction of slavery on a large scale tied Texas economically, culturally, and politically to the Old South. The original Austin Colony consisted of 1,347 whites and 443 slaves.[23] Over time, more southern whites and African American slaves poured into Texas.[24] By 1850, the overall population of Texas had climbed to 212,592, including 58,161 slaves, or 27.4 percent of the total population. By 1860, the eve of the Civil War, Texas's population had surged to 604,215. The slave population had grown even faster, to 182,566, or 30.2 percent (Table 2.1). Most Texans, especially slaves, remained concentrated in the southeastern portion of the state (Figure 2.1).

Texas would pay a steep price for embracing slavery. One early cost was northern resistance to annexation. Soon after Texas won independence from Mexico, most Texans, including its first president, Sam Houston, hoped the new Lone Star Republic would quickly become part of the Union. In Washington, D.C., however, the question of Texas annexation became engulfed in the national conflict over slavery. During these years, many southerners hoped to expand slavery into the West, while many in the North wanted to contain it to its existing geographic limits. The admission of Texas would massively expand the slave-owning portions of the United States and tilt the nation's political balance to the South. Moreover, many feared that annexing Texas would lead to war with Mexico. Southern sympathizers, including President John Tyler, supported

Table 2.1 1860 Census Total Population and Slave Population for Seceding States

State	Total Population	Slave Population	Percentage Slave Population
Virginia*	1,596,260	534,239	33.5
Tennessee	1,109,801	275,719	24.8
Georgia	1,057,286	462,198	43.7
North Carolina	992,622	331,059	33.4
Alabama	964,201	435,080	45.1
Mississippi	791,305	436,631	55.2
Louisiana	708,002	331,726	46.9
South Carolina	703,708	402,406	57.2
Texas	604,215	182,566	30.2
Arkansas	435,450	111,115	25.5
Florida	140,424	61,745	44.0

*Includes portion of the state that became West Virginia
Source: U.S. Census Bureau

annexation, while many northerners, including New Englander John Quincy Adams and other prominent abolitionists and northern Whigs, resisted.[25]

The question came to a head in 1844, when President Tyler negotiated an annexation treaty with Texas but the Senate rejected the deal. The treaty's defeat thrust the Texas question to the center of the 1844 U.S. presidential election. Democrats nominated Polk, the advocate of Manifest Destiny and Texas annexation, while Whigs nominated Henry Clay, who opposed annexation. When Polk defeated Clay, Tyler claimed a mandate for his Texas policy. He brought the issue back to Congress, this time in the form of a joint resolution to annex the Republic of Texas as a state. In early 1845, the Whig-controlled Senate narrowly approved the resolution, 27 to 25, with all Democrats and enough southern Whigs voting in the affirmative. The Democratic House concurred.[26]

In May 1845, a desperate Mexico offered to recognize Texas's independence, so long as it remained a separate republic and did not join the United States. The Texas Senate rejected Mexico's final bid and both houses unanimously approved the U.S. offer of annexation and statehood.[27] On July 4, a convention gathered in Austin and began work on the Texas statehood constitution. Almost all of the 57 delegates were natives of the South, including eighteen from Tennessee, eight from Virginia, seven from Georgia, six from Kentucky,

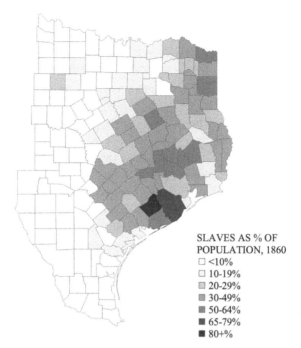

Figure 2.1. Slaves as a percentage of the Texas population, 1860

Note: Map uses current county boundaries, some of which have been modified since 1860.

Source: University of Texas, Austin, *Atlas of Texas* (1976)

and five from North Carolina. The only Texas-born delegate was José Antonio Navarro of San Antonio.[28] The convention drew from several models, including the constitutions of the Texas Republic and southern states, especially Louisiana. Like those models, it explicitly protected the institution of slavery.[29] In late 1845, Texas voters approved annexation and the statehood constitution. Congress concurred, and President Polk signed the Texas Admission Act on December 29, 1845. In a ceremony on February 19, 1846, the Republic's last president, Anson Jones, delivered a valedictory address. "The Lone Star of Texas, which ten years since arose amid clouds, over fields of carnage" was now "fixed forever in that glorious constellation" of the American Union. "The final act in this great drama is now performed," he concluded. "The Republic of Texas is no more."[30]

The 1845 agreement between Texas and the United States had several distinctive features. First, Texas retained ownership of its expansive public lands. This provision was noteworthy because the federal government normally retained ownership of a new state's public lands—and, indeed, it continues to own large tracts in many western states today. On the other hand, the federal government did not assume the Republic's substantial public debts. The agreement also left

Texas's geographic boundaries unsettled. In 1845, Texas claimed one-third more land than it possesses today, including some lands that extended north of 36° 30′ latitude, known at the time as the Missouri Compromise Line. Congress decided to reserve the boundary question for a later date. Finally, the resolution provided that Texas could later divide itself into as many as five states, pursuant to congressional approval.[31]

The settlement of the state's boundaries required five more years and several intervening events. The Mexican War (1846–1848) and the Treaty of Guadalupe Hidalgo (1848) fixed the Rio Grande as the state's border with Mexico. Thereafter, the Compromise of 1850 resolved the other boundary issues by requiring Texas to cede to the United States one-third of its claimed territory, including all lands above 36° 30′ and its far western lands. In exchange, the federal government agreed to pay Texas $10 million to relieve the state's debts.[32]

The annexation and statehood controversies further bonded the Lone Star State to the South, and it sided with its southern neighbors in the sectional tensions of the 1850s and the secession crisis of 1860–1861. To be sure, not all Texans supported secession. The state was home to many unionists, prominently including German immigrants in the Hill Country. Moreover, its leading citizen, Sam Houston, was a staunch defender of the Union and did all he could to prevent Texas from exiting. By the mid-1850s, Houston had predicted a grim fate if the "clamor for secession" prevailed: "Alas! I see my beloved South go down in the unequal contest, in a sea of blood and smoking ruin."[33] In early 1861, however, fire-eaters forced the question and Texas voters supported a secession referendum by a 46,153 to 14,747 margin. The effective date was March 2, 1861, the twenty-fifth anniversary of Texas independence. Governor Houston argued that if Texas must secede, it should reestablish itself as an independent republic. The Secession Convention rejected that view. It voted to join the Confederate States of America and required officeholders to swear an oath of allegiance to the Confederacy. Houston refused and was replaced in office.[34]

Texas's decision to cast its lot with the Confederacy committed it to the southern side in the Civil War. Although the war inflicted less destruction on Texas than on some other parts of the South, the state suffered thousands of casualties as well as deep economic losses. Thereafter, the state experienced nearly a decade of federal occupation and Reconstruction. Newly freed slaves benefited from the federal presence, but many Anglo Texans, like whites in other states, resisted Reconstruction. In 1866, the state legislature rejected ratification of the Fourteenth Amendment and enacted laws known as black codes, which restricted the freedoms of African Americans. In 1869, bowing to increased federal pressure, the state adopted a Reconstruction constitution and elected the radical Republican E. J. Davis as governor. In 1870, to satisfy a condition for readmission to the Union, the Texas legislature ratified the Thirteenth, Fourteenth, and Fifteenth Amendments. Governor Davis, meanwhile, advanced the Reconstruction project by pursuing an ambitious reform agenda. Many Anglo Texans responded by hardening their opposition to Republicans, Reconstruction, and activist government.

By the mid-1870s, federal enthusiasm for Reconstruction waned and Texas Democrats reasserted control over the state. They ousted Davis in 1874 and, in 1876, adopted a new "redeemer" constitution that repealed Reconstruction policies and placed new limits on state government powers.[35] Despite the upheavals of Civil War and Reconstruction, in many ways Texas remained the same in the mid-1870s as it was in 1860—a geographically vast, culturally southern, independent-minded, rural society with a traditional racial caste system, sitting at the intersection of the Old South, Mexico, and the western frontier.

California's Northern Identity

Unlike Texas, with its clearly defined southern demographics, California was formed by a diverse mix of newcomers from around the world. Northern migrants were more numerous, but southerners were politically active, and thus California's sectional loyalties were unsettled. Soon after the Mexican War ended, California statehood became a topic of intense interest, and the discovery of gold added a sense of urgency. Congress's polarization over slavery and its competing visions of California's future complicated the question. At the time, the Union consisted of fifteen free states and fifteen slave states; admitting California as a free state would tip the balance. While most northerners advocated the early admission of California as a free state, many southerners resisted. As historian Hubert Howe Bancroft noted: "The question of the admission of California had become the chief topic in Congress; and whenever the word 'California' was pronounced close after came the word 'slavery.' All through 1849, the subject of providing a government for California was discussed, and at every point it was met by objections originating in a fear of disturbing the balance of power in the Senate to the prejudice of slavery."[36]

California residents complained that indecision in Washington prevented them from establishing a legitimate government. In mid-1849, they persuaded the military governor, Bennet C. Riley, to allow them to call a constitutional convention. In August 1849, voters selected a diverse group of forty-eight delegates. Twenty-two had emigrated from the northern states; fifteen from southern and border slave states; four were foreign-born; and seven were native *Californios*.[37] When the delegates gathered in Monterey in September 1849, they understood that the weight of public opinion opposed slavery in the new state, and all of them, including those from the South, agreed to a ban.[38] The slavery issue resurfaced, however, in the debate over California's boundaries. Some southern sympathizers hoped to divide California in two at the 36° 30' line. Under that plan, Northern California would be admitted as a free state, but Southern California would be admitted with no restriction on slavery. Others wanted to extend California's borders far to the east beyond the Sierra Nevada, to include some or all of the lands acquired in the Mexican War, on the premise that those regions could later be divided into additional states, with some becoming slave states. In the end, the convention rejected these ideas, drew the boundaries of the state as they exist today, and applied for admission as a free state.[39]

The congressional debate over California's admission was long and contentious, with many southerners angrily protesting against it.[40] In the end, Congress approved California's admission as the nation's thirty-first state as part of the broader Compromise of 1850.[41] In the Senate, the vote was 34–18, with the no votes coming from southern members. The House concurred, 150–56, will all opposition again coming from the South. After the Senate voted approval, ten southern senators signed a protest resolution and several sought, without success, to block the swearing-in of the new delegation from California.[42]

The debates over statehood, in both California and Washington, D.C., helped secure California's identity as a northern state in the lead-up to the Civil War. However, Californians themselves remained divided in their sectional sympathies. As newcomers flooded into the state from both regions, many brought with them their old allegiances. The division in public opinion found expression in the state's politics. During the late 1850s, the state's two U.S. senators were bitter rivals who took opposite sides on the North-South conflict. Senator David Broderick (a former New Yorker) fiercely opposed slavery, while Senator William Gwin (a native of Tennessee who owned a plantation in Mississippi) was the leader of the state's "Chivalry," or southern Democrats, and supported slavery and the South.[43] The national North-South divide was reflected in the Golden State's political geography. During the 1850s, most residents of sparsely populated Southern California aligned with the South and agitated to allow Southern California to separate from the rest of the state, become a territory, and then, later, a slave state. In 1859, the legislature passed, and voters in Southern California approved, the Pico Act, which would have authorized such a North-South division—a project that was superseded by the Civil War.[44]

As the secession crisis neared, the growing tensions produced a clash between Senator Broderick and the chief justice of the state supreme court, David S. Terry. During the 1850s, Terry had emerged as one of California's most prominent defenders of the South and the institution of slavery. A Kentucky native who moved to Austin's colony in the 1830s, Terry fought in the Battle of San Jacinto and the Mexican American War, and often brandished a Bowie knife. He emigrated to California during the gold rush, was elected a justice of the California Supreme Court in 1855, and became chief justice in 1857. In 1859, the California Democratic Party denied Terry renomination to the court due to divisions between its pro- and anti-slavery factions. Terry blamed Broderick, the state's leading free-soil Democrat and, after an exchange of insults, challenged him to a duel. On September 13, 1859, Terry shot and killed Broderick in "the interview at Lake Merced" outside of San Francisco.[45] Broderick was venerated in California as a martyr in the fight against slavery; his death mobilized anti-slavery sentiment in the state, with many viewing Terry and other southern sympathizers as assassins.[46]

In addition to Broderick, many of California's most prominent northern-born leaders, including the Unitarian minister Thomas Starr King and the lawyer-politician Edward Baker, advanced the case for the Union.[47] Their public advocacy helped build support for Abraham Lincoln in the presidential election of 1860. In a four-way contest, Lincoln won California's electoral votes by a thin margin—734 votes of nearly 120,000 cast, with most of his support coming from San Francisco and the surrounding region.[48] Following that momentous election, some Californians persisted in pro-Confederate activities, but the state as a whole remained loyal to the Union throughout the secession crisis and Civil War. California contributed to the federal defense of the West Coast, sent troops to New Mexico to block Confederate incursions from Texas into that territory, shipped other soldiers to the east to fight alongside northern regiments, and, significantly, helped finance the Union war effort with millions of dollars in gold.[49]

After the Civil War, California was poised for further growth and development, but remained limited by its geographic isolation from the rest of the United States. Its prospects were transformed by the completion of the Transcontinental Railroad in 1869. During the 1850s, sectional rivalry had prevented Congress from approving legislation for the project. Both North and South saw the importance of establishing a direct rail connection to the Pacific, but they sharply divided on what route it should take. Southern states wanted the railroad to cross the Southwest to Southern California. One proposal would have built the line from Texas's western border at El Paso across the New Mexico and Arizona Territories to San Diego. The northern states demanded either a central or northern route to Sacramento and San Francisco. The factions could not agree before the Union split in 1861.

When secession caused most advocates of the southern route to exit Congress, northern lawmakers adopted the Union Pacific Act, which President Lincoln signed in July 1862. The Act called for the route to extend across the continent to Sacramento from an eastern terminus on the Missouri River at or near Omaha, Nebraska, and connect from there to Chicago. The eastern tracks would be laid by the Union Pacific Railroad Company, the western portions by the Central Pacific Railroad Company, controlled by prominent California businessmen known as the "Big Four"—Leland Stanford, Mark Hopkins, Collis Huntington, and Charles Crocker. Through an epic achievement of engineering and construction, the two lines met at Promontory Point, Utah, on May 10, 1869. Stanford hammered home the final, ceremonial golden spike.[50]

The arrival of the railroad ended California's isolation. By providing passengers direct connection between the eastern United States and Sacramento, it dramatically reduced the time, effort, and dangers of travel between the rest of the country and the Pacific Coast. The railroad also changed the state's economy by opening eastern markets to California's agricultural bounty and other goods. California quickly transformed from a remote frontier society into a far more integrated region of the United States. Moreover, as the South had feared, the initial transcontinental route strengthened California's connections with the upper Midwest and the Northeast. In the years that followed, additional rail lines linked Northern and Southern California and connected Southern California directly to an expanding railroad network to the east, which, in turn, opened the southern part of the state to rapid population growth and economic development.[51]

The Importance of Origins

This chapter contends that origins matter—that identities are shaped by early experiences. The origins of Texas and California, from the period of Spanish and Mexican rule, through American conquest to early statehood, to the crucible of the Civil War era and its aftermath, help explain why these states have become what they are today. In these origins, one can see similarities, but also critical differences that set the siblings on rival paths. The similarities present themselves in their common experiences as remote borderlands of Spain and Mexico, as targets of westward expansion and conquest by Americans, and in their common entry into the United States in the middle years of the nineteenth century.

The primary differences are evident in the circumstances of their settlement and the identity of the settlers. Texas was settled by southerners who entered into a vast frontier and quickly engaged in series of fights—against hostile Native American tribes, the Mexican government and its soldiers, American opponents of annexation, the Union army, and the implementers of Reconstruction. In addition, because the climate could be severe, Texans often had to wrestle with the land itself. Partly as a result of these struggles, the earliest Texans were marked by a remarkable tenacity, independence, and deep loyalty to one another and to their state. They were distinguished from other southerners by their connections to Mexico and the western frontier and by their experiences as an independent republic. At the same time, their identities were closely tied to the South—with its strengths as well as its shortcomings. Texas joined the South in embracing slavery, secession, and war against the Union—choices for which it would pay a price for years to come.

By comparison, California was a remote land, thinly settled by Americans before the Conquest of 1846–1847. The earliest settlers came by sea and land and from North more than South. At the very moment California was passing from Mexican to American sovereignty, gold was discovered in Northern California. Almost immediately, hundreds of thousands of newcomers converged on California from across the United States and around the world. The gold rush reinforced the perception (shared by no less than Karl Marx) that California was an exceptional place in the world—uniquely blessed with natural beauty, resources, and wealth. These extraordinary advantages helped California quickly achieve statehood. And, despite the mixed origins of its settlers and their competing sympathies, California rejected slavery and remained solidly aligned with the North during the secession crisis and Civil War, a position that was reinforced when the railroad connected California to the rest of the nation by way of the North.

Of course, circumstances of birth and early growth did not fully determine the destinies of Texas and California. Origins have had enduring influence, but later developments from the twentieth century forward—including long-term demographic changes, economic transformations, and shifting cultural currents—have further shaped their identities and directed their political and policy choices. The following chapters explore how developments in these areas have contributed to the rivalry between the two states.

3

People

Political analysts have suggested that "demography is destiny"—that is, a place's population characteristics determine its political orientation.[1] This chapter tests this premise by examining how the population characteristics of Texas and California have developed over time and, further, whether they help explain the rival states' political divisions. The theory presents a puzzle because, at first glance, the demographics of the two states look remarkably alike. Most obviously, California and Texas have experienced spectacular growth that have made them the nation's two most populous states. Moreover, both states have urbanized, with a large share of their residents now living in major metropolitan areas. Finally, both have become racially and ethnically diverse, joining the short list of "majority-minority" states in which non-white residents (mainly Hispanics, blacks, and Asians) constitute a population majority. If demography is, indeed, destiny, how can two states with outwardly similar demographic traits have developed such deep political differences? This chapter considers this question and concludes that, while it influences political outcomes, demography alone is not destiny. We must look beyond demography to economic and cultural factors to understand why these two rivals have become so profoundly polarized.

National Demographic Trends

The demographics of the two states can be better understood by placing them in national context over the long term. In assessing U.S. demographic trends since 1900, the most notable feature is, again, growth. The nation's population more than tripled during the twentieth century—from 76 million to 281 million. By 2020, the U.S. population expanded to approximately 330 million, an average growth rate of about 2.4 million per year in the new century.[2] Americans can credit immigration for much of their nation's robust growth. Net immigration to the United States totaled nearly 40 million people during the twentieth century and about 20 million more in the first two decades of the twenty-first. Second, the nation's population shifted, on average, south and west, due to large-scale domestic migration to the Sunbelt and heavy foreign immigration into that region.

Texas vs. California. Kenneth P. Miller, Oxford University Press (2020). © Oxford University Press.
DOI: 10.1093/oso/9780190077402.001.0001.

In 1900, the mean center population of the United States was located in eastern Indiana; during the 1970s, it crossed the Mississippi River; by 2000 it had moved to south-central Missouri; and over the next two decades, it continued to travel south and west toward the borders of Arkansas and Oklahoma.[3] Third, the nation urbanized. In 1900, about 60 percent of Americans lived in rural areas and 40 percent on farms; a century later, less than 20 percent lived rural lives and only 1 percent worked the plow. Conversely, the nation's urban population grew from about 40 percent in 1900 to more than 80 percent in the early twenty-first century. Much of the urban growth occurred in the suburbs of major cities. By 2000, one in two Americans lived in suburbia.[4]

Most important for this analysis, the nation has become far more racially diverse. Classifying people on the basis of race is controversial, in part because racial distinctions are determined not only by biology or genetics, but also through social construction.[5] For most of the nation's history, two racial groups—whites and blacks—were numerically dominant. The 1900 Census reported that nearly 88 percent of Americans were white, most of whom could trace their ancestry to northern Europe. In the Census calculation, the "white" category also included the then-small Hispanic population.[6] Waves of immigrants from southern and eastern Europe diversified the white population until anti-immigrant sentiment led Congress to impose strict immigration quotas in the 1920s, adding to earlier restrictions on immigration from Asia.[7] From the 1920s through the 1960s, U.S. immigration rates remained low, and the percentage of foreign-born Americans declined. In 1900, blacks were by far the nation's largest racial minority group (11.6 percent), although nearly nine in ten still lived in the South. However, beginning around 1915, many blacks joined the "Great Migration" out of the South in search of economic opportunities and social and political freedom. By 1970, nearly half of the black population lived outside the South, adding diversity to the nation's northern and western regions.[8]

The growth of the U.S. Hispanic population is more difficult to measure because the Census Bureau counted Hispanics in a number of conflicting ways before standardizing its approach after 1970. For most of the nation's history, the decennial Census provided no separate category for people of Hispanic descent; instead, it treated the nation's relatively small Hispanic population as "white." The best estimate of the nation's Hispanic population came from data on foreign-born residents, which included residents born in Mexico. In 1930, for the first and only time, the Census Bureau created a separate racial category for people of Mexican origin. That year, it also retroactively estimated the nation's Mexican-origin population in 1910 and 1920. In 1940, the Bureau eliminated the

Mexican racial category and again included the Hispanic population with the white population.

In 1970, the Bureau made its first attempt to enumerate the entire Hispanic population. That year, it used three different methods to identify the Hispanic population: (1) native language or "mother tongue"; (2) heritage (including surname); and (3) self-identification. In later decades, the Bureau relied on self-identification and used full counts rather than samples. Most important, the Census Bureau has chosen not to treat the Hispanic-origin category as a race. Instead, it maintains that Hispanics can be of any race and that Hispanic identity is an ethnicity rather than a race. The Census Bureau's view has merit, but it creates difficulties when comparing the Hispanic population to non-Hispanic whites, blacks, and Asians. Some demographers, including William Frey of the Brookings Institution, have chosen to treat Hispanics (or Latinos) as a distinctive racial group. While noting that this (indeed, any) racial classification is problematic, this book follows that approach.[9]

Although many immigrants from Latin America (especially Mexico) entered the United States throughout the twentieth century, as late as 1970 the nation remained largely white and black. That year, non-Hispanic whites made up more than four-fifths (83.5 percent) of the U.S. population, followed by blacks, at 11.1 percent. Hispanics represented only 4.5 percent, and Asians and Native Americans were less than 1 percent.[10]

The landmark Immigration and Naturalization Act of 1965 radically transformed the nation's racial and ethnic mix.[11] By replacing the old restrictive quotas that favored immigrants from northern and western Europe with a system that prioritized unifying families and attracting workers, the law opened the door to large-scale immigration from non-European regions, including Asia, Africa, and Latin America. Over the next half century, the nation experienced what Frey has called a "diversity explosion."[12] The Census Bureau reported that in the five decades after 1970, the white share of the population fell from more than 80 percent to about 60 percent, while the percentages of all other groups increased. The share of black people grew modestly, to about 13 percent while the Hispanic share jumped to more than 18 percent, making Latinos the nation's largest minority group. Meanwhile, the fast-growing Asian population increased from less than 1 percent to about 6 percent during this time. Demographers predicted that the number of white Americans would actually start falling in the 2020s, and that any growth in the nation's population would come from other groups. Whites were projected to become a minority of the U.S. population by the middle of the twenty-first century—just one group among many in a very diverse mix.[13] Texas and California have driven these national demographic trends.

Population Growth in Texas and California

Numbers

During the twentieth century, the two states added people at remarkable rates—California grew by a stunning 32.4 million and Texas by 17.8 million. Combined, those 50 million people accounted for nearly one-fourth of the nation's population increase during the century.[14] The rivals' rapid population growth translated into economic and political power. Consider one measure: California's seats in the U.S. House of Representatives increased by more than sixfold during the twentieth century—from eight after the 1900 Census to 53 after 2000. The latter figure was the largest allocation of U.S. House seats in the nation's history. Meanwhile, the Texas delegation doubled from 16 after the 1900 Census to 32 after 2000, further rising to 36 after 2010.[15]

If population growth is a competition, the contest between Texas and California can be divided into three distinct periods—the nineteenth, twentieth, and twenty-first centuries. Texas won the first round. The Lone Star State had a larger population than California at the time of admission, and it extended its lead for the rest of the nineteenth century. By 1900, Texas ranked sixth in the nation and California twenty-first, both well behind first-place New York. California dominated the second round, as its population exploded from 1.5 million in 1900 to 34 million in 2000. The Golden State blew past Texas in the 1930s and caught New York in the early 1960s. It kept growing thereafter, with foreign immigration driving its population gains after 1970. During the 1980s alone, California added more than six million people, the greatest one-decade increase by any state in U.S. history. Although Texas fell behind California in the twentieth century, it also grew rapidly, expanding from three million to 21 million. In 1994, Texas passed New York to become the nation's second most populous state.

When round three began in 2000, the competition shifted back in Texas's favor as its growth accelerated while its rival's declined. California's fall from a high- to a low-growth state was striking. The change was driven by a drop in foreign immigration, a reduced birth rate, and a net outflow of residents. In contrast to the days when the Golden State drew waves of newcomers from all corners of the country, it was now losing more residents to other states than it was gaining. The Census Bureau reported that between 2007 and 2016, approximately 6 million California residents moved out of the state, with a net out-migration of about 1 million. A 2019 U.C. Berkeley poll of California voters reported that more than half of those surveyed had considered such a move, citing high housing costs, taxes, and the state's political culture as the leading reasons. This exodus was producing a large California diaspora—including, increasingly, in Texas.[16] For some time, the migration of Californians to other states was masked by high rates of foreign immigration and natural increase, but these rates also started to fall near the turn of the millennium. By 2019, California's demographers estimated that the state's population was growing at a rate of only 0.35 percent per year, the slowest rate in its history, and the Census Bureau estimated that the state's population was growing even more slowly. Demographers were forced to lower their projections of the state's future growth. As late as the mid-1990s, both the U.S. Census Bureau and state demographers had predicted that California's population would reach 50 million by 2020; in fact, it was struggling to reach 40 million. California now faced the prospect of joining New York and Illinois as a shrinking state.[17]

The story was the opposite in Texas. After the turn of the millennium, the Lone Star State grew rapidly, consistently adding more people than any other state and ranking near the top of the nation in percentage population gains. Texas's growth could be attributed to foreign immigration, natural increase, and, notably, net domestic in-migration. Nearly half of its increase came from people arriving from other states, most numerously from California, New York, Illinois, and Florida. Moreover, the number of younger Texans was growing rapidly. While California's population of residents under age eighteen fell by more than 400,000 between 2010 and 2019, in Texas that group grew by more than 500,000. After Utah, Texas could now boast the nation's second highest percentage of residents under age eighteen.

Overall, in rough numbers, Texas gained more than four million residents from 2000 to 2010 (from nearly 21 million to 25 million) and almost five million more between 2010 and 2020 (from 25 million to close to 30 million)—in all, a one-third increase in just two decades. Consequently, it gained four congressional seats after the 2010 Census and was poised to gain more after 2020. In terms of the competition, Texas was narrowing the population gap with California and was on pace to pass it later in the century (Figure 3.1).[18]

Urbanization

Both rivals have urbanized, but California did so more quickly than Texas (Figure 3.2). From the early days of statehood, a large share of Californians clustered in urban areas. The state's urban identity began in San Francisco. As late as the mid-1840s, San Francisco was a quiet village with only a few hundred residents, but the discovery of gold in 1848 transformed it forever. The primary point of entry for the gold rush, San Francisco became the Pacific Coast's leading center of commerce, finance, and trade. Within just a few years, the small village grew to become one of the nation's twenty-five largest cities. By 1870, San Francisco had reached the

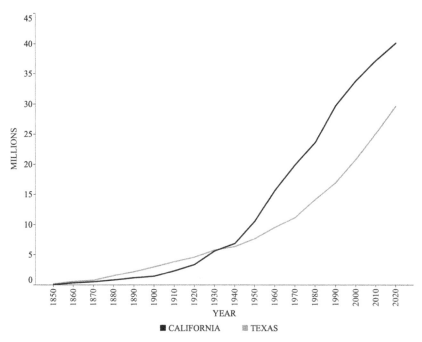

Figure 3.1. California and Texas population, 1850–2020

Sources: U.S. Census Bureau, California Department of Finance, Texas Demographic Center (2020 projected)

150,000 mark, which made it the nation's tenth largest city and, by 1900, its population had expanded to more than 340,000, ranking ninth. Meanwhile, when the railroads opened Southern California to development in the 1880s, Los Angeles also became a major city. Between 1900 and 1930, its population exploded from just over 100,000 to more than 1.2 million, surpassing San Francisco to rank first in California and fifth in the nation. In 1984, Los Angeles passed Chicago to become, after New York, the nation's second largest metropolis. Over time, quickly growing San Diego and San Jose joined Los Angeles in the nation's top-ten cities, and suburbanization vastly expanded the population of the state's urban regions. By the end of the twentieth century, 95 percent of Californians were packed into urban areas that collectively occupied less than 6 percent of the state's geographic area, with two-thirds of the state's residents clustered in the densely urbanized coastal regions of the San Francisco Bay Area and Southern California.[19]

By contrast, Texas long remained rural. None of its towns topped 20,000 residents until Galveston and San Antonio in 1880. Ten years later, at a time when San Francisco had nearly 300,000 residents, Texas's largest towns were Dallas and San Antonio, with approximately 38,000 residents each. By 1900, San

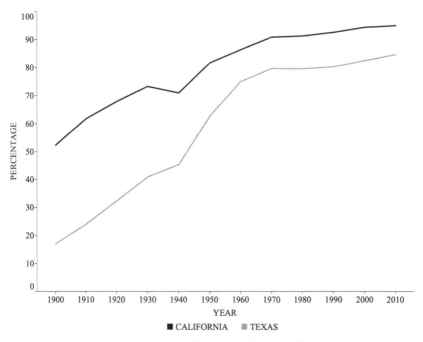

Figure 3.2. Urban percentage of population, California and Texas, 1900–2010
Source: U.S. Census Bureau

Antonio had grown to 53,000, followed by Houston and Dallas, each with less than 45,000. The state as a whole remained agrarian, with 83 percent of Texans living in rural areas.

During the twentieth century, however, Texas transformed into an urban society. The change began at the turn of the century and accelerated during World War II and the postwar years, driven at first by movements of rural Texans into cities in search of economic opportunities. Later, newcomers from across the country and around the world flooded into the state's urban areas for similar reasons. By 1970, both Houston and Dallas ranked among the nation's ten largest cities—San Antonio later joined that group, and Austin rose to eleventh. In the early twenty-first century, these major cities—plus Fort Worth and El Paso—ranked among the nation's fastest growing. By that point, nearly 85 percent of Texas's population lived in urban areas, reversing the state's old rural orientation. Most Texans were choosing to live in the geographic triangle formed by Dallas–Fort Worth in the north, Houston in the southeast, and San Antonio in the southwest, an area that includes Austin, Waco, and other large population centers. This triangle became one of the most densely populated areas in the United States—and had virtually unlimited room to grow.[20]

Diversity Explosion in Texas and California

Texas and California also were among the leading contributors to the nation's "diversity explosion." In the half-century after 1970, both rapidly changed from overwhelmingly white societies into two of the nation's most diverse states. This transformation can be better appreciated by reviewing the histories of their four largest population groups—whites, blacks, Hispanics, and Asians.

Whites

As noted in the previous chapter, the Americans who first settled in Texas were almost exclusively southern whites and African American slaves. A smaller number came from Europe (largely Germany), most of whom gravitated to the Hill Country. In the latter half of the nineteenth century, whites (often called "Anglos" in Texas) increased their share of the population, as they poured into the state in numbers that exceeded other groups. By 1900, the Census reported Texas had 2.4 million whites, which translated to 80 percent of the state's residents. Again, the 1900 Census included Hispanics when counting whites, but other sources indicate that the number of Hispanic Texans remained small at the time.[21]

Deep into the twentieth century, nearly all Anglo Texans had southern roots; few northern whites, including the turn-of-the-century European immigrants, migrated to the Lone Star State. This old North-South sectional barrier began to break down during World War II and the postwar period. Northerners began to move to Texas in large numbers, attracted by economic opportunities, increasing urbanization, and even by the spread of air conditioning, which helped mitigate the region's hot summer climate.[22]

A representative member of this migration was George Herbert Walker Bush. In 1948, this Connecticut Yankee and World War II veteran moved with his family to Odessa, Texas, to pursue opportunities in the oil business. Many northern whites made similar moves, creating in the second half of the twentieth century waves of migration from the North to the Lone Star State. By the early twenty-first century, Texas was attracting newcomers from all corners of the United States, including large numbers from California. Thus, while it remained true that most white Texans had their roots in the South, the state's population was now far more diverse—more northern and western—than it used to be.

Even as their numbers grew, whites declined in percentage terms. As late as 1970, they accounted for about 70 percent of Texas residents, but their share of the population fell sharply thereafter. In 2004, for the first time in the nearly two centuries since the establishment of the Texas Republic, Anglo Texans dropped below 50 percent of the state's population. Texas thus became the nation's fourth "majority-minority" state, joining Hawaii, New Mexico, and California. The trend continued in the years that followed. By 2020, whites had declined to just over 40 percent of the state's population, and demographers predicted they would drop below Hispanics by 2022. The white population's older age structure and decreasing birth rates suggested that its share would shrink for the foreseeable future.[23]

By comparison, for most of its history California was whiter than Texas, largely because it had fewer blacks and its population of other minorities (Hispanics, Asians, and Native Americans) remained relatively small. On the other hand, the white population was more diverse in California than in Texas. Early on, San Francisco became home to a variety of white ethnic and religious groups, including Irish and Italian Catholics as well as a substantial German Jewish community.[24] By the end of the nineteenth century, California's ethnic diversity was comparable to the urban areas of the East, and unlike anything then existing in Texas.

In the twentieth century, California absorbed further waves of white immigrants, with the largest numbers coming from the Midwest. By 1910, approximately 60 percent of California residents had midwestern origins. The tendency of midwesterners to settle in Southern California reinforced divisions between Northern and Southern California, with the northern part (and especially the San Francisco Bay Area) being more ethnically diverse and Catholic than the overwhelmingly midwestern and Protestant Southland.[25] During the Great Depression, another river of white migrants arrived from the southwestern plains to escape the Dust Bowl. These impoverished newcomers, memorialized in John Steinbeck's *Grapes of Wrath* and the photographs of Dorothea Lange, settled in near-equal numbers in the agricultural areas of the Central Valley and in Los Angeles, helping to make Los Angeles, by the mid-twentieth century, one of the whitest major cities in the United States.[26]

At the same time, California absorbed new waves of Europeans, including Italians, Greeks, Armenians, and central and eastern European Jews. Some of these groups formed cohesive communities in the state. One example is the Armenian community, which first formed in Fresno and the Central Valley, and later concentrated in and near Los Angeles. In time, half of all Armenian Americans came to live in Los Angeles County, and Los Angeles became home to the largest concentration of Armenian émigrés in the world. Similarly, in the first half of the twentieth century, many Jewish immigrants settled in Los Angeles— to the point where the Jewish community of Los Angeles became the nation's second largest (after New York City); similarly, California could claim the second largest Jewish population (after the State of New York).[27] As of 2018, the Jewish population of California was estimated to be 1.2 million, a far larger presence than the estimated 167,000 in Texas.[28] These waves of ethnic whites contributed to the state in distinctive ways. For example, European Jewish immigrants helped establish Hollywood; immigrants from Italy and France created California's wine industry; and newcomers from Ireland founded the state's labor movement.

As late as 1970, whites constituted more than three-quarters of California's population. That year, about 15.6 million whites resided in California, compared to about 2.4 million Hispanics and a lesser number of blacks and Asians.[29] After 1970, however, the white percentage of the population fell sharply, as it did in Texas and elsewhere—but more strikingly, the absolute number of white Californians declined, as well. According to Census estimates, by 2019 the number of whites had fallen to 14.5 million—a decrease of about a million from the 1970s level. As a result of net-outmigration and declining birth rates, especially compared with other demographic groups, the white share of California's population was reduced by more than half in less than 50 years, from 78 percent in 1970 to 36.8 percent in 2019 (Figure 3.3).[30]

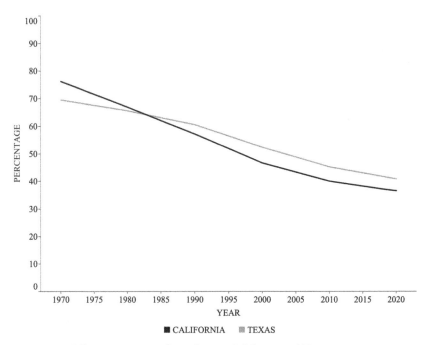

Figure 3.3. White percentage of population, California and Texas, 1970–2020

Sources: U.S. Census Bureau, California Department of Finance, Texas Demographic Center (2020 projected)

African Americans

African Americans have generally maintained a larger presence in Texas than in California, although the gap has fluctuated over time. As noted in the prior chapter, slavery was a central feature of Texas's early history; by the end of the Civil War approximately 250,000 black slaves resided in Texas, constituting just under one-third of the state's population.[31] On June 19, 1865, a date now widely celebrated as "Juneteenth," Union forces in Galveston declared that all slaves were emancipated.[32] Yet African Americans continued to struggle for basic freedoms—after the brief period of Reconstruction, Texas and the rest of the South reimposed a racial hierarchy.[33]

In time, the weight of Jim Crow caused many black Texans to join the Great Migration, which reduced their share of the state's population. The black percentage declined from 18 to 13 percent between 1910 and 1950, but remained stable thereafter.[34] Blacks had long constituted a smaller percentage of the population in Texas than in the states of the Deep South. In his classic *Southern Politics in State and Nation* (1949), Texas-born political scientist V. O. Key Jr. contended that the state's comparatively small black presence made white Texans less "obsessed" about maintaining segregation than were whites in states where blacks constituted a majority.[35] Yet Texas enforced segregation deep into the twentieth century and became the site of several important battles in the civil rights movement, including cases that overturned the white primary system and racial segregation in public law schools.[36]

More recently, a "reverse Great Migration" of blacks to the post–civil rights South revitalized Texas's African American population. Houston and Dallas became, after Atlanta, the nation's most popular places for African Americans to relocate. As of 2019, approximately 3.5 million blacks resided in Texas, which placed the state among the nation's leaders in black population, along with New York, Florida, and Georgia. Most black Texans lived in the state's largest urban areas—more than two-thirds in the metropolitan areas of Houston and Dallas–Fort Worth, with smaller concentrations in Austin and San Antonio.[37]

By comparison, for much of its history, California was home to modest numbers of African Americans. During the gold rush, a small contingent of blacks came to California but found the state an unwelcoming place for people of African descent. Unlike many northern states that resisted the federal Fugitive Slave Act of 1850, California enacted an aggressive fugitive slave law of its own and placed other restrictions on African Americans. As of 1860, only about 4,000 blacks resided in California, compared to about 183,000 in Texas. For the rest of the nineteenth century, California's black population remained low, slowly growing to only about 11,000 (or 0.7 percent of the population) in 1900. The first waves of the Great Migration increased those numbers, as the black share of the population doubled between 1900 and 1930.[38]

During these years, a black middle class began to form in Los Angeles and Oakland. As terminuses on the transcontinental railroads, these cities became home to railroad porters, some of the highest paid African Americans at the time, and both communities began to support black professionals and black-owned businesses. One emigrant in this period was Tom Bradley, the future five-term mayor of Los Angeles. Born in 1917 in Calvert, Texas, Bradley was the grandson of a slave and son of a railroad porter. In 1924, his family moved to Los Angeles. Bradley attended UCLA as a classmate of Jackie Robinson, rose to a high rank in the Los Angeles Police Department, and achieved distinction as the first African American mayor of a predominantly white major city.[39]

In the 1940s, a larger wave of African Americans entered California, with many seeking work in the state's war industries. In a single decade, the state's black population increased from about 124,000 in 1940 to more than 462,000 in 1950—or, in percentage terms, from 1.8 to 4.4 percent of the state's population. The state's African American community continued to grow after the war. In part due to racial housing restrictions, blacks continued to cluster in a few urban areas, mainly in Los Angeles County and the eastern edge of the San Francisco Bay. By 1970, as many blacks lived in California as in Texas (approximately 1.4 million in each state) and for at least the next two decades the number of African Americans in California actually exceeded the number in Texas. The black share of California's population never surpassed Texas, however, and peaked at 7.7 percent in 1980. In the 1990s, the number of black Californians plateaued as many began exiting the state for more affordable locations. By 2010, California's black population fell below that of Texas.[40]

Hispanics

By virtue of history, geography, culture, and numbers, Hispanics—especially those of Mexican descent—hold a distinctive place in both Texas and California. Heavy immigration from Mexico and Central America over the course of the twentieth century revived the Hispanic identity of both states. In the first decades of the twenty-first century, Hispanics achieved numerical superiority in California for the first time since the American conquest, and they were on pace to do so in Texas as well. In both states, most Hispanics were Mexican in origin, with smaller numbers tracing their ancestry to Guatemala, Honduras, El Salvador, and other Central American countries.

In the decades after the conquest, the Mexican presence had declined in both states but never disappeared. In Texas, a remnant survived along the border and maintained a resilient Mexican subculture. In California, the writer and social critic Carey McWilliams noted a similar remnant. "At the turn of the [twentieth] century it appeared—in fact it was generally assumed—that the Mexican influence had been thoroughly exorcised," he wrote, "but the number of Spanish-speaking residents in Southern California was at all times sufficient to keep vestiges of the earlier life and culture alive."[41]

Indeed, in the first decades of the twentieth century, Mexicans began expanding their presence in both states though temporary visits and permanent settlement. Texas and California became the primary gateways for immigration from Mexico to the United States. The flow of people across the border was driven by mutual economic advantage. Mexico had a large pool of poor people who wanted work, and the border states sought low-cost labor. Between 1900 and 1930, nearly one-tenth of the entire population of Mexico crossed the border, with the largest number locating in Texas, followed by California, Arizona, and New Mexico (Figure 3.4). This wave of immigration was driven in part by unsettled conditions in Mexico, but also by U.S. employer demand for workers.[42]

By the 1920s, growers in the Southwest had become highly dependent on Mexican labor. Congress thus exempted that workforce from the immigration quotas it enacted during the decade.[43] But when the Great Depression wiped out

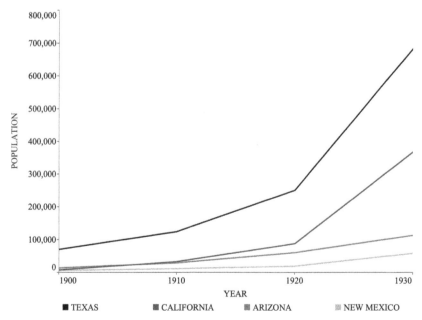

Figure 3.4. Number of Mexican-born residents in Texas, California, Arizona, and New Mexico, 1900–1930

Source: U.S. Census Bureau

U.S. demand for Mexican workers, the federal government forced thousands of them, most of whom lived in Texas or California, to leave the country. Some left voluntarily, but others were forcibly removed. Some who departed were not actually "repatriated," because they were born in the United States and thus had U.S. citizenship.[44] Before long, U.S. policy shifted again as the nation entered World War II and needed laborers to maintain agricultural production in the Southwest. In 1942, the United States established the Bracero program, which authorized Mexicans to come to the United States as temporary guest workers. After the war, employers successfully lobbied to preserve the arrangement.

In the 1950s, the United States continued to administer the Bracero program even as growing numbers of unauthorized Mexican immigrants crossed the border into the Southwest. Public sentiment turned against large-scale immigration from Mexico, and in 1954 the United States launched a military-style action to deport hundreds of thousands of Mexican immigrants from California, Texas, and other parts of the Southwest.[45]

After Congress let the Bracero program expire in 1964, the nation lacked a functioning guest worker program and, over time, millions crossed the Mexican border into the United States without authorization. In 1986, Congress enacted legislation that effectively provided amnesty to about 2.7 million immigrants, most of Mexican origin, who were in the country illegally, while also increasing border enforcement. Like earlier reforms, however, this law failed to stem Mexican immigration, which remained high through the 1990s and the early 2000s. The levels eventually fell after the Great Recession of 2007–2009, and thereafter the nation's Hispanic population grew more by natural increase than by immigration.[46]

The Census Bureau has documented the remarkable growth of the Hispanic population in both Texas and California in the half-century from 1970 to 2019 (Figure 3.5). In Texas, the number of Latinos expanded from 1.8 million to nearly 11.8 million during that time (a 6.5-fold increase); in California, from 2.4 million to more than 15.5 million (also about a 6.5-fold gain). Back in 1970, Latinos comprised a larger share of the population in Texas than in California (16.4 percent vs. 11.9 percent). California soon caught up and in the four decades between 1980 and 2019, the Hispanic share of the population rose almost identically in Texas and California, approaching the 40 percent mark in both states. Demographers estimated that California reached a milestone in 2014, when Hispanics displaced non-Hispanic whites as the state's largest population group, and they expected a similar moment to occur in Texas in the early 2020s.[47]

California and Texas have become the co-capitals of Hispanic America. Los Angeles County is home to the largest Hispanic concentration in the United States, and dozens of cities throughout Southern California and the Central Valley have large Latino majorities. Similarly, in Texas the Hispanic population

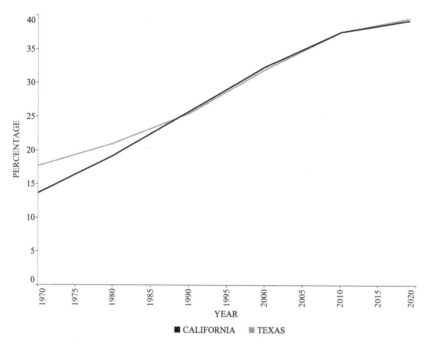

Figure 3.5. Hispanic percentage of population, California and Texas, 1970–2019
Source: U.S. Census Bureau

has spread beyond its traditional communities in San Antonio, El Paso, and the Rio Grande Valley to become a major presence in Houston and Dallas and throughout the state. California and Texas are now home to eight of the nation's top ten metropolitan areas based on Mexican-origin population—with four in each state (Figure 3.6 and 3.7).[48]

Asians

No Asians emigrated in significant numbers to the United States until the discovery of gold in California. From its earliest days of statehood in the 1850s, California has attracted Asian immigrants, making it the first U.S. state with a significant Asian presence. Over time, California attracted waves of immigrants from all corners of the Asian continent, with its multitude of nations, languages, and cultures, making the Golden State the capital of Asian America.

The first large wave came from China. In 1852, approximately 20,000 Chinese crossed the Pacific and arrived in San Francisco, with many heading directly to

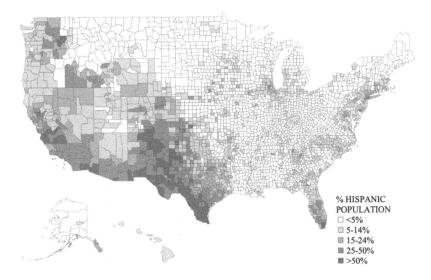

Figure 3.6. Hispanic percentage of population by county, 2010
Source: U.S. Census Bureau

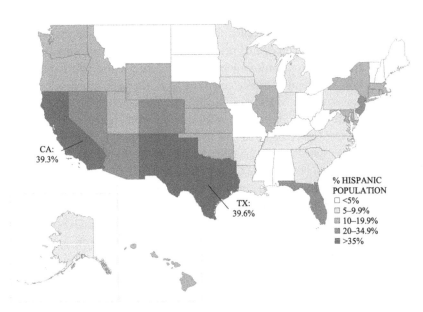

Figure 3.7. Hispanic percentage of population by state, 2019
Source: U.S. Census Bureau (2019 estimates)

the gold fields. These immigrants quickly constituted approximately one-fifth of the population in the mining regions and one-tenth of the state's total non-native population.[49] In the mid-1860s, the Central Pacific Railroad turned to China for a labor force to construct the Transcontinental Railroad. The company eventually hired nearly 20,000 Chinese workers to complete the colossal project.[50] Later, the Southern Pacific Railroad employed Chinese labor to build its network of rail lines, especially in California. Chinese men were also employed in other sectors, including light industry and agriculture.

By 1880, one-third of the state's agricultural labor force was Chinese.[51] California initially welcomed immigrants from China as useful contributors to an undeveloped frontier society, but soon many feared that the Chinese were becoming a distinct racial laboring caste. The social reformer Henry George worried that "what the blacks of the African coast were to the great land lords of the Southern States, the Chinese coolies may be, in fact are already beginning to be, to the great land lords of our Pacific slope."[52] In the 1870s, an anti-Chinese movement emerged in California, led by the Workingmen's Party. The movement caused the state to impose restrictions on Chinese labor in its constitution of 1879, and pressured Congress to pass the Page Act of 1875 and the broader Chinese Exclusion Act of 1882, the nation's first racially restrictive immigration laws.[53]

Immigrants from other Asian countries also made their way to California in the nineteenth century, with significant numbers arriving from Japan and the Philippines. The Japanese excelled in agriculture and many bought or leased farms. By 1910, they constituted nearly half of the state's farm workforce. This success bred opposition. A movement to exclude Japanese from the state resulted in the 1907 "Gentlemen's Agreement" between Theodore Roosevelt and the Japanese government, which curtailed further immigration of male Japanese workers to the United States while allowing for family reunification. In 1913, California passed an Alien Land Law to prevent Japanese from purchasing real property in the state. California's underlying hostility toward the Japanese contributed to tension between the United States and Japan in the years leading up to World War II. After the Japanese attack on Pearl Harbor, most Californians readily accepted President Franklin D. Roosevelt's infamous Executive Order 9066, which led to the removal and internment of tens of thousands of California residents of Japanese descent, regardless of their citizenship or loyalty to the United States.[54]

Despite a long history of racial restriction and hostility, people of Asian descent have always maintained a substantial presence in California. When the nation liberalized its immigration policies in 1965, the state became a natural gateway for new Asian immigrants. Large numbers arrived from across the Asia-Pacific region, greatly multiplying and diversifying the state's Asian population. By 2017, Asian Californians' leading countries of ancestry were China (including

Taiwan) (1.5 million), the Philippines (1.3 million), India (713,000), Vietnam (643,000), Korea (466,000), and Japan (276,000)—followed by substantial numbers from countries including, in descending order, Laos, Thailand, Pakistan, Indonesia, Burma, and Sri Lanka.[55]

As their numbers rose, Asians became the majority of residents in several cities near Los Angeles and San Francisco. They also accounted for about one-third of the population of San Francisco, Alameda, and Santa Clara Counties in Northern California.[56] Overall, by 2019, more than six million people of Asian descent lived in California, or about 15 percent of the state's residents. California's Asian population was by far the nation's largest and was growing faster than any of the state's other demographic groups.

By comparison, Asians long struggled to establish a significant presence in Texas. The earliest settlers were Chinese laborers brought in by the Southern Pacific and other railroads to construct rail lines. A few of these workers remained and settled in the state, but the 1900 Census reported that the total Chinese population of Texas was fewer than 1,000—a number that stayed low for the next half century.[57] Meanwhile, Japanese began to settle in Texas in the late nineteenth century, locating in rural areas to farm rice and other crops. The population of Japanese Texans remained small, due to restrictions on immigration and land ownership, among other obstacles. As of 1940, Texas's Asian population was limited mainly to people of Chinese and Japanese descent and collectively numbered fewer than 2,000. After World War II, and especially after the 1965 Immigration and Naturalization Act, the Asian presence in Texas grew and diversified. One important development came in the 1970s, when the collapse of governments in Southeast Asia drove refugees out of Vietnam, Cambodia, and Laos. By the mid-1980s, more than 50,000 Southeast Asian immigrants had settled in Texas, many in Houston and the Gulf Coast region.

By the turn of the millennium, Texas had become a magnet for immigrants from across Asia, many arriving as students or professionals, with some accompanied by family members. According to Census estimates, the Asian population of Texas was on pace to more than double between 2010 and 2020, expanding to approximately 1.5 million, or more than 5 percent of the state's total population. Suddenly, Texas was home to the nation's third largest Asian population, trailing only California and New York. These new immigrants could trace their origins to the full range of Asian countries, including, increasingly, South Asia. Immigrants from India and their offspring were the largest Asian group in Texas (estimated 422,300 in 2017), followed by people of Vietnamese, Chinese, Filipino, Pakistani, Korean, Burmese, and Japanese descent.[58]

Forty percent of Asian immigrants in Texas had first settled in another state then relocated to Texas, with many citing economic opportunities as the reason for their move. Asian Texans were now overwhelmingly urban dwellers. As of 2010, 90 percent lived in the state's top four metropolitan areas—Houston (41 percent), Dallas–Fort Worth (36 percent), Austin (9 percent), and San Antonio (5 percent). No Texas city, however, had a majority-Asian population—the closest was the Houston suburb of Sugar Land, where, as of 2019, 37 percent of residents claimed Asian ancestry.[59]

Is Demography Destiny?

We now return to the question, is demography destiny? To be sure, the rivals' demographics have shaped their destinies in many ways. Most fundamentally, massive population growth has helped California and Texas emerge as the nation's most powerful and consequential states. But has demography determined their political orientations? That question is more complex.

Looking at their basic population characteristics, one would expect the two states to be more politically aligned than they have turned out to be. By the early twenty-first century, both states had large, urbanized populations and both were at the forefront of the nation's diversity explosion. The most notable similarity was Hispanics' almost identically large and fast-growing population share in both states. One could also find differences. Texas was still more rural than California, and although it had become majority-minority, it remained somewhat more white. At the same time, Texas had a larger black population than California, offsetting California's larger percentage of Asian residents. But, overall, the two states' demographic similarities were more striking than their differences.

Many large, urban, racially diverse states have aligned with the Democratic Party. California reinforced this pattern by turning deep blue at the same time its population became majority-minority. However, Texas did not follow this script—at least not as quickly as some had expected. Instead, even as it urbanized and its minority population surged, the Lone Star State remained solidly Republican. This divergence suggested that at least some demographic groups must have been voting differently in California than they were in Texas. And, indeed, some were. Most notably, by the early twenty-first century a huge gap had opened between white voters in the two states, with those in California far more Democratic and progressive than those in Texas. Latinos also leaned further to the left in California than in Texas and participated in elections at higher rates. The gaps were smaller among blacks and Asians, with both groups voting heavily Democratic in the two states.

Such differences are most commonly measured through surveys that ask people their voting preferences and categorize respondents by various characteristics, including race. The National Election Pool's exit polls, funded by major media organizations, have applied this method for decades and thus reveal racial voting patterns over time both within and across states. To be sure, exit polls should be viewed with caution as a measure of the voting behavior of subgroups of the electorate (such as Asian voters in Texas). These surveys are designed primarily to predict election outcomes at the national and state level rather than to provide fine-grained estimates of voting by subgroups. In part because the surveys' samples of various subgroups are relatively small, they can be vulnerable to sampling errors and other distortions. Some critics have charged, for example, that national exit polls have consistently overstated Latino support for Republican candidates by oversampling Latino voters who are more conservative than the Latino electorate as a whole.[60] Nevertheless, comparing exit poll data across states and over time is a useful way to identify broad differences in racial voting patterns between Texas and California (Table 3.1).

Most notably, polling data highlight the wide and persistent gap between white voting patterns in the two states. During the first decades of the twenty-first century, these surveys indicated that whites in Texas consistently supported GOP candidates by 40 points or more, while in California they evenly divided their votes between Republican and Democratic presidential candidates. In 2004, for example, white voters in Texas supported George W. Bush over John Kerry by a 49-point margin (74–25 percent) and in 2008 supported John McCain over Barack Obama by 47 points (73–26 percent). The National Election Pool did not conduct a separate exit poll for Texas in 2012, but in 2016 whites in Texas supported Donald J. Trump over Hillary Clinton by a familiar 43 points (69–26 percent). In stark contrast, Obama won the white vote in California in 2008 by six points (52–46 percent), and in 2016 Clinton defeated Trump among white voters in California by five points (50–45 percent).

The results of the 2016 presidential election bear repeating because they illustrated the difference between the white vote in the two states as vividly as possible. In California, whites supported Clinton by five points; in Texas, they supported Trump by forty-three.

The gap in the white vote appeared in other races, as well. In Texas, Republican candidates for governor and U.S. Senate regularly ran up the score among the white electorate. In 2014, for example, white voters supported Republican Greg Abbott over Democrat Wendy Davis by 47 points (72–25 percent). In the hotly contested 2018 U.S. Senate race, Republican incumbent Ted Cruz won the white vote against Democratic Congressman Beto O'Rourke by a narrower 32-point margin (66–34 percent), but that same year whites supported Abbott for governor by 40 points (69–29 percent). By contrast, in California, Democratic candidates frequently won a majority of the white vote. In the 2010 governor's election, for example, Jerry Brown defeated Republican Meg Whitman among white voters by five points (50–45 percent). Eight years later, Democrat Gavin Newsom won the white vote in the race for governor over Republican John Cox

Table 3.1 Presidential Election Exit Poll Results by Race/Ethnicity in U.S., Texas, and California, 2004–2016

2004	Texas		California	
	Kerry	Bush	Kerry	Bush
White	25	74	47	51
Black	83	17	81	18
Hispanic	50	49	63	32
Asian	N/A	N/A	66	34
2008	Texas		California	
	Obama	McCain	Obama	McCain
White	26	73	52	46
Black	98	2	94	5
Hispanic	63	35	74	23
Asian	N/A	N/A	64	35
2012	Texas		California	
	Obama	Romney	Obama	Romney
White	N/A	N/A	45	53
Black	N/A	N/A	96	3
Hispanic	N/A	N/A	72	27
Asian	N/A	N/A	79	21
2016	Texas		California	
	Clinton	Trump	Clinton	Trump
White	26	69	50	45
Black	84	11	88	9
Hispanic	61	34	71	24
Asian	72	26	70	17

Source: National Election Pool Exit Polls 2004–2016 via CNN. N/A = not available. NEP did not conduct an exit poll in Texas in 2012.

by a 14-point margin (57–43 percent). Certainly, the white electorate in the two states had persistently different partisan preferences.

As noted, the data on Latino voting was more controversial, but also revealed a partisan gap between the two states. Although Latinos in both California and Texas consistently supported Democratic candidates, in California the margins were wider. In the 2004 presidential election, for example, exit polls reported that in California Latinos supported Democrat John Kerry by a wide 63–32 percent margin over Republican George W. Bush, but in Texas Latinos divided their votes evenly between the two candidates (50–49 percent). Again, critics argued that the 2004 poll overestimated Latino support for the Republican candidate, but there was no doubt that a higher percentage of Latinos voted for Bush in Texas than in California.[61] The gap persisted in later presidential elections as well. In 2016, for example, the exit poll found that Latinos supported Hillary Clinton by 71–24 percent in California, but by a lesser 61–34 percent in Texas.[62] The divide between the two states could be seen in non-presidential elections, as well. For example, Texas governor Greg Abbott won 44 percent of the Latino vote in 2014 and 42 percent in 2018, but no Republican candidate in California could match those numbers.

Moreover, Latinos turned out at higher rates in California than in the Lone Star State. Between 2006 and 2018, the U.S. Census Bureau's Current Population Surveys reported that, on average, 41.9 percent of eligible Hispanics (citizens 18 and older) voted in California, compared with only 31.8 percent in Texas.[63] It is evident that Latinos in California were, on average, more politically engaged as well as more decidedly Democratic (Figure 3.8).

African Americans, by comparison, have voted in similar ways in Texas and California. Blacks began to align with the Democratic Party during the Great Depression and solidified their support during the 1960s. This pattern has extended equally to the two states. In 2008, for example, exit polls reported that African American voters supported Barack Obama over John McCain by 94–5 percent in California, and by 98–2 in Texas. In 2016, Hillary Clinton won the black vote over Donald Trump by 88–9 percent in California and by 84–11 in the Lone Star State. Other races produced similar results. This rock-solid African American alignment with the Democratic Party far overshadowed any state-level differences.

Meanwhile, Asian American voting patterns were more complex. Through the last decades of the twentieth century, Asians voted at comparatively low rates and had established no definitive partisan orientation. Over time, however, they began voting more heavily Democratic, a change that has been called the "Asian realignment."[64] California's Asian voters, now more than one-tenth of the state electorate, were at the forefront of this trend. In 2016, exit polls reported that Hillary Clinton defeated Donald Trump by 70–17 percent among Asian

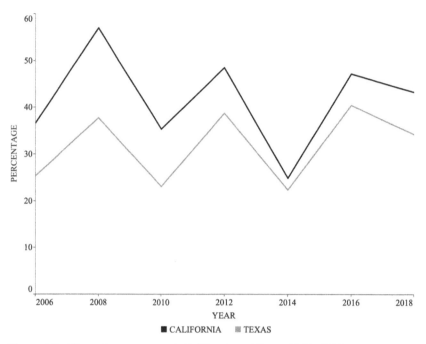

Figure 3.8. Hispanic voter turnout, California and Texas, 2006–2018
Source: U.S. Census Bureau

voters in the Golden State, nearly identical to her margin among Hispanics. Asian voting patterns in Texas are harder to discern, largely because until recently the group's voting population was too small to provide reliable survey samples. The limited evidence suggests, however, that Asian voters in Texas leaned heavily Democratic—indeed, more so than the state's Latinos. The 2016 exit poll reported that 72 percent of the state's Asian electorate supported Clinton over Trump, compared to 61 percent of Latinos. Put another way, Asian voters seemed to hold similar political preferences in Texas and in California, and in that way were more akin to blacks than to whites or Latinos.

Looking at these patterns as a whole indicates that demography certainly influences political outcomes in meaningful ways, but that it cannot alone explain why Texas and California have polarized. We need to look to other explanations. In the following chapters, we will examine two—the rivals' economic systems and their political cultures.

4

Economy

Economics helps explain why California and Texas have become such powerful states—and also why they have polarized. The rivals have built highly productive economies in very different ways. The Texas economy has both reflected and reinforced the state's conservative political model, while California has aligned its economy with its increasingly progressive social and political values.

The two economies are the nation's largest—and among the largest in the world (Figures 4.1 and 4.2). In 2019, California generated nearly $3.2 trillion in GDP, which exceeded runner-up Texas by more than $1 trillion. If California had been an independent nation, its economy would have ranked fifth in the world, ahead of India, Britain, and France, and trailing only the United States, China, Japan, and Germany. Texas boasted the nation's second largest economy, having surpassed New York in 2006.[1] The Lone Star State yielded nearly $1.9 trillion in GDP in 2019, which would have ranked ninth in the world, behind Italy, but ahead of Brazil, Canada, and the Russian Federation.[2] The two states ranked high on the global list even though they had far smaller populations than most nations in this elite group.

The two states have taken different paths to economic growth. Texas has relied on business-friendly free-market principles and a commitment to keeping costs low. Indeed, its greatest advantage over California and many other states has been its ability to maintain comparatively low costs across the board—in land, energy, labor, taxes, and regulatory compliance. Texas has also developed world-class strength in a few critical sectors, including, most importantly, energy and energy-related industries.

Conversely, California long ago lost the ability to compete on cost. Instead, it has developed a high-cost, high-value economy, a feat it accomplished largely by dominating the New Economy of high technology and other creative enterprises. The amazing phenomenon of Silicon Valley, combined with the state's strength in other creative sectors such as the entertainment industry, has attracted entrepreneurs, highly skilled workers, and investment capital. Partly as a result of the New Economy's success, California's workers are among the most productive in the United States. At the same time, the state's businesses have been forced to pay a high price for energy, labor, taxes, and regulatory compliance, and many have chosen to leave California in search of more affordable locations, taking with them many middle-class jobs.

Texas vs. California. Kenneth P. Miller, Oxford University Press (2020). © Oxford University Press.
DOI: 10.1093/oso/9780190077402.001.0001.

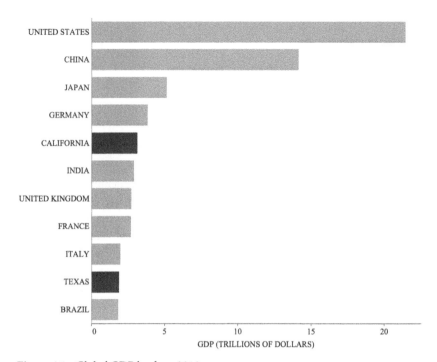

Figure 4.1. Global GDP leaders, 2019

Sources: World Bank, U.S. Bureau of Economic Analysis

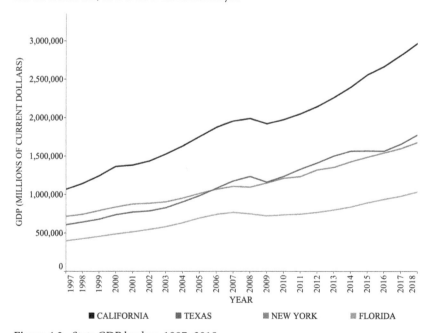

Figure 4.2. State GDP leaders, 1997–2019

Sources: U.S. Bureau of Economic Analysis, California Department of Finance

The divergent economic models of Texas and California have contributed to the rivals' political polarization. Most of Texas's economic foundations, including dominance of the energy sector and cost competitiveness, have relied upon and reinforced its conservative red state politics and policies. The main countertrend is the growing technology sector, which has introduced a streak of progressive social and political values to the Lone Star State.

Meanwhile, California's economic model has increasingly aligned with its progressive politics. Both ends of California's stratified economy have reinforced its blue state orientation. At the high end, New Economy elites have embraced much of the state's progressive political agenda, while at the bottom, many low-income residents have supported government intervention to redress the state's chronic income inequality, which is compounded by its high cost of living. This chapter explores these differences by briefly discussing the nature of state economies within the federal system and then describing the development and political implications of the rivals' economic models.

National Context

Like all fifty states, Texas and California have enjoyed the benefits of participating in a powerful national economy. With a GDP of more than $21 trillion as of 2019, the U.S. economy remained by far the world's largest—one-third greater than runner-up China.[3] The nation's economic dynamism could be attributed in part to its original design, which promoted the free flow of people, capital, goods, and services across state lines. Moreover, the federal system's common currency, monetary policy, legal code, tax rules, transportation networks, and other unifying elements have helped form a strong, integrated, national economy.

At the same time, states have retained distinctive economic models. Within the broad confines of federal law, they have pursued their own tax, labor, regulatory, and spending policies and have specialized in different economic sectors. The various approaches have produced uneven results over time. Early on, northern states were the first to industrialize and thus achieved the nation's highest levels of economic development and wealth. Southern states, by contrast, remained agrarian and poor. Eventually, however, the old regional gaps narrowed. As the North's industrial base eroded, the nation's center of economic gravity moved south and west. By the end of the twentieth century, the nation's regions were competing on more even terms for corporate headquarters, production facilities, skilled workers, and other drivers of economic growth. This competition often divided along red and blue lines. Red states, especially in the South, attracted and retained businesses by promising business-friendly tax, labor, and regulatory policies, while higher-cost blue states, mostly on the coasts, promoted their urban amenities, highly educated workers, and progressive social values.[4]

Modern economies are highly complex, and many factors determine their performance. Economists generally agree, however, that both red and blue states have gained a competitive advantage when industries within their borders have developed "clusters" that specialize in producing high-value, tradable goods and services. Clusters form when a group of producers in a given industry brings together highly skilled workers, suppliers, service providers, and investors into a small geographic area. Many clusters also draw on universities and other institutions for specialized education, research, training, and technical support. Successful clusters drive innovation, increase productivity, generate new businesses, create high-paying jobs, attract skilled workers, amass capital, and raise incomes and wealth throughout the regions where they are located.[5] Clusters exist throughout the United States. One can think of finance on Wall Street, auto making in Detroit, music in Tennessee, and oil and gas in Texas. The information technology industry has formed clusters as well, most prominently in Silicon Valley, but also in other parts of the country including Boston, Seattle, Austin, and the North Carolina Research Triangle.

High-tech clusters, in particular, have produced winners and losers. Critics note that although such clusters have generated great wealth, they have also deepened economic inequality by unevenly distributing incomes and raising housing and other costs.[6] The consequences have been especially acute for those who are less educated, lower skilled, and lower paid, thus fueling a national debate over how to promote economic growth in a fair and sustainable way. Texas and California come to that debate with different economic histories and contrasting strategies for the future.

Texas

Especially considering its early limitations, Texas has excelled at developing a dynamic, modern economy. Throughout the nineteenth century, the Lone Star State was much like the rest of the South—poor and agrarian, dominated by subsistence farming and the large-scale production of a few agricultural commodities. According to historian T. R. Fehrenbach, "Texas entered the twentieth century with its basic society a full two generations, or about sixty years, behind the development of the American mainstream. Industry was in its infancy; among the people themselves, the norms and patterns of industrial society had no root."[7]

Early Economy

The state's early economy relied heavily on cotton. By 1900, growers were culti-vating more than 3.5 million bales of cotton on more than seven million acres of Texas land, making the state the nation's largest cotton producer.[8] Cattle also featured prominently. In the years after the Civil War, Texas cattlemen drove herds hundreds of miles to northern markets, searing into the state's identity the image of the cowboy on the open range. Transportation by rail soon replaced the cattle drive, but ranching continued to grow. By 1890, Texas boasted the nation's largest herds, together totaling some 8.5 million head. Meanwhile, the timber industry—centered in East Texas—remained the state's other major economic activity. At the turn of the twentieth century, Texas was producing more than two billion board feet of lumber per year and the industry was employing more workers and generating more income than any other business in the state.[9] Yet, the production of cotton, cattle, and lumber was not a winning formula for cre-ating a modern industrial economy. As of 1900, Texas, like the rest of the South, remained an underdeveloped agricultural colony of the North, with no clear prospect for closing the gap.

Oil!

The state's economic prospects brightened dramatically in 1901, when oil was discovered in East Texas. This breakthrough quickly made petroleum Texas's most important industry and put the state's economy on a path to become one of the world's most powerful. The discovery came with a bang. At the dawn of the twentieth century, in a quiet corner of southeastern Texas, a prospector named Anthony Lucas suspected that oil might be lurking under a hill called "Spindletop." Lucas worked with other wildcatters to erect a derrick and send a drill nearly a thousand feet below the surface, through layers of dirt, sand, and rock. On January 10, 1901, the drill hit its target. Tons of steel pipe exploded from the well, followed by a massive eruption of mud, rocks, gas, and oil. The gusher made a deafening roar and reached hundreds of feet in the air. Lucas's well had tapped into a massive pool of oil. Soon, the discovery produced a frenzy not un-like the California gold rush. A multitude of drillers, investors, and swindlers converged on the area to get a piece of the action. Speculators fought to buy leases to nearby property, and within six months more than one hundred sepa-rate enterprises had drilled 214 separate wells on the Spindletop Hill. Texas was suddenly home to the world's greatest oil boom.[10]

Spindletop erupted at a propitious time, just as oil was becoming the planet's most valuable commodity. The United States and other countries were reaching higher levels of industrialization and needed new sources of energy to fuel their economies. Oil would soon replace coal as the leading source to meet that need. For many years, oil had been used mostly to produce kerosene, a fuel used for lighting. After Thomas Edison created the incandescent bulb, electricity displaced kerosene as the preferred fuel for illumination. This disruption could have destroyed the oil industry, but new uses for the resource quickly emerged. Railroad locomotives and ship engines began converting from coal to oil and the advent of the automobile promised a huge market for gasoline.

After Spindletop, other discoveries solidified Texas's leadership of the industry. The most important came in 1930, when a wildcatter named "Dad" Joiner tapped into what would become known as the great East Texas oil field. Although its size was not immediately apparent, the field turned out to be the largest of its time, a vast pool stretching more than forty miles north-to-south and up to twelve miles wide. Before its full extent was known, Joiner sold his interest to another wildcatter, H. L. Hunt, who came to symbolize the self-made, risk-taking, independent Texas oilman—a description shared by such figures as Hugh Roy Cullen, Clint Murchison, Sid Richardson, and Glen McCarthy.[11]

The East Texas oil field produced huge yields and soon became a critical resource for the Allies during World War II. Over the course of the war, Allied forces consumed seven billion barrels of oil, six billion of which came from the United States, and much of that from Texas. To securely transport petroleum from the oilfields, the U.S. government ordered construction of two massive pipelines from Texas to New Jersey—a distance of more than 1,200 miles. Long after the war, those pipelines continued to transport oil and gas from Texas to the Northeast, part of a dense web of oil and pipelines that linked Texas to the rest of the United States.[12]

In the postwar period, the Texas oil and gas cluster matured and became increasingly dominant. Whereas in 1900, the American oil industry was based in the East and was largely controlled by John D. Rockefeller's Standard Oil Company, by the mid-twentieth century, Texas had established itself as the world's energy capital. Centered in Houston with a strong presence in Dallas and other parts of the state, the cluster developed a vast network of major oil and gas companies, smaller independents, refineries, pipeline and storage companies, engineering and construction firms, specialized suppliers, financial institutions, and professional programs at the state's top universities.

The large number of energy-related Fortune 500 companies headquartered in Texas reflected the cluster's strength. As of 2019, the list included major oil companies Exxon-Mobil, Phillips 66, Valero Energy, Conoco Phillips, Occidental, Anadarko, Apache, and Marathon; companies that refined petroleum or provided pipeline services, such as Energy Transfer LP, Plains GP Holdings, Holly Frontier, and Targa Resources; and companies that provide engineering, construction, or technical services for the industry, such as Halliburton and Quanta Services. Although the list changes from year to year, about fifty Fortune 500 companies were headquartered in Texas and more than half of them were linked—directly or indirectly—to oil and gas.[13] As in other clusters, large companies were surrounded by a network of other, smaller firms. Houston alone was home to five thousand energy-related companies.[14]

Texas's energy cluster attracted a world-class community of geologists, petroleum engineers, and other experts who specialized in discovering, extracting, refining, and transporting oil and gas around the globe. This community developed innovations in exploration and production as well as downstream processes. Perhaps the most consequential breakthrough came near the turn of the millennium, when engineers developed a sophisticated new form of hydraulic fracturing, or "fracking," that could extract oil and gas from shale rock. As discussed further in Chapter 11, this discovery allowed the industry to expand oil and gas production to stunning new levels. Texas was at the center of the revolution.[15] Between 2007 and 2019, it increased crude oil production from 336 million barrels to more than 1.8 billion barrels per year, by far the largest increase of any U.S. oil-producing state.[16] The state's enormous spike in production, combined with its technical expertise and innovations, reinforced its position as the capital of the global energy industry.

Like successful clusters elsewhere, the Texas energy industry strengthened the state's economy, with benefits flowing to real estate development, manufacturing, trade and logistics, finance, and more. One of the cluster's most notable contributions was the development of the petrochemical industry. Petrochemicals are products derived in whole or in part from petroleum and natural gas. During World War II, the U.S. military demanded new petroleum-based products, including synthetic rubber and chemicals used in explosives. The government worked with oil companies to build plants along the Texas Gulf Coast that could convert petroleum into these and other products. After the war, the government's involvement receded, but private enterprises invested heavily in the fast-growing petrochemical industry. The industry soon made countless consumer and industrial products, ranging from plastics and synthetic fibers to fertilizers and pharmaceuticals.[17] The Texas Gulf Coast became the world's largest petrochemical cluster—by the 1970s, the region was producing more than 40 percent of the nation's basic petrochemicals. The industry generated innovations, turned out high-value tradable goods, attracted highly skilled workers, and pulled in investment capital.

Although it is hard to overstate the importance of oil to Texas's historical economic development and future economic health, the state's reliance on this resource has created vulnerabilities. One long-term threat is the rising environmentalist challenge to fossil fuels, a topic discussed at length in Chapter 11.

Another more immediate problem is price volatility in oil markets. For decades, the steep rise and fall of oil prices caused the Texas economy to go through cycles of boom and bust. When oil prices were high, the industry's bounty rippled through the whole Texas economy; but when oil prices collapsed, the economy sagged. Dramatic examples of these effects occurred in the 1970s and 1980s. During the 1970s, Middle East conflicts and embargoes by the Organization of Petroleum Exporting Countries (OPEC) caused the price of oil to spike. This shock harmed the economic fortunes of the United States as a whole, but caused the oil industry, and the Texas economy, to flourish. Conversely, in 1986, oil prices fell sharply. This price decline provided a boost to the U.S. economy, but the oil industry suffered—and the pain spread throughout the broader Texas economy. The state's unemployment rate rose, consumer spending and real estate values fell, and financial institutions and other businesses throughout the state faltered.[18]

Diversification

Texas pursued economic diversification to offset to its overreliance on oil. Over time, Texans developed competitive clusters in numerous other sectors, including aircraft manufacturing, air transportation, aerospace, finance, construction, trade and logistics, information technology, and green energy. The Dallas–Fort Worth air transportation cluster, for example, became home to one of the nation's highest-volume airports (DFW) and the corporate headquarters of two of the nation's largest airlines—American and Southwest. The Port of Houston became one of the nation's busiest, and Texas established itself as the national leader in exports, exceeding California and New York combined. The Houston aerospace cluster, centered on NASA's Johnson Space Center, generated many innovations and pulled billions of dollars into the state's economy.[19] And the Texas information technology cluster, centered in Austin, became one of the nation's most powerful, tracing its success to early breakthroughs by Texas Instruments, innovations by Dell Computers, and the development of a dense network of tech firms. As this cluster grew, Texas came to export more technology products—from semi-conductors to telecommunication equipment—than California or any other state.[20]

By the beginning of the twenty-first century, the Texas economy was more diversified than it had been in the 1980s, and thus better able to withstand yet another major oil shock. Between June 2014 and January 2016, a global surplus caused the price of oil to collapse from $115 to less than $30 per barrel. A wrenching crisis ensued—many oil and gas producers filed for bankruptcy, and companies throughout the cluster were battered. This time, however, diversification paid off as the Texas economy continued to grow. Although Houston, Midland-Odessa, and other energy-producing regions were hard-hit in 2015–2016, their weakness was offset by strength in Dallas–Fort Worth, Austin, and other metropolitan areas with more broad-based economies.[21]

Most of all, Texas has pursued economic development through what it calls the "Texas Model." As discussed in detail in later chapters, the model has spurred growth by keeping costs low. Texas has been famously steadfast in keeping a lid on taxes—it has no state income tax, and its overall tax burden remains among the nation's lowest. More broadly, Texas has consistently kept its cost of living below the national average, an impressive achievement for a highly urbanized state. As of 2019, the cost of living in Texas was 9 percent less than in the United States as a whole—and dramatically less than in California, which was a staggering 40 percent above the national average.[22] Much of that difference could be attributed to Texas's comparatively low housing costs. As Texas's population surged in the first decades of the twentieth century, housing demand increased and home prices rose, but far less than in California and other high-cost states. Texas became a "home building machine" and expanded its housing supply nearly on pace with demand.[23] As a result, one could buy a house for half the price, or less, in Texas's large metropolitan areas than a similar home in California's major cities. Texas thus put ownership of a home within reach for many who could not afford one in California or other high-cost states. That difference alone made relocation to Texas attractive for many workers. Finally, Texas's political and civic leaders were hungrier to build the state's economy than officials in many other states. Former governor Rick Perry set the tone when he went on "hunting trips" to recruit businesses in California and elsewhere to relocate to Texas.

The state's efforts to grow its economy produced strong results. In the three decades between 1990 and 2019, the Texas economy grew at a faster pace than the national economy and created more jobs than any other state. Texas also succeeded in convincing many large corporations to relocate their headquarters to the state or expand their operations there. These developments solidified Texas's reputation for being business friendly, and the state consistently ranked at or near the top of national lists of the best places for doing business.[24]

Of course, Texas also had economic challenges. Although the gap had narrowed, Texas was still not as wealthy as California or some other states, as measured by per capita income. Taking costs into account further narrowed the gap, but did not eliminate it. Moreover, Texas's commitment to low taxes and limited government necessarily produced trade-offs. The state struggled to provide public goods, such as education and health care, to its quickly growing and diversifying population. Yet, despite these challenges, millions clearly wanted to participate in the Texas economy, and were voting with their feet.

California

While the Texas economy got off to a slow start, California quickly became an economic power. To be sure, the Golden State enjoyed many natural advantages—access to the Pacific, eight hundred miles of coastline, one of the world's great natural harbors, fertile soil, mineral wealth, and one of the most temperate climates on earth. The state exploited these natural assets by investing heavily in economic development, with capital flowing from both public and private sources. Builders established rail connections to the East; a huge harbor complex in Los Angeles; world-class bridges across the San Francisco Bay; dozens of dams and aqueducts to capture, store, and transfer water to farms and urban areas; a vast system of roads and highways; public and private universities; scientific and cultural institutions; and more.

Early Economy

California's early investments caused its economy to excel in many sectors, including agriculture, energy, manufacturing, trade, entertainment, and tourism. Agriculture is a prime example. California's first settlers knew that the region's fertile soils and mild climate could support a flourishing agricultural economy, but only if water could be found to sustain crops during the state's long dry seasons. The state made large-scale investments in dams and aqueducts, and those projects allowed agriculture to flourish across a range of climate zones. California became, by far, the nation's most productive agricultural state.[25]

California also achieved early success in the oil industry. Before Texas became the nation's dominant oil producer, California held that title. The state's first large-scale oil production began in the 1890s with major discoveries in Los Angeles and the San Joaquin Valley. By 1910, California was producing more than seventy million barrels a year, the most in the United States and more than any foreign nation. In the 1920s, the industry built derricks throughout the Los Angeles region, along the coast, offshore, in interior canyons, and even in downtown Los Angeles and Beverly Hills. Large reserves were discovered north of Los Angeles in the San Joaquin Valley and on the Santa Barbara coast. Standard Oil of California (later Chevron) and Union Oil of California were the largest producers, while some independent oil men, such as Edward Doheny, made fortunes in the California oil fields. Oil quickly became the leading export of the new Port of Los Angeles.[26]

California also developed early strength in manufacturing. In the first decades of the twentieth century, Los Angeles became the manufacturing capital of the West Coast in part by investing in large-scale infrastructure (including petroleum-based power generation, a deep water port, and an extensive highway and rail system), and in part by keeping costs low. At the time, land was cheap in Southern California, and the region enforced the open shop, which held its labor costs below the more heavily unionized San Francisco Bay Area. By 1920, Southern California was one of the nation's most productive manufacturing hubs, generating large volumes of tradable goods, including automobiles, garments, glass, furniture, tires, and airplanes.

California developed strength in other sectors as well, including finance, real estate development, trade, entertainment, and tourism. Its vibrant economy made it a magnet for newcomers from across the country and around the world seeking a better life. The different fates of three California economic clusters—aviation and aerospace, entertainment, and information technology—help explain why the state's economy has become what it is today.

Aviation and Aerospace

As part of its flourishing manufacturing economy, Southern California developed the world's greatest aviation cluster. In the first decades of the twentieth century, industry pioneers Glenn Martin, Malcolm and Allan Loughead (later Lockheed), Donald Douglas, Jack Northrop, and T. C. Ryan set up operations in the region. Local businessmen, led by *Los Angeles Times* publisher Harry Chandler, supplied start-up capital to the emerging ventures. In the 1920s, the California Institute of Technology (Caltech) created the Guggenheim Aeronautical Laboratory, which provided the new industry with research, technical support, and engineering talent. The region's low cost of land and labor also helped the industry get off the ground. The cluster locked in its dominance in the 1930s, when it achieved a series of breakthrough innovations. Most importantly, Lockheed's L-10 Electra and Douglas's DC-3 made possible widespread commercial aviation. By the mid-1930s, the Southern California cluster ruled the nation's aircraft market, with Douglas accounting for nearly 60 percent of total sales and Lockheed more than 30 percent.[27]

World War II supercharged this cluster. Factories in and around Los Angeles operated on round-the-clock shifts to supply thousands of aircraft for the war effort. At the peak of production, this massive enterprise employed 280,000 workers in the Southern California region.[28] The war's end could have devastated the industry—and, indeed, the military canceled contracts and many workers lost their jobs. But the war years had expanded the cluster's capacities and strengthened its ties to the Department of Defense. Soon, the Pentagon turned to Southern California to produce most of the nation's Cold War arsenal of jet fighters, bombers, and missiles.

The state's aviation industry successfully transitioned to new specializations in aerospace and electronics. Its network expanded to include new suppliers, subcontractors, and academic institutions, such as the Jet Propulsion Laboratory (JPL) near Pasadena and the RAND Corporation in Santa Monica (created at Douglas Aircraft Company in late 1945 and established as an independent nonprofit in 1948), as well as expanded graduate programs at the University of Southern California and the University of California at Los Angeles. The cluster also made prominent contributions to the nation's space program. Southern California plants built many of the icons of U.S. space flight, including Saturn rockets, the Apollo command modules, Skylab, and the Space Shuttle, as well as associated advanced guidance and communications technologies. Meanwhile, JPL designed and guided NASA's unmanned space missions. This hive of activity drew billions of federal dollars to the region's economy, created hundreds of thousands of well-paying jobs, and produced positive spillover effects throughout the state. The cluster experienced a final extraordinary surge in the 1980s, as the massive Reagan-era defense buildup pumped capital and workers into the system.

However, after the Cold War ended, the cluster collapsed. For decades, the region's aerospace industry relied heavily on federal dollars, and was unable to adapt when that funding dried up. In the 1990s, many plants went dark and major firms consolidated, downsized, or shut their doors. More than two hundred thousand aerospace workers in the region lost their jobs, including many engineers and other workers with specialized skills. Thousands could find no comparable employment and many left the state.[29] To be sure, Southern California's aviation and aerospace cluster did not completely die. After the collapse, a remnant of the industry remained in the Los Angeles area and new ventures such as Elon Musk's SpaceX stirred hopes for a revival.[30] But few believed aerospace would ever again provide such a bountiful source of jobs, economic development, and wealth for the region or the state.

Hollywood

The entertainment industry has been one of California's most durable economic clusters. Thomas Edison invented motion pictures in New Jersey in the 1890s, and the earliest commercial filmmaking centered in New Jersey and New York. Early in the twentieth century, however, filmmakers migrated to Southern California, drawn by the region's temperate climate, diverse landscapes, and comparatively low land and labor costs.[31] D. W. Griffith, a transplant from Kentucky, asserted early leadership. He developed many film-making techniques, including the close-up, the flash-back, and the fade-out, and in 1915 released the industry's first blockbuster, *The Birth of a Nation*. In 1913, Cecil B. DeMille arrived from New York and soon become the world's most successful filmmaker. A talented group of immigrants, including Samuel Goldwyn, Adolph Zukor, William Fox, and Carl Laemmle, also moved to Southern California. Together, these men created the studio system, an efficient, vertically integrated means for financing, producing, distributing, and screening motion pictures.[32]

The emerging cluster attracted a talented community of writers, directors, actors, artists, musicians, and technical workers. It soon achieved stunning success. By 1920, millions of Americans each week attended Hollywood-produced movies in more than twenty thousand movie theaters around the country. Hollywood also dominated the global film industry, producing 90 percent of movies shown in foreign countries. Early stars such as Mary Pickford, Douglas Fairbanks, and Charlie Chaplin became the first global celebrities and were treated like royalty in foreign capitals.[33] By the mid-1920s, filmmaking had become the nation's fifth-largest industry.[34]

The studio system continued to thrive through the Great Depression and World War II, but soon thereafter was disrupted by a number of forces. The first was the Supreme Court's decision in *U.S. v. Paramount Pictures* (1948), which held that various elements of the studio system violated U.S. antitrust laws.[35] The rise of television in the early 1950s further unsettled the film industry by introducing new competition. The old studio system could not survive these challenges, but the industry creatively adapted. Studios reduced the number of films they produced, cut their payrolls, and began to rely on a new pool of independent contractors. The new model was much more fluidly organized than the old studio system, less vertically integrated, more flexibly networked, and oriented toward individual projects. Indeed, Hollywood developed an early version of the organizational models of the New Economy. Under the new system, much of the filming moved out of Los Angeles (in part due to lower costs and higher subsidies in other locations), but the region maintained its dominance over the industry.[36]

More recently, the entertainment sector has adapted to new innovations, such as home video and streaming. Through it all, Los Angeles has remained the hub of deal-making, financing, pre- and post-production work, and technical support in the motion picture industry and for similar activities in television production and music recording. A century after establishing itself as the capital of the entertainment industry, Hollywood still attracts a creative class of actors, writers, directors, musicians, and agents, and generates economic wealth for the region and the state.[37]

Silicon Valley

Silicon Valley became the most powerful economic cluster in California—and, arguably, in the world—through its mastery of the technology industry and the New Economy. The cluster's ascendancy is comparatively recent. As late as the 1950s, the region remained a quiet agricultural valley south of San Francisco; one had to look hard to see signs of its extraordinary future. The origins of that success can be traced to a community of engineers and entrepreneurs associated with Stanford University. Early in the twentieth century, that community began exploring the new technologies of radio and electronics. A Stanford professor named Frederick Terman believed that scientific innovations in these and other fields should find commercial application.

In the late 1930s, two of Terman's students, William Hewlett and David Packard, started developing new innovations in a Palo Alto garage and launched the Hewlett-Packard Company. After World War II, Terman and others at Stanford helped incubate HP and other early tech start-ups by establishing the Stanford Industrial Park (now Stanford Research Park), which became home to companies engaged in research and development. Terman also encouraged Stanford to create Stanford Research Institute (later named SRI International), which had a mission "to pursue science for practical purposes [that] might not be fully compatible internally with the traditional roles of the university."[38]

The emerging cluster soon formed a pattern of rapid business formation and spin-offs. The pattern can be traced to an engineer named William Shockley, a Stanford graduate who, in the late 1940s, co-invented a small device for semiconducting electric signals while working at Bell Labs in New Jersey. In 1955, Shockley returned to Palo Alto, formed a firm called Shockley Transistor Corporation, and attracted a group of talented engineers to his company. Two years later, eight of those engineers left Shockley to establish their own firm, the Fairchild Semiconductor Company. Fairchild developed a way to make transistors from silicon, thus creating the first silicon integrated circuit. In time, Fairchild produced dozens of spin-offs of its own, including Intel and AMD. By the early 1970s, the region's preeminence in developing silicon-based semiconductors led a journalist named Don Hoefler to bestow on it the name "Silicon Valley."[39]

Part of the Valley's genius was its ability to make repeated technological breakthroughs and bring these discoveries to market, largely because it had a concentration of highly skilled, creative, and ambitious people working in close proximity on similar problems. Time and again, when the cluster commercially advanced one innovation, such as semiconductors, it did not rest, but developed another—from personal computers, video games, servers, and the Internet to digital media, smart phones, apps, autonomous cars, and more. This culture of perpetual technological innovation and commercial development attracted money (in the forms of government contracts, venture capital, and, eventually, crowd funding) as well as human talent.[40]

Indeed, Silicon Valley drew in some of the best talent from across the United States and around the world. Young technologists migrated to a place that celebrated innovation and generated wealth, but also tolerated failure, and even valued it, because it was seen as an essential part of the creative process. Newcomers moved freely from start-up to start-up and capital flowed to young people with new ideas. The paradigmatic migrant to the Valley was Mark Zuckerberg, a New York native who developed the concept for Facebook while still an undergraduate at Harvard. Zuckerberg could have tried to launch his venture anywhere, but realized that no place could match Silicon Valley's dense cluster of venture capitalists, information technology firms, and young tech workers. In 2004, Zuckerberg moved to California—first to downtown Palo Alto, then to Stanford Research Park, before establishing a new headquarters in Menlo Park. Silicon Valley provided Zuckerberg start-up funding, including an early angel investment from Peter Thiel, as well as a deep pool of highly skilled creative workers steeped in the local entrepreneurial tech culture.[41]

As the technology cluster grew and diversified, many Internet start-ups such as Twitter, Uber, and Pinterest chose to locate in San Francisco rather than in the suburban towns of Palo Alto, Menlo Park, Mountain View, or Cupertino, in part because many young tech workers preferred to live and work in a more urban environment. By the early twenty-first century, San Francisco rivaled Silicon Valley as a hub of tech innovation.

In 2019, the largest concentration of Fortune 500 companies headquartered in California came from the tech sector—including Apple, Alphabet, Intel, Hewlett-Packard, Cisco, Oracle, Facebook, Qualcomm, Synnex, Western Digital, PayPal, Applied Materials, eBay, Netflix, Salesforce, Adobe, and NetApp. In 2018, Apple had become the first to top $1 trillion in market capitalization, making it for a time the world's most valuable publicly traded company. Google's parent Alphabet and Facebook also ranked in the world's top 10.[42] The founders of these and other high-flying tech companies quickly rose from obscurity to become some of the richest people in the world, and many early employees of top tech firms also achieved great wealth. Many companies in the cluster were dominating new sectors, and start-ups were constantly emerging. Although most of this activity remained centered in the Bay Area, it also spread to other parts California, including "Silicon Beach" on the west side of Los Angeles, the biotechnology cluster in San Diego, and an emerging green energy industry in locations throughout the state.

The different fates of these three clusters were part of California's larger economic and demographic sorting at the turn of the twenty-first century. California's stunning success in technology, combined with its strength in entertainment and other creative and knowledge-based industries, generated much of the state's economic growth, productivity, high-paying jobs, and wealth.[43] These successes were matched, however, by weaknesses elsewhere. The collapse of the state's aerospace cluster represented a broader decline in high-end manufacturing and other sectors that had once sustained a strong middle class.[44]

California's economy became highly stratified. At the top, it produced incredibly attractive opportunities for elite "knowledge workers"—that is, computer programmers, engineers, designers, scientists, venture capitalists, attorneys, and other highly educated professionals—and, at the bottom, ample work for low-skilled laborers in the service industries and other fields.[45] But the middle hollowed out as the supply of well-paying, middle-class jobs declined. The main exception was public employment. The public sector continued to grow in California and provided a large numbers of jobs. California's public employees generally received substantial salaries and benefits, situating most of them in the middle class. But a good number of them also struggled to make ends meet.

The state's middle-class crisis was intensified by rising costs. A cost of living 40 percent higher than the national average drove many Californians to their limits. Housing became the major stressor, accounting for 80 percent of the state's higher costs.[46] For decades, California had failed to build enough single- and multi-family residences to meet demand, especially in its coastal areas, due to restrictive zoning and environmental laws and high land, labor, regulatory, permitting, and related costs.[47] As a consequence, by 2019, the median home value in California had surpassed half a million dollars—more than double the national median and more than 2.5 times the median in Texas.[48] Along large stretches of California's coastal areas, the cost of a home was far higher. In San Francisco, for example, the median house price reached $1.7 million.

The state's home ownership rates fell to their lowest levels since the 1940s, and were now among the lowest in the United States. California's Latino and African American populations had the hardest time achieving home ownership.[49] California renters struggled as well, especially in the state's coastal areas. In many places, the median monthly rent for a one-bedroom apartment was over $2,000, and in San Francisco, it was approaching $4,000, the highest in any major U.S. city. The state's tax and regulatory policies added further cost burdens—for utilities, transportation, and more. The winners in the California's New Economy were able to pay these premiums, but many middle- and working-class families— let alone the poor—could not. One-third of Californians said that the high cost of housing alone was causing them to consider leaving the state.[50]

California's economic sorting was reflected in migration patterns. Most of those entering the state came from one of two groups—either highly educated workers from other states or abroad who were attracted to California's tech, entertainment, and other high-end knowledge jobs, or low-skilled immigrants who were destined for work at the low end of the employment ladder. The Golden State no longer attracted many middle- and working-class people from other parts of the United States; to the contrary, its stratified economy was causing millions of them to leave.

At the same time, California's high cost of doing business caused many firms to move to lower-cost states, with the largest number going to Texas. Occidental Petroleum relocated from Los Angeles to Houston, and a long list of corporations moved from California to the Dallas area. These firms included Toyota USA, the North American subsidiary of the world's largest automaker; McKesson, the nation's largest pharmaceutical distributor and sixth largest company; Fluor Corporation and Jacobs Engineering Group, two major international design and construction firms; Omnitracs, a company that manages operations for the trucking industry; Core-Mark, a supplier to convenience stores; and Jamba Juice, the maker of popular smoothies. In late 2019, the massive brokerage firm Charles Schwab announced that it, too, was moving its headquarters from San Francisco to the Dallas area. The company's founder and chairman, Charles "Chuck" Schwab, explained that "the costs of doing business here are so much higher."[51] Moreover, many companies that kept their headquarters in California moved the majority of their employees to Texas and other cost-competitive places. This exodus even hit the state's tech sector. Many California-based tech firms, such as Apple, Google, and Facebook, were shifting a larger share of their operations out of state, and a growing number of start-ups were moving to tech hubs in less expensive places.[52]

Economic Models and Polarization

These economic differences have contributed to the rivals' political polarization by reflecting and reinforcing the two states' political orientations. The Texas economy has helped align the state with the Republican Party in several ways. First, its dominant clusters—the ones that for years have provided it the greatest economic advantage over other states—are oil and gas, petrochemicals, and related enterprises. These industries depend on state and national support for (or at least tolerance of) fossil fuels, a position Republicans embrace but Democrats increasingly do not. Second, the Texas economic model relies on low taxes. Throughout its history, Texas has kept taxes comparatively low, firmly believing that maintaining a low tax burden provides the state an essential competitive advantage. That conviction naturally aligns with Republican philosophy and has created obstacles for Democrats. Third, the Texas Model's commitment to light regulations more closely aligns with the Republican than the Democratic conception of government. And fourth, the Texas Model's support for low labor costs and the "right to work" has severely weakened the state's unions. This circumstance has deprived the Texas Left of a primary means of mobilizing public employees, as well as low-income and minority workers (especially Latinos) to support Democratic candidates and progressive causes.

On the other hand, the success of the Texas Model has not exclusively benefited Republicans. The state's vibrant economy, plentiful jobs, and low costs have made it a magnet for newcomers who have brought with them a range of social and political perspectives. To be sure, many new Texans have been attracted by the state's conservative political culture and politics. Yet, other new residents are more progressive and would like to change the Texas Model and make it more like the blue states from which they came. Migrants flowing into the state's fast-growing technology sector are one such group. Compared to workers in the state's more traditional industries, technologists tend to hold progressive social and political views and often support Democrats and progressive causes. The surge in tech workers has provided new energy to the Texas Left—and a potential disruption to the close relationship between business and conservative politics in the Lone Star State.[53] Nevertheless, although the future is uncertain, the dominant structures of Texas's economy will likely continue to align with conservative policies and the Republican Party.

Conversely, one can see several ways the California economy has helped align the state with the Democratic Party. First, the collapse of aerospace and other middle-class jobs in the 1990s thinned the ranks of Republican voters. Many Republican suburbs in Southern California quickly flipped to the Democrats as these older, more conservative workers departed, and a new, more liberal population moved in.[54] Second, as California became more heavily unionized in certain sectors, organizations such as the California Teachers Association (CTA), the California Nurses Association (CNA), and the Service Employees International Union (SEIU) helped mobilize public employees, hotel and restaurant workers, and other groups to bring them into the Democratic fold. The state's strong unions also gave critical organizational and financial backing to Democrats and to progressive causes. Third, California's large-scale public spending provided direct economic benefits to a large number of the state's residents—and many of them naturally aligned with the party more committed to maintaining that support. And fourth, as discussed further in the next chapter, Hollywood, Silicon Valley, and other flourishing sectors of the New Economy produced a sizable, well-resourced, progressive-leaning constituency for Democratic candidates and their social and political causes.[55]

The rivals' contrasting economic models, and the many disparate effects that flow from them, thus help explain why the two states have divided politically. But, like demographics, economics provides only a partial explanation for the polarization of Texas and California. Cultural differences offer further clues.

5

Culture

For millions around the world, the names "Texas" and "California" evoke vivid cultural images. In the popular imagination, Texas is the land of grit and swagger, of cowboys, oilmen, and Friday night lights; California, the land of glitter and dreams, of hippies, starlets, and endless summers. Beneath these surface images lie deeper cultural identities. More than demographics or economics, these identities have shaped the two states' political rivalry. To be sure, both Texas and California are complex places with enormous cultural diversity. This chapter does not seek to describe this diversity in detail; instead, it presents in broad strokes the rival states' dominant cultural traits and discusses how these tendencies have influenced their politics.

Texas's dominant culture is a fusion of southern and western elements. The state's southern orientation can be seen in its religious fervor and respect for tradition; its western character shows through in its pragmatism, individualism, and toughness. At the same time, Texas belongs to the borderlands shared with Mexico. The state's fast-growing Mexican American population, with its own deep roots and cultural traditions, has made the Texan identity more complex, but in many ways has aligned with the state's dominant conservative perspective. Recent waves of newcomers have helped make Texas's urban centers more diverse and progressive than they used to be, but these blue islands have not yet overtaken the red Texas sea. Finally, Texas's cultural identity is shaped by populist forms of Lone Star patriotism—the view that Texas is a unique place, a state unlike all others, a nation within the nation. Texans' visceral love for their state is central to the Lone Star identity.[1]

In *Travels with Charley*, John Steinbeck described what he called Texans' "obsession" with their state. "Texas is a state of mind," he wrote. "Texas is an obsession. Above all, Texas is a nation in every sense of the word. . . . For all its range of space, climate, and physical appearance, and for all the internal squabbles, passions, and strivings, Texas has a tight cohesiveness perhaps stronger than any other section of America. Rich, poor, Panhandle, Gulf, city, country, Texas is the obsession, the proper study, and the passionate possession of all Texans."[2]

California, by comparison, has absorbed a broad range of cultural influences and, over time, has increasingly embraced a progressive worldview. From its origins, the Golden State was more northern, urban, and cosmopolitan than

Texas vs. California. Kenneth P. Miller, Oxford University Press (2020). © Oxford University Press.
DOI: 10.1093/oso/9780190077402.001.0001.

Texas. It was also less tied to tradition than other parts of the nation, and more intent on inventing the future. In the 1960s, the writer Wallace Stegner captured this characteristic when he described California as "Innovationville."[3]

At the same time, California has experienced internal cultural fissures. In broad terms, the San Francisco Bay area was always the state's most culturally progressive region, a global capital of the cultural left. Southern California and the rural interior were more conservative, in part because they absorbed larger streams of migrants from the Midwest and South who brought with them traditional religious and cultural perspectives.[4] Yet Southern California also had a strong progressive streak, centered in Hollywood and west Los Angeles, that more closely aligned with the Bay Area's values than with the cultural right. Moreover, California's Latinos were assimilated in ways that facilitated their adoption of progressive views. Finally, California's cultural right has receded in recent decades, thus narrowing the state's internal divides—and widening the gap that distinguishes it from Texas.

These developments in the rival states have contributed to the nation's broader cultural polarization. In the last decades of the twentieth century, America's cultural consensus eroded and its divisions escalated to the point of culture war. Combatants on both sides sought to win the war by gaining political power. As the Republican and Democratic Parties split more sharply on social issues, voters across the country tied their political choices more closely to their cultural values. By large margins, social conservatives aligned with the Republicans and cultural progressives sided with the Democrats.[5] Texas and California reinforced this cultural-political divide. California saw itself as the vanguard of cultural progressivism, and Texas concluded that its conservative values were under siege and needed to be defended.

This chapter explores these ties between culture and politics by describing how the nation's diverse cultural traditions have been given political expression and how political cultures have distributed geographically. It then shows how the cultural differences between Texas and California have deepened the rivalry between these states.

The Nation's Cultural Geography

Like demographics and economics, culture has a geographic dimension. "Culture" has been defined as "the way of life of a particular people, especially as shown in their ordinary behavior and habits, their attitudes toward each other, and their moral and religious beliefs."[6] Put more simply, culture is *the way we do things around here*. The concept implies that people in a particular place often share common ideas, beliefs, behaviors, habits, customs, and ways of life. But can it be said that millions of people who live in a state the size of Texas or California share a common culture?

According to the cultural geographer Wilbur Zelinsky, a large community, even one as large as a state or a nation, can have a distinctive cultural identity. At the same time, not all members of the community necessarily share its cultural traits, and "statements about the character of the larger community cannot be, indeed should not be, transferred to individuals."[7] Thus, while some people may not conform to the dominant pattern, a state (and even the nation as a whole) possesses a culture "with a certain coherence and personality of its own."[8]

One might think that modern transportation, telecommunications, media, commerce, and other integrating forces would break down cultural distinctions between geographic regions. Yet, the nation still has well-defined "culture areas"—places where most people share a common cultural heritage and identity.[9] Cultural regions are not necessarily tied to political boundaries. For example, a Mormon culture area extends from Utah into parts of several other western states. In that greater region, the Mormon community's religion, history, and traditions form the dominant culture. Many scholars similarly describe a New England cultural region that embraces part or all of several northeastern states. Moreover, multiple culture areas can exist within the same state.[10]

Political Cultures

Culture can assume political forms, and varying patterns of political culture appear in different sections of the country. In the mid-twentieth century, political scientist Daniel Elazar developed a typology of three basic forms of American political culture, which he labeled "traditionalistic," "individualistic," and "moralistic." According to Elazar, one or more of these cultures could be found in every state. States with a traditionalistic political culture tended to defend long-standing social and cultural values and the political status quo, and often had low levels of citizen political participation. By comparison, states with an individualistic political culture viewed politics as a marketplace and focused on sorting out individuals' competing interests. Finally, states with a moralistic political culture believed that government should identify and promote a concept of the common good, and that citizens should actively engage in political life.[11]

In Elazar's view, many states contained more than one of these political cultures, but one could identify a state's dominant type (or synthesis of types). Moreover, political cultures clustered geographically. States with traditionalistic cultures could be found mostly in the South; those with individualistic cultures appeared mostly in the mid-Atlantic region, the Midwest, and the intermountain

West; and those with moralistic cultures spread from New England across the upper Midwest to the Pacific Coast. Writing in 1972, Elazar concluded that Texas had a dominant traditionalistic political culture with a strong individualistic strain, while California had mix of all three, but the moralistic form predominated.[12]

Since Elazar articulated this typology, new factors, including migration, urbanization, and other social changes, have modified state-level political cultures. While one must be mindful of these changes, the basic categories still help explain the geography of American political culture. As discussed in the following chapter, nearly all states with strong traditionalistic cultures became "red"; many (but not all) states with dominant moralistic cultures became "blue"; and states that had individualistic political cultures divided more evenly between the two political parties.[13]

Religious Belief and Practice

In the decades surrounding the new millennium, changes in the nation's religious characteristics deepened its cultural and political divides. Although Americans remained one of the most religiously observant people in the developed world, the percentage who believed in God, identified with Christianity, or regularly attended religious services fell, and the share of those who had no religious belief was on the rise. These changes varied along geographic lines. The South, long known as the nation's "Bible Belt," still strongly identified with traditional Christian faith, while many urban areas, especially in the Northeast and Pacific Northwest, became increasingly "post-Christian" (Figure 5.1).

A large national study conducted in 2014 by the Pew Foundation found that 71 percent of Americans described themselves as Christian (Table 5.1). Among the states, Alabama had the largest percentage of self-identified Christians (86 percent) and Vermont the lowest (54 percent). Texas was tied with several other states in eleventh place, at 77 percent.[14]

In addition, a comparatively high percentage of Texans identified as evangelical Protestant (31 percent), a figure lower than several southern states, but well above the national average. By comparison, lower percentages of Californians identified as Christian and as evangelical. California ranked higher than several Northeastern states in these categories, but trailed Texas and, even more, Texas's southern neighbors (Figure 5.2).[15]

Conversely, 23 percent of Americans said they had no religion—that is, they were atheist, agnostic, or had "no religion in particular." Among the states, Vermont had the highest percentage of religious "nones" (37 percent) and Alabama the lowest (12 percent). California tied for ninth, with more than one-fourth

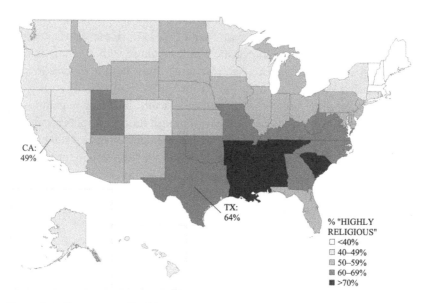

Figure 5.1. Percentage of highly religious by state, 2014
Source: Pew Research Center

Table 5.1 Religious Affiliation in the United States, Texas, California, Dallas, and San Francisco (2014)

	U.S.	Texas	California	Dallas	San Francisco
Christian	71	77	63	78	48
—Evangelical	25	31	20	38	10
—Mainline Protestant	15	13	10	14	6
—Catholic	21	23	28	15	25
—Historically Black Protestant	7	6	2	7	4
—Other Christian	3	4	3	4	3
Non-Christian Faiths	6	4	9	4	15
None	23	18	27	18	35

Source: Pew Research Center

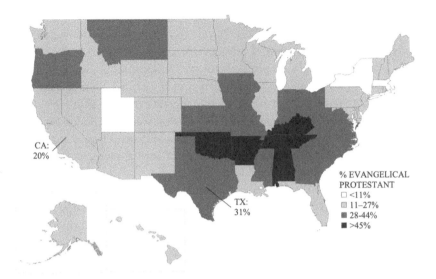

Figure 5.2. Evangelical Protestants by state, 2014
Source: Pew Research Center

(27 percent) of its residents claiming no religion, while Texas had one of the nation's lowest percentages of "nones."[16]

The contrast between the rivals' religious characteristics was more pronounced when one compares two of their largest cities, Dallas and San Francisco. Seventy-eight percent of Dallas residents said they were Christian, and 38 percent evangelical. Conversely, less than half of San Francisco residents identified as Christian and only 10 percent evangelical. More than one-third of San Franciscans had no religion, while the 15 percent who identified with non-Christian faiths was more than double that of the nation as a whole.[17]

According to the study, Americans' religious beliefs and practices closely tracked with their views on social issues. For example, those who identified as evangelical Christian were far less likely than "nones" or most other religious groups to support same-sex marriage, to believe that abortion should be legal in all or most cases, to believe that government aid to the poor does more good than harm, or to believe that stricter environmental laws and regulations are worth the cost.[18]

These religious differences contributed to the nation's partisan divide. Beginning in the 1970s, a large share of committed evangelicals as well as conservative Catholics and others with orthodox faith shifted their partisan allegiance from the Democratic to the Republican Party.[19] According to the 2014 study, Americans who identified as evangelical or were religiously observant—that is, frequently attended religious services, read scripture, or prayed—were far more likely to align with the Republican Party. Conversely, citizens who belonged to more liberal faith communities, infrequently attended religious services, or had no religion at all were far more likely to vote Democratic. The study found that evangelical Christians leaned Republican by nearly a thirty-point margin (56 to 28 percent). Conversely, "nones" leaned Democratic by more than thirty points (54 to 23 percent), and a large percentages of Jews, Muslims, Hindus, Buddhists, and others who belong to major non-Christian faiths also leaned Democratic. Mainline Protestants, Catholics, and Orthodox Christians were more closely divided between the two parties.[20]

Exit polls from the 2012 and 2016 presidential elections found an even stronger tie between religious orientation and partisan voting patterns. According to these polls, 78 percent of those who identified as white evangelical or "born again" Christian supported Republican Mitt Romney in 2012, and 80 percent voted for President Donald Trump in 2016. Conversely, religious "nones" voted for the Democratic candidate at high rates, with 70 percent backing President Obama in 2012 and 67 percent supporting Democrat Hillary Clinton in 2016. In both elections, the Republican candidate won by more than 10 points among those who attended religious services weekly. Sixty-two percent of voters who did not attend any religious services backed the Democrat in both elections.[21]

The tight relationships among religion, culture, and partisanship have deepened divisions between Texas and California—and between red and blue states across the nation.

Texas Culture

Texas's cultural identity is a matter of long-standing debate. Is the Lone Star State primarily southern, rooted in southern-style religious cultural values? Or does it have a more libertarian western identity? Or is it distinctively southwestern? Should it be seen as part of the borderlands with Mexico? Or can Texas be said to be a place unique unto itself—a cohesive cultural entity distinct from all others?[22]

The question allows for various responses. As we have seen, Texas's early cultural influences came primarily from Spain, Mexico, and the American South. Through the nineteenth century, the southern influence grew through emigration from the region, a common agrarian economy, the slave system, secession, confederacy, war, Reconstruction, post-Reconstruction race relations, and a shared religious heritage. As political scientist Cal Jillson argues, "Texas's southern roots were never in question during the nineteenth century. From the initial settlement of the Austin colony through the post–Civil War exodus of southern whites to Texas, the state's population stock and its political and social instincts were overwhelmingly southern."[23]

Rebranding Texas

By the early twentieth century, however, a growing number of influential Texans concluded that the state's southern identity was a barrier to progress. At the time, a large divide still existed between the South and the rest of the nation. The region's lingering attachments to the "Lost Cause," antebellum culture, and agrarian economics impaired its ability to integrate with the North and achieve northern levels of economic development and modernization. After the discovery of oil, Texas's economy began to outpace the rest of the South. To accelerate this development, the state's leaders believed Texas needed to shed its southern cultural identity. The question became how to do so. Their solution was to redefine Texas as fundamentally western.[24]

This cultural makeover progressed in the years leading to 1936, the centennial of Texas independence. As part of the centennial celebration, the state staged pageants and other commemorative events and built more than one thousand physical memorials—including exposition buildings, museums, murals, statues, markers, and monuments.[25] The most imposing was a 567-foot, star-capped column at San Jacinto—taller than the Washington Monument and still the highest masonry column in the world. In these commemorations, the state downplayed its Southern identity and developed a narrative in which Anglo settlement, the revolution, the Alamo, and San Jacinto became metaphors for American Manifest Destiny and the winning of the West.

The effort culminated in the Texas Centennial Exposition, a world's fair held in Dallas from June to November 1936. The exposition was designed to introduce the world to a new Texas by presenting a western-oriented account of the state's past and an optimistic view of its future. Among other attractions, visitors were treated to the Cavalcade of Texas, a massive open-air pageant that portrayed the state's history with a western flavor, as well as "Rangerettes," young women clad in ten-gallon hats, colorful bandannas, plaid shirts, boots, and spurs. (In one memorable moment, the Rangerettes lassoed FBI director J. Edgar Hoover.) Texas native Gene Autry, the famed singing cowboy, filmed the movie *The Big Show* at the exposition, thereby introducing audiences around the world to the centennial's western themes. President Franklin D. Roosevelt paid a visit and saluted "the Empire of Texas."[26]

According to Texas historian Light Townsend Cummins, the makeover was a remarkable success. "As a result of the intellectual changes and official sanctions provided by the Centennial Celebration," Cummins wrote, "the public image of Texas had been rebranded as western by the late 1930s. . . . Texans increasingly viewed themselves as westerners."[27] This shift was not merely symbolic. As it moved deeper into the twentieth century, Texas increasingly embraced the values of pragmatism, self-sufficiency, and libertarianism often associated with the American West. By the late 1940s, the political scientist V. O. Key Jr. said that changes in the state had "weakened the heritage of southern traditionalism, revolutionized the economy, and made Texas more western than southern." In his view, Texas was less attached to the Old South and more concerned about "money and how to make it, about oil and sulfur and gas, about cattle and dust storms and irrigation, about cotton and banking and Mexicans."[28]

Southern-Style Religion

Many scholars have resisted characterizing Texas as western, insisting that the state's true identity remains deeply rooted or "moored" in the South. They argue that Texas has a "stubborn southernness" that is reinforced by numerous factors, including southern demographics, cultural conservatism, and religiosity.[29]

Indeed, religion has provided an especially durable cultural bond between Texas and the rest of the South. Although the earliest Texans were not particularly religious, later waves of southerners inspired by the Second Great Awakening caused Protestant Christianity to flourish in the state.[30] Methodist and Baptist churches attracted the largest numbers. By the close of the nineteenth century, nearly three-quarters of Texas Protestants belonged to these two denominations.[31] When both the Baptists and Methodists divided into northern and southern camps over the issue of slavery, Texas churches joined the southern side, reinforcing the state's religious connection to the rest of the South.[32] Over time, the Southern Baptist Convention (SBC) became Texas's largest and most influential Protestant denomination, with more than four million members in the state. Although immigration from Latin America has increased the size and influence of the Roman Catholic Church (nearly five million members in Texas), Protestants remained the state's dominant religious group.[33]

Even as it modernized, Texas was still part of the Bible Belt, because millions of its residents held fast to traditional Christian beliefs, values, and practices. According to the 2014 Pew study, Texas ranked eleventh on the list of most religious states, based on its comparatively high percentage of residents who believed in God (88 percent); believed that religion is very important in one's life (63 percent); attended religious services at least once per week (42 percent) or once or twice a month or a few times a year (33 percent); and attended prayer, scripture study, or religious education groups at least once a week (30 percent).[34]

And, with nearly one-third of Texans identifying as evangelical Protestant, that tradition remained a formidable force.

Evangelical institutions assumed a central place in Texas culture. The state became home to some of the nation's largest and most influential evangelical "megachurches." These institutions engaged in a wide range of activities, and their pastors became well-known public figures with flourishing broadcasting and publishing ministries. The largest congregations were surrounded by thousands of smaller churches, each with its own community of members. Texas was also home to an abundance of Christian colleges, universities, seminaries, radio and television stations, nonprofit organizations, and ministries—an elaborate evangelical ecosystem.[35]

Evangelicals have long exercised political clout in the state. Although federal tax laws limit the ability of churches and other religious nonprofit organizations to endorse political candidates or contribute to their campaigns, the state's evangelical ecosystem has provided essential support to Republican candidates and conservative causes. In the 1970s, evangelical political activism intensified in response to gains by the cultural left. The emergent Christian right viewed political power as a necessary means of defending their values, and a close alliance with the Republican Party as the best way to achieve that power. The movement became a juggernaut when the Southern Baptist Convention politically mobilized in the 1980s.[36] Evangelical pastors throughout the state addressed cultural and political themes in their sermons and mobilized their congregations to engage in grassroots activism. As elsewhere in the nation, evangelicals tied their hopes closely to the Republican Party, and became the party's most important constituency.[37]

Tejano Culture

Tejano culture is an essential part of Texas's cultural identity. At nearly 40 percent of the total population, Latinos live in all areas of the state, but their cultural influence is strongest in the areas bordering Mexico. The borderland known as South Texas extends from Corpus Christi on the Gulf Coast to San Antonio, the region's unofficial economic and cultural capital. Latinos constitute the large majority of South Texas, and some cultural geographers consider the region a distinct culture area within the state—a unique Mexican American cultural province. By virtue of its proximity to Mexico, large Latino population, and mix of language, religion, art, and music, South Texas is as culturally Mexican as it is American.[38]

Although the demographics of Texas Latinos are similar to those in California, the two groups are culturally and politically distinct. According to Albert

Morales, senior political director for the polling firm Latino Decisions, "Texas Latinos are different from those in California. They just don't think the same as those in more liberal states."[39]

Why are Latinos more conservative in Texas than in California and other blue states? At least part of the answer can be found in the fact that culture is transmitted to new residents. Although waves of newcomers can change a culture, the reverse is also true. Cultural psychologists have observed that people are influenced by their surroundings, and when they move to a new location, they often adopt, over time, that place's dominant cultural and political views.[40] As Latinos have arrived in Texas, they have become part of a broader cultural matrix that generally embraces religious and social conservatism and does not seek to transmit progressive values. Because Texas has weak unions, for example, organized labor has had less influence on Latinos there than it has in California. And because Texas has a strong religious culture, many of its Latino residents have held fast to their religious commitments. Indeed, Texas Latinos' high levels of religious belief and practice have earned the state a reputation as "the heart of the Latino Bible Belt."[41] These religious commitments help explain why Latinos are less progressive and less solidly aligned with the Democratic Party in Texas than they are in California.

Urban Texas

Several of the state's fast-growing urban centers—including, especially, Austin, Houston, and Dallas—have become more racially diverse, multicultural, and cosmopolitan than the rest of the state. As these cities have attracted waves of migrants from more progressive parts of the nation and around the world, they have increasingly embraced blue state values. Austin, home to the state government, the University of Texas, a burgeoning tech industry, and a thriving music scene, has long nurtured the state's most progressive political culture. The city has been called "the Berkeley of Texas" and "the San Francisco of the South." According to writer Lawrence Wright, a resident of Austin, the city "sees itself as standing apart from the vulgar political culture of the rest of Texas, like Rome surrounded by the Goths."[42]

Meanwhile, Houston has quietly become one of the nation's most diverse metropolises. Houstonians speak at least 145 different languages at home, and the city has developed an increasingly international outlook.[43] Even long-conservative Dallas has begun to adopt a more progressive identity. In 2017, for example, the chambers of commerce of Dallas and Fort Worth prepared a promotional video as part of the region's bid to win the second Amazon headquarters (HQ2). The video flashed a series of words and images designed to represent the DFW area. The words included *diversity, acceptance, choice, creativity, culture, sustainability, trendy,* and *progressive*—cultural associations that an earlier generation of the region's leaders would have been slow to embrace.[44] These emerging urban cultures represent a growing challenge to the state's dominant cultural conservatism, but they have not, as yet, supplanted it.

Texas Nationalism

Given its internal variations—southern, western, Evangelical, Mexican, rural, urban cosmopolitan, and more—one might believe that Texas lacks a common culture. Yet, from these diverse elements, the state has forged a distinctively Texan cultural identity. Many Texans feel as much loyalty to their state as to the nation. Allegiance to the Lone Star State is instilled in young Texans in numerous ways—through public commemorations of the Texas Revolution, school curricula featuring heroes of Texas history, and even the recitation of a pledge of allegiance to the Lone Star Flag.[45] Various forms of social reinforcement deepen the attachment over time. Although other Americans feel strong local attachments, few can match the intensity of Texans' devotion to their state.

One can say, then, that Texas's dominant political culture is largely traditionalistic, rooted in southern-style religious and social conservatism—leavened, however, by a more "western," or libertarian, commitment to individual freedom and responsibility. In addition, a populist form of Texas nationalism fosters loyalty to the state and an aversion to interference from outsiders—especially the federal government and coastal elites. In combination, these characteristics have created a distinctive and durable political conservatism in the Lone Star State.

California Culture

California brings to mind a large and often conflicting mix of cultural images. From this great diversity, can one identify overarching characteristics or a common "California culture"? Sociologists, historians, and cultural geographers have struggled with this question. Some say California has developed a multitude of cultures that have little in common. Others point to significant cultural differences between Northern and Southern California and between the state's coastal and inland regions. Still others believe that, despite their many differences, Californians share certain characteristic attitudes and a common cultural identity with "a coherence and personality of its own."[46]

The following discussion separately addresses the cultural development of Northern and Southern California and argues that Northern California's more progressive cultural identity has come to dominate the state's diverse cultural mix.

Northern California

The northern part of California—especially the area surrounding the San Francisco Bay—has long been known for its cultural progressivism. This cultural region has several interconnected subparts that include the City of San Francisco itself; Berkeley, across the Bay; and, to the south, the Silicon Valley. Although the region's progressive identity continues to evolve, its roots can be traced back to the American settlement of San Francisco.

Early Cultural Vision
As noted in Chapter 2, many of the first American immigrants to San Francisco arrived hoping to create a second New England—a "Massachusetts of the Pacific"—through the transmission of New England's forms of religion, education, and literature.[47] The gold rush overwhelmed this project because most of the newcomers were more interested in digging for mammon than in building a religious commonwealth. Moreover, these new arrivals from around the world brought a range of perspectives that, together, produced a strain of individualistic political culture. Yet, as California historian Kevin Starr noted, "New Englandism remained a key element of regional identity."[48] The New England legacy can be found in the Bay Area's devotion to intellectual life, public education, literature, and the arts. It can also be found in the region's leading universities—the University of California and Stanford—which looked to Yale and Harvard for inspiration. Most notably, the New England legacy is evident in the region's commitment to social reform.[49]

An early expression of the Bay Area's high-minded, moralistic culture was its environmental activism. In 1892, the naturalist John Muir, professors from Berkeley and Stanford, and like-minded friends met in San Francisco to establish the Sierra Club. With Muir as their first president, the members resolved to protect California's wilderness areas from exploitation. In time, the Club expanded to become the world's first large-scale, grassroots environmental organization and served as a model for other environmental groups, many also founded in and around San Francisco.[50]

By the turn of the twentieth century, this reformist strain compelled many in Northern California to support the rising Progressive movement. Across the nation, the movement was strongest in New England, the upper Midwest, and the West Coast—that is, in areas dominated by what Elazar called a "moralistic" political culture. The early twentieth-century Progressives advanced a large reform agenda, with the underlying conviction that government is responsible for pro-moting the common good. Progressives believed that special interests, such as corporations, labor unions, and political party organizations, had become too powerful and needed to be checked by "good government" reforms, such as nonpartisan elections; campaign finance regulation; independent regulatory agencies and commissions; and direct democracy tools such as initiative, refer-endum, and recall.

By that time, waves of newcomers from the mid-Atlantic states and Europe (especially Ireland and Italy) had diversified the region's culture, making San Francisco more ethnic and Catholic than the rest of the state and more con-ducive to labor activism and left-wing social movements. In the Bay Area, the reformers' moralistic vision existed in tension with ethnic communities and labor movements that had a more transactional view of politics—a tension that would exist for years.[51]

Counterculture

Through this period, San Francisco also earned a reputation for challenging cul-tural norms. The region's countercultural identity deepened in the 1950s, when Allen Ginsberg, Jack Kerouac, and other beat writers arrived from New York and joined the local avant-garde poetry scene. Beat culture spread through the Bay Area, promoting anti-materialism, exploration of Zen Buddhism and other eastern religions, experimentation with hallucinogenic drugs, and sexual liberation.[52]

Beat culture also reinforced San Francisco's emergent movement for gay and lesbian liberation. In 1955, San Franciscans Phyllis Lyon and Del Martin founded the Daughters of Bilitis, the first national lesbian advocacy organiza-tion. At the same time, the Mattachine Society, founded in Los Angeles in 1950 to advance the rights of gay men, moved its headquarters to San Francisco. Both groups attracted a large following through their magazines, *The Ladder* and *The Mattachine Review*. These developments helped lay a foundation for San Francisco to become an international center of gay and lesbian culture and activism.[53]

By the 1960s, the San Francisco Bay Area was thus immersed in social critique and experimentation and naturally assumed leadership of the decade's cultural revolution. Berkeley was at the epicenter. In the summer of 1964, a number of University of California students, including a charismatic leader named Mario Savio, participated in civil rights activism in Mississippi and were eager to begin political organizing when they returned to the Berkeley campus in the fall. They soon learned, however, that the university administration had restricted political activism on campus. Savio and other students believed these restrictions violated their First Amendment rights and responded with what became known as the

Free Speech Movement. In December 1964, a massive gathering of students and their supporters, including folk singer Joan Baez, surrounded the university's main administration building to protest the policies. More than one thousand protestors occupied the building and, after a tense standoff, police arrested nearly eight hundred of them. The episode radicalized Berkeley and launched several years of intense student activism and protest.[54]

In 1965, activists turned their focus to the Vietnam War. That year, they organized mass peace rallies and marches in Berkeley and neighboring Oakland, some of the nation's first large scale demonstrations against the war. Major antiwar protests continued in and around Berkeley for the next several years. In addition to resisting the war, student activists more broadly protested what they considered the "machines" of American society—universities, the military, corporations, conventional careers, and the traditional values that supported them. Dissent soon found new forms of expression in the hippie counterculture. In 1967, the Haight-Ashbury district of San Francisco attracted thousands of young hippies from around the world who came to join "the Summer of Love"—a drug-infused celebration of rock music, sexual liberation, and radical utopian visions.[55]

Legacy of the Sixties

The ferment of activism in the Bay Area during the 1960s fueled countless social movements, including second-wave feminism; the black power movement; movements to empower Latinos, Native Americans, gays and lesbians, and disabled persons; new efforts to protect the Earth; and many more. The leaders of these movements sought to break down old hierarchies, authorities, and customs, believing that these forces impeded human enlightenment and social progress. Many activists considered organized religion the greatest obstacle to liberation.[56] The San Francisco Bay Area had long been less religiously observant than other parts of the country, but the Sixties emboldened its resistance. Although it embraced eastern religions and other forms of spirituality, the region became increasingly unreceptive to traditional western religious beliefs and practices.[57]

The secularism, non-traditional spirituality, cultural experimentation, egalitarianism, and activism that infused the San Francisco Bay area in the 1960s remained vital features of the region's character. More than half a century after the Free Speech Movement and the Summer of Love, Berkeley, San Francisco, and surrounding areas continued to generate progressive thought and action.

One enduring legacy of the 1960s counterculture was its profound influence on the culture of Silicon Valley. For decades, the technology industry had been relatively conservative, driven by business-minded engineers who built semiconductors and other components for the military and other customers. Many of the industry's early leaders, including William Hewlett and David

Packard, held centrist views, and the region frequently elected moderate Republicans to the state legislature and Congress. In the late 1960s, however, utopian visionaries introduced a new element to the industry's culture.

Stewart Brand was perhaps the most important contributor to this change. Brand's *Whole Earth Catalog* envisioned a new society liberated from oppressive institutions and focused on individual empowerment and self-actualization through the application of what it called "appropriate technology." First published in fall 1968, the *Catalog* proclaimed in its statement of purpose:

> We *are* as Gods and might as well get good at it. So far, remotely done power and glory—as via government, big business, formal education, church—has succeeded to the point where gross defects obscure actual gains. In response . . . a realm of intimate, personal power is developing—the power of the individual to conduct his own education, find his own inspiration, shape his own environment, and share his adventure with whoever is interested. Tools that aid this process are sought and promoted by the *WHOLE EARTH CATALOG.*[58]

The thick *Catalog* combined poetry, photography, ads and reviews for esoteric books (including the futurist Buckminster Fuller's *No More Secondhand God*, a do-it-yourself manual for constructing "The Indian Tipi," a book authored by five English schoolboys titled *We Built Our Own Computer,* a guide to self-hypnosis, and a book titled *The Fundamentals of Yoga*), as well as ads for Zen mediation cushions, buckskin, and solar panels. The *Catalog* developed a cult following and became a bible for many future leaders of the tech and Internet industries, including the founders of Stripe and Airbnb, early employees of Facebook, and most, notably, Steve Jobs, the co-founder of Apple and founder of Pixar. The *Catalog*'s underlying values—a mix of progressive and libertarian thought, experimentation, and self-empowerment—became Silicon Valley's guiding philosophy.[59] By fusing this and other legacies of the 1960s with other elements of progressive thought and action, the San Francisco Bay Area became the nation's most thoroughly progressive cultural region.

Southern California

Southern California developed along different cultural lines than the northern part of the state. The division was, in part, a result of geography. Southern California sits four hundred miles south of San Francisco and is insulated by mountain ranges north of Los Angeles. To the east, lies a vast desert, to the west, the Pacific Ocean, to the south, Mexico. The writer Carey McWilliams called Southern California "an island on the land"—a geographic region distinct from all that surrounds it.[60] During the first decades of the state's history, this island was sparsely populated, rural, and remote. In the 1880s, new transcontinental rail lines reached Southern California, and the region began to grow and take on a cultural identity of its own. Most early newcomers sought economic opportunity and the promise of a healthful life in a Mediterranean climate. In time, millions were attracted by images of perpetual sunshine, oranges ripening in midwinter, and palm trees waving in a mild ocean breeze.

Emigrants to Southern California brought with them a middle-class Protestant culture that, for a time, set the tone for the region. By 1910, 60 percent of the state's total population had come from the Midwest, and the concentration in Southern California was even higher.[61] These newcomers recreated a midwestern society by the sea, blanketing the region with citrus groves that were punctuated by well-ordered towns with single-family homes, small businesses, public schools, libraries, and churches. Los Angeles liked to boast that it had more churches than any other city of its size in the nation.[62] By 1900, Southern California had developed a midwestern-style "good government" political culture that provided fertile soil for the reformist Progressive movement of the early twentieth century.

Voluntary Culture

The era of small-town Southern California would not—indeed, could not—last. The region was too attractive to remain sparsely settled, especially as its boosterish leaders actively promoted growth. By building water delivery systems and other infrastructure to support a large population, Southern California was able to absorb waves of new immigrants bearing diverse cultural traits. Zelinsky noted that as Southern California saw ceaseless waves of immigration, its cultural personality underwent "constant redefinition" with "the formulation of new attitudes and cultural entities."[63] The island on the land developed what McWilliams called internal "islands" and "archipelagos" that together created a complex and fluid cultural mix.[64] Although it would be impossible to describe all of these subcultures, three in particular have powerfully defined Southern California's identity: suburbia, Hollywood, and the Latino community.

Suburbia

In the years after World War II, Southern California real estate developers paved over thousands of acres of agricultural land to create one of the world's most expansive suburban societies. New developments radiated from Los Angeles to nearly every corner of the region to accommodate millions of newcomers, many of them veterans who had passed through Southern California during the war years and decided they wanted to stay. A typical suburbanite was white and middle class, worked in a stable job, drove to that job on a new freeway, and lived in a comfortable, if modest, tract home—possibly featuring a swimming pool in the back yard.

Southern California's mass suburban society developed a dominant conservative culture. Many postwar suburbanites held conservative economic, cultural, and religious values, which were reinforced by robust conservative institutions, including defense firms, chambers of commerce, service clubs, churches, and newspapers.[65]

This conservative suburban ecosystem most clearly manifested in Orange County, located just south of Los Angeles. The county developed rapidly in the decades after World War II and absorbed a large population of white middle-class residents. As in many parts of Texas, Orange County fused religious conservatism and libertarian ideology. It nurtured evangelical institutions and charismatic movements, taking southern-style religion and making it more accessible to modern, middle-class suburbanites. It also fostered conservative political activism and provided a solid financial and organizational base for conservative candidates at the local, state, and national levels.[66]

Near the turn of the millennium, however, this conservative cultural ecosystem collapsed in Orange County and throughout Southern California. At the same time that the region lost much of its industrial base, many of its conservative institutions disappeared. Most notably, numerous evangelical ministries left Southern California for other states or shut down altogether. A representative example was Robert Schuller's Crystal Cathedral. In the 1950s, Schuller built a church in the Orange County suburb of Garden Grove. He began by holding services in a drive-in movie theater next to the Santa Ana Freeway and soon started broadcasting his sermons. By the 1970s, his "Hour of Power" was the nation's most-watched religious program. In 1980, Schuller's church opened a three thousand–seat, glass-encased "Cathedral." For years thereafter, the Crystal Cathedral was a focus of evangelical activity in the region. In the early 2000s, however, the church's attendance declined and the ministry was forced into bankruptcy. In 2012, the Roman Catholic Church bought the Crystal Cathedral and recommissioned it to serve the region's growing immigrant Catholic population.[67]

Similarly, all across suburban Southern California, older conservative institutions and ways of life were yielding to a new, more diverse cultural mix.

Hollywood

Carey McWilliams observed many years ago that Hollywood is more of a state of mind than a geographical entity: "One of the most famous place-names in the world, Hollywood is neither a town nor a city; it is an integral part of Los Angeles." In McWilliams's view, Hollywood profoundly influenced Southern California culture—it "liberated" Los Angeles from religious fundamentalism, shaped its "manners and morals," and served as its arbiter of taste and style. Its "glamour" and "slickness" permeated the rest of the region.[68] Of course, Hollywood's cultural power has always reached far beyond Southern California. Its movies, television programs, music, and related media influence culture across the United States and around the world.

How should one characterize Hollywood's cultural values? Some caution should be used when describing the cultural inclinations of a creative community that has existed for more than a century and produced an enormous amount of cultural content—especially when it has always sought to appeal to broad audiences. Early on, producers strove to avoid transgressing mass cultural norms by establishing the Hays Office and the Motion Picture Code. These and other self-imposed regulations caused the entertainment industry to produce movies and television programming that adhered to conservative cultural standards.[69] Moreover, for much of the twentieth century, many of Hollywood's leading actors, directors, and producers publicly embraced conservative values.[70] However, the social ferment of the 1960s and 1970s led much of Hollywood's creative class to rebel against cultural constraints and to test their limits. In the decades that followed, the industry shifted more consistently to the left. This change could be seen in the more progressive content of movies and television programming, celebrity activism, the politicization of awards shows, and contributions to political campaigns and causes. By the late twentieth century, Hollywood—like the San Francisco Bay Area—was closely aligned with progressive cultural and political values.[71]

Latino Culture

Many racial and ethnic groups have contributed to Southern California culture, but Mexican Americans have established such a strong cultural presence in the region that they may be said to have created a "culture area." Mexican identity has a special place in Southern California, distinguishable from other Latin American identities, for it was Mexico that provided the region its original cultural matrix and—despite opposition—has always maintained a cultural presence. Over the past century, that presence has been reinforced by millions of immigrants. The evidence suggests that Mexican Americans and other Latinos in Southern California have largely aligned with the region's dominant culture—that is, they are less religious and more politically progressive than Latinos in Texas. As discussed in later chapters, community organizers, union activists, Spanish-language media, public officials, government agencies, Latino advocacy groups, and the Democratic Party have nurtured a progressive Latino political culture in Southern California and helped instill in millions of Latino residents the region's progressive cultural and political perspectives. These efforts have helped forge a different, more progressive Latino identity in Southern California than in Texas.[72]

A California Culture?

Amid all of this diversity, can we say that California, like Texas, has a unified culture? Does the state foster a set of recognizable attitudes and beliefs that distinguishes it from other states? One can conclude that if Californians do have a common trait, it is their commitment to experimentation and innovation. When Stegner called California "Innovationville," he emphasized that it was not "Traditionburg." Unlike other parts of the country that highly value tradition and familiar ways, California's impulse is to discard the old and try something new. According to Stegner, the state's motto is "Why not?"[73]

The ideology of "why not" can be found in all corners of California. It can be seen most easily in places like Hollywood, which created the modern entertainment industry; or in Berkeley and San Francisco, which have launched countless social movements; or in Silicon Valley, which has transformed the way people live around the world. But for most of the state's history, the spirit of innovation could be found elsewhere as well—even in places that might be called "conservative." It was California, for example, that invented the modern suburb and suburban culture. And it was California that converted the nation's "old-time" religion of evangelical Protestantism into a modern, media-savvy phenomenon.

For many years, a creative tension prevailed between the cultural left and cultural right, between Berkeley radicals and Southern California suburbanites, for example, or between Hollywood liberals and conservative evangelicals. These competing forces produced internal cultural counterbalances. Now the state's cultural right has declined, and progressivism has become dominant not only in the San Francisco Bay Area but throughout of the rest of the state as well.

Competing Cultures

Two chapters ago, we asked why two states with such seemingly similar demographics could be so deeply divided. We can now see that the rivals' economic structures and their contrasting cultural identities go a long way toward providing an answer. The explanation for the rivals' polarization, however, is incomplete. Texas and California have long had contrasting political cultures—sometimes described as "traditionalistic" versus "moralistic"—but they have not always been polarized along partisan lines. In the following chapters, we turn to the story of how the two states moved into the Republican and Democratic camps and became the leaders of red and blue America.

6

How Texas Turned Red

Texas has always had a predominantly conservative political culture, but it was not always Republican. To the contrary, for most of its history, the Lone Star State was part of the solid Democratic South and felt no love for the Republican Party—or, as it was sometimes called, "the party of northern aggression." The story of Texas's abandonment of the Democratic Party and shift to the Republican ranks is intimately connected to the broader realignment of the American party system during the second half of the twentieth century—a gradual process whereby conservative states became Republican and progressive states became Democratic. Although Texas's conversion resembled similar moves by other southern states, it had its own distinctive character.

In Texas, the Republican Party endured decades of defeat and marginalization before clawing its way to parity, and finally, majority status. By the early twenty-first century, Texas Republicans regularly delivered a large bloc of electoral votes for GOP presidential candidates, dominated Democrats in statewide races, and won stable majorities in the legislature and congressional delegation. Moreover, with unified control over all branches of Texas government, Republicans were able to enact a thoroughly conservative vision of public policy in the Lone Star State.

That being said, the state Republican Party has never established the same level of control that Democrats enjoyed during their era of one-party rule. Instead, even as Republicans gained control of politics at the state level, Democrats maintained a power base in some of the state's largest urban areas and in its borderlands with Mexico. Moreover, the state's growing demographic, economic, and cultural diversity fueled Democrats' hopes of turning Texas blue. This possibility presented one of the great political questions of the day: Will Republicans retain their control over the Lone Star State? This chapter explores the nation's broad partisan realignment, Texas's transition from the Democratic to Republican ranks, and the question of whether the state will remain in the Republican fold.

The Nation's Big Partisan Sort

Over the past half century, the ideological polarization of the Democratic and Republican Parties has defined American politics. Earlier in the twentieth

Texas vs. California. Kenneth P. Miller, Oxford University Press (2020). © Oxford University Press.
DOI: 10.1093/oso/9780190077402.001.0001.

century, the parties' guiding philosophies were hard to pin down because both contained such broad internal diversity. The Democratic Party had especially profound ideological and sectional divisions. With a legacy extending back to Thomas Jefferson, Andrew Jackson, and John C. Calhoun, the party had deep roots in the South—and, by virtue of their seniority and political skill, conservative southerners maintained a formidable presence within the national Democratic coalition. At the same time, as waves of immigrants settled in the industrial centers of the North, the Democratic Party's numbers in that region surged, strengthening the party's northern wing. During the 1930s, Franklin D. Roosevelt expanded the Democratic tent to accommodate a diverse coalition—southern conservatives, northern liberals, immigrants, Jews, Catholics, African Americans, union members, intellectuals, artists, blue collar workers, and the poor. The coalition was truly national and diverse in its demographics, cultural orientation, and ideology. For years, the glue of the New Deal held the coalition together.[1]

By comparison, the Republican Party was established in the 1850s as a sectional party—it was strong in the North and West, but had virtually no presence in the South. The GOP briefly governed the South as part of Reconstruction, but it quickly lost power there when the federal troops withdrew. As V. O. Key noted, as late as the mid-twentieth century, the Republican Party of the South was so weak it "scarcely deserve[d] the name of party."[2]

Although it lacked a southern element, the Republican Party experienced its own internal divisions, including a long-running conflict between its conservative establishment and progressive wing. Conservative Republicans had a more transactional view of politics and believed government should support the nation's rapid industrialization and economic development; progressive Republicans promoted a moralistic political culture focused on social and political reform. Many of this latter group, including Theodore Roosevelt, Robert La Follette, and Hiram Johnson, provided leadership to the early twentieth-century Progressive movement. The conflict between the GOP's conservative and progressive factions surfaced repeatedly—for example, in 1912, when conservatives denied Theodore Roosevelt the party's nomination for president and TR's followers bolted to form the Progressive Party, and again in the 1960s, when the party was divided between Goldwater conservatives and Rockefeller liberals.

Due to their internal divisions, neither party spoke with one voice on many policy matters. Northern Democrats often formed alliances with liberal Republicans on civil rights and other issues, while right-of-center Republicans forged a durable "conservative coalition" with southern Democrats. This blurring of ideological distinctions led Alabama governor George Wallace to complain in the 1960s that there wasn't "a dime's worth of difference" between the two parties.[3]

Many scholars agreed, arguing that the parties needed to become more distinct in order to give voters clearer policy choices. In 1950, a committee of the American Political Science Association issued a report calling for the nation to move "toward a more responsible two-party system"—a system in which the two parties would be more easily distinguishable and more disciplined.[4] In the decades that followed, this ideological separation did, in fact, occur—as Democrats became more clearly the party of the American left and Republicans the party of the right.

The national partisan sorting occurred along sectional lines. Once it became apparent to all that the Democratic Party was moving to the left across multiple issue domains—on civil rights, national defense, social and cultural issues, and more—southern states, with their traditionalistic, conservative political cultures, started exiting for the Republican Party. This movement began in the 1960s and 1970s, solidified at the presidential level with the election of Ronald Reagan in 1980, and later extended down the ballot to congressional and state-level offices through the 1990s.

Conversely, most of the progressive states of the Northeast, upper Midwest, and Pacific Coast—states with moralistic political cultures or at least a strong moralistic strain—moved from the Republican Party to the Democrats. Near the end of the Reagan years, and especially with the election of Bill Clinton in 1992, several states that had regularly voted for Republican candidates in presidential elections decisively shifted to the Democratic Party. These states included Oregon and Washington in 1988 and California, Connecticut, Illinois, Maine, New Jersey, and Vermont in 1992.[5]

Comparing national electoral results from an earlier era with recent election maps reveals remarkable inversion (Figures 6.1 and 6.2). Sectional partisan realignment caused most states to switch their historic party allegiance. The former solid Democratic South became a Republican stronghold, and the once-Republican Northeast, Pacific Coast, and part of the Midwest (namely, Illinois) became reliably Democratic. Texas (like California) has contributed to this massive realignment.

Democratic Texas

For most of its history, Texas was squarely aligned with the Democratic Party. Sam Houston was a protégé of Andrew Jackson, and he helped transmit a Jacksonian-style Democratic political identity to the Lone Star State. The experiences of Civil War and Reconstruction led most white Texans to deepen

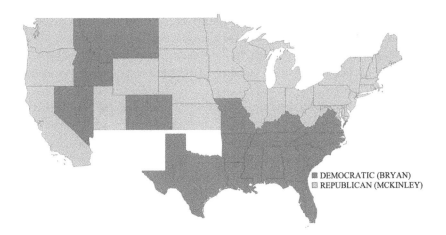

Figure 6.1. Presidential vote by state, 1900

Source: American Presidency Project

Note: In 1900, Alaska, Arizona, Hawaii, New Mexico, Oklahoma, and the District of Columbia did not yet vote in presidential elections.

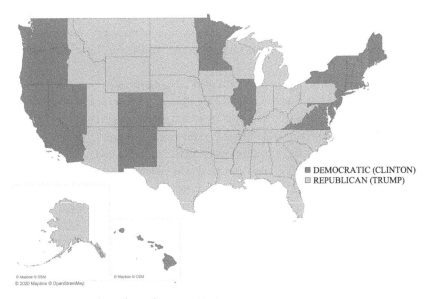

Figure 6.2. Presidential vote by state, 2016

Source: American Presidency Project

their loyalty to the Democratic Party—and their hostility to the GOP. According to University of Texas political scientist Roscoe C. Martin, "the Democratic Party was looked at, rightly or wrongly, as the defender of all that was dearest to the hearts of Texans, and those not members of that party were regarded virtually as traitors to the State."[6]

Republicans won elections in Texas during the brief period of Reconstruction, but once the federal troops withdrew, Democrats quickly reestablished one-party rule. For nearly a century thereafter, the Democratic Party exercised hegemony over the state's politics. The Texas Republican Party barely survived at the margins—small, weak, and internally divided. African American Republicans, known as "Black and Tans," remained active but faced opposition from "Lily White" Republicans who worked to marginalize them.[7] The party paid closer attention to these internal divisions than to competing in elections. In the 1880s and 1890s, the GOP failed to field candidates in about half of the state's congressional races and, by 1900, elected zero representatives to the state legislature.[8]

Republican weakness created an opening for new parties and political movements to challenge the state's Democratic monopoly. A few third-party insurgencies surfaced in the late nineteenth century, the most powerful of which were the Populists. The movement tapped into the economic, social, and political grievances and aspirations of the agrarian South and West. Populists advanced an ambitious agenda. Among other proposals, they advocated fiat money, public ownership of railroads and telegraph and telephone systems, and government support for farmers. Because it sought to regulate corporate power and redistribute wealth, the Populist revolt has generally been viewed as a movement of the left.[9]

Texans were at the heart of the Populist movement. They organized county, district, and state conventions, held educational campaigns, circulated tracts, and attracted large crowds to revival-style camp meetings.[10] For a brief time, it seemed they might credibly challenge the Democrats' hegemony in the Lone Star State. In 1894, twenty-four Populists won election to the Texas Legislature and, in 1896, the Populist nominee for governor won 44 percent of the vote.[11] However, the national Populist Party's ill-fated decision to "fuse" with the Democrats in 1896 in nominating William Jennings Bryan for president led to electoral defeat and recrimination. The Populists soon faded away as an organized political movement both in Texas and across the nation, but the populist impulse remained an enduring feature of Lone Star politics.[12]

In the wake of the Populist revolt, Democrats across the South looked to prevent further attacks on their political monopoly by placing new restrictions on voting—a move consistent with the traditionalistic impulse to limit political participation.[13] The Populist movement had weakened in-formal restrictions on black voting and had drawn to the polls many other citizens who had never voted in the past. Texas Democrats sought to remove these groups from the electorate—especially blacks, but also Latinos and poor whites. Between 1902 and 1904, the state established a poll tax and enacted the "Terrell Election Law," which, among other provisions, authorized local elec-tion officials to impose restrictions—including racial restrictions—on voting in party primaries.[14] Representative Alexander Watkins Terrell defended these laws as a means to "eliminate the thriftless, idle, and semi-vagrant ele-ment of both races."[15]

The restrictions contributed to a sharp decline in voting. In the 1896 election, held at the peak of the Populist era, about 80 percent the state's eligible voters went to the polls, a historically high turnout. By contrast, in 1904, after Texas enacted new voting restrictions, turnout plummeted by nearly two-thirds, to 33 percent. In 1920, it fell further, to 20 percent, the state's all-time low for a presidential election.[16]

In 1923, the Texas Legislature explicitly banned African Americans from voting in Democratic Party primaries. The state's white primary statute declared that "in no event shall a negro be eligible to participate in a Democratic party primary election held in the State of Texas, and should a negro vote in a Democratic primary election, such ballot shall be void and election officials are herein directed to throw out such ballot and not count the same." [17] These voting restrictions generated decades of legal and political struggle. Several challenges to the white primary system ultimately resulted in the U.S. Supreme Court's decision in *Smith v. Allwright* (1944), which declared that racial restrictions in primary elections violated the U.S. Constitution.[18] The state's poll tax remained in place for federal elections until 1964, when it was abolished by the Twenty-Fourth Amendment and, for state elections, until 1966, when courts held that it was fully invalidated by the Voting Rights Act of 1965.[19] For decades, however, restrictions on participation helped ensure the Democratic Party's domination of Texas politics.[20]

Democratic Party Divisions

A crack in the state's Democratic Party edifice appeared in the 1920s. In 1928, the Democratic National Convention met in Houston and nomi-nated for president New York governor Al Smith, the preferred candidate of the party's ascendant northern, urban wing. The Texas delegation bitterly opposed the convention's choice of a Catholic and a "wet."[21] In that year's general election, most southern states remained loyal to the Democratic Party and voted for Smith, but Texas bolted to the Republican nominee, Herbert Hoover, marking the first time it had supported a Republican for president. The episode demonstrated that Texas would not always vote in lockstep with its southern neighbors and the Democratic Party.[22] Yet, Texas's defection remained an isolated exception for the next quarter century. In the next presidential election, Texans abandoned Hoover and returned to the Democratic fold, supporting Franklin D. Roosevelt by an 88–11 percent margin.

FDR's presidency created a split within the Texas Democratic Party between those who supported the New Deal and those who opposed it. Prominent Texas New Dealers included Governor James Allred, who helped implement New Deal programs from 1935 to 1939; Houston businessman Jesse Jones, who headed up the Reconstruction Finance Corporation; Sam Rayburn, who shepherded much New Deal legislation through Congress and was elevated to House Majority Leader in 1937 and Speaker in 1940; and Rayburn's protégé, Lyndon Baines Johnson, who first won a seat in Congress on a New Deal platform in a 1937 special election. LBJ aligned himself with Roosevelt so closely that, according to biographer Robert Caro, "no Fundamentalist preacher, thundering of fire and brimstone in one of the famed Hill Country revival meetings, had called the people of the Hill Country to the banner of Jesus Christ more fervently than Lyndon Johnson had called them to the banner of Franklin Roosevelt."[23]

On the opposite side, Texas oilmen and industrialists led the state's anti–New Deal faction. They attacked many elements of FDR's program, especially the National Labor Relations Act (1935), which gave the federal government power to intervene in the relationship between employers and their employees and to protect the right of employees to unionize. In 1936, businessman John Henry Kirby formed a group called the "Constitutional Democrats of Texas," the first organized effort to challenge Roosevelt in the state. In the 1936 election, FDR brushed aside this challenge, winning 87 percent of the vote in Texas as part of a forty-six-state landslide.[24]

The anti–New Deal faction was undeterred. Several leading Texas Democrats resolved to oppose the president more boldly, including, most remarkably, FDR's own vice president, John Nance Garner. In 1937, Garner broke with Roosevelt over the president's court-packing plan and ended up challenging him, unsuccessfully, for the Democratic presidential nomination in 1940.[25] Finally, in 1944, the faction formed a group called the "Texas Regulars" to try to derail FDR's bid for a fourth term. Led by conservative U.S. senator (and former governor) W. Lee "Pappy" O'Daniel and backed by a group of wealthy businessmen, the Texas Regulars attacked the New Deal as "communist-controlled."[26] In the 1944 presidential election, more than 135,000 Texans (about 12 percent of the electorate) cast their votes for the third party Texas Regular ticket.

Texas's pro– and anti–New Deal factions were engaged in what V. O. Key called the "most bitter intra-Democratic fight" of any state in the South. That conflict would eventually lead to the development of a two-party system in the state.[27]

Republican Stirrings

The long-hibernating Texas GOP finally began to stir during the presidential election of 1952.[28] That year, the Democrats nominated Illinois governor Adlai Stevenson, while the Republicans put forward General Dwight D. Eisenhower. Texas's conservative Democratic governor, Allan Shivers, endorsed the Republican nominee.[29] Many were surprised by the endorsement, but, in truth, Eisenhower was the candidate better suited for postwar Texas, with its strong military presence, fast-growing population (including many Republicans from the Midwest), modernizing economy, and conservative political culture. Moreover, although Eisenhower grew up in Kansas, he was born in the north Texas town of Denison, and thus could claim to be a native Texan. Ike won the Lone Star State in 1952 by 53–47 percent, and again in the 1956 rematch by 55–44 percent. In both elections, Texas split from the Deep South, which backed Stevenson.

Eisenhower's back-to-back Texas victories laid a foundation for later Republican successes in the state. These campaigns helped the Texas GOP gain valuable expertise and introduced future Republican leaders, including George H. W. Bush, to Texas politics.[30] Moreover, the general's popularity helped destigmatize a long-hated political party, showed Democrats that they could "ticket split" and at least occasionally vote for a Republican, and gave Republicans reason to believe they could actually win elections in the Lone Star State.

Moreover, during the 1950s many Texans were attracted to conservative movements that advocated anti-communism, limited government, and traditional American values. Activists in these movements shared an intense concern about the threat of international communism at home and abroad. They also opposed what they saw as government intrusion in economic and social spheres, including but not limited to federal interventions to enforce civil rights. Many also decried what they saw as the nation's cultural decline. One of the more prominent activists was the Dallas-based oil magnate H. L. Hunt, who used his wealth to advance a conservative, anti-communist worldview through newsletters, magazines, and radio and television shows. Hunt's programs, including "Facts Forum" and, later, "Life Line," were broadcast on more than five hundred radio and fifty television stations to an estimated listening and viewing audience of five million. Called "a Voice of America in the heart of the country," this programming established a model for conservative talk radio and Fox News.[31]

At the time, however, it was still not certain whether these conservative movements would fuse with the Republican Party. The two parties had not yet separated along ideological lines, and the Democratic Party still had a large right wing. Many conservative Texans supported Republican candidates for president, but most still retained their Democratic identity.

A False Spring

In 1961, the Texas GOP achieved a critical breakthrough—the election of John Tower as the first Republican U.S. senator from Texas since Reconstruction. Tower's historic victory could be attributed in part to the ideological feud within the Texas Democratic Party. The senate election came down to a run-off between Tower and William Blakley, a conservative Democrat. Frustrated by conservative domination of their party, many liberals decided to oppose Blakley. Their goal was to rid the Democratic party of its conservative elements and rebuild it along liberal lines. The left-wing *Texas Observer* urged its readers to cast a "conscious liberal vote for Tower." Through a combination of sincere conservative support and strategic liberal voting, Tower narrowly won the election. One Republican activist called the outcome a political "earthquake that shook the entire state of Texas."[32] After Tower's victory, many Republicans believed they were poised to expand their gains and create a legitimate two-party system in the Lone Star State.

Texas Republicans had good reasons for optimism in the early 1960s. "Resignation rallies" were spreading across the state for those who had decided to leave the Democratic Party and join the GOP. The state's two largest cities, Dallas and Houston, were rapidly moving in a Republican direction. In Houston, a young George H. W. Bush was preparing a 1964 race against Democratic senator Ralph Yarborough in what was expected to be a referendum on Yarborough's liberalism. And many were eager to join Barry Goldwater's nascent campaign for president. Texas GOP chairman Peter O'Donnell, leader of the national Draft Goldwater Committee, believed Goldwater could wrest the nomination from New York governor Nelson Rockefeller and the Eastern Establishment, remake the Republican Party along Sunbelt-conservative lines, and defeat President John F. Kennedy.[33] These goals were ambitious but not entirely unrealistic. A November 1963 *Houston Chronicle* poll reported that if the election were held then, Goldwater would defeat Kennedy by approximately fifty thousand votes in the Lone Star State. One Republican operative later recalled, "Those were heady days for Texas Republicans. The momentum was strong and getting stronger every day."[34]

The momentum collapsed, however, in November 1963, when President Kennedy visited Dallas. The president's assassination on the streets of that city shocked the nation in a way that had profound consequences for Dallas, for the state of Texas, and, not least, for the Texas Republican Party. In the weeks after the shooting, Dallas faced intense national scrutiny. The city's streak of conservative activism and anti-Kennedy sentiment was blamed for creating a "climate of hate" that had inspired the crime. The blame was unjust, considering that the president's assassin, Lee Harvey Oswald, was not a right-wing extremist, but rather an enigmatic loner with left-leaning views. Nevertheless, many Texans felt compelled to distance themselves from the Republican Party and from conservative activism and instead rally around the Democratic Party and the Texan in the White House, Lyndon Johnson.[35]

As a result, the 1964 election was a disaster for Texas Republicans. Johnson beat Goldwater in the state by a landslide, 63–37 percent; Democrat Ralph Yarborough defeated George H. W. Bush in the Senate race, 56–44 percent; the state's two Republican members of Congress both went down in defeat; and Republicans lost ten of their eleven seats in the Texas House of Representatives. When the dust settled, only one Republican remained in the lower house of the legislature (out of 150 members), and no Republicans held office in the state senate, executive branch, or congressional delegation.[36]

Slow Conservative Exodus

As these results show, Texas did not rise up in protest against the Democratic Party in 1964. Although it is often said that Democrats lost Texas and rest of the South when President Johnson signed the Civil Rights Act of 1964, in reality the story is more complicated.[37] In 1964, five deep southern states—South Carolina, Georgia, Alabama, Mississippi, and Louisiana—cast their votes for Goldwater, the only states to do so other than Goldwater's home state of Arizona. In the conventional account, these states supported Goldwater to protest the leftward movement of the Johnson administration, especially the president's backing of the Civil Rights Act. This view was reinforced in 1968 when a similar group of states—Georgia, Alabama, Mississippi, Louisiana, and Arkansas—supported the third-party candidacy of segregationist Alabama governor George Wallace. But that year Texas again split from its southern neighbors, supporting the Democratic nominee, Hubert Humphrey, over Republican Richard Nixon.

Wallace received 19 percent of the vote in Texas (compared with 66 percent in Alabama and 64 percent in Mississippi), with most of the state's Wallace vote concentrated in a cluster of counties in East Texas.

These results indicate that Texas had a different political orientation from that of much of the South. To be sure, segregation, race relations, civil rights, and states' rights were contested issues in Texas during the 1960s, but they did not dominate political debate to the same degree in Texas as they did in several other southern states, and did not, by themselves, separate Texas from the Democratic Party in the mid-1960s. Instead, Texas's conversion took longer and involved a broader set of factors.[38]

By 1968, the national Democratic Party was deeply divided, not only over civil rights, but also over the war in Vietnam, the revolution in cultural mores, and social unrest in the nation's cities. The 1968 Democratic convention was marked by massive conflict between traditional Democrats and insurgents, producing sharp debate in the convention hall and rioting in the streets. Traditional Democrats were able to secure the nomination of Hubert Humphrey, but when Humphrey lost to Nixon in the general election, progressives mobilized and moved the party to the left.

In 1972, Democrats nominated for president one of the most liberal members of the U.S. Senate, George McGovern of South Dakota. The party's lurch to the left helped Nixon win one of the largest landslides in U.S. history, amassing 61 percent of the national popular vote and 49 states. McGovern captured only Massachusetts and the District of Columbia. If the 1972 Democratic ticket and platform had moved too far to the left for the rest of the country, they were even more objectionable in Texas. Nixon won the Lone Star State by a 66–33 percent margin, carrying 246 of the state's 254 counties and many traditional Democratic groups.

By the 1970s, it was clear that a values gap was growing between the national Democratic Party and Texas voters. While many Texans could still embrace an old-style, New Deal liberalism, few were attracted to the Berkeley-style New Left of antiwar protests and social and cultural radicalism. Republicans were able to stigmatize Democrats as the party of "acid, amnesty, and abortion."[39]

Beyond the Democratic Party's shift to the left, other factors strengthened the position of Texas Republicans during the 1970s, including waves of migration from the Midwest; prosperity in the state's oil, tech, and other economic sectors; the spread of middle-class suburbs; the growth of evangelical churches; and the political mobilization of social conservatives around a range of issues, including opposition to the Supreme Court's decision in *Roe v. Wade*.[40] Finally, a charismatic visitor from California helped Republicans achieve parity in the Lone Star State.

Reagan's Invitation

Ronald Reagan was perfectly suited to convert Texans to the Republican fold. He was a Sunbelt conservative and a westerner who tapped into the state's populist resentments against the Eastern Establishment, liberal elites, and the federal government. At the same time, he came across as less radical than Goldwater and spoke in a way that was particularly welcoming to conservative Democrats. He often reminded voters that he, too, had once been a Democrat, and that he understood it was hard to change parties. He argued, however, that principle was more important than party. If the Democratic Party no longer shared Texas values, he reasoned, Texans should no longer give it their allegiance. "You know," he would say, "a lot of Democrats around the country are saying that their party leadership has swung so far to the left, so far out of the mainstream, that the national Democratic leadership has lost touch with the rank and file of the Democratic Party. Now, I'm a former Democrat, and I have to say: I didn't leave my party; my party left me."[41]

In 1976, Reagan sought the presidency through a direct challenge to the incumbent president from his own party, Gerald R. Ford. In Texas, as across the nation, the Republican establishment backed Ford, while the conservative base mobilized for Reagan. Ford's Texas supporters included Senator John Tower, James A. Baker III, and Robert Mosbacher, the head of the campaign's national finance committee. The state's grassroots conservatives, by contrast, dismissed Ford as an establishment man and a career insider who had committed the sin of making the liberal Nelson Rockefeller vice president. They loved Reagan with an almost religious devotion and invested themselves in his campaign.[42]

After Ford established a lead in early-voting states, Reagan needed a victory in the Texas primary to remain in the race. After a spirited campaign, more than 400,000 Texans participated in the Republican primary, a turnout nearly three times higher than in any Republican primary in the state's history. Combining the support of Republicans and independents with a large Democratic crossover vote, Reagan won Texas in a landslide, beating the incumbent president in all of the state's twenty-four congressional districts, with margins of two-to-one in nearly every district.[43] Reagan was awarded all 96 of the state's delegates to the 1976 Republican convention. In the end, however, he narrowly lost the nomination to Ford, who, in turn, lost the general election to Georgia governor Jimmy Carter.

Although Reagan's 1976 campaign fell short, his victory in the Texas Republican primary strengthened the GOP's appeal to conservatives in the state. He won the Texas primary again in 1980, this time defeating Texan George H. W. Bush on his way to securing the Republican presidential nomination. After

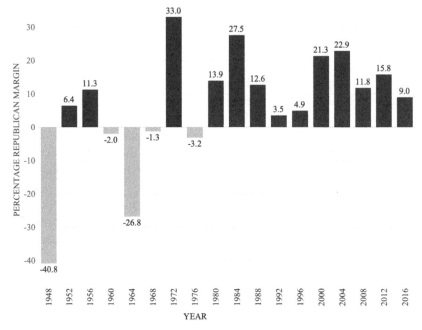

Figure 6.3. Margin between Republican and Democratic percentage of presidential vote in Texas, 1948–2016

Source: American Presidency Project

Reagan selected Bush as his running mate, the ticket defeated President Carter by 55–41 percent in Texas as part of its national landslide victory. In 1984, Texans backed Reagan again, this time by a massive 64–36 percent vote. These victories marked the beginning of an era in which Texas would provide a critical foundation for Republicans in the Electoral College. Moreover, Reagan helped make it not only acceptable, but expected, for Texas conservatives to support Republican presidential candidates (Figure 6.3).[44]

Two-Party Competition

Despite their increasing success in presidential politics, Texas Republicans struggled to achieve victories farther down the ballot. With the exception of John Tower's seat in the U.S. Senate, Democrats continued to control almost all of Texas's congressional and state legislative seats as well as all statewide offices, including attorney general, lieutenant governor, and the state's largest political prize, governor. A long line of centrist Democrats, including John

Connally (1963–1969), Preston Smith (1969–1973), and Dolph Briscoe (1973–1979), maintained their party's hold on the state's highest office until, in 1978, a Republican oilman named William Clements broke through, narrowly winning election as Texas's first GOP governor since Reconstruction.[45]

Many point to Clements's victory as a particularly important moment in the state's partisan realignment. At the time of Clements' death in 2011, journalist Carolyn Barta wrote that he had proved a Republican could be elected governor of Texas, and "could function in the traditionally Democratic environment that was state government. [Clements'] ability to deal successfully with conservative Democrats created the environment that made conservatives comfortable with switching parties."[46] Former governor George W. Bush agreed: "[Clements] broke the ice. . . . He showed Texas that a Republican could bring to the governor's office a philosophy that was acceptable to most Texans. He began the change at the state level for conservative Democrats to vote Republican for governor."[47]

Karl Rove, a political consultant to Clements who later served George W. Bush in Austin and Washington, D.C., has argued that the key to the GOP's success in Texas from the 1970s onward was its ability to tap into Texans' populist impulse. According to Rove, during these years, Texans "went from being economic populists, who thought the system was rigged against them by Wall Street, to being social and conservative populists, who thought that government was the problem."[48]

Although they had found a winning electoral formula, Texas Republicans still had much work to do to narrow the Democratic Party's advantage in the state. When Clements took office as governor in 1979, Democrats controlled all of the state's other elected executive offices, all seats on the state's elected supreme court and criminal appeals court, and, by large margins, both houses of the state legislature. The state's House of Representatives seated 125 Democrats and 22 Republicans that year; the Senate, 27 Democrats and only four Republicans. For the next two decades, Democrats put up a strong fight in statewide elections. Democrat Mark White defeated Clements for re-election in 1982, and the office switched back and forth between the two parties until George W. Bush unseated Democratic governor Ann Richards in 1994, ushering in a long period of Republican control.

After the 1994 election, Democrats still held other statewide offices and controlled both houses of the legislature, but it was clear the state's political balance was shifting and that Democratic power was quickly eroding. In 1996, Republicans achieved two more breakthroughs—for the first time, more Texans voted in the Republican than the Democratic state primaries and Republicans gained control of the state senate (Figure 6.4). In 1998, Bush won re-election in a landslide, and Republicans achieved their first sweep of all statewide offices.

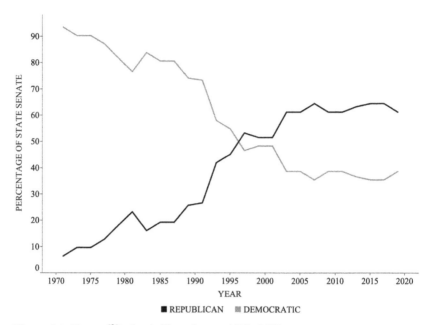

Figure 6.4. Party affiliation in Texas Senate, 1971–2019

Source: Legislative Reference Library of Texas

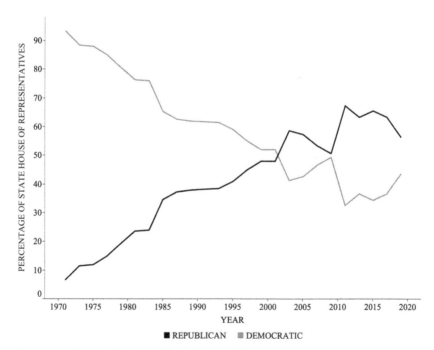

Figure 6.5. Party affiliation in Texas House of Representatives, 1971–2019

Source: Legislative Reference Library of Texas

And, in 2002, Republicans won their first majority in the Texas House of Representatives (Figure 6.5).[49]

Finally, in 2003, the Texas Legislature's new Republican majority proceeded to break one last Democratic power base—the state's congressional delegation. Texas's 2001 redistricting process had created a congressional map that preserved a 17–15 majority of Democratic seats. Once Republicans gained unified control of the legislature, however, U.S. House Majority Leader Tom DeLay urged them to redraw the map to make it more favorable to Republicans. The legislature did so, and the new districts had their intended effect. In the 2004 election, Republicans picked up six seats, gaining a 21–11 majority.[50]

Red State

Texas's partisan realignment was thus complete—the state had replaced the period of competitive two-party politics with an era of Republican dominance. The new arrangement resembled the old one-party Democratic monopoly in many ways. Republicans controlled all branches of state government (including the elected state supreme court), set the state's policy agenda; and contributed to their party's strength at the national level. Yet, the GOP lacked the degree of control Democrats enjoyed during their long period of one-party rule. In the old days, Republicans were excluded not only from statewide office, but also from nearly all positions in Congress, the state legislature, the state courts—all the way down to the lowest local office. By contrast, in the new era of Republican ascendancy, Democrats maintained strongholds throughout the state, especially in urban areas and among minority communities. In South Texas and the state's largest cities, Democrats continued to win local offices as well as races in state legislative and congressional districts.

In the early twenty-first century, Texas's rapid demographic changes and rising levels of urbanization and cultural diversity gave Democrats hope they could re-establish two-party parity, or even Democratic control, in the Lone Star State. This hope expanded during the Obama years, inspired by President Obama's mobilization of a winning coalition of minorities, urban progressives, women, and young voters. After Obama's 2012 re-election, some members of his campaign team created a venture called "Battleground Texas." The group sought to mobilize an Obama-like coalition in Texas and thereby make Democrats fully competitive in the state. Its premise was that it could "make Texas a battleground by treating it as a battleground."[51] The group targeted the 2014 election cycle to roll out the organizing tactics honed in the Obama campaigns. After investing a great deal of time and resources in 2013–2014, however, the effort fell short as Republicans rang up another big victory.[52]

In 2016, Democrats hoped the GOP's choice of Donald Trump as its presidential nominee would alter the electoral dynamics in the state, based on Trump's inflammatory rhetoric on immigration and his uneasy relationship with the party's establishment. Many believed that Trump's presence on the ballot would mobilize more Latinos to vote for Democrats and cause moderate Republicans, especially women, to defect from their party. As it turned out, Hillary Clinton lost Texas by nine points—a smaller deficit than the previous four Democratic nominees, but greater than Bill Clinton's losing margins in the 1990s.[53] Again, the Democratic ticket performed best in the state's largest urban areas and along the border with Mexico. Trump handily won the rest of the state (Figure 6.6).

Two years later, Democrats sensed yet another opportunity for a breakthrough. The 2018 midterm election was widely considered a referendum on President Trump. Across the nation, many Democratic candidates benefited from a surge of anti-Trump sentiment among minorities, suburban women, and other groups. In Texas, the election also featured a candidate for U.S. Senate, Congressman Beto O'Rourke, who generated a great deal of enthusiasm. The election saw a large turnout—more than 8.3 million Texans voted in 2018 compared with only

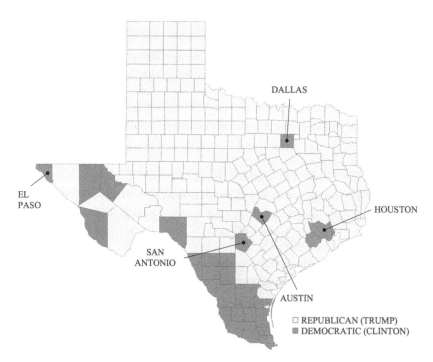

Figure 6.6. Presidential election results in Texas by county, 2016
Source: Texas Secretary of State

4.6 million in 2014. This surge helped Democrats gain ground. They picked up a number of legislative seats in longtime Republican areas such as North Dallas, and narrowed the gap in several statewide races. O'Rourke posed a credible threat to incumbent Republican Senator Ted Cruz, but ended up losing by a narrow 50.9–48.3 percent margin. O'Rourke ran up the score in the state's largest metropolitan areas and made inroads in long-established Republican suburban counties around Austin, Dallas, and Houston (Figure 6.7). Despite these developments, however, Texas Republicans again rallied to win all statewide offices and maintained their majorities in the state legislature and congressional delegation, even in a challenging political year for the GOP.[54]

Looking forward, one can imagine various possible political futures for the Lone Star State. Demographic, economic, and cultural changes indeed may cause Texas to become a true battleground, with Democrats again competing at parity with Republicans. Even if so, however, Texas's underlying conservative political culture will likely prevent the state from become truly "blue" in the manner of California or other progressive states. Indeed, to compete effectively in Texas, Democrats will need to distance themselves from the national party's increasingly progressive political and policy commitments. This will be a tall order in an

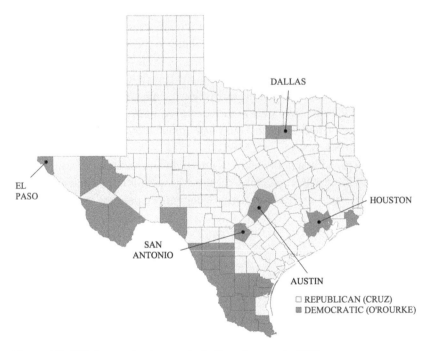

Figure 6.7. U.S. Senate election results in Texas by county, 2018
Source: Texas Secretary of State

era of polarization in which politicians have great difficulty differentiating themselves from their national party. The resulting dynamic provides Republicans an ongoing advantage in Texas just as it gives Democrats an edge in California and other progressive states.

Thus, while becoming more competitive, Texas will likely remain red for some time to come. The preceding chapters help explain why. To briefly summarize, Texans still hold more conservative views than residents of blue states and, indeed, than Americans as a whole. This difference is especially strong among whites, but can be seen among Latinos as well. Economic factors help explain Texas's Republican orientation. Texas's economic strength depends upon business-friendly economic policies, such as low taxes and light regulations, and this reality naturally points the state's politics in a conservative rather than a progressive direction. Moreover—and most important—Texas's predominantly conservative political culture more easily aligns with Republicans than with the Democratic Party.

Finally, in addition to these underlying advantages, the Texas GOP possesses a set of institutional powers that will help it maintain control over the state's politics. Like majority parties elsewhere, Texas Republicans have found ways to entrench their incumbency. For example, if they maintain their legislative majorities, they will have redistricting authority—and thus the power to draw congressional and state legislative district lines in ways that benefit Republican candidates.[55] Similarly, they will have the ability to preserve state laws that make it comparatively difficult in Texas to register and vote—a traditionalistic policy that narrows the electorate in ways that tend to benefit Republicans.[56] To be sure, these types of advantages operate primarily at the margins and would make little difference if the electorate were to turn decisively against the GOP. Under most circumstances, however, they should help Republicans maintain their control over the Lone Star State.

Accordingly, although the future is uncertain and various scenarios are possible, Texas likely will remain for some time the nation's largest and most consequential red state—and California's most determined political rival.

7

How California Turned Blue

California also took part in America's great partisan inversion. Like other
northern and western states with relatively progressive political cultures—states
like Oregon, Washington, Connecticut, New Hampshire, Vermont, Maine, New
Jersey, and Illinois—California had deep roots in the Republican Party and had
long maintained balanced two-party competition. In the 1990s, however, each
of these states joined the Democratic ranks—and, by many measures, California
became the bluest of them all. How did a state with such a strong Republican
streak convert so decisively to the Democratic Party?

This chapter places California's transformation into national context by briefly
describing the broader late twentieth-century movement by formerly Republican
states into the Democratic fold. It then explains how the interplay between these
national trends and California's distinctive demographic, economic, and cultural
characteristics drove the Golden State to the left and made it the leader of Blue
America.

The Formation of Blue America

Even as Texas and other conservative southern states famously left the Democratic
Party to join the GOP, a similar number of northern and western states moved
the opposite way, shifting from the Republican to the Democratic ranks.

As noted in the last chapter, most states in the North and West aligned with
the Republican Party in the decades after the Civil War. Near the end of the nineteenth century, most of them (including California) deepened their allegiance to
the party, and Republicans thus dominated American politics through the 1920s.
In the 1930s, the crisis of the Great Depression and the popularity of the New
Deal greatly strengthened the Democratic Party and weakened the GOP. By the
1950s, Republicans recovered, reasserting their presence across the northern tier.

Many of the old Republican states had progressive political cultures—or, at
least, strong progressive streaks—and were able to harmonize their progressivism with their support for the GOP. Through 1960, Republicans nominated
for president establishment figures Wendell Willkie, Thomas E. Dewey, Dwight
Eisenhower, and Richard Nixon. In 1964, however, the party experienced a sharp
division between its insurgent Sunbelt conservative wing and its more liberal

Texas vs. California. Kenneth P. Miller, Oxford University Press (2020). © Oxford University Press.
DOI: 10.1093/oso/9780190077402.001.0001.

establishment. That division was manifest in the contest for the 1964 presidential nomination between Arizona senator Barry Goldwater and New York governor Nelson Rockefeller.

As noted earlier, Rockefeller was a committed liberal who sought to preserve the Republican Party's progressive character. Among other positions, he supported federal intervention to ensure civil rights for African Americans, government efforts to alleviate poverty, and an internationalist foreign policy. Goldwater, by contrast, wanted the Republican Party to become more consistently conservative. In the summer of 1964, he was one of only six Republican senators (out of thirty-three) to oppose the Civil Rights Act, claiming that he was not defending racial discrimination, but rather constitutional principles of federalism and individual liberty. Goldwater also sought to scale back the size and powers of the federal government and to pursue a more nationalist, anticommunist foreign policy. He complained that establishment Republicans had done too little to roll back the expansion of federal power under two decades of Democratic rule. The Eisenhower administration, he said, had offered a "dime store New Deal." He wanted to give Americans "a choice, not an echo."[1]

Goldwater narrowly defeated Rockefeller in the pivotal California primary, then fended off a late "stop Goldwater" effort to secure the GOP presidential nomination. At the national convention in San Francisco, Goldwater's supporters drafted a conservative party platform and shouted down Rockefeller during his speech to the delegates. Longtime establishment figure Henry Cabot Lodge asked, "What in God's name has happened to the Republican Party?"[2]

As it turned out, Lodge was witnessing the early stages of the nation's partisan polarization. As the Democratic Party was moving to the left on civil rights and other social issues, the Republican Party was becoming more conservative. And just as southern conservatives were starting to feel out of place in the Democratic Party, northern liberals were beginning to wonder whether they belonged in the GOP.

The shift by northern and western Republican states to the Democratic Party took years to complete. Each of these states (save Arizona) voted for the Democratic ticket in 1964, but most returned to the Republican fold in 1968 and generally remained there through 1970s and 1980s. By the late 1980s, however, the Republican Party was clearly moving geographically to the South and ideologically to the right. The party's increasing focus on social issues aligned with its emerging southern-style, conservative orientation.

Pat Buchanan's address to the 1992 Republican National Convention in Houston reflected the GOP's new emphasis on cultural issues. After denouncing the Democratic Party's progressive positions on abortion, same-sex marriage, feminism, environmentalism, and church-state relations, Buchanan said: "This election is about more than who gets what. It is about who we are. It is about what we believe, and what we stand for as Americans. There is a religious war going on in this country. It is a cultural war, as critical to the kind of nation we shall be as the Cold War itself, for this war is for the soul of America."[3] Buchanan's speech was well received by social conservatives and helped deepen the Republican Party's connection with conservative voters. On the other hand, as the GOP took a harder line on social issues, it struggled to compete in more culturally diverse, secular, and progressive parts of the country—in particular, the Northeast and the Pacific Coast. The Democratic Party was able to convince voters in these regions that it was more closely aligned with their values.

In 1988, Oregon and Washington shifted to the Democratic column, joined by states that sometimes had voted Republican in presidential contests—Hawaii, Massachusetts, New York, and Rhode Island. In 1992, this stream became a flood, with California, Connecticut, Delaware, Illinois, Maine, New Hampshire, New Jersey, and Vermont joining the Democratic ranks. For decades after 1992, all of these states (with the brief exception of New Hampshire) maintained unbroken support for Democratic presidential candidates (Figure 7.1).

The states that joined Democratic fold in 1988 and 1992 established the core of Blue America. And California was the most important convert of all.

California's Early Party System

California had a long journey to become the nation's bluest state because, for much of its history, it aligned with the GOP. To be sure, the Golden State's affinity for the Republican Party was never absolute. In 1856, for example, Republicans fielded their first presidential candidate, John C. Frémont, in a three-way contest. One might think that the legendary "Pathfinder" and hero of the American conquest of California would have captured the Golden State, but that was not the case. Although he won 114 electoral votes in eleven states in the Northeast and upper Midwest, Frémont finished a distant third in California, receiving only 20,704 votes, or less than 20 percent of the total cast. Four years later, in the critical presidential election of 1860, California supported the Republican candidate, Abraham Lincoln, but only by a narrow margin.[4]

During the 1860s, the new party began to take root in the state. In 1861, Leland Stanford won election as California's first Republican governor, and for the balance of the century, the state had six Republican and five Democratic governors, in addition to one governor from the Unionist Party. In eleven presidential elections between 1860 and 1900, California voted for the Republican ticket nine times and for Democrats only twice.[5] Like most of the North and West, California became more solidly Republican following the realigning election of 1896. From the last years of the nineteenth century through the 1920s,

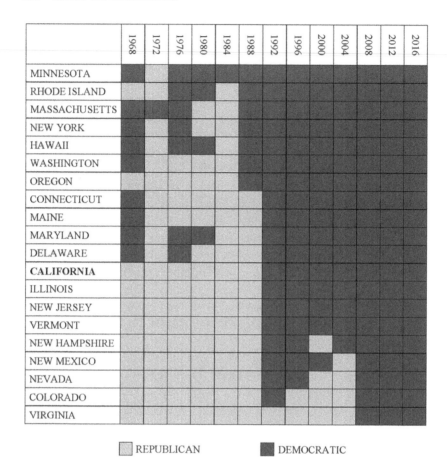

Figure 7.1. Shift in partisan vote in presidential elections, 1968–2016
Source: American Presidency Project

Republicans maintained large majorities in the California Legislature and regularly won statewide elections. During this era, California's most important political competition occurred within the ranks of the state GOP.

California Progressives

At the turn of the twentieth century, the California Republican Party was internally divided between the political machine of the Southern Pacific Railroad and reformers who sought to break the machine's power. For years, the Southern Pacific (successor to the Central Pacific Railroad) had leveraged its economic power to gain extraordinary influence over California politics and government. Stanford, one of the "Big Four" who controlled the railroad, held office as governor (1862–1863) as well as U.S. senator (1885–1893). Stanford's elections were but a small manifestation of the Southern Pacific's enormous political power. The company's political bureau rivaled New York's Tammany Hall in its control over candidate selection, party nominations, legislative politics, and policy at the state and municipal levels. According to one of the railroad's critics, "From the village constable to the governor of the state . . . the final selection of the people's officials lay with . . . the railroad machine."[6]

In 1907, a group of political reformers met in Los Angeles to pursue the "emancipation of the Republican Party in California from domination by the Political Bureau of the Southern Pacific Railroad Company and allied interests."[7] The group identified with the nation's emerging Progressive movement and, as part of its mission, advocated a broad range of Progressive reforms.

California Progressives of that era were mostly upper-middle class urban professionals—academics, clergy, lawyers, doctors, and journalists, as well as owners and managers of independent businesses. They tended to be young, white, midwestern, Protestant, and college educated.[8] They also fully embodied what Elazar called a moralistic political culture—that is, they believed the state should pursue a vision of the common good that transcends individual private interests, and that citizens should actively participate in government. Most Progressives sought to rein in railroads and other large corporations, but many also opposed organized labor in the belief that unions constituted a special interest, as well. Although most California Progressives came from the Republican Party, the movement also featured prominent Democrats, including James Phelan, the mayor of San Francisco (1897–1902) and U.S. senator (1915–1921).[9]

The movement achieved a breakthrough in 1910. That year, California voters elected a Progressive Republican prosecutor named Hiram Johnson as governor and sent a large group of Progressives to the legislature. In 1911, Johnson and the legislature called a special election and presented voters a long slate of constitutional amendments that represented the heart of the Progressive agenda. Voters approved nearly all of these goals, including women's suffrage, direct democracy (initiative, referendum, and recall), regulatory powers over railroads and other corporations, authorization for public ownership of utilities, workers' compensation laws, and more.[10] The 1911 Special Election effectively refounded California state government on Progressive principles.

These accomplishments vaulted Hiram Johnson onto the national stage. In 1912, Johnson joined Theodore Roosevelt in defecting from the GOP and forming the National Progressive ("Bull Moose") Party, and he accepted the new party's nomination for vice president. The Roosevelt-Johnson ticket narrowly defeated Democrat Woodrow Wilson in California, but lost the national election.[11] The Progressives soon disappeared as a third-party movement, but their ideals deeply influenced both Republicans and Democrats in California for decades to come.

After the Progressive Era, the GOP dominated the state's political landscape. By the middle of the 1920s, Republicans held a three-to-one advantage over Democrats in voter registration and maintained control over all statewide offices, both U.S. Senate seats, and the vast majority legislative seats, including seventy-five of eighty seats in the state assembly, thirty-seven of forty in the state senate, and nine of eleven in the congressional delegation. In 1928, Republican Herbert Hoover, a Stanford University graduate who made his home in the state, won the presidency—the first Californian to do so.[12] Based on these successes, the GOP expected to dominate California politics for a long time to come.

1930s: Great Depression and EPIC Vision

The Great Depression shattered that expectation. The cataclysm broke the GOP's tight grip on California politics, revived the state Democratic Party, and introduced a period of close two-party competition. In 1932, Franklin Roosevelt defeated Hoover in California by 58–37 percent, launching a streak of five straight Democratic victories in California's presidential contests (1932–1948). During the 1930s, Democrats also won a U.S. Senate seat, a majority of the state's congressional delegation, and temporary control of the state assembly. Moreover, they surpassed Republicans in voter registration, due partly to the waves of new Democratic voters entering the state, and partly to the conversion of Republicans to the Democratic Party.[13] Yet, despite these gains, Democrats struggled to assert broader control over state government.

The California Democratic Party's most spectacular failure came in the 1934 gubernatorial race.[14] That year, the party selected Upton Sinclair, the celebrated socialist author of *The Jungle*, as its nominee. Sinclair based his campaign on a radical pledge to "End Poverty in California," also known as "EPIC." His campaign manifesto (written in the form of a fable) was titled, *I, Governor of California, and How I Ended Poverty—A True Story of the Future*. The EPIC program sought to repeal the state sales tax and replace it with personal income, property, and inheritance taxes; increase taxes on banks, public utilities, and other corporations; establish state pensions for the elderly, blind, disabled, and widows with dependent children; and, most radically, create state-managed cooperative colonies. This last goal was designed to provide immediate employment for the state's seven hundred thousand unemployed workers and to create the foundation for a broader cooperative economy. The EPIC campaign generated great enthusiasm. By the fall of 1934, nearly two thousand EPIC clubs formed in the state and EPIC News achieved a circulation of two million.[15]

Sinclair met massive resistance from the state's political establishment. Republicans unleashed a new innovation, the political consulting firm, to attack both the candidate and the EPIC movement.[16] Most of the state's major newspapers, including the then-conservative *Los Angeles Times*, joined in the assault. Sinclair was pilloried as a communist, an atheist, and an authoritarian menace. The election was an international spectacle, one of the highest-profile and most hotly contested elections in the state's history. FDR and other Democratic leaders distanced themselves from Sinclair, considering him too radical. In the end, the state's establishment turned back the EPIC challenge.[17]

Some Democrats believed the 1934 EPIC campaign was a disastrous detour to the far left that cost the party a winnable election; others considered it an important catalyst for Democratic activism in the state. Although a more moderate candidate with the full backing of President Roosevelt and the national Democratic Party might have won the 1934 governor's race, it is also true that the lively EPIC campaign inspired and mobilized many future leaders of the California Democratic Party.[18]

Four years later, EPIC supporter Culbert Olson captured the governor's office for Democrats for the first time in the twentieth century. Like Sinclair, Olson was a man of the left—an advocate of progressive taxation, universal health care, regulations on industry, and protections for organized labor. He was also an avowed atheist who later became president of the United Secularists of America. Despite his resemblances to Sinclair, Olson was perceived as less radical than the socialist author and won the backing of FDR and the Democratic Party establishment. Once in office, he faced heavy opposition from the legislature and the state's attorney general, Earl Warren, and was able to achieve only a fraction of his agenda during his one-term administration.[19] Yet Olson's brief tenure, like the EPIC campaign that preceded it, gave a rising generation a vision of progressive Democratic government in the Golden State.

Earl Warren's Midcentury Consensus

In 1942, Earl Warren recaptured the governor's office for the GOP, ushering in sixteen more years of Republican control of the state. Like many other California Republicans of his day, Warren was no orthodox conservative, but instead a committed California progressive. Born in Los Angeles in 1891, Warren reached maturity just as the Progressive movement swept through the state. As a student at Berkeley, he volunteered to work for Hiram Johnson and enthusiastically backed his election as governor in 1910. Progressivism became Warren's guiding philosophy.[20]

Throughout his ascent from county prosecutor to attorney general to governor, Warren occupied the state's political center. As a law-and-order prosecutor, he attracted right-leaning voters; but he also appealed to liberals with views that foreshadowed his later career as chief justice of the United States. Warren surrounded himself with Democratic advisors and built alliances with key Democratic constituencies, including the American Federation of Labor. He cultivated a reputation for bipartisanship and flourished in a political culture that rewarded centrism.[21]

A Progressive Era innovation called "cross-filing" reinforced Warren-style bipartisan politics. Under the system, candidates could compete for the nomination of multiple parties for the same office. Warren won both the Republican and Democratic nominations for governor in 1946—and he was far from alone in exploiting the system. Candidates from both parties cross-filed, but Republicans used the process to greatest advantage. Because Democrats had surpassed Republicans in voter registration, Republicans needed to win Democratic votes. Competing in Democratic primaries, Republicans often downplayed their party affiliation and tailored their message to appeal to moderate Democrats. With Warren as their model, California Republicans of this era occupied the political center, accepting most New Deal domestic programs and supporting public investments in education and infrastructure for the state's fast-growing suburbs.[22]

During the postwar years, California Republicans also featured prominently at the highest levels of national politics. Governor Warren was a leading presidential contender in 1948 and 1952 before leaving elective politics to join the Supreme Court as chief justice of the United States in 1953. A young Richard Nixon soon replaced Warren on the national political scene. Nixon won a Southern California House seat in 1946 and a Senate seat in 1950, on his way to election as vice president in 1952. Through the 1950s, Nixon set his sights on the top office.[23] At the same time, Goodwin Knight (Warren's successor as governor) and U.S. Senator William Knowland also eyed runs for the presidency. At midcentury, fast-growing California had established itself as one of the nation's most dynamic Republican states.[24]

1958: Democratic Breakthrough

California Democrats were hungry to break the GOP's lock on power. In January 1953, a group of liberal Democratic officials and activists held a conference to tackle the question: "How to End the Republican Stranglehold in California."

They outlined plans for a new organization called the California Democratic Council (CDC), which would develop an explicitly progressive platform and endorse like-minded candidates in Democratic primaries. The CDC held its first annual convention in early 1954 and soon became a force in the state party. At the same time, activists began forming clubs in communities throughout the state to provide local organization and fundraising support for Democratic candidates. By late 1954, 425 local Democratic clubs had been established, consisting of approximately thirty thousand members.[25] Democrats became more organized and disciplined by the day. Democratic clubs spread throughout the state and the CDC approach—ideological and issue-oriented—was mobilizing voters. Democrats registered new voters at a rapid clip, with 72 percent of new registrants joining the Democratic ranks.[26]

Republican missteps also provided Democrats an opening. In 1958, GOP senator Knowland decided to challenge Goodwin Knight, the incumbent Republican governor. Knight abandoned his re-election bid and ran for Knowland's Senate seat—an awkward attempt to swap offices. More importantly for the party's future, Knowland broke from Earl Warren's tradition of centrist, bipartisan politics. A hardline conservative, he tied his campaign for governor to a statewide ballot measure to mandate the open shop throughout California. In the postwar years, however, the state's industrial unions were at the peak of their power and contributed millions of dollars and countless volunteer hours to defeat the ballot measure, as well as Knowland and other Republican candidates.[27]

For their part, Democrats fielded a talented slate in 1958, led by their candidate for governor, Edmund G. "Pat" Brown.[28] In many ways, Brown was the Democrats' answer to Earl Warren—a natural politician deeply influenced by early twentieth-century Progressivism. After his conversion in the mid-1930s to the New Deal and the Democratic Party, Brown rose through the party ranks, winning office as district attorney of San Francisco and, later, state attorney general, before running for governor.[29]

The 1958 election proved to be a critical stage in the California Democratic Party's long rise to power. That year, Democrats finally shattered Republican dominance in the state. Brown defeated Knowland for governor by more than a million votes, while the Democrats also captured Knowland's old U.S. Senate seat. In state legislative races, Democrats gained control of the state assembly for the first time since 1942 and the state senate for the first time since 1890. Democrats also gained an edge in the state's congressional delegation. And, for good measure, voters soundly defeated the Republicans' anti-union ballot measure.[30]

This landmark election severed the ties Warren had formed between the GOP and organized labor and solidified the alliance between unions and the Democratic Party. It also permanently shifted partisan control of some parts of the state—including Berkeley and parts of Los Angeles—to the Democratic Party. Finally, it marked the beginning of the end of California's mid-century consensus. As evidenced by the stark contrast between Knowland and the open shop initiative on one side and the CDC on the other, the parties were sorting ideologically.[31]

Pat Brown's victory in 1958 also laid the foundation for one of the nation's most enduring political dynasties. Brown went on to serve two terms as governor (1959–1967) and was later succeeded by his son, Edmund G. ("Jerry") Brown Jr., who served an unprecedented four terms in the office (1975–1983 and 2011–2019). Jerry's younger sister, Kathleen, also held the office of state treasurer (1991–1995) and won the Democratic nomination for governor in 1994. All told, members of the Brown family appeared on the state's general election ballot no fewer than fifteen times (including eight times for governor), and held statewide office with only occasional interruptions for nearly seven decades between 1951 and 2019.[32]

In the aftermath of the 1958 election, the California Democratic Party became more consistently a party of the left—an alliance of organized labor, social liberals, intellectuals, racial minorities, and government workers—focused on promoting social democracy, civil rights (including fair employment and housing), public works, economic regulation, state-funded health care, and a broad range of other government services. In the late 1950s and early 1960s, California Democrats sought to complete the unfinished agenda of the New Deal and expand it to new circumstances. In their view, a fast-growing state was generating new needs that demanded an activist state government. Their agenda left little room for the party's conservative wing. As conservatives drifted away, nearly all California Democratic activists and leaders in the state came to share a left-leaning approach to politics and government.[33]

At the same time, the California Republican Party was moving rightward from its Warren-era centrism. In one key indicator of that movement, the state GOP narrowly chose Goldwater over Rockefeller in the 1964 presidential primary. The Goldwater campaign energized the rising suburban conservative movement in Southern California and helped lay a foundation for Ronald Reagan's later political successes.[34] Again, these developments further differentiated the state's two major parties—providing voters increasingly clear and contrasting choices.

1958–1998: Partisan Parity

As California's political parties sorted ideologically, they engaged in a long period of balanced competition. In the four decades after 1958, neither party could establish dominance (Figure 7.2). Many voters shifted their allegiances back and

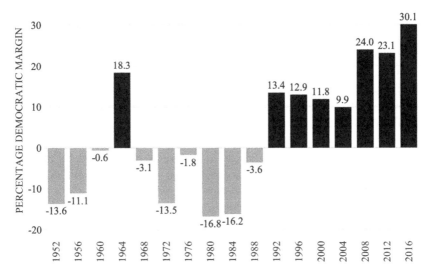

Figure 7.2. Margin between Democratic and Republican percentage of total presidential vote in California, 1952–2016

Source: American Presidency Project

forth, splitting tickets and voting for a Republican in one race and a Democrat in another. During these years, Republicans held the edge in most top-of-the-ticket races, with their largest advantage in presidential elections. With the lone exception of Lyndon Johnson's victory over Goldwater in 1964, Republican presidential candidates won the other seven presidential contests in California between 1960 and 1988, before Democrats began their long streak of victories in 1992. The presence of Californians on the ballot boosted the GOP's performance in presidential elections—Richard Nixon won the state three times (1960, 1968, and 1972) and Ronald Reagan twice (1980 and 1984). Democrats held a narrow edge in U.S. Senate contests, winning six of eleven elections between 1958 and 1988 before locking down both seats in 1992, but Republicans won six of eleven governor's races between 1958 and 1998, including four straight elections between 1982 and 1994.

Republicans achieved most of their success in this four-decade period by appealing to California's broad, moderate center. Although the state GOP was becoming more conservative than it had been during the Warren era, its leading figures maintained a progressive streak. Ronald Reagan was a prime example. Although he became a conservative icon during his years as governor (1967–1975), Reagan nevertheless endorsed policies—including income tax hikes, environmental regulations, expanded access to abortion, and establishment of a full-time, professionalized legislature—that placed him within the state's progressive tradition and political mainstream.[35] Reagan's Republican successors during this period, George Deukmejian (1983–1991) and Pete Wilson (1991–1999), also appealed to the state's political center.

At the same time, Democrats consistently maintained an advantage in the state's legislative contests. After winning control of both houses of the legislature in 1958, the party retained them, with few interruptions, thereafter.[36] Similarly, after 1958, Democrats held a majority of the state's congressional seats with the brief exception of the 104th Congress in 1995–1996, when the delegation was evenly divided, 26–26. As a consequence, throughout this period of two-party parity, the legislature was a center of Democratic strength. Powerful Democratic Assembly Speakers Jesse Unruh (1961–1969) and Willie Brown (1980–1995) made the legislature an engine for progressive policies.[37]

Finally, during these years the California Supreme Court was dominated by liberal justices, most of whom were appointed by Democratic governors Culbert Olson and Pat and Jerry Brown. The state's high court earned a reputation as the most activist in the nation as it adapted the common law to progressive ends, especially in the field of torts, and expanded state constitutional rights in areas including racial desegregation, abortion, criminal procedure, criminal punishment, free speech, school funding, and gender equality.[38]

As is common in a divided government, both parties were often frustrated in their efforts to achieve their policy goals. For years, Democratic majorities in the state legislature thwarted Republican priorities, and Republican governors Reagan, Deukmejian, and Wilson blocked or modified much of the Democratic agenda. At the same time, the state's strong forms of direct democracy placed additional limitations on the Democrats' power. The most important of these tools was the initiative process, which allows citizens to propose a statute or constitutional amendment, place it on the ballot, and enact it through simple majority vote. The Progressive architects of the initiative process designed it to give popular majorities the power to override the legislature, the governor's office, and the special interests that they believed often control those institutions.[39] They expected citizens would employ the system to overcome the power of corporate interests; but over time, citizens and groups used it for a wide range of purposes. From the 1970s through the 1990s, conservative groups frequently relied on ballot initiatives to counter progressive policies.

A famous example occurred in 1978, when citizens invoked the initiative process to slash their property taxes. Overriding the state's political establishment, voters approved Proposition 13, a measure that cut existing taxes and strictly limited government's ability to raise them in the future.[40] Similarly, from the 1960s through the 1990s, voters approved a long list of initiatives that reversed the legislature and progressive judges on issues including fair housing, busing, criminal procedure, the death penalty and other criminal punishments, bilingual policies, affirmative action, and term limits.[41]

Finally, in 1986, voters used the ballot to unseat three liberal state supreme court justices, Rose Bird, Cruz Reynoso, and Joseph Grodin, in one of the state's periodic judicial retention elections—a move that transformed the court from a catalyst of progressive policy into a more conservative institution.[42]

The Critical 1990s

After nearly four decades of balanced competition between the state's conservative and progressive forces, the scales shifted in the 1990s. One could see the first signs of change in 1992. That year, California joined other formerly Republican states to support the Democratic presidential ticket. In the Golden State, Bill Clinton defeated George H. W. Bush by 46 to 33 percent, with Ross Perot, the Texan third party candidate, taking 21 percent of the vote. Clinton's victory broke the GOP's string of six straight wins in presidential contests in California, dating back to 1968, and began a long streak of Democratic dominance.

Democratic success at the top of the ballot also extended downward. In 1992, Democrats nominated former San Francisco mayor Dianne Feinstein and Congresswoman Barbara Boxer for the state's two U.S. Senate seats. In what became known as the "Year of the Woman," Feinstein and Boxer handily defeated their Republican rivals. Once in office, the two Democrats remained there for decades. When Boxer retired in 2017, she was succeeded by fellow San Francisco Bay Area Democrat Kamala Harris.

As the 1990s progressed, California experienced the extraordinary range of demographic, economic, and cultural changes described in prior chapters. Immigrants continued to arrive in large numbers, causing many older suburbs to become majority-minority. At the same time, the end of the Cold War hollowed out the state's aerospace industry—contributing, in the short run, to a deep recession, and, in the longer term, to the permanent disappearance of many high-wage manufacturing jobs. Moreover, the state experienced rising crime rates and other social ills. The number of residents migrating out of California rose sharply in the early 1990s, to more than 600,000 per year.[43]

In 1994, amid these stresses, California held what turned out to be a pivotal election. The incumbent governor, Pete Wilson, was running for re-election, hoping to extend the GOP's control of the governor's office for another four years. Early polls showed, however, that Wilson was trailing his Democratic challenger, Kathleen Brown, by a large margin. To climb back into contention, the moderate

Wilson shifted right and focused on two hot-button issues, crime and immigration. And, to underscore his hardline positions on these issues, he endorsed two controversial ballot initiatives.[44]

The first was a tough-on-crime measure known as the "Three-Strikes-and-You're-Out" initiative, which promised to lock up recidivist criminals with three qualifying offenses for twenty-five-years-to-life.[45] That initiative went on to pass by an overwhelming 72 percent vote. The second, Proposition 187, was more deeply polarizing. The measure promised to deny undocumented immigrants public services (including public education, non-emergency health care, and social services) and to require public employees to report persons they suspected to be in the country illegally. The campaign surrounding Proposition 187 produced strong feelings on all sides. Proponents provocatively called Proposition 187 the "Save Our State" initiative and aired ads featuring black and white video of immigrants running through a border checkpoint. In one ad, a narrator said: "They keep coming—two million illegal immigrants in California. The federal government won't stop them at the border, yet requires us to spend billions to take care of them." Governor Wilson then appeared onscreen and said: "I'm suing to force the federal government to control the border. And I'm working to deny state services to illegal immigrants. Enough is enough."[46]

Proposition 187's opponents argued that the measure would cruelly deny essential services to vulnerable residents, including children; turn school teachers, nurses, and other public employees into immigration cops; and stigmatize all immigrants, not just those in the country unlawfully. In the weeks before the election, immigrant rights groups organized demonstrations throughout the state, including a massive rally in downtown Los Angeles. After a tense campaign, California voters approved Proposition 187 by a 59–41 percent vote.[47]

Opponents immediately challenged the measure in federal court, and most of its provisions were never implemented.[48] Instead, Proposition 187's true power was in its symbolism. In the short run, the initiative provided the California GOP political benefits by contributing to a Republican wave in the 1994 election.[49] Wilson rallied to win re-election over Kathleen Brown by a sizeable margin. Republican candidates won a majority of other statewide offices and secured a narrow majority in the state assembly for the first time in decades. And in the state's congressional races, Republicans achieved parity, winning twenty-six seats compared to twenty-six for the Democrats.[50]

In time, however, it became apparent that the California Republican Party's harsh tone on immigration had created a long-term political liability—and that the party's success in 1994 had been less a revival than a last gasp.

Post 1994: Democratic Surge

Soon after their setback in the 1994 election, Democrats regrouped and began to establish their dominant position in the state. This sequence of events led many political observers to conclude that Republican support for Proposition 187 caused California to turn blue. This conventional wisdom was based on the perception that backlash against the measure caused Latinos and other immigrants to mobilize and align more tightly with the Democratic Party.[51] And, indeed, Latinos did become a more powerful presence in the Democratic Party and in California generally in the wake of the 1994 election.

The effort to unlock the power of the Latino vote proceeded on various fronts, with organized labor taking the lead. Labor organizer Miguel Contreras, a protégé of Cesar Chavez, was particularly effective in strengthening the alliance among Latinos, organized labor, and the Democratic Party. In 1996, Contreras assumed leadership of the Los Angeles County Federation of Labor, which was comprised of 325 local unions with more than 600,000 members. Contreras brought new energy to the federation by tapping into immigrant communities. He focused on organizing low-wage Latino maids, janitors, restaurant employees, and other service workers. At the same time, he recruited talented Latinos in the labor movement to run for public office and encouraged rank-and-file union members to participate in their campaigns. In the years after 1994, Contreras and his allies mobilized in the Latino community a new generation of activist, progressive Democratic voters and elected officials.[52]

Moreover, despite many attempts by Governor Wilson and other Republicans to draw distinctions between legal and illegal immigrants, the GOP's support for Proposition 187 reinforced the perception that Republicans disliked not only illegal immigration but also the state's rapidly changing demography. Many immigrants and other minorities hardened their belief that the GOP did not welcome them—surely a problem for a political party in a majority-minority state.

That being said, the causal connection between Proposition 187 and the state's partisan realignment is often overstated.[53] Indeed, just as the Civil Rights Act of 1964 did not, by itself, realign the South, neither did one ballot measure in 1994 realign California. Instead, Proposition 187 was one factor among many that caused California to turn blue. One can ask the question another way: What would have happened if California Republicans had never endorsed Proposition 187 or taken a hard line on immigration? Most probably, California still would have become heavily Democratic. As discussed in prior chapters, many other factors were pulling the state to the left, including its underlying progressive political culture, its increasing secularization, the rise of the New Economy, the hollowing out of the middle class, and the changing character of the national political parties. Yet, while many factors were conspiring to turn California blue, the reaction to the GOP's positions on immigration policy and, more, its rhetoric on the issue, moved the state more deeply and permanently into the Democratic column.

The shift from two-party parity to Democratic dominance gathered momentum in the late 1990s. In 1996, Democrats started growing their majorities in the state legislature and, in 1998, they reclaimed the governor's office through a landslide victory by Democrat Gray Davis. At that point, all signs suggested that Democrats would establish long-term control over the state. This culmination was temporarily delayed, however, by the 2003 recall of Governor Davis and election of Arnold Schwarzenegger.

By 2003, another recession (the dot-com bust), a budget crisis, and a failed attempt to deregulate the state's electricity industry had eroded Davis's support, and citizens seized on another direct democracy device, the recall, to force him from office. In October 2003, voters removed Davis (only the second recall of a state governor in the nation's history), and replaced him with the "governator."

Arnold Schwarzenegger won the governor's election as a Republican, but in many ways resembled an old California Progressive more than a contemporary conservative. He had little interest in advancing conservative positions on social issues, and instead focused on economic growth, environmental protection, and political reform. By the end of his second term, he found himself frequently aligning with Democrats on climate policy, LGBT rights, and other matters. Meanwhile, during Schwarzenegger's seven years in office, the California GOP continued to atrophy. In one of his favorite lines, Schwarzenegger said that his fellow Republicans were "dying at the box office."[54] Schwarzenegger's personal popularity did not revive the state GOP, and he turned out to be a transitional figure on the path to Democratic dominance. Once he left office, the field was cleared for Democrats to assert unchallenged power in the state.

Deep Blue California

Democrats soon tightened their grip on California politics. For the next several election cycles, they won all statewide offices and a growing number of legislative districts. The imbalance grew so great that, in some races—including for the U.S. Senate—the November election featured two Democratic candidates and no Republican. These outcomes could occur because under the state's "top-two" primary system (established in 2010), the two candidates receiving the most votes effectively advanced to a run-off in the general election. Democrat-versus-Democrat general election contests highlighted the weakness of the state GOP, but even when Republican candidates appeared on the November ballot, they typically lacked enough name recognition, talent, organization, and money to run a competitive campaign. Democrats thus routinely won statewide elections against Republican challengers with little effort and by large margins. Indeed, Gavin Newsom was safely able to measure new drapes for the governor's office well before his election in 2018.

California's 2016 presidential contest further highlighted Democratic strength and Republican weakness. By nominating Donald Trump for president, the GOP tied its fate to a candidate who uniquely repelled most California voters. Trump's core constituency of working-class whites had been exiting California for decades, and his personal manner, policy positions, and rhetoric were antithetical to the state's increasingly progressive political culture. In November 2016, California voters dealt Trump the largest state-level raw popular vote defeat in the nation's history (Figure 7.3). Hillary Clinton outpolled Trump in the

Figure 7.3. Presidential election results in California by county, 2016
Source: California Secretary of State

state by more than four million votes—an unprecedented figure that alone fully accounted for Clinton's winning margin in the national popular vote.[55]

As the GOP embraced Trumpism, the party label became increasingly toxic for California Republican candidates down the ballot. In 2018, anti-Trump sentiment helped Democrats capture several formerly safe Republican districts in Orange County, San Diego County, and the state's interior, further expanding their dominance in the state. Through this surge, Democrats achieved what some called a "giga-majority"—two-thirds supermajorities in both houses of the state legislature, a margin that allowed them to raise taxes, propose constitutional amendments, and exercise other powers with no Republican votes. They also controlled a historic forty-six of fifty-three seats in the state's congressional delegation, while retaining both U.S. Senate seats and all statewide offices (Figures 7.4 and 7.5).

At the same time California voters were giving Democrats supermajority control of state government, they were taking more progressive positions on policy matters. In past decades, Californians had adopted conservative ballot initiatives to constrain the legislature; now the electorate was more closely aligned with

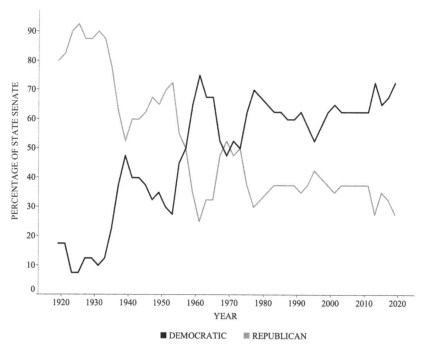

Figure 7.4. Party affiliation in California Senate, 1919–2019
Source: California Secretary of State

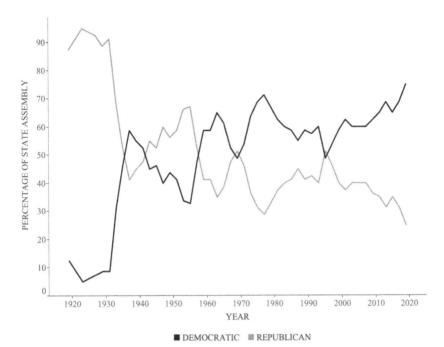

Figure 7.5. Party affiliation in California Assembly, 1919–2019
Source: California Secretary of State

the legislature's progressive policy agenda. From 2010 to 2018, voters approved measures to raise taxes on the state's highest earners, reduce criminal penalties, restore bilingual education, impose gun control, legalize marijuana, and protect animal rights, among other progressive goals.

Finally, California Democrats began establishing a larger presence in national politics. Throughout the nation's history, few Democrats from the West had risen to the highest levels of the American political system. For example, through 2016, no Democrat from west of the Rocky Mountains—let alone from California— had ever been selected as a presidential or vice-presidential nominee. Similarly, no California Democrat had served as Senate Majority Leader or Speaker of the House until Nancy Pelosi won the election as Speaker in 2007.[56] As California Democrats came to dominate the nation's largest state, they began developing a pipeline of talented politicians with national ambitions—including Kamala Harris, Gavin Newsom, and Eric Garcetti. Moreover, by 2019, Californians constituted nearly one-fifth of the House Democratic Caucus, opening up new opportunities for the state's Democratic politicians to exert leadership in Congress.

By all of these measures, California had become the nation's most powerful blue state. And, as they moved deeper into the twenty-first century, California Democrats were setting their sights high. With no meaningful partisan competition within the state, they were developing an ambitious progressive agenda at home with the hope of exporting it to the rest of the nation—and, indeed, to the world.

Why Did the Siblings Divide?

To summarize, numerous factors have caused Texas and California to divide. Although the two states share underlying similarities, they also possess various characteristics that have driven them apart. These differences can be seen in the states' origins, with Texas initially embracing a southern economic and cultural identity and California assuming more northern and cosmopolitan traits. The differences have persisted over time. Texas has become more modern and "western," but has maintained its southern roots and conservative identity. Described in broad strokes, its economic system is market-oriented, based on low costs, light regulation, and opposition to organized labor, while its dominant cultural instincts are rooted in traditional values. By contrast, California has always had a progressive streak, which has evolved and deepened over time. The Golden State's economy includes higher levels of government regulation, unionization, and redistribution than its rival, and its cultural traits have become increasingly secular and liberal. The states' divergent economic and cultural characteristics have contributed to their contrasting political cultures. Critically, however, for much of the twentieth century, the Democratic and Republican Parties were not as ideologically distinct as they are today, and the two states' differences in political culture did not neatly translate into competing party loyalty. In more recent decades, as the parties polarized along ideological lines, Texas converted to the GOP and California shifted emphatically to the Democratic camp. Once they separated in this way, the nation's largest and most powerful states became the natural leaders of red and blue America. What are the consequences of Texas and California engaging in direct competition for the nation's future? The following chapters explore that question.

PART II
COMPETING VISIONS

8

Rival Models

Even as partisan polarization drove a political wedge between Texas and California, it allowed the rivals to develop ideologically coherent policy models and to promote them within the federal system. The empowerment of Texas and California during this age of partisan division illustrates how polarization has operated differently in the states than in Washington, D.C.

By the turn of the millennium, polarization had created chronic gridlock at the federal level because, critically, the nation was split fifty-fifty—Republicans and Democrats were not only deeply divided, but also evenly matched. Neither party was able to establish a lasting advantage. Control of the presidency and Congress swung back and forth between the two camps, as Republicans often seized one branch of government and Democrats the other. Each party could generally block or reverse the other's national policy agenda. In frustration, both parties attempted to make policy through unilateral action, such as presidential executive orders, but the federal constitutional system generally prevented either side from achieving durable change in the absence of broader consensus. As a consequence, federal policymaking experienced cycles of paralysis, instability, and confusion.

Polarization affected the states in a different way. Although the nation as a whole was split evenly between the two parties, most states aligned decisively with one side or the other. This was a change. For years, most states had experienced internal partisan balance (as in California) or split-ticket voting (as in Texas). But near the turn of the millennium, a large number of states sorted into one of the two partisan camps.[1] In these one-party states, party cohesion and discipline facilitated policymaking. Unlike the evenly divided, gridlocked politics of Washington, D.C., states with polarized one-party control could develop and implement their policy agendas in near-parliamentary fashion, without obstruction by the minority party.

Texas shifted to unified Republican control in 2003. Freed from the constraints of divided government, Republicans in the Lone Star State were able to pursue policies that fully conformed to their conservative views. In California, Democrats began exercising one-party control in 2011. Starting that year, they were able to ignore Republican objections and pursue an ambitious progressive policy agenda across the board. Both Texas and California believed it was developing a model for other states and the nation to follow.

Texas vs. California. Kenneth P. Miller, Oxford University Press (2020). © Oxford University Press.
DOI: 10.1093/oso/9780190077402.001.0001.

This chapter introduces the book's policy discussion by examining how the rivals' models have developed within the nation's polarized political system. It describes the expansion of one-party government in the states, then explains how Republicans in Texas and Democrats in California have pursued their competing policy visions.

The Rise of the Trifecta

For much of the twentieth century, most states (at least those outside of the South) experienced long stretches of two-party competition and divided government. Near the turn of the millennium, however, partisan sorting along geographic lines caused one party or the other to gain control in most states. Republicans made the largest gains. Back in 1990, Democrats controlled both houses of the legislature and the governor's office—sometimes called a "trifecta"—in 14 states and the GOP in only four (Figure 8.1). In 2020, however, Republicans could claim trifectas in 20 states and Democrats in 15. As a result, more than two-thirds of all state governments were controlled by one party (Figure 8.2).[2]

This sorting followed familiar geographic patterns. Most states in the South and the plains became more solidly Republican; most states in the Northeast and on the Pacific Coast became more deeply Democratic.

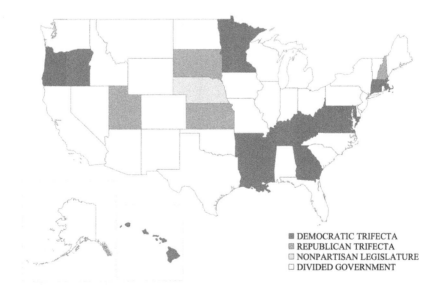

■ DEMOCRATIC TRIFECTA
▨ REPUBLICAN TRIFECTA
□ NONPARTISAN LEGISLATURE
□ DIVIDED GOVERNMENT

Figure 8.1. One-party control of state governments, 1990
Source: National Conference of State Legislatures; Barone and Ujifusa (1990)

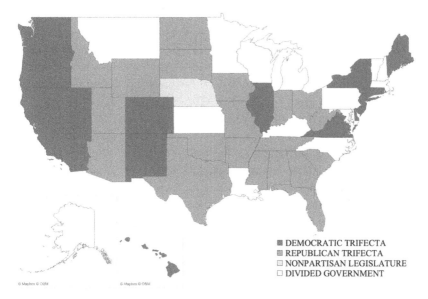

Figure 8.2. One-party control of state governments, 2020
Source: National Conference of State Legislatures

In addition, in several states, one party was able to gain two-thirds control of both houses of the legislature. After the 2019 elections, Republicans could claim trifectas with two-thirds legislative supermajorities in eleven states—Alabama, Arkansas, Idaho, Indiana, Missouri, North Dakota, Oklahoma, South Dakota, Tennessee, Utah, and Wyoming. Democrats had trifectas with legislative super-majorities in three states—California, Hawaii, and Rhode Island.[3]

When it achieved a trifecta, especially with supermajority control, a state's dominant party often was able to dispense with compromise and unilaterally enact policies that advanced its ideological agenda. Polarization thus paved the way for states to experiment with very different policy models. Red states adopted a range of conservative economic and social policies, while blue states enacted starkly contrasting programs.[4]

Limits on Red and Blue State Powers

Although one-party state governments enjoy much freedom to make policy, they still can face constraints from three directions—above, below, and within.

The first constraint comes from above—that is, from the federal government. Although state governments can enact laws on most topics of public concern, they cannot, as a rule, make policies that conflict with the U.S. Constitution or federal law. In some policy areas, such as trade tariffs, the federal government has exclusive lawmaking authority. But even when the state is not completely pre-empted, the principle of federal supremacy requires state laws to yield to federal law when the two conflict. This federal constraint has defeated many state policies.

The second source of resistance comes from below—that is, from local governments. Even when one party dominates state-level government, the opposing party may have strongholds at the local level. This dynamic has occurred most commonly in situations where Republicans run the state government and Democrats control cities within the state. In these cases, local officials often have advanced progressive local ordinances that conflict with statewide policies.[5] Local governments are creatures of the state, and thus state governments can block local laws that conflict with state policy. Even so, local partisan resistance has posed challenges for many state governments.

Finally, a third limitation comes from within—that is, from inside the ranks of the dominant party. Although the nation's major parties have become more cohesive and disciplined in recent decades, they still contain internal factions. In red states, social and "tea party" conservatives have separated on some issues from the more moderate, business-minded Republican establishment. In blue states, committed progressives (or self-avowed socialists) have sometimes split with moderate Democrats. When a dominant party expands to include a larger share of the electorate, it typically becomes more internally diverse and thus vulnerable to factional divisions. Management of those factions has become a challenge for leaders in both red and blue states.

Formation of Red and Blue State Blocs

To defend their respective models and enhance their power in the federal system, states have formed red and blue alliances to pursue common ends, most visibly through joint action in the federal courts. States have a long history of cooperating in federal litigation, but near the turn of the millennium, the practice expanded dramatically and became explicitly partisan. In 1999, representatives from twelve red states formed the Republican Attorneys General Association. This organization aimed to increase the number of Republican attorneys general across the nation and to coordinate red state efforts to advance conservative goals through the legal system. Three years later, Democratic attorneys general formed their own association to promote progressive objectives through the courts.[6]

During the Obama years, red states filed dozens of federal court challenges against administration policies. In some of the most prominent cases, twenty-six states, led by Florida, challenged the individual mandate and Medicaid expansion provisions of the Affordable Care Act; twenty-six states, led by West Virginia and Texas, challenged the Environmental Protection Agency's Clean Power Plan; and twenty-six states, led by Texas, challenged the Department of Homeland Security's policies deferring deportation of undocumented immigrants.[7] Texas and its red state allies believed that these and other lawsuits were a necessary way to defend their interests against a hostile administration. In response, blue states regularly filed briefs defending the challenged policies.[8]

When control of the White House shifted from Barack Obama to Donald Trump, blue states immediately adopted the Texas playbook and brought a flood of litigation against Trump administration policies. California attorney general Xavier Becerra took the lead in many of the challenges. And, on cue, red states lined up on the other side, filing briefs supporting Trump policies.[9] The stated goals of those lawsuits was to prevail on the law; given the slow pace of federal litigation, they frequently ended up achieving the "next best" outcome of delaying implementation of the policies until the next election.

It is worth noting that states are not always divided—indeed, they continue to have bipartisan, cooperative relationships on many matters of common concern. But on an expanding array of highly salient issues, including climate policy, health care, labor law, immigration, gun regulation, abortion, LGBT rights, immigrant rights, and more, red and blue states have developed deep and often irreconcilable differences. By forming and defending radically opposed policy models, the two blocs have intensified national polarization.[10] Texas and California have been at the center of that struggle.

Texas Red State Model

Texas's conversion to one-party Republican control in 2003 paved the way for the Texas Model to achieve its full potential. That year, Texas government finally aligned with the state's underlying political culture and constitutional structure. As discussed in Chapter 6, the state's political culture more easily harmonized with the contemporary GOP than with the modern Democratic Party. So did the Texas Constitution.

The Lone Star Constitution places many shackles on state government. These constraints can be seen most clearly in the design of the legislative branch. Texas is one of the few large states that maintains a part-time legislature, and one of only four states where the legislature convenes every other year rather than annually. Texas lawmakers meet for a maximum of one hundred forty days (or just under five months) in odd-numbered years to pass a two-year state budget and to consider all legislation for the biennium. The governor may also call special sessions lasting no more than thirty days for the legislature to consider specific topics the governor deems critically important to the state, but the general principle is that lawmaking should not be a full-time pursuit. Texas legislative salaries reflect the state's modest expectations for the lawmaker's role—as of 2019, the base annual salary for a member of the Texas Legislature was only $7,200, an amount that had not changed for decades. Even with per diem payments for days in legislative session, the state's compensation for its lawmakers was among the lowest in the nation.[11]

The Texas Constitution further caps the state government's powers through its strict spending limitations, which include a pay-as-you-go rule, a spending limit, a welfare spending limit, and a debt limit, as well as its restriction on imposing a state income tax.[12] These and other constitutional provisions have entrenched the principle of limited government. Contemporary Democrats will have great difficulty overriding this principle if they ever gain control of the Lone Star State.

Texas Republicans agree on many issues and remain universally committed to preserving the state's model of small government, light regulation, and low taxes. Like most majority coalitions, however, they have experienced internal factional divisions—most notably on social issues. Social conservatives have worked to move the state rightward on a range of topics, including abortion, guns, undocumented immigration, and LGBT policies—with some successes as well as some notable setbacks.[13]

In 2017, social conservatives advanced a proposal that deeply divided the party—namely, a "bathroom bill" that would have required transgender persons to use bathrooms in public buildings based on their "biological sex"—defined as the sex on the person's birth certificate. The bill also would have prohibited local governments from authorizing transgender persons to use the bathroom that corresponded with their gender identity.[14]

Many members of the party's establishment believed this bill (and others like it) were bad for business. They knew that most of the nation's largest corporations affirmed LGBT rights and that some would punish states that, in their view, discriminated against LGBT persons. Tech companies featured prominently in this debate. As the bill was pending, fourteen of the nation's leading tech CEOs, including Tim Cook (Apple), Michael Dell (Dell), Mark Zuckerberg (Facebook), Meg Whitman (Hewlett-Packard), and Sundar Pichai (Google), wrote a letter to Governor Greg Abbott personally opposing the legislation. The letter stated:

> As large employers in the state, we are gravely concerned that any such legislation would deeply tarnish Texas's reputation as open and friendly to businesses and families. Our ability to attract, recruit, and retain top talent, encourage new business relocations, expansions and investment, and maintain our economic

competitiveness, would all be negatively affected. We strongly urge you and the Texas legislature not to further pursue legislation of this kind.[15]

Several CEOs, including Apple's Tim Cook, personally lobbied against the bill. The message was clear: if Texas leaders wanted the technology sector to continue to grow in the state, they had to forgo divisive social legislation.[16] Many large corporations outside the tech sector sent similar messages.

The controversy divided the state's top Republican officials. On one side, Governor Abbott and Lieutenant Governor Dan Patrick (leader of the state senate) backed the bill, but the more moderate speaker of the house of representatives, Joe Straus, opposed it. Over the objections of social conservatives, and to the relief of the business community, Straus and his chamber killed the bathroom bill. At the same time, they defeated a number of other conservative, senate-backed measures. These moves embittered social conservatives. Lieutenant Governor Patrick denounced Straus, and the state Republican Executive Committee formally censured him.[17]

The factional divide within the Texas GOP spilled over into primary elections. Social conservatives, backed by Lieutenant Governor Patrick, West Texas billionaires Tim Dunn, Farris Wilks, and Dan Wilks, and a network of conservative advocacy groups, competed in Republican primaries against more moderate candidates supported by Straus and business interests.[18] In early 2018, Patrick disparaged the moderate faction. "I don't want our state to be in the hands of moderates, liberals, and progressives," he said, "because if it is, we'll be California and the country will be in trouble."[19] However, GOP losses (and close calls) in the 2018 general election caused party leaders to tamp down internal struggles and focus on the growing Democratic threat. During the 2019 legislative session, Republicans turned their attention to matters that unified the party, such as improving public schools and reducing property taxes.[20]

Meanwhile, Republican state officials faced a separate challenge from below. Democrats controlled most of Texas's largest cities, including Austin, Houston, Dallas, San Antonio, and El Paso, and the leaders of these and other cities sometimes sought to advance progressive policies. A number of local governments raised property tax rates, expanded pensions for public employees, increased minimum wages for employees under public contract, banned plastic bags, and prohibited fracking within city limits. In addition, in the wake of Donald Trump's election as president, progressives in Austin and elsewhere began pushing for sanctuary city policies that would prevent local law enforcement officers from cooperating with federal immigration officials.[21]

Governor Abbott objected to these local measures, arguing that they were undermining the Texas Model and threatening to make Texas more like California. He warned:

Texas is being Californianized and you may not even be noticing it. It's being done at the city level with bag bans, fracking bans, tree-cutting bans. We're forming a patchwork quilt of bans and rules and regulations that is eroding the Texas model. Large cities that represent about 75 percent of the population in this state are doing this to us, and unchecked overregulation by cities will turn the Texas miracle into the California nightmare. That is contrary to my vision for Texas. My vision is one where individual liberties are not bound by city limits. I will insist on protecting unlimited liberty to make sure Texas will continue to grow and prosper.[22]

Abbott and the legislature enacted a series of laws overriding progressive local policies.[23]

Even as it was beating back challenges from local governments, Texas was exercising leadership within the red state bloc. During the Obama years, the state set a new standard for litigiousness, bringing nearly fifty lawsuits against the administration.[24] As noted, the lawsuits were the primary means by which Texas and other red state governments resisted President Obama's agenda. During his tenure as attorney general, Abbott filed thirty-one of these legal challenges and participated in many others. Some of the most consequential cases challenged various provisions of the Affordable Care Act. Abbott remarked, "When the sun sets on [the ACA cases], the Obama administration will scoff no more at the resolve and ability of state attorneys general." As the list of lawsuits lengthened, he took pleasure in saying, "I go to the office. I sue the federal government. Then I go home."[25] Abbott's successor as attorney general, Ken Paxton, filed seventeen more lawsuits against the Obama administration. After President Obama left office, Paxton continued to challenge laws and regulations adopted during the Obama years, including the Affordable Care Act (ACA) and the Deferred Action for Childhood Arrivals (DACA) program.[26]

Thus, even as they divided on some issues, Texas Republicans were disciplined in adhering to their shared governing philosophy and defending it against challenges from above and below. Indeed, Texas maintained an amazingly steadfast commitment to the Texas Model.

What are the essential features of that model?

First, Texas has sought to keep taxes low. It has proudly remained one of a small group of states with no income tax, and its political culture would need to change massively for one to be imposed. Even in times of fiscal distress, the state has cut spending before it has considered raising other taxes, and it has flatly rejected the income tax option. Conservative Texans believe that limiting taxes serves two salutary purposes: first, it reduces the costs of living and doing business in the state, and, just as important, it caps the size of government because keeping revenues low places a natural limit on government growth.

Second, Texas has kept regulations light. Most Americans agree that some government regulation is necessary, but they disagree on how extensive it should be. Progressives generally embrace regulation as a means of promoting greater social equality, protecting the environment, safeguarding public health, and achieving other social goals, but conservatives object that government overregulates in a way that impairs individual freedom and economic growth. The Texas Model takes the latter view and broadly seeks to limit regulation, especially in the economic sphere.

Third, Texas has maintained the view that citizens should be self-sufficient and not rely on government to provide for their needs. Many progressives believe that government should ensure the material well-being of all members of the community. Texas disagrees. It resists ambitious progressive plans for a comprehensive social welfare state on the view that overreliance on government saps individual initiative, personal responsibility, and private charity.

These elements—low taxes, light regulation, and low social spending—represent the quasi-libertarian, business-minded core of the Texas Model. At the same time, many traditionalistic Texans believe the model should also advance conservative values on cultural matters such as marriage, abortion, gender identity, drugs, immigration, and the like. But even as the state's governing coalition has split over the inclusion of social issues in the state's policy agenda, Republican leaders have managed to maintain a coherent and powerful governing model in the broad areas where the party agrees.

California Blue State Model

In 2011, California Democrats seized the opportunity to implement their progressive vision for the state. Until that year, Republicans could still place a check on Democratic ambitions because Arnold Schwarzenegger remained in office and the legislature needed a two-thirds vote (and thus some Republican support) to approve the state budget and any tax increases. In 2010, voters eliminated the two-thirds requirement for the budget bill and elected Democrat Jerry Brown as governor—thus creating conditions for unfettered, one-party Democratic rule.[27] Over the next decade, Democrats solidified their position by achieving two-thirds margins in both houses of the legislature and retaining control of all statewide offices.

With Democrats in charge, California government aligned with the state's underlying political culture. It was harder to say, however, whether the state's increasingly progressive government harmonized with the state's constitutional design. Unlike the conservative, limited-government Texas Constitution, the California Constitution does not demonstrably lean left or right. On the one hand, it contains a surprisingly long list of conservative elements—most of which were added in an earlier era through the initiative process. These provisions include restrictions on state and local taxing powers; term limits on state elected officials; a ban on race- or gender-based affirmative action; protection of capital punishment; restrictions on the procedural rights of criminal defendants; a limitation on court-ordered busing; and a statement that English is the state's official language.[28]

On the other hand, unlike its Texas counterpart, the California Constitution has a robust view of government. Early twentieth-century Progressives had an appreciation for government and believed it should be highly professionalized. In this spirit, California voters amended the state constitution in 1966 to establish a full-time, professional legislature. In part due to that reform, the California Legislature now meets year-round; creates annual budgets; has a well-compensated, professional staff; and pays its members the highest salaries, by far, of any state. In 2019, California legislators earned base salaries of $110,459 per year, not including per diems and other benefits. California's lawmakers actually received a lower salary than many of their staff members, but they took home about $20,000 per year more than legislators in runner-up Pennsylvania, and *fifteen times* more than lawmakers in Texas.[29] Most California legislators view their positions as full-time work and devote more time and attention to policymaking than part-time lawmakers can.

Beyond the legislature, California state government conforms to blue state expectations. California state departments and agencies are largely staffed by career civil servants, most of whom belong to public sector unions and identify with the Democratic Party.

When Democrats gained control of California in 2011, they began a golden era of progressive policymaking. At the time, Barack Obama occupied the White House, and California leaders worked closely with officials in his administration on a range of policy initiatives, including implementing the Affordable Care Act, expanding Medicaid, developing climate policy, establishing new protections for undocumented immigrants, and recognizing LGBT rights (including the right of same-sex couples to marry). The state was an indispensable partner to the White House and federal agencies in advancing these shared goals and defending them against attack by Texas and other red states. California justifiably viewed itself as the vanguard of progressive policies—pushing the country forward in the pursuit of progressive goals.

A few examples illustrate the ambitious scope of California's agenda as it developed during this period.

First, the Golden State was deeply green. Long a leader in environmental policy, California moved to the forefront of the effort to combat climate change. Frustrated by a lack of progress in Washington, D.C., the state set its own regulatory standards for reducing carbon emissions, created its own cap-and-trade system, established aggressive goals for decarbonizing its economy, promoted the development of a green energy industry, negotiated directly with the automobile industry over emissions standards, and participated in international climate diplomacy. In addition to overseeing its signature climate efforts, California pursued a broad range of other policies to protect the environment.[30]

Second, California sought to provide all residents access to health care. The state was one of the earliest and most enthusiastic implementers the Affordable Care Act. To provide health insurance to those who lacked it, the state quickly set up the "Covered California" plan and opted in to Medicaid expansion. Unsatisfied with continuing gaps in coverage, California continued to look for ways to provide universal health care to all residents, including its undocumented population.[31]

Third, California embraced undocumented immigrants—a stance that was, for the state, a complete reversal. As noted in the previous chapter, in 1994 California voters had famously adopted Proposition 187, one of the nation's harshest attempts to curb illegal immigration. Once Democrats gained power, however, they fully repudiated that policy. Governor Davis immediately abandoned the legal defense of Proposition 187. In the years that followed, the state provided undocumented immigrants an expanding body of statutory rights and benefits, to the point that they enjoyed quasi-legal status. In a series of enactments, the California Legislature authorized them to obtain driver's licenses and professional licenses, to receive in-state tuition to state colleges and universities, and to obtain government-sponsored health care, including full Medi-Cal coverage for the young.[32]

Fourth, California asserted leadership of the LGBT rights movement. In the years before the U.S. Supreme Court established a federal constitutional right of same-sex couples to marry, California's leaders worked to overturn the state's voter-approved constitutional definition of marriage, in part by refusing to defend that provision when it was challenged in federal court. More broadly, California sought to expand a wide range of protections to LGBT persons and pressured other states to do the same. In 2016, the California Legislature enacted a law banning most state-sponsored and state-funded travel to states that "authorize or require discrimination on the basis of sexual orientation, gender identity, or gender expression." In the legislature's view, "California must take action to avoid supporting or financing discrimination against lesbian, gay, bisexual, and transgender people."[33]

California's progressive ambitions spread beyond these areas to nearly every corner of public policy. As they gained firmer control of state government, Democrats expanded the powers of labor unions, raised the minimum wage to the highest level in the nation, increased funding for public welfare, created new programs for the homeless, placed new regulations on guns and ammunition, reduced criminal penalties and prison sentences, placed a moratorium on capital punishment, legalized marijuana, authorized physician-assisted suicide, mandated progressive public school curricula, and raised taxes, especially on the state's wealthiest residents. California was implementing a huge body of progressive ideas, pushing policy into new, uncharted territory, and creating a map for progressives in other states and at the national level to follow.

The state's governing Democratic coalition was so strong (and the Republicans so weak) that on many issues the blue juggernaut faced no meaningful resistance. On a limited range of issues, however, the coalition had internal divisions. The party was highly progressive overall, but it also contained a more moderate element, largely representing the interior part of the state, that did not support all elements of the progressive agenda.

Within the legislature, the centrist faction became known as the "mod squad." The group did not create a formal caucus or circulate a membership list. Indeed, some were unwilling to acknowledge publicly that they belonged to the squad. Nevertheless, some moderate Democrats did break from the party and vote with Republicans on several economic, environmental, and other policies. Business interests took note and supported squad members (or prospective members) in Democratic primary contests. And, at least for a time, moderates exercised a partial check on some policies, including the state's climate laws.[34]

Meanwhile, the state's Democratic coalition struggled to manage conflict between two important constituencies—the technology sector and labor unions. The tech sector holds progressive views on many issues, including universal health care, environmental regulations, immigration, and higher taxes on the wealthy. But it also has an entrepreneurial, libertarian streak that clashes with organized labor, the party's most powerful constituency.[35] From time to time, the conflict broke out into the open, such as when Governor Newsom signed a union-backed bill (AB 5 of 2019) that redefined many gig economy and other contract workers as employees, which, in turn, caused them to fall within a wide range of state labor regulations. App-based companies such as Uber, Lyft, DoorDash, and Postmates, as well as many other businesses, considered AB 5 a threat to their economic models, lobbied furiously against it, and vowed to overturn it after it became law. The controversy exposed a broader divide within the party between the purveyors of the New Economy on one side and organized labor and its allies on the other.[36] A similar conflict emerged in education policy. While New Economy reformers favored innovation in public education, the state's powerful teachers' unions sought to preserve older models of the public school.[37] These types of disputes created tensions within the state's Democratic coalition, but did not threaten to break it apart.

Another potential source of opposition came from below. Although Democrats had an iron grip on state government, some regions of California resisted parts of the progressive agenda. One flashpoint was immigration. In 2017, the legislature passed a bill declaring California a "sanctuary state"— meaning that state and local officials could not, in most cases, inquire about a person's immigration status or cooperate with federal immigration officials. A number of local governments in Orange County and the state's interior passed resolutions denouncing the move; some joined a challenge by the Trump administration to the state's sanctuary policy. Many local governments also resisted a state law that required them to zone for higher-density housing as a way to address the state's housing crisis.[38] These conflicts showed that not all Californians embraced the state's progressive policies, but again they did not rise to the level of a powerful resistance.

Similarly, the state's progressive model did not face consistent opposition from citizens exercising the power of direct democracy. In the past, California voters frequently invoked the initiative and referendum to counter the legislature's liberal agenda. In the recent era of Democratic dominance, however, the electorate has generally declined to do so, rejecting several conservative or business-backed ballot measures that attempted to overturn progressive policies. For example, voters rejected Proposition 23 of 2010, which sought to suspend the state's landmark climate policy; Proposition 67 of 2016, which sought to repeal the state's plastic bag ban; and Proposition 6 of 2018, which sought to repeal an increase to the state's gas tax. Instead, in the decade after 2010, voters reinforced the state's progressive agenda by approving ballot measures that increased taxes, reduced criminal penalties, restored bilingual education in the public schools, legalized marijuana, and tightened controls on guns and ammunition.[39]

If the California Model encountered little resistance from within the state, it met massive opposition from above—that is, from the federal government. As soon as Donald Trump was sworn in as president of the United States, the state confronted a direct threat from his administration. For the preceding eight years, the Obama administration had closely cooperated with California and nurtured its progressive policies. Once President Trump took office, however, the close partnership among California, the White House, and federal agencies abruptly ended. It was soon evident that the new administration would work to roll back Obama-era policies such as the Affordable Care Act and climate policy, and also take aim at long-standing pillars of California's blue state model—from the state's power to set automobile emissions standards to its residents' ability to deduct state and local taxes on their federal tax returns.

California wasted no time announcing that it would resist Trump. On the day after the president's election, Assembly Speaker Anthony Rendon and Senate President Pro Tem Kevin de León issued a joint manifesto declaring their intentions. The document began with a lament: "Today, we woke up feeling like strangers in a foreign land" because the rest of the nation had made a choice "clearly inconsistent with the values of the people of California." It then commended Californians for rejecting "politics fueled by resentment, bigotry, and misogyny" and insisted that "while Donald Trump may have won the presidency, he hasn't changed our values." It concluded with a vow that California would "lead the resistance" using "every tool at our disposal," because "California was not a part of this nation when its history began, but we are clearly now the keeper of its future." [40]

California leaders immediately worked to build a "firewall" around their blue state model, defending its progressive policies with "every tool at [their] disposal." Whenever the administration issued a new policy, California counterpunched. When President Trump announced his decision to pull the United States out of the Paris Climate Agreement, Governor Jerry Brown issued new climate goals and met with foreign leaders to assure them that California would continue the fight against climate change. When the Department of Homeland Security announced its intention to end the DACA program, California sued the administration to protect DACA and declared itself a sanctuary state. When the president signed legislation effectively ending the Affordable Care Act mandate, California passed its own mandate, and expanded its efforts to achieve state-level universal health coverage. When the Environmental Protection Agency announced plans to weaken fuel economy rules, California again sued, and its regulators directly negotiated independent standards with automakers.[41]

Like Texas during the Obama years, California repeatedly challenged the Trump administration in federal court. Early on, the legislature hired former U.S. attorney general Eric Holder to plot legal strategy, and it set aside extra funds for the state attorney general's office to support the anti-Trump litigation effort. In the years that followed, California regularly led the blue state coalition to challenge Trump administration policies in federal court. By January 2020, three years into the Trump presidency, California had filed more than 65 lawsuits against the administration, far surpassing the record set by Texas during the full eight years of the Obama administration. The California cases challenged a wide range of Trump administration policies, including its "travel ban," its attempts to end DACA and the Clean Power Plan, its effort to add a citizenship question to the 2020 Census, its plan to build a wall on the border with Mexico, its decision to cut federal funds from cities and states with sanctuary policies, its plan to deny green cards to prospective immigrants who use (or are deemed likely to use) public assistance, its decision to ban openly transgender people from the U.S. military, and its refusal to ban certain pesticides, to name a few.[42] California was not only defending its progressive policy model, it was also reinforcing the nation's new form of polarized, sectional federalism, by which blocs of dissident states resist the federal government's policy agenda through litigation and other tools at their disposal.

The Competition

The nation's partisan polarization has empowered Texas and California to develop opposite approaches to public policy. Texas has cultivated a comprehensive conservative model and California has advanced an ambitious progressive program. These governing strategies are near-perfect antitheses. The rivals have been deeply committed to their respective visions, and both have tenaciously defended them within the federal system, especially when the opposing party has controlled the federal government.

The intensity of the competition suggests that its outcome matters greatly. What, exactly, *are* the stakes? To help answer that question, the following chapters closely examine five policy areas—tax, labor, energy and the environment, poverty, and social issues—that highlight the stark differences between the two rival models.

9

Taxes

Taxation offers a prime example of how the rivals have transformed their competing visions into policy—and highlights the high stakes of their different models. For decades, Texas and California have approached taxes differently, and the gap between them is only widening. Texas has vowed to keep taxes low and assess them in a "business-friendly" manner, acting on this oath by refusing to authorize an income tax—even though this decision has left billions on the table. Instead, the state has managed to get by on other revenues—including taxes on sales, property, oil and gas, and a few other sources. California, by contrast, has embraced its identity as a high tax state and a place where the rich pay the largest share. It has imposed the nation's top personal income tax rates (including a surcharge on millionaires) and a hefty tax on corporate income. The state also has raised outsized revenues through sales taxes and gasoline taxes, both among the highest in the nation. Although California voters capped property tax rates in the 1970s, the state's high-priced real estate has produced substantial property tax revenue for local governments. Overall, state-level tax receipts have been nearly *three times* higher in California than in Texas. According to official reports, in 2018, California collected a total of $178 billion in state-level taxes (income, sales and use, personal property, license, and other taxes), while Texas collected only $60.3 billion.[1] That year, nearly $108 billion of the Golden State's revenues came from the income tax—a tax Texas refuses to assess. Of course, at that time, California had slightly more than a four-to-three population advantage over Texas; but even measured on a per capita basis, state tax collections were more than twice as high in California than in the Lone Star State.[2]

The rivals' radically opposing tax policies reflect their different underlying values and priorities. Texas believes that high taxes are wicked because they threaten individual freedom and economic opportunity. Keeping taxes low is thus imperative, even if it stresses public budgets. Texas also taxes consumption rather than income, believing that this choice promotes economic growth. As a result, businesses and wealthy individuals pay a far smaller share in Texas than in California or other states with highly progressive tax systems. Even as it has raised concerns about fairness, the Texas tax model has attracted new residents and businesses seeking lower tax burdens.

By contrast, California believes that high taxes serve the public good by funding a large and well-resourced public sector. It also maintains that taxing

Texas vs. California. Kenneth P. Miller, Oxford University Press (2020). © Oxford University Press.
DOI: 10.1093/oso/9780190077402.001.0001.

rich people and businesses at high rates ensures that they pay their fair share. California's overall tax approach has promoted a liberal vision of distributive justice, but also has risked chasing off some of the state's most productive residents and corporations. This chapter asks: Among the range of options, why have Texas and California adopted such different tax policies? And what are the consequences of their choices?

The Range of State Tax Options

In the nineteenth century, states performed far fewer tasks than they do today. Generally, they got by on modest revenues derived from taxes and fees on property and a few other sources.[3] On rare occasions, including the Civil War, some states enacted emergency income and other taxes, but repealed them soon after the crisis passed. Not until the twentieth century did a state maintain a permanent income tax or broad-based sales tax.

Income Tax

Wisconsin adopted the first modern income tax in 1911. The tax was designed to provide long-term revenues and shift the tax burden to those most able to pay. It quickly became a model for other states.[4] Within the next two decades, thirteen of them enacted taxes on income. In the 1930s, California and sixteen other states adopted the income tax as a means to finance Depression-era government programs. More than forty states now have some form of income tax—with Texas one of the few exceptions.[5] As of 2019, nine states applied a flat income tax, but most used tiered formulas that imposed higher rates on higher incomes. For example, as of 2019, California had ten different brackets—with a rate of 1 percent for income up to $8,809 for single filers, all the way to a marginal rate of 12.3 percent for incomes over $590,742, plus an additional 1 percent add-on for incomes of more than $1 million. California's top income tax rate of 13.3 percent was the highest in the nation (Figure 9.1).[6]

Sales Tax

No state enacted a broad-based sales tax until the 1930s. During the Depression, twenty-three states adopted such a tax, with California and twelve other states signing on in the peak year of 1933.[7] Over time, forty-five states have enacted a statewide sales tax, which applies to most material goods, sometimes excepting

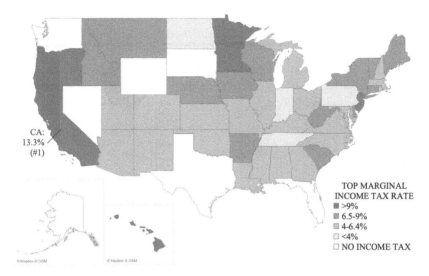

CA:
13.3%
(#1)

TOP MARGINAL
INCOME TAX RATE
■ >9%
■ 6.5-9%
■ 4-6.4%
□ <4%
□ NO INCOME TAX

Figure 9.1. Top marginal personal income tax rates, 2020

Source: Tax Foundation

Note: As of 2020, Colorado, Illinois, Indiana, Kentucky, Michigan, North Carolina, Pennsylvania, and Utah had a flat tax. New Hampshire and Tennessee taxed interest and dividend income only; Tennessee was scheduled to eliminate this tax in 2021.

necessities such as groceries and prescription medicines. Many states have also exempted nonmaterial goods such as services and digital products.[8]

Sales taxes vary both between and within states. Neighboring states can have widely different rates. New Jersey, for example, assesses a substantial sales tax while next-door Delaware has none, thus putting New Jersey retail businesses at a competitive disadvantage. A similar imbalance exists on the border between Vermont (with a sales tax over 6 percent) and tax-free New Hampshire. Most states have allowed their local governments to tack on a separate sales tax, which has created a proliferation of ten thousand sales tax jurisdictions nationwide. In many parts of the country, combined state and local sales taxes range from about 6 to 9 percent, although in many cities the combined tax has surpassed 10 percent (Figure 9.2).

Property Tax

Property taxes are the largest source of tax revenue in the states. These taxes are assessed on residential and commercial real property as well as on certain forms of personal property such as automobiles.[9] The real property tax is typically a

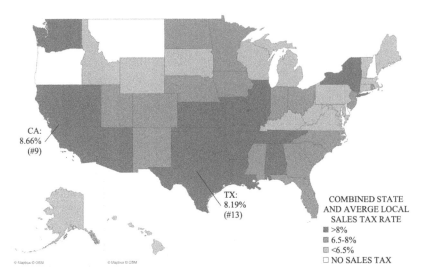

Figure 9.2. Combined state and average local sales tax rates, 2020

Note: As of 2020, Alaska had no state sales tax but allowed a local sales tax.

Source: Tax Foundation

local tax. Local jurisdictions assess property values, collect the tax, and use the revenues to fund local services, such as schools and police and fire protection.[10] Taxes on personal property generally go to the state. The property tax is considered the most stable source of revenue because property values tend to fluctuate less rapidly than sales, wages, and incomes. Although all states rely on property taxes, they do so to differing degrees. For example, as of 2016, Alabama derived less than 20 percent of its state and local revenues from the property tax, while New Hampshire (which has no sales tax) relied on the property tax for nearly two-thirds of its state and local revenues. The property tax constituted a much larger share of total tax revenues in Texas (43.8 percent) than in California (25.7 percent).[11]

Like other taxes, property taxes vary from state to state, and one can use several methods to draw comparisons. A common way is to focus on one class of property, such as owner-occupied residences, and calculate the average amount a homeowner paid in taxes compared to the average home value. Using this figure, called the "average effective rate," New Jersey had the highest property tax in the nation, as of 2017, imposing an average effective property tax rate on owner-occupied housing of 2.13 percent per year. Texas ranked seventh, with an average effective rate of 1.62 percent. Largely due to the constraints of Proposition 13 (a property tax limitation measure discussed in a later section), California ranked thirty-fifth, with an average effective property tax rate

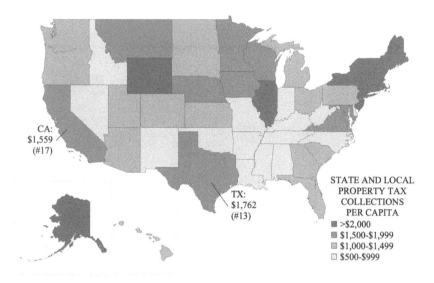

Figure 9.3. State and local property tax collections per capita, 2016
Sources: U.S. Census Bureau, Tax Foundation

of 0.7 percent.[12] By itself, however, this rate does not provide a full comparison of property tax burdens. Because the rate is applied to the taxable value of the property, a state with high property values will generate large property tax receipts even if it has a comparatively low tax rate. As a result, a more meaningful measure of a state's comparative property tax burden is total property tax collections per capita. Using this measure, as of Fiscal Year 2016, Texas (with comparatively low real estate prices) dropped from seventh to thirteenth in the national ranking, and California (with high real estate prices) jumped from thirty-fifth to seventeenth. The gap in per capita property tax collections between Texas and California was $203—a meaningful but relatively narrow difference (Figure 9.3).[13]

Other Revenue Sources and Overall Fiscal Philosophy

States can raise revenue by other means, such as taxes and fees on businesses, taxes on inheritances, severance taxes on natural resources, excise taxes on gasoline or other products, professional license fees, fees for services (including university tuition), fines, road and bridge tolls, lottery proceeds, sale of public assets, and more. In addition, states rely on federal transfers to help finance many programs. In sorting through their revenue options, states must ask: How much do we need to meet our spending goals? Do we want to be a low-tax state, or do we want to impose higher taxes? And, importantly: To what sources should we turn for revenue? What are the trade-offs of relying on sales taxes, for example, rather than income taxes to finance government programs? The following sections take a closer look at how Texas and California have approached these questions and why they have developed such starkly different policies.

Texas Taxes

Texas has always attracted residents with the promise of low taxes. As discussed in Chapter 2, the earliest American settlers were eager to acquire land that was both cheap and tax-free, and they remained devoted to low taxes after Texas gained independence. Unfortunately, the Republic's revenues were too low to meet expenses and, by the mid-1840s, its accumulated debt exceeded $10 million. Upon annexation, Texas hoped to pay down this debt through the sale of public lands, but land prices were so low that the strategy failed. In 1850, Congress offered a fiscal lifeline. As part of the Compromise of 1850, the federal government agreed to pay Texas $10 million in exchange for the state's pledge to release its claim to 67 million acres in the Upper Rio Grande Valley, land that would later become parts of New Mexico and Colorado. As a further condition, Congress required Texas to use these funds to retire its debt. This infusion of federal money, followed by additional payments later in the decade, helped Texas stabilize its finances, but also reinforced its tendency to rely on windfalls rather than ordinary taxes to pay its bills.[14]

During the Civil War, Texas again was desperate for revenue and resorted to a range of taxes, including property taxes, the poll tax, and taxes on liquor and financial transactions. The state also enacted what has been described as a "partial" tax on income, which applied to certain professions, including dentists, lawyers, and doctors as well as railroad company presidents, directors, conductors, engineers, and secretaries.[15] After the war, the Reconstruction legislature and administration of Governor E. J. Davis further raised taxes to fund public education, the expansion of roads and rail lines, and other public investments. This unprecedented tax burden helped harden Anglo-Texan opposition to the Reconstruction government.

Once Democrats regained control, they systematically dismantled Reconstruction policies. Texas historian T. R. Fehrenbach called this effort "a long, detailed, and exhaustive program that was nothing short of a rebellion against government itself."[16] The post-Reconstruction government slashed government spending across the board and made corresponding tax cuts. The Texas Constitution of 1876 locked in a number of restrictions on state spending, borrowing, and taxation. Among other provisions, the constitution placed specific limits on property taxes.[17]

In the first half of the twentieth century, as other states adopted a general sales tax, an income tax, or both, Texas resisted. Depression-era governors Ross S. Sterling, Miriam A. Ferguson, James V Allred, and W. Lee O'Daniel promoted these options, but the legislature rejected them. The lawmakers could hold out because they kept spending low and had access to a resource most other states lacked—oil. In 1905, four years after the gusher at Spindletop, Texas adopted an oil severance tax. For many years thereafter, severance taxes on oil and gas, plus other revenue from the state's energy industry, helped fill the state treasury, accounting for fully one-third of state tax receipts by the 1950s. The state supplemented these revenues with other sources, including a state property tax, modest business taxes, a franchise tax on capital investment, and an inheritance tax.[18] The legislature gradually extended taxes to other sources, but stood firmly against a broad-based sales tax or an income tax.

In time, this resolve wavered. As Texas faced chronic budget shortfalls, it became harder for officials to defend a revenue system that had neither a general sales tax nor an income tax.[19] By the late 1950s, support for adoption of a general sales tax reached a critical mass. Governor Price Daniel (1957–1963) opposed the idea, believing that such taxes are regressive and place too large a burden on the poor, but could offer no workable alternative. In 1961, he allowed a sales tax bill to become law without his signature. The first Texas sales tax was set at a modest 2 percent rate and included a number of exemptions. Once in place, however, the rate increased—doubling to 4 percent by 1971. Beginning in 1967, the legislature also authorized local governments to add on local sales taxes, with the maximum local rate eventually capped at 2 percent.

During the 1970s, surging oil prices caused the Texas economy to boom and state revenues to grow. As a result, the legislature was able to freeze the sales tax, eliminate the state-level property tax altogether, and create new exemptions to the oil severance tax. The collapse of oil prices in the 1980s produced the opposite effect, forcing the state to scrape together new revenues to balance the budget. In 1987, Republican governor Bill Clements and the Democratic legislature agreed to hike the state sales tax to 6 percent, extend that tax to a range of services, raise taxes on gasoline and tobacco, and increase corporate franchise fees.[20] In 1990, the state raised the sales tax one more time, to 6.25 percent. For decades thereafter, the sales tax did not budge, even during tight budget cycles. As of January 2020, with most local jurisdictions tacking on the maximum 2 percent local sales tax, Texas's average combined state and local sales tax was approximately 8.2 percent. This rate placed Texas in the top quartile of states for sales tax, but below California's average state and local sales tax of 8.66 percent.

As of 2019, the sales tax accounted for nearly 60 percent of Texas state tax revenues. Additional consumption taxes (on motor vehicle sales and rentals, motor fuels, insurance, tobacco, alcoholic beverages, hotel occupancy, utilities, and the like) added about 25 percent more. Consumption taxes thus accounted for nearly 85 percent of all Texas state tax receipts. Taxes on businesses and on oil and gas production provided most of the rest. Although Texas had no corporate income tax, it imposed a business franchise tax, called a "margins" tax, on a relatively small percentage of the state's businesses. Assessed through a complex formula, the margins tax generated approximately $4.2 billion in revenues, or 7 percent of state tax receipts.[21] Oil and gas severance taxes supplied a similar amount. Many mistakenly assume that Texas's large-scale oil and gas production generates most of the state's revenues and is the main factor allowing Texas to keep other taxes low. Although oil and gas severance taxes once supported a large portion of the state budget, they accounted for only 9.3 percent of state tax revenues in Fiscal Year 2019.[22]

Like other states, Texas has relied heavily on property taxes to generate revenue for local governments, including cities, counties, school districts, and special-purpose districts.[23] Although rates varied throughout the state, the average effective property tax rate for owner-occupied housing was approximately 1.6 percent. This rate was one of the highest in the nation, but, as noted previously, the overall property tax bill was moderated by the state's comparatively low real estate prices. As those prices have risen, however, property taxes have also increased, sparking new anti-tax movements throughout the state. In 2019, Governor Abbott and the legislature responded to this unrest by enacting a law to prevent local jurisdictions from increasing property taxes by more than 3.5 percent per year without voter approval. This development suggested that the property tax was reaching its upper limits as a revenue source. If so, the state faced a larger problem because property taxes generated a substantial share of public revenues, with the majority used to fund schools.[24] Limiting this source would make it even harder for the state to make ends meet.

Although Texas has been willing to tolerate substantial sales and property taxes, it has fervently opposed income taxes, almost as an article of faith. In the early 1990s, one of the state's leading Democrats, Bob Bullock, tested that creed. As a longtime state comptroller and, later, lieutenant governor, Bullock was a legendary figure in state government and could boast a deep knowledge of state finance. In 1991, Bullock stood before a group of reporters in the governor's mansion and proclaimed, "Texas needs an income tax!" When he introduced a bill to achieve this goal, public reaction was "swift, clamorous, and negative," with opponents flooding the state capitol with angry calls, letters, and faxes. According to one account, rumors spread that the lieutenant governor was terminally ill—why else would he so forcefully attempt political suicide?[25] In the face of this opposition, a chastened Bullock surrendered, dropped his bill, and instead backed a state constitutional amendment to limit any future income tax. The amendment stated that no income tax would be enacted without a vote of the people, and that two-thirds of any revenue from such a tax be set aside to reduce property taxes, with the other one-third earmarked for education.[26] In 1993, Texans approved these new limitations by a resounding 69 to 31 percent vote.[27] Since then, no Texas political leader has dared to promote such a tax—and, indeed, Governor Abbott doubled down in the opposite direction, calling for a constitutional amendment to further prevent any future state income tax.

In November 2019, voters approved Proposition 4, an amendment to the Texas Constitution that explicitly bans income taxes. Any income tax proposal would now need to repeal the amendment, which, in turn, would require a two-thirds vote of both houses of the legislature and a majority vote of the people. Before the election, Abbott tweeted a video of himself tearing up a California income tax return and declaring, "I never want to see one of these in the great state of Texas!" Three-fourths of Texas voters approved the amendment, demonstrating the strength of the bipartisan consensus against income taxes in the Lone Star State.[28]

Clearly, low taxes have become the central tenet of the Texas Model. Since the GOP gained unified control of the Texas government in the 1990s, the state has hardened its anti-tax policy. It has rejected tax increases, expanded exemptions, and reduced or even eliminated a variety of other taxes. The state's strong economy and willingness to live with a lean government have allowed it to maintain this low tax policy even during economic downturns—a stance that surely will be tested in the years ahead.

California Taxes

It took time for California to become a high tax state. Through the nineteenth and early twentieth centuries, the state's legislature and local governments were content to get by on a mix of property taxes and a few other modest revenue sources. When Wisconsin and other states embraced the income tax in the 1910s and 1920s, California demurred.[29] Likewise, California declined to adopt a general sales tax. In the early 1930s, however, the state changed its position. As the Depression wiped out revenues and stirred public demand for relief programs, the state faced a massive deficit. In 1933, the legislature responded to the crisis by adopting both a retail sales tax (at an initial 2.5 percent rate) and a graduated income tax. Governor James Rolph signed the sales tax into law but vetoed the tax on income.

In the tumultuous gubernatorial election of 1934, Upton Sinclair and his "End Poverty in California" ("EPIC") campaign called for radical policies to redistribute the state's wealth. Notwithstanding Sinclair's defeat, EPIC's broad appeal prompted many of California's business and political leaders to accept an income tax as a less threatening alternative. In 1935, Republican governor Frank Merriam endorsed an income tax modeled on the federal Revenue Act of 1934, with rates ranging from 1 percent at the low end to 15 percent for residents with the highest incomes. The California Legislature rejected EPIC-backed proposals to make the rates much steeper, but the compromise 15 percent top rate (on top of the federal income tax) was quite high—even higher than California's top marginal rate today.[30]

Some Californians hotly resisted the new tax. The sharpest complaints came from one of the state's most prominent men, William Randolph Hearst. Hearst owned a media empire that included dozens of newspapers and magazines, as well as operations in Hollywood. He watched over these enterprises from his perch high above the California coast in one of the world's most opulent homes, popularly known as "Hearst Castle." For months, Hearst and his newspapers savaged the income tax bill; when the governor signed it into law, Hearst declared he would be forced to leave the state. In October 1935, he published a letter in *Variety* to make the following announcement:

> I hope still to be able to spend some time in California, but I am compelled to close my places and live entirely in New York. Heaven knows I do not want to leave California. No one does, least of all a native son whose father was a pioneer; but it is utterly impossible for me to remain here and occupy a place like San Simeon . . . it is absolutely necessary for me to eliminate the high income tax in California.[31]

Hearst argued that other high earners, especially in the movie industry, would follow, especially if "some alert motion picture company should establish studios in Florida or Delaware or New York." Hollywood producer Louis B. Mayer agreed. "Mr. Hearst's leaving evidences the fear in all our minds of the disastrous consequences of reckless and discriminatory tax legislation," he said. "It seems inevitable that others will be obliged to follow, regardless of our great love for this state."[32]

Hearst's dramatic exit in 1935 highlighted the danger that high taxes could drive individuals and businesses out of a state. But his personal story also demonstrated the limits of the danger—at least in California. By the end of the decade, the man known as "the Chief" swallowed his opposition to the state's income tax and re-established his residence at San Simeon. Similarly, despite their protests, most other high earners did not flee. Instead, the tax's opponents gathered enough signatures to qualify a proposal to repeal the new law. Appearing on the November 1936 ballot as Proposition 2, the measure would have voided the income tax and amended the state constitution to prevent the legislature from enacting a new one without a vote of the people.[33] On Election Day, however, voters soundly rejected the repeal measure by a 62–38 percent margin. California has maintained a substantial income tax ever since.[34]

Over time, California has repeatedly increased its income and sales tax rates. The main exception was in the 1940s, when the booming wartime economy swelled state coffers and allowed Governor Earl Warren and the legislature to cut the top personal income tax rate from 15 percent to 6 percent, the sales tax from 3 percent to 2.5 percent, and the corporate income tax from 4 to 3.4 percent.[35] By the late 1950s, however, demands for higher spending on state programs led officials in both parties to support tax increases. In 1959, the state faced a deficit, but Governor Pat Brown and the new Democratic legislature were eager to increase spending. Without great controversy, they raised the top personal income tax rate from 6 to 7 percent, increased the corporate income tax, and hiked taxes on tobacco.

By 1967, when Ronald Reagan assumed office as governor, the state budget was again out of balance. Reagan closed the gap partly through spending cuts but even more by agreeing to what was then the largest state tax increase in the nation's history. The 1967 tax package raised the state's top personal income tax rate from 7 to 10 percent (a rate that Reagan and the legislature would later increase to 11 percent) and made other adjustments that put more taxpayers in the top bracket. Reagan also agreed to raise the sales tax from 4 to 5 percent (and later to 6 percent); the corporate income tax rate from 5.5 to 7 percent (and later to 9 percent); the alcohol tax from $1.50 to $2 per gallon; the cigarette tax from 3 cents to 10 cents per pack; and the inheritance tax from a top rate of 10 percent to 15 percent.[36] In connection with these changes, Reagan secured some property tax relief, but the bottom line of his tax policies was a sharp increase in the overall state tax burden. Although Reagan and his administration blamed these large increases on the deficit they inherited, the new taxes produced more revenue than was needed to close the gap. As Reagan biographer Lou Cannon noted, "An economist who analyzed the tax bill without knowing its political background might conclude that it had been crafted by a New Deal Democrat" because of the ways it raised taxes overall and made the system more progressive.[37] Reagan's willingness to raise taxes at these levels demonstrates that, as governor, he was far from a doctrinaire anti-government conservative, but rather fit within California's broad Progressive and New Deal traditions. Moreover, all but one of the state's Republican legislators voted for the 1967 tax hikes, underscoring that tax policy was far less polarized along partisan lines than it is today.[38]

Reagan's successors, Jerry Brown and George Deukmejian, were able to hold California's income and sales tax rates steady through the 1980s.[39] In the early 1990s, however, the economic downturn caused by the end of the Cold War

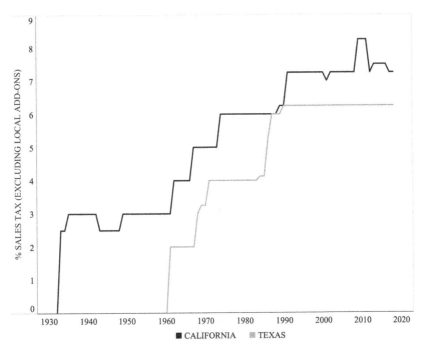

Figure 9.4. California and Texas sales tax rates (excluding local add-ons), 1932–2020

Sources: California Department of Tax and Fee Administration; Texas Comptroller of Public Accounts

again created a gap between the state's revenues and its spending commitments. In 1991, the newly elected Republican governor Pete Wilson negotiated a budget deal with the Democratic legislature that included increases to the income and sales tax as well as other taxes. More recent governors, including Democrat Gray Davis, Republican Arnold Schwarzenegger, and Democrat Jerry Brown, resorted to tax increases as well. Overall, for decades, the trend lines of California taxes have pointed upward (Figures 9.4 and 9.5).

The Golden State's history of raising taxes was interrupted by the property tax revolt of the 1970s and the ballot measure known as Proposition 13. During the 1970s, California home prices rapidly inflated, producing sharp increases in property assessments and tax bills. This burden was especially heavy for working-class and fixed-income homeowners. The state's political establishment, including Governor Jerry Brown and other officials from both parties, failed to redress the problem. While government stalled, a citizen activist named Howard Jarvis declared he was "mad as hell" and used the state's citizen initiative process to propose a far-reaching property tax limitation measure. The Jarvis initiative,

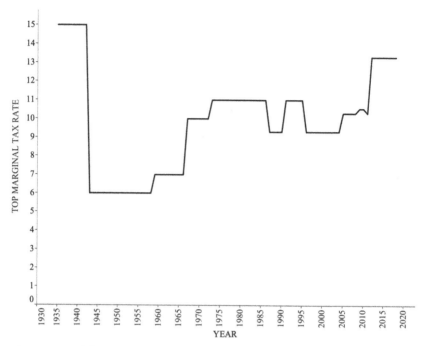

Figure 9.5. California income tax top rate, 1935–2020
Source: California Franchise Tax Board

known as Proposition 13, was brief and powerful. It permanently capped the property tax rate at 1 percent; limited increases in the property's assessed value to 2 percent per year until the property is sold; and required a two-thirds vote in the legislature for any future state taxes and a two-thirds voter approval for future local taxes for designated purposes. Proposition 13 tapped into a growing populist, anti-government sentiment in the electorate and, in June 1978, voters approved it by an overwhelming 65 percent margin.[40]

This single measure transformed California's fiscal policy. Among other effects, it limited local revenues, forced the state to bail out local governments, and required both state and local government to rely more heavily on an alternative mix of taxes and fees. Yet one can overstate how much Proposition 13 defunded government. Even under the measure's constraints, California's property taxes have continued to produce large receipts. In Fiscal Year 2019, local governments collected total property tax revenues of $71 billion, a higher take than any other state.[41] As noted earlier, however, on a per capita basis, California's property tax receipts ranked seventeenth in the nation as of 2017, which was lower than the state's ranking in other tax categories. Proposition 13 did not gut the property tax, but kept it lower than it otherwise would be.

For decades, progressives have wanted to amend or repeal Proposition 13's restrictions but have feared that attempting to do so would mean touching the third rail of California politics. As the state's electorate has shifted leftward, a coalition of organized labor and other groups has become emboldened to challenge the measure, beginning with a proposal to eliminate its limits on commercial property taxes.

Proposition 13 ultimately has proven to be an exception (albeit an important one) in the history of California taxation. The larger themes are California's willingness to identify as a high-tax state and to embrace a progressive income tax to fund state spending. The state's heavy reliance on the income tax is relatively new. For many years, California considered the sales tax to be its real workhorse (it produced about 60 percent of state receipts), while the income tax was expected to pull less weight. It took until 1983 for the income tax to surpass the sales tax as the revenue leader, $9.3 billion to $8.8 billion. By 2019, the trend lines had radically split—sales tax receipts had grown to $28 billion, but income tax revenues had surged to more than $100 billion—or about two-thirds of the state's total general fund.[42]

California's income tax is so prodigious partly because it casts such a wide net. The state captures a taxpayer's ordinary income, partnership income, pass-through income from businesses, capital gains, dividends, and more. It also targets upper-income residents with steeply graduated rates. California has targeted corporate income through a tax that generated an additional $14 billion in Fiscal Year 2019, more than three times what Texas collected through its margins tax on business. Because California is home to super-high earners in the technology, entertainment, and other sectors, its income tax has yielded huge revenues in times of economic plenty. For example, Facebook's initial public offering in 2012 produced such massive profits for founder Mark Zuckerberg and other early investors that it generated an estimated $2.5 billion income tax windfall for the state treasury.[43] In many years, the top 1 percent of the state's tax filers have paid nearly half of the state's income tax, and the top tenth nearly 90 percent. Unfortunately, however, the year-to-year income of high earners is highly variable, rising and falling with price fluctuations in stocks and other investments. Although the tax has produced an enormous bounty in rising economic cycles, it has dried up when markets falter.

In 2012, Governor Jerry Brown increased the state's reliance on this unstable source by promoting Proposition 30, a ballot measure that temporarily increased income taxes, especially for the highest earners.[44] Voters approved the measure and, in 2016, extended the income tax increases for another twelve years. Even as he was doubling down on taxes on the state's wealthiest residents, Brown warned that these revenues were highly volatile. His solution to this problem was to create a "rainy day fund" to help the state endure the time when a recession hit and the top 1 percent of taxpayers claimed losses not gains. Voters approved the rainy day concept in 2014, and before the economic crisis of 2020, the fund was bumping up against its cap of 10 percent of state general fund revenues.

The Rival Tax Models

The two states' tax policies are consistent with their underlying values. Texas's approach closely aligns with its conservative political culture. Throughout its history, Texas has kept its overall tax burden low, a policy it believes attracts businesses and promotes economic freedom. Texas also shows little interest in making the rich pay what some would call their fair share. The state has many super-affluent residents, but has never demanded that they fill the state coffers. As a result, critics say, Texas's tax structure raises too little money and does so in a regressive way.[45] A critical mass of Texans rejects this liberal critique and believes that the low-tax policy is a big reason why the Lone Star State has produced economic growth and attracted new residents and businesses.

The central question Texas faces is whether it can sustain its beloved low-tax model. Put another way, can the state's limited tax system, with zero income taxes, produce enough revenue to fund its residents' expanding demands for public services, especially in times of economic stress? The following chapters explain how Texas has kept its spending low, thereby requiring far less tax revenue than California and other high-cost blue states. But its margin for error is thin. If Texas cannot keep a lid on spending, it will face a major fiscal crisis—and possibly an existential one as well. The state appears to be approaching the upper limits of its major revenue sources (sales and property taxes) and would be hard-pressed to extract much more from them. But where else can it turn? In the years after Bob Bullock proposed an income tax, Texans' opposition to this heresy has only hardened, as evidenced by their recent three-fourths popular vote for the anti–income tax state constitutional amendment. Indeed, adherents of the Texas Model resist the income tax with a commitment that resembles the defense of the Alamo. If Texas wants to sustain this resistance, it will need to raise revenue from other sources, maintain spending discipline, and get a bit lucky.

On the other side of the divide, California has closely aligned its tax policy with its increasingly progressive political culture. The state's governing coalition believes that high taxes are a social good and that those with the greater resources should be willing to pay their "fair share." As a result, the state is committed to collecting prodigious revenues in a way that shifts the burden to high-income taxpayers. The state's signature tax is the personal income tax, with its heavy draw on those in the highest brackets. That tax alone has earned California the distinction of being the state with the nation's most progressive tax system.

Critics have attacked California's tax system from several angles. Some say a system that relies so heavily on the investment income of a small group of wealthy people is terribly unstable. For years, the state acknowledged this vulnerability, but failed to address it in a meaningful way by broadening the tax base or pursuing other structural reforms. Instead, it hoped the "rainy day fund" would ease the pain the next time markets tumbled.

Others have argued that California's tax burden is too expensive for everyone. While Texas runs the danger of collecting too little revenue, California risks taxing its residents too heavily. The fear is that the Golden State's high taxes will limit economic growth and, moreover, force people to leave. As we have seen, this concern dates to the 1930s, when William Randolph Hearst reacted to the tax by exiting the state. The question remains a critical one: in a federal system where people and capital can freely cross boundaries, do big tax disparities lead to migration? Economists have debated the issue. Studies of high earners have suggested that high taxes have caused some to move.[46] However, the exodus of high earners has not been as large as some expected, in part because location can be "sticky."[47] Once a person becomes established in a place, it is not always easy to leave. Someone who owns a business in the area, has family nearby, belongs to the local professional community, or appreciates the region's climate or cultural amenities has good reasons to stay—even if that means paying a premium to do so. The more affluent the person, the easier it is to absorb the extra cost. In California, many wealthy residents have been willing to pay this premium—from Hearst (ultimately) and Louis B. Mayer to Mark Zuckerberg, Larry Ellison, Larry Page, Sergei Brin, and Elon Musk. But not every Californian is a Hollywood mogul or a tech oligarch. For residents who don't command Zuckerberg's income, it is a struggle to pay the price to live in the Golden State. The total "California premium" includes the high cost of housing, utilities, gasoline, and more—all capped off by high taxes. For many in the middle class, it has become too much, and they have made the fateful call to the moving company.

Competing in the Federal System

A final point is that the two states are pursuing their very different tax models within a federal system that can disrupt their preferred policies. Consider Texas. To preserve its low-tax model, it must limit spending. This task is difficult under any circumstances, but becomes impossible if the federal government forces the state to assume unfunded mandates or to spend beyond its means. Texas faced this threat during the Obama years, when the president and Congress pressured states to increase their spending on health and welfare programs. The stimulus package, the Affordable Care Act, and other initiatives offered large infusions of federal dollars, but at a cost: state governments would have to contribute more to these programs as well.

As discussed further in Chapter 12, the most consequential mandate was Medicaid expansion under the Affordable Care Act (ACA). Congress promised the states billions of dollars in new Medicaid funding on the condition that they extend coverage to many currently uninsured residents. For the first few years, the federal government would pay the full cost of covering these new recipients, but states would soon be required to pay up to 10 percent. Any state that opted out would lose not only these new federal subsidies but *all* of its federal Medicare funding.[48] California and other blue states quickly accepted this deal, but Texas and other red states balked. Texas estimated that it would be on the hook for $27 billion in new state spending over the first ten years and that its existing revenue models could not support the added spending the commitment would require. If the state agreed to the deal, it would have no choice but to raise taxes.[49] Texas joined twenty-five other states to challenge the ACA as part of the landmark case of *National Federation of Independent Business (NFIB) v. Sebelius*. In that case, the Supreme Court upheld many parts of the ACA, but sided with the red state petitioners on the Medicaid expansion issue.[50]

Shortly after the ruling, Governor Rick Perry announced that Texas would opt out of the deal—even though doing so left millions of Texas residents uninsured and billions of federal dollars on the table. In his view, buying in to Medicaid expansion would threaten the Texas Model itself.[51] The episode demonstrated the depth of the state's commitment to low taxes—as well as its model's vulnerability to federal intervention.

Meanwhile, California's tax model also has proven vulnerable to federal policy. The top example is Congress's capping of the federal deduction for state and local taxes, or "SALT." For decades, California and other high-tax states benefited from a federal provision that allowed taxpayers who itemize deductions to claim the full amount of their state and local taxes on their federal tax returns. Thus, for example, a wealthy California resident who paid $100,000 in state and local taxes could deduct the entire $100,000 from his or her federal income taxes. The policy subsidized high-tax states and shielded their residents from bearing the full cost of their state and local taxes. Taxpayers in California and other deep blue states—New York, Connecticut, New Jersey, Massachusetts, Illinois, Maryland, Rhode Island, and Vermont—gained the most from this policy, taxpayers in low-tax red states the least.

In 2017, President Trump signed a sweeping Republican-backed tax reform bill that, among other provisions, capped the SALT deduction at $10,000. The new law dealt a well-aimed blow to the blue state model. It cut off the old subsidies, laid bare the full cost of blue state tax burdens, and widened the gap between red and blue state tax policies. Red states welcomed the policy, but blue states howled. Governor Jerry Brown said the bill would "divide the blue states from the red, the Democrats from the Republicans. It is evil in the extreme."[52]

The full effects of the SALT cap would take time to develop, but it clearly demonstrated that changes in federal law could disrupt tax policies in California as well as in Texas. This reality highlighted the stakes of the struggle between the rivals and their allies to control the federal government and its policies.

10

Labor

For more than a century, labor policy has occupied a central place in the nation's political debates. Liberals have argued that government should support unions and protect their rights while conservatives have countered that the workplace should be free of union control. Left and right have also clashed over employment regulations such as minimum wage and health and safety standards. Although Congress has enacted a body of federal employment law that navigates these differences, states have the ability to favor one side or the other. And the rivals have, indeed, taken opposite positions, with California enacting the nation's most progressive employment laws and Texas maintaining a conservative, business-oriented stance. Texas and California have made their labor policies central to their governing models and to their identities as leaders of the red and blue states.

Texas has led the charge for limiting the power of organized labor. Texans were early advocates of the "open shop," which bans making union membership a condition of employment. A Dallas newspaperman later popularized this principle by calling it the "right to work." Further, Texas was an early opponent of public sector unionism and continues to deny most government employees the right to bargain collectively and to strike. The state has dismissed most other elements of the labor agenda, declining, for example, to adopt a state minimum wage above the federal minimum. Through these policies, Texas has reinforced its reputation as an employer-friendly state. It boasts one of the nation's lowest levels of union density—that is, the percentage of the workforce that belongs to unions—as well as low private sector labor costs and low government spending on public employee salaries and benefits.

California, by contrast, has become one of the nation's most union-friendly states and the most aggressive in regulating employers. It has rejected various attempts to limit union power, recognized the right of groups such as farm workers and public employees to unionize, and enacted a wide range of other rules designed to benefit workers. For example, California frequently has set its minimum wage above the federal level and was the first state to adopt a statewide $15 per hour requirement. It also willingly pays its public sector workers comparatively generous salaries, pensions, and other benefits. California is proud to rank high nationally in the percentage of its workforce that belongs to unions.

Texas vs. California. Kenneth P. Miller, Oxford University Press (2020). © Oxford University Press.
DOI: 10.1093/oso/9780190077402.001.0001.

This chapter places the rivals' sharply contrasting labor policies into national context and shows how these policies are central to the competing red and blue state models.

Private Sector Unionism: The Labor Movement and Its Opponents

The national struggle over the rights of labor reached a point of crisis during the Great Depression. In 1935, in the midst of widespread labor unrest, Congress enacted the National Labor Relations Act (NLRA), also known as the Wagner Act.[1] Hailed by union leaders and New Dealers as the "Magna Carta of labor," this landmark law guaranteed most workers the right to organize, collectively bargain, and strike. The Wagner Act created rules for union elections and required employers to negotiate exclusively with the employees' elected representatives. It prohibited employers from engaging in unfair labor practices such as intimidation, interference in union elections, or other actions that undermine workers' ability to exercise these rights. Finally, the act established the National Labor Relations Board to interpret and enforce its provisions.[2]

Implementation of the Wagner Act, combined with rapid military industrialization and a tight wartime labor market, produced large union gains in the 1940s. By the end of the war, organized labor represented more than one-third of the American workforce—five times its share in the early 1930s. Labor made gains even in the South and other places that had resisted its advances.[3] After the war, unions began to assert their growing power. Released from pledges to protect wartime production, labor engaged in a wave of postwar strikes and work stoppages.

Business leaders and other conservatives responded by pressing Congress and state legislatures to limit union power.[4] This countermovement achieved its greatest victory in 1947, when a coalition of congressional Republicans and conservative Democrats overrode President Truman's veto to pass the Taft-Hartley Act. Unlike the Wagner Act, which empowered unions, Taft-Hartley limited union strength. The new law prohibited unions from engaging in secondary boycotts, secondary or mass picketing, wildcat strikes, solidarity or political strikes, and jurisdictional strikes. It established a national ban on the "closed shop," a system that requires employers to hire union members and forces employees to remain in the union or lose their jobs. Perhaps most important, Taft-Hartley confirmed that states can limit union power by enacting "right-to-work" laws.[5]

A right-to-work law bans union contracts that force workers to either become a dues-paying member of the union or pay the union a fee, known as an "agency fee," as a condition of employment. Unions argue that they need to collect agency fees to prevent workers from free-riding—that is, benefiting from union representation without paying anything for it. They say that agency fees should be considered "fair share" fees.[6] Advocates of right-to-work laws counter that no one should be forced to make payments to a union as a condition of employment.[7] With the blessing of the Taft-Hartley Act, several states enacted the first wave of right-to-work laws in the 1940s (Table 10.1). Other states followed, creating a group that would eventually include even formerly union-friendly Michigan (2013) and Wisconsin (2015). More than half of all states have now embraced the right-to-work principle (Figure 10.1).[8]

Although debate persists about the costs and benefits of right-to-work laws, most agree that these laws have weakened unions and contributed to the national decline of private sector unionism. At the same time, union density has diminished in all states, including those that have rejected right-to-work laws. In the 1950s, one-third of nation's workforce was unionized. By 2018, union membership had fallen to just over one-tenth (10.5 percent) of the national workforce and only 6.4 percent of private sector workers—the lowest levels of union membership in more than a century.[9] Deindustrialization of the U.S. economy, changing work patterns, management opposition, and failures by unions themselves have contributed to this trend. Public policies such as right to work have reinforced the view that union membership should be by choice.[10]

Texas

Early in the twentieth century, Texas seemed to be the South's most promising target for labor organizing, mainly because it was the region's most rapidly industrializing state. The Texas State Federation of Labor (TFSL) formed in 1900, and unions soon spread to several sectors of the Texas economy. Movement leaders successfully lobbied the Texas Legislature to enact several labor-friendly laws.[11] In 1919, business interests responded by establishing the Texas Open Shop Association (TOSA), a group devoted to defeating unionization and government regulation of employers. TOSA and other conservative forces effectively countered unions in Texas during the 1920s. When the Wagner Act stimulated new organizing efforts in Texas, including activity by the left-wing Congress of Industrial Organizations (CIO), the state's conservatives redoubled their opposition.

Houston-based oil industry lobbyist Vance Muse emerged as a leader of these efforts. In 1936, Muse formed an organization called the Christian American Association to oppose the New Deal and advance a conservative counter-agenda.

Table 10.1 States with Right-to-Work Laws by Year

State	Year
Arkansas	1944
Florida	1944
Arizona	1946
Nebraska	1946
Georgia	1947
Iowa	1947
North Carolina	1947
South Dakota	1947
Tennessee	1947
Texas	1947
Virginia	1947
North Dakota	1948
Nevada	1952
Alabama	1953
Mississippi	1954
South Carolina	1954
Utah	1955
Kansas	1958
Wyoming	1963
Louisiana	1976
Idaho	1985
Oklahoma	2001
Indiana	2012
Michigan	2013
Wisconsin	2015
West Virginia	2016
Kentucky	2017

Source: National Right to Work Committee

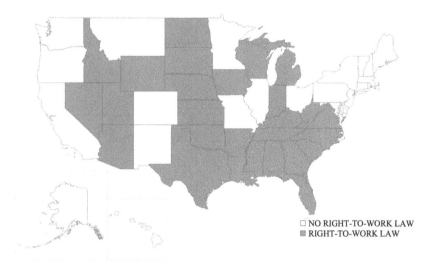

Figure 10.1. States with right-to-work laws, 2019
Source: National Right to Work Committee

He soon focused on combating organized labor. In 1941, Muse and his allies persuaded the Texas Legislature to pass an "anti-violence bill," a measure that made strikers criminally liable for violence on the picket line. Mississippi, Florida, Arkansas, and Alabama soon enacted bills modeled on the Texas law. In 1943, the Texas Legislature imposed further regulations on labor organizations. Encouraged by these successes, Muse and his allies pushed for broader restrictions, including a ban on the union shop.[12]

William Ruggles, an editorial writer for the *Dallas Morning News*, bestowed on this cause a powerful name—"right to work." The term framed resistance to unions in the language of worker's rights—a strategic rhetorical move. Ruggles unveiled the phrase in a *Dallas Morning News* editorial on Labor Day in 1941, in which he advocated a right-to-work amendment to the U.S. Constitution. According to Ruggles, such an amendment would

> guarantee . . . the right of the individual to work with or without membership in an organized union. If submitted and adopted, that amendment would indeed be the Magna Carta of labor, all labor, not a particular division of labor. It would . . . guarantee the open shop as that American institution should be, a shop in which the union man has his organization and bargains with it as he pleases. And in which the non-union man has his rights, free of coercion to join an organization that he does not want.[13]

The term "right to work" quickly spread from Texas across the country, providing an attractive rationale for state legislatures and Congress to limit union power. This development greatly frustrated unions. They embarked on an effort to amend the term to "right to work *for less*," which they believed more accurately characterizes the policy.[14]

Although Texans were at the vanguard of the right-to-work movement, the Lone Star State was not the first to adopt a right-to-work law. The movement achieved earlier breakthroughs in Florida, Arkansas, and other states. In Texas, opponents blocked the right-to-work proposal in the state senate during the 1945 session. In 1947, however, the Texas Legislature adopted not only a right-to-work law, but also a comprehensive package of nine laws to limit union power. Among other restrictions, these laws required unions to obtain written consent before collecting dues, limited picketing, outlawed boycotts, and subjected unions to antitrust laws.[15] At the same time, Texans broadly supported Taft-Hartley. Although House Minority Leader Sam Rayburn opposed the bill, most Texans in Congress voted for it, including Congressman Lyndon Johnson and both of the states' U.S. senators, Tom Connally and Pappy O'Daniel. Taken together, these developments in the 1940s cemented Texas's reputation as a pro-business, anti-union state—a reputation it has maintained ever since.

California

By contrast, unions established a stronghold in California, especially in the San Francisco Bay Area. During the nineteenth century, San Francisco became a hive of union activity, with seamen, dockworkers, tradesmen, and other laborers organizing and leading protests. The city was home to activist Denis Kearney and the Workingmen's Party, an offshoot of the International Workingmen's Association, which agitated in the 1870s for a more worker-friendly state constitution. In 1901, the California State Federation of Labor held its first convention in San Francisco and helped launch a campaign to make the city adopt the closed shop.[16]

In these early years, organized labor was much stronger in Northern California than in the southern part of the state. Los Angeles, in particular, was hostile to unions. *Los Angeles Times* publisher Harrison Gray Otis and other business leaders strenuously argued that the region needed the open shop in order to develop its industry and compete with San Francisco and cities in the East. And, indeed, the large wage gap between unionized San Francisco and anti-union Los Angeles helped Southern California industrialize more quickly than the Bay Area in the early years of the twentieth century.[17] The split in the state between the pro-union north and anti-union south narrowed when the Great Depression, the Wagner Act, and wartime industrialization weakened Southern California's opposition to organized labor.

By the end of World War II, most California leaders, including Republican governor Earl Warren, accepted the presence of a strong labor movement in the state. In 1944, as other states were beginning to adopt right-to-work laws, conservatives placed a similar proposal on the California state ballot. Warren opposed the measure, and voters decisively rejected it.[18] In 1958, conservative U.S. Senator William Knowland spearheaded a similar effort to mandate the open shop through a statewide ballot initiative. Most of the state's political establishment, including all prominent Democrats as well as many moderate Republicans, opposed this initiative. Organized labor mobilized to defeat it, spending more than $2.5 million on the campaign—a huge sum at the time. When California voters rejected the open shop proposal by nearly a million votes, they confirmed the state's pro-union identity.[19]

In the years that followed, California became a national leader in extending collective bargaining rights and other workplace protections to new groups. Farm workers were a notable example. When the architects of the Wagner Act drafted the "Magna Carta of labor," they excluded agricultural employees from its protections. As a consequence, farm workers often toiled in fields and orchards for long hours, at low wages, under harsh working conditions, with little ability to negotiate better terms. Efforts to organize farm workers and to strike for higher wages and better working conditions almost invariably failed—until organizers achieved a breakthrough in California in the 1960s.

In 1962, Cesar Chavez, Dolores Huerta, and other activists formed the National Farm Workers Association (NFWA) in California's Central Valley. The organization would become the United Farm Workers of America (UFW), the nation's first enduring agricultural union.[20] Chavez and Huerta had been trained by Fred Ross, an associate of the famed community organizing theorist Saul Alinsky, and became known for their mix of community organizing methods, nonviolent activism, and sophisticated public relations strategies. The UFW soon gained the trust of farmworkers and the attention of the broader public. Chavez led a 340-mile march up the Central Valley to the state capitol in Sacramento, launched a five-year public boycott of grapes, and engaged in hunger strikes, among other high-profile tactics. The grape boycott showed how the UFW could turn a weakness into a strength. The exclusion of farm workers from the National Labor Relations Act created many barriers to UFW organizing, but it also exempted the union from the act's prohibition on secondary boycotts. Through the grape boycott and other direct action, UFW forced growers to agree to contracts that improved pay and working conditions. By the mid-1970s, nearly one hundred thousand farm workers in California and other states were covered by union contracts. The union enjoyed the support of California's increasingly progressive Democratic Party. In 1974, Democrat Jerry Brown won his first election as governor and the following year signed the state's Agricultural Labor Relations Act, which established the nation's first comprehensive bargaining rights for farm workers. The act also created the California Agricultural Relations Board, modeled on the National Labor Relations Board, to enforce its provisions.[21]

Although the UFW later struggled to meet the high expectations of its early years, the *causa* achieved the lasting legacy of fusing the labor movement to the emerging movement for civil rights for immigrants, especially the fast-growing Mexican American population. In later decades, many activists trained and inspired by the UFW shifted their focus to organizing immigrant workers in the state's urban centers, especially in Los Angeles County. As noted, Miguel Contreras and Maria Elena Durazo, disciples of Chavez and Huerta, led impressive efforts to organize the Los Angeles region's largely immigrant workforce of janitors, hotel and restaurant workers, and construction workers.[22] As deindustrialization hollowed out California's traditional industrial unions, a combination of the state's union-friendly policies and the labor movement's decision to organize immigrant workers helped unions establish new strength in other sectors, especially the state's large service industry.

Through these efforts, California has maintained one of the nation's highest levels of private sector unionization. In 2018, approximately 1.2 million Californians belonged to private sector unions out of a private sector workforce of 13.9 million. Those figures translated to a union density of 8.3 percent, which ranked tenth in the nation. The California levels looked especially strong when compared with those in Texas. In 2018, only about 272,000 Texans belonged to private sector unions out of a private sector workforce of 10.3 million. Texas's 2.6 percent private sector union density was the nation's eighth lowest.[23]

Public Sector Unionism

The national decline in private sector unionization was offset by a surge in union membership by federal, state, and local government workers, placing public sector unions at the heart of the labor movement. In 2009, for the first time, the number of unionized government workers in the United States (7.9 million) exceeded the number of private sector union members (7.4 million).[24] By that time, more than one-third of all government workers had joined unions, with the highest concentrations in blue states. Governments in these states generally supported public sector unions by granting them expansive bargaining rights and requiring nonunion employees to pay agency fees. The U.S. Supreme Court's 2018 decision in *Janus v. AFSCME* threatened this surge in public sector unionism by banning agency fee rules and effectively creating a national right-to-work rule for government employment.[25]

The rise of government unions was a relatively new development because public employees were long denied the right to bargain collectively or to strike. In 1935, the Wagner Act reinforced this limitation by excluding public employees from its provisions. President Franklin Roosevelt agreed with this exclusion, pointing to "the special relationships and obligations of public servants to the public itself and to the Government." According to Roosevelt, "government employees should realize that the process of collective bargaining, as usually understood, cannot be transplanted into the public service."[26] Many public employees agreed, believing that union membership and collective bargaining were incompatible with their status as public servants. Rather than organizing labor unions, public employees formed professional associations. These organizations lacked power to bargain collectively, but they advanced their members' interests by other means, including legislative advocacy and the provision of benefits such as legal representation and access to credit unions and retirement plans.

The political consensus against public sector unionism eventually eroded as more government workers pushed for collective bargaining rights and a new generation of elected officials came to support their cause. In 1959, Wisconsin adopted the nation's first state law granting public employees collective bargaining rights.[27] In 1962, President John F. Kennedy advanced the movement by signing Executive Order 10988, which allowed most federal employees to engage in collective bargaining with respect to working conditions.[28] In the 1960s and 1970s, California led other states in authorizing full unionization for government workers, while Texas and other conservative states resisted. To this day, the division has largely adhered to ideological lines. Conservatives have argued that public employees enjoy civil service protections and do not need unions to protect their rights, and, further, that public unions can easily gain too much power by helping to elect public officials who then support union demands. Strong public unions, in this view, cause government to overspend on public employee salaries, pensions, and other benefits. Progressives have countered that public employees need collective bargaining rights to ensure that government employers treat them fairly, and, further, that public employees should have the same collective bargaining rights as any other workers.

As of 2018, the share of public employees that belonged to unions was 34 percent nationwide, with a wide gap between red and blue states.[29] The differences can be attributed, in part, to state policies. Red states have generally restricted public sector collective bargaining while blue states have embraced it. Texas and California again represent these opposite positions.

Texas

Texas has long been a leader in opposing public employee unionism. The legislature's 1947 package of anti-union laws included an explicit ban on public sector collective bargaining. The statute declared that state and local authorities "may not recognize a labor organization as the bargaining agent for a group of public employees" and "may not enter into a collective bargaining contract with a labor organization regarding wages, hours, or conditions of employment of public employees." The law further mandated that "[p]ublic employees may not strike or engage in an organized work stoppage" against the state or local governments and that any public employee who does so "forfeits all civil service rights, reemployment rights, and any other rights, benefits, and privileges the employee enjoys as a result of public employment or former public employment." Finally, the law established a right-to-work rule for public employees, stating that "an individual may not be denied public employment because of the individual's membership or nonmembership in a labor organization."[30]

These long-standing restrictions remain in place, with two important exceptions. First, in 1973, the Texas Legislature opened the door for police and firefighters to engage in collective bargaining with local governments. The process requires local voter approval and voters in approximately thirty Texas cities—including Houston, Dallas, San Antonio, and Austin—have authorized their local governments to engage in collective bargaining with either police unions, fire unions, or both.[31] Second, in 2005, the legislature authorized collective bargaining for municipal employees in cities of over 1.5 million residents, a provision that currently applies only to Houston.[32] Otherwise, Texas has firmly maintained its ban on public sector unionism.

Most Texas public employee associations thus cannot exercise the most important function of a labor union—collective bargaining. Public school teacher associations fall into this category. Texas is one of only five states—the others are Georgia, North Carolina, South Carolina, and Virginia—that prohibit teachers from engaging in collective bargaining. At the same time, Texas school districts employ more than 350,000 teachers, the most of any state. Nearly two-thirds of Texas teachers belong to professional associations. The largest of these groups is the Association of Texas Professional Educators (ATPE), an independent association with approximately one hundred thousand members. The ATPE embraces an older understanding of what a teacher's association should be. It provides services to members and lobbies on their behalf, but flatly opposes unionism based on exclusive representation and collective bargaining, arguing that "educators have a right to work in public schools without being forced to join any particular organization," and insisting that "collective bargaining policies create an adversarial relationship between employees and employers that can compromise students' education."[33] Whether they belong to ATPE or more union-oriented groups like the NEA-affiliated Texas State Teachers Association (TSTA), Texas teachers cannot collectively bargain or strike. Indeed, under Texas law, teachers who strike can be fired from their jobs and stripped of all of benefits, including their pensions. These limits and sanctions mean that teachers in Texas have less traditional bargaining power than in almost any other state.[34]

Most other Texas public employees find themselves in a similar position. They can belong to associations such as the Texas Public Employee Association (TPEA), but those organizations have little power to force public employers to respond to salary and other demands. Due to their special legal status, police, fire and some other municipal employee unions have broader bargaining powers, but they remain an exception among the state's public employees. Overall, the state's policies have helped it limit public sector union density to 14 percent as of 2018, the ninth lowest in the nation.

California

Although California is now home to formidable public sector unions, it was not always so. Before the 1960s, California's public employee associations looked much like Texas's are today—they were voluntary membership organizations that lacked collective bargaining power. Some of the largest associations included the California Teachers Association (founded in 1863 as the California Educational Society), the California School Employees Association (founded in 1927), and the California State Employees Association (established in 1931). In its early years, CTA was a model for other non-union public employee associations. It offered its members access to a credit union, insurance programs, training, and other services, and it lobbied for teachers and K–12 public education in the state capital. In the early twentieth century, CTA persuaded the legislature to provide free textbooks to elementary school students, establish teacher tenure, and create the California State Teachers Retirement System (Cal-STRS). CTA also opened its membership to management, including school administrators, superintendents, and even elected school board officials. For years, CTA opposed collective bargaining—an attitude many other public employee associations shared.

By the 1960s, however, these views began to change. A growing number of California's public employees objected to their pay and working conditions and envied the ability of private sector unions to win concessions from employers. Some government workers also were inspired by the political and cultural activism of the day and wanted to launch their own rights movement. The state's social workers were among the most militant. They engaged in several stand-offs with their county employers, affiliated with national unions such as SEIU and the American Federation of State, County, and Municipal Employees (AFSCME), and went on strikes to demand higher pay, lower caseloads, and, above all, collective bargaining rights. According to one organizer, social workers wanted the right to collectively bargain, "just like they had in the automobile industry."[35] Soon, the drive for union rights spread throughout California's public sector, most consequentially in the public schools.

For many years, the California Federation of Teachers (CFT), a state affiliate of the American Federation of Teachers (AFT), had challenged CTA's opposition to collective bargaining. In the mid-1960s, many California teachers came to embrace the CFT view that they should demand these rights. Facing unrest in its ranks and competition from CFT, the California Teachers Association finally converted to the pro-union position. In 1971, the CTA removed school administrators from its membership and embraced collective bargaining, a momentous decision that set it on course to become one of the state's most powerful unions, and perhaps the most powerful teachers' union in the nation.[36] Meanwhile, other California public employee associations had similar conversions and began to press for full union status.

In 1968, California became the second state, after Wisconsin, to authorize large-scale public sector unionization. That year, the legislature enacted—and Governor Reagan signed—the Meyers-Milias-Brown Act (MMBA), which legalized collective bargaining for California's city and county government employees.[37] Although the 1968 law explicitly excluded teachers and state employees, one union victory led to others. When Democrats gained unified control of state government in 1975, the legislature quickly extended collective bargaining rights to a full spectrum of public employees, including teachers in 1976, state employees in 1978, and university employees in 1979.[38] California also established a quasi-judicial body called the Public Employee Relations Board (PERB) to enforce these new rights on the model of the National Labor Relations Board.[39] As California embraced unionism for public employees, it began requiring non-union members covered by a union contract to pay agency fees—the very requirement that the U.S. Supreme Court would declare unconstitutional in 2018.[40]

California's public sector unions are now among the strongest in the nation. In 2017, on the eve of the *Janus* ruling, more than half of all California public employees belonged to unions. Union membership was far higher in some sectors, including public education, where approximately 94 percent of California schoolteachers held union cards. This high membership rate made the California Teachers Association, with more than 300,000 members, one of the state's largest and most powerful unions. Others included the California Federation of Teachers (CFT), the California School Employees Association

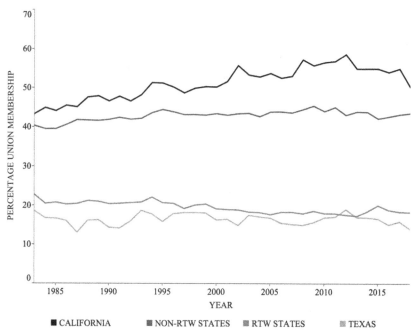

Figure 10.2. Public sector union density in California, Texas, and other states, 1983–2018

Source: U.S. Census Bureau

(CSEA), the American Federation of State, County, and Municipal Employees (AFSCME), SEIU Local 1000, the California Nurses Association (CNA), the California Correctional and Peace Officers Association (CCPOA), and local police and professional firefighter unions. Approximately 1.2 million California state and local government workers belonged to these and other unions. California's public sector union density was higher than the average for "union-friendly," non-right-to-work states, and far above the levels in Texas and other right-to-work states (Figure 10.2).[41]

Workplace Regulations

In addition to the National Labor Relations Act, Congress has established a large body workplace rules. Examples include the Fair Labor Standards Act of 1938, the Occupational Safety and Health Act of 1970, and the Family and Medical Leave Act of 1993.[42] In setting standards that all U.S. employers must follow, Congress has generally sought to balance the interests of employers and employees, while often allowing states to increase their regulations above the federal floor. State-level regulation generally corresponds to the influence of organized labor. Red states with weak unions tend to go no further than the federal minimums require, while blue states with strong unions frequently raise the bar. Again, Texas and California stand on opposite sides of this divide.

Minimum Wage

The minimum wage provides a useful illustration. Congress established the first federal minimum wage in 1938 at 25 cents an hour and later raised the minimum numerous times. In 2009, it set the federal minimum wage at $7.25 per hour, the last increase for many years. As Congress resisted further increases, a growing number of states chose to raise their rates. As of 2019, twenty-nine states had set their minimum wage above the federal level, while twenty-one had declined to do so.

Texas has explicitly limited its minimum wage to the federal baseline.[43] Moreover, the state's lawmakers have prohibited local governments from setting higher minimum wages. In 2003, when San Francisco and Santa Fe, New Mexico became the first U.S. cities to set local minimum wages above their state levels, the Texas legislature quickly blocked local jurisdictions from following the trend.[44] Similarly, when a wave of other states raised minimum wages to $10 an hour or more, the legislature rejected Democratic proposals to join the movement.

By contrast, the Golden State has frequently set its minimum wage above the federal level. In 1913, it became one of the first states to adopt a minimum wage, and for decades after Congress adopted a national floor, it typically maintained a slightly higher rate.[45] The gap between the California and federal minimums remained narrow until the twenty-first century, when California embraced the concept of the "living wage." By 2012, labor-backed movements such as "Fight for 15" emerged in various parts of the country pushing for a minimum wage of $15 an hour. San Francisco became the first major U.S. city to adopt a $15 minimum wage. In 2014, San Francisco became the first major U.S. city to adopt a $15 minimum wage (effective 2018), and other California cities soon followed. In 2016, California's SEIU–United Health Care Workers union gathered enough signatures to qualify a ballot initiative to raise California's statewide minimum to $15 per hour by 2021. On April 4, 2016, before the measure reached a vote, Governor Jerry Brown signed a bill that committed California to a $15 minimum wage by 2022 for larger employers and 2023 for smaller ones, with the rate indexed to inflation thereafter.[46] The same day, New York governor Andrew Cuomo signed a bill to raise the hourly wage to $15 per hour in the New York City area, with lesser increases in other parts of the state. California lawmakers took pains to say that their minimum wage law, not New York's, set the national standard. Senate

President Pro Tem Kevin de León proclaimed that California's $15 minimum wage law "is first in the nation, period.... Ours is more progressive and ours is a smarter way to go about it." According to de León, "We don't look towards New York for leadership, I think the rest of the country looks toward California for leadership on this issue."[47] California had, indeed, set itself apart by raising the minimum wage to $15 not only in its urban centers but in all corners of the state. Soon, all of California would have a minimum wage that was more than double the federal minimum—and thus double the minimum wage in Texas and most other red states (Figure 10.3).

The large minimum wage gap between Texas and California can be explained in part by the relative strength of organized labor in the two states. In California, as elsewhere, organized labor has been the driving force for minimum wage increases. In addition to their progressive ideological commitments, unions have a strong financial interest in raising minimum wages. Although most union members already earn more than the minimum wage, union contracts often contain formulas that link increases in the minimum wage to increases in union pay scales. Even without an explicit contract guarantee, a rising minimum

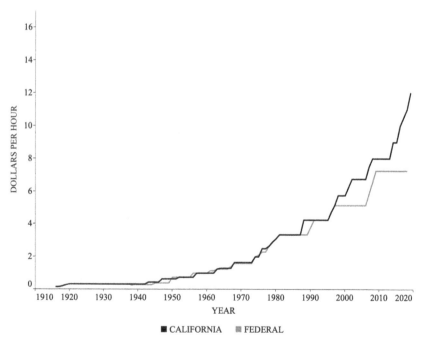

Figure 10.3. California vs. U.S. (and Texas) minimum wage, 1916–2020

Sources: U.S. Department of Labor, California Department of Industrial Relations

Note: California minimum wage scheduled to increase to $15 per hour, fully effective 2023.

wage provides unions leverage to demand higher pay several rungs up the wage ladder.[48] It is not surprising that California and a small number of the nation's most densely unionized states have driven the movement for the $15 per hour minimum wage—and, also not surprising that Texas and other states with weak unions are have consistently defeated minimum wage increases.

Other Workplace Regulations

Texas generally follows federal minimums for other employment regulations, maintaining that mandates above that level would excessively burden businesses. California, by contrast, has been much more willing to raise its requirements above the federal floor. The California Legislature has expanded rules for employment nondiscrimination, accommodations for pregnant and disabled workers, overtime pay, rest breaks, meal breaks, paid sick leave, paid family leave, workers compensation, unemployment insurance, and more. For example, as noted earlier, in 2019 California enacted AB 5, which applied state labor regulations to gig-economy and other contract workers. Moreover, the state has created powerful mechanisms for enforcing its labor laws. In particular, in 2003, the legislature enacted the Private Attorney General Act (PAGA), which allows employees to hire private lawyers to sue their employers for alleged labor code violations. By permitting plaintiffs to recover damages for even minor violations, the law likely improved compliance, while also creating profits for employment lawyers and increasing costs for many businesses.[49] Organized labor has led the push for these measures, and, more broadly, for creating in California the nation's most expansive system of workplace regulation.[50]

Consequences of Contrasting Labor Policies

Private Sector

The Texas and California approaches to private sector labor policy present basic trade-offs. The conservative Texas Model has promoted economic growth by keeping labor costs low, but also has forced many workers to survive on comparatively low wages and benefits. Conversely, California's progressive model has increased employee pay, benefits, and workplace protections, but also has placed stress on employers—especially small businesses—to meet higher costs. Studies by the U.S. Census Bureau and the Department of Labor's Bureau of Labor Statistics have shown that, in almost every job classification, unionized private sector employees receive more generous compensation than comparable nonunion members. This "union premium" includes both higher pay and more frequent coverage by employer-provided medical care and retirement plans.[51] With a larger unionized private sector workforce, more California workers have reaped the benefits of this premium. Moreover, California's high minimum wage has elevated most workers in the state above the federal minimum wage, while in 2018 approximately 226,000 Texas workers were paid the federal minimum—or even below, if their work fell within an exception to the law.[52] Overall, the median wages and benefits of California workers have consistently outpaced those in Texas.[53] The other side of the coin, of course, is the cost of doing business. The price of California-level wages and benefits, as well as compliance with the state's workplace regulations, directly hits an employer's bottom line. Many employers have been able to absorb these expenses, but others have struggled to do so. Labor costs have been a major factor in causing employers to exit California—or, if they stay, to reduce their payrolls and rely more heavily on lower-cost part-time workers. By contrast, Texas's lower labor costs have encouraged employers to locate and expand in the Lone Star State.

Public Sector

The consequences of the two approaches are even greater in the public sector, where the presence or absence of strong unions has influenced not only worker salaries and benefits, but also the size and character of public budgets and of government itself. In Texas, restrictions on public sector collective bargaining have helped keep government pay scales low, with most of the state's public employees compensated below the national average. According to the U.S. Department of Labor, in 2018, Texas's full-time state employees earned an average of $59,947 per year, slightly beneath the national average for state employees of $60,751 per year. A separate study of public school teacher salaries showed that, in 2018–2019, Texas teachers earned an average salary of $54,155 per year, which ranked well below the national average of $61,730 per year.[54] By contrast, California's public employees received much larger paychecks. According to the Department of Labor, in 2018, California state workers earned on average $80,316 per year, making them the best compensated of their peers in other states, including in New York and other high-cost states. Similarly, California teachers in 2018–2019 earned $82,282 per year, about 50 percent more than Texas teachers, and second only to New York for the nation's highest teacher pay.[55]

In addition to their wide gaps in pay scales, Texas and California provide different levels of public employee benefits, the most consequential of which are pensions. Most public employees, in both red and blue states, enjoy defined benefit retirement plans. These systems differ from the defined contribution plans—typically 401(k)s—that cover most private sector employees. In a 401(k)-type plan, both the employer and the employee contribute to the account over time, the employee controls how the account's funds are invested, and the employee can draw down the accumulated funds—and only those funds—upon reaching retirement age. By contrast, a defined benefit plan promises an employee a guaranteed retirement income, with payouts based not on contributions or investment returns, but rather on a separate set of factors such as the employee's years of service and salary history. The danger is that the public pension systems will have insufficient funds to meet promised payouts. Expanded benefits, lengthening life expectancy, and other developments have created pension debt in nearly all states, but the gaps are most worrisome in states with the most generous pension guarantees, the most stringent legal limits on reducing them, and the strongest public sector unions defending the status quo. On that basis, the pension crisis is greater in California than in Texas—indeed, greater in California than in most other states.

In 1999, Gray Davis took office as California's first Democratic governor in sixteen years. At the same time, the "dot-com boom" was pouring revenues into state treasury and generating high investment returns for the state's retirement funds. Public sector unions saw an opportunity to win greater benefits for their members. They rallied support for SB 400, a bill that greatly enhanced public sector pensions.[56] Among other provisions, SB 400 granted many state workers large retroactive pension increases and introduced new, generous pension formulas. The state gave highway patrol officers the best deal—a "3 percent at 50" formula, which allowed them to retire at age fifty and receive a lifetime pension equaling 3 percent of their highest salary times the total number of years worked. Officers who served ten years, for example, would now receive a pension equaling 30 percent of their highest annual salary; and those with 30 years on the job would get a pension equaling 90 percent of their highest pay. The law established generous new formulas for many other state workers, as well. At the same time, California allowed employees to increase their long-term pension payouts by "spiking" their salaries in a single year through increased overtime and other means. After enactment of SB 400, other state and local government workers demanded and received enhancements to their retirement plans. Many public employees could now retire expecting to receive more than $100,000 per year for the rest of their lives. By promoting these changes, California's public sector unions thus helped their members secure some of the nation's most generous pension benefits.

Proponents of expanded pension benefits originally claimed that they would cost taxpayers nothing—because, they said, pension fund investment gains would fully cover the increased payouts. This rosy forecast quickly collapsed when the dot-com bubble burst. In the years that followed, the state and many local governments were forced to pay far greater contributions to pension funds, which consumed a growing share of public budgets and crowded out spending on other programs. Unfortunately, even these increasing contributions failed to keep pace with rising costs. By 2012, the California cities of Stockton and San Bernardino had filed for bankruptcy, with public employee labor costs, including pension commitments, contributing to their insolvency.[57] Other governments in California faced similar stresses as the cumulative state and municipal pension debts continued to grow.

Many California public officials—including some prominent progressives—realized that existing pension systems are unsustainable and have called for reforms. Their efforts faced two major obstacles. The first limitation was the "California Rule," a judicial doctrine that has long prevented the state's government employers from reducing pension benefits for existing employees (the rule doesn't prevent cutting benefits for new hires). California is one of a minority of states to lock in the pensions of existing employees in this way.[58] More fundamentally, California's public sector unions consistently resisted any meaningful reductions in public employee pensions. A coalition of public unions blocked all of Governor Schwarzenegger's efforts to change pension rules and were able to limit the scope of Governor Jerry Brown's later pension reform efforts. In 2012, Brown proposed and the legislature approved the Public Employees' Pension Reform Act (PEPRA). This act banned some methods for spiking pension benefits and made other adjustments for new hires, but did not touch core benefits for existing employees or fundamentally change the state's approach to public pensions.[59] After the reform, California still faced a massive unfunded pension liability that totals hundreds of billions of dollars.[60]

Texas also provides its public employees with defined benefit retirement plans, but the size of pensions—and the costs and liabilities government incurs—is far lower than in California. Several factors help explain the difference. First, Texas's lower public sector pay has the effect of reducing retirement benefits because pensions are calculated based on an employee's salary history. Second, Texas uses smaller multipliers for its pension formulas, further limiting retirement pay. Third, Texas makes its public employees pitch in a larger share of total pension funding than California does, with Texas governments contributing 57 percent to employee pension funds compared to California's contribution of 73 percent. All of these factors have helped keep pension obligations lower and more manageable in Texas than in California.

The magnitude of the difference can be seen by comparing the two states' total contributions to pension funds and payouts to retirees. In Fiscal Year 2018, Texas governments chipped in $8.3 billion to public employee pension plans, while California state and local governments contributed $39.3 billion—nearly five times as much. Also in Fiscal Year 2018, Texas pension systems paid out $18.9

billion in benefits and other payments, while California pension payouts totaled $59.3 billion—more than a threefold difference.[61] Looking to the future, both Texas and California will need to increase pension contributions, reduce payouts, or both, but the challenge will be far less in Texas than in the Golden State.

Moreover, Texas has greater flexibility to reduce the pension benefits of existing employees. Texas has never adopted the California Rule, but instead has treated state employee pension benefits as "gratuities" that can be reduced or eliminated at will (although locally administered pensions enjoy greater protection).[62] Texas also has not had to face California levels of union resistance when it seeks to alter public employee pension benefits. Despite these advantages, Texas has struggled to keep some of its local pension systems financially sound. In recent years, the cities of Dallas and Houston have experienced pension crises involving multibillion-dollar funding shortfalls. In 2017, the state intervened and Governor Greg Abbott signed bills requiring higher employee contributions and limiting future pension increases for current employees in those cities.[63] Although the episode showed that even a fiscally conservative state can struggle to keep public pension funds solvent, Texas was able to address the problem in a way that would have been harder to do in California.

Labor Policy and the Competing Models

The rivals approach labor policy with similar premises as they do tax policy— and, as with taxes, their competing labor policies present fundamental trade-offs. California seeks through its labor laws to redistribute resources and power from the higher to the lower rungs of the economic ladder—namely, from employer to employee—even if doing so places stress on businesses and drives some out of the state. California also uses labor policy to empower government employees and their unions—even if that means imposing unsustainable costs on public budgets. Conversely, Texas believes that private sector labor policy, like tax policy, should aim to reduce employer costs—even if doing so depresses worker wages and benefits. And in the public sector, Texas labor policy seeks to limit the power and costs of the government workforce—even if that approach inadequately funds public employee salaries and pensions.

One might think that within the federal system, both sides would be content to peacefully pursue their preferred labor policies within their respective states; in practice, they have found reasons to disrupt the other side's model. The minimum wage again provides an example. Even though California already has adopted a $15 minimum wage, it has backed efforts to impose this rate on the nation as a whole, which would have the effect of driving up red state wages (and labor costs) to blue state levels.[64] At the same time, Texas and other red states have worked to disrupt the blue state labor model by advancing federal policies that weaken unions. Although it already bans agency fees and thus had no direct stake in the litigation, Texas joined eighteen other red states in filing a brief promoting the anti-union position in the *Janus* case.[65] These and other signs suggest that the rivals will continue seeking to impose their preferred labor policies on the other side.

11

Energy and Environment

Meeting the nation's energy needs in a way that both sustains the economy and protects the environment has become one of the most pressing challenges of our day. The task gained urgency near the turn of the millennium as most scientists concluded that carbon-based fossil fuels—the lifeblood of the modern world—threaten the earth's climate. An international movement to combat climate change emerged and set its sights on the fossil fuel industry. In the United States, the conflict reinforced the right-left political divide. Conservatives downplayed climate fears. They argued that the nation should take full economic advantage of all of its domestic energy resources (including coal, oil, and natural gas, as well as renewables), and insisted that climate regulations not override the free market and consumer choice. Progressives countered that climate change is an existential threat that demands an immediate response, including rapid decarbonization and a wholesale shift to alternative energy sources. Texas and California asserted national—even global—leadership on opposite sides of this high-stakes contest.

As the nation's largest energy producer and the hub of the global energy industry, Texas has fought for an "all-energy" policy. Even as the state has embraced new energy sources, it has tenaciously fought efforts to restrict fossil fuels. Indeed, Texas has radically revitalized U.S. oil and gas production capacity by pioneering new, highly productive extraction technologies. California, by contrast, has become an international leader in the fight against climate change. Driven by its progressive ideology, the Golden State is at the forefront of efforts to reduce carbon emissions, in large part by mandating conversion from fossil fuels to renewable energy sources. Energy and environmental policies now divide the rival states as deeply as any other issue. This chapter provides an overview of the nation's energy options, demonstrates how Texas and California present competing visions of the nation's energy future, and compares the costs and benefits of their energy models.

Energy in the United States

In the late nineteenth century, coal replaced wood as the nation's largest energy source; ever since, carbon-based fossil fuels (coal, petroleum, and natural gas)

Texas vs. California. Kenneth P. Miller, Oxford University Press (2020). © Oxford University Press.
DOI: 10.1093/oso/9780190077402.001.0001.

have supplied most of its energy needs. Plentiful, portable, scalable, cheap, and efficient, fossil fuels made industrial economies possible and, in so doing, helped create the modern world. Nearly all transportation now relies on petroleum and most electricity is generated by natural gas and coal. Despite the push for alternatives, in 2018, fossil fuels still accounted for about 80 percent of all U.S. energy consumption—led by petroleum, at 36 percent, natural gas, at 31 percent, and coal, at 13 percent (Figure 11.1).[1]

Yet fossil fuels have shortcomings. Among other limitations, these resources are finite, non-renewable, and constantly depleting. In the 1970s, this scarcity produced a crisis, as the United States started tapping out its conventional oil and gas reserves. U.S. oil output steadily declined from 1970 until 2008, even as demand continued to rise. To compensate, the United States was forced to import large quantities of oil, mainly from the Middle East.[2] The domestic supply of natural gas also failed to meet demand. Fearing a natural gas shortage, Congress in 1978 banned construction of gas-fired power plants, a restriction that lasted for nearly a decade. U.S. coal reserves were comparatively plentiful (nearly

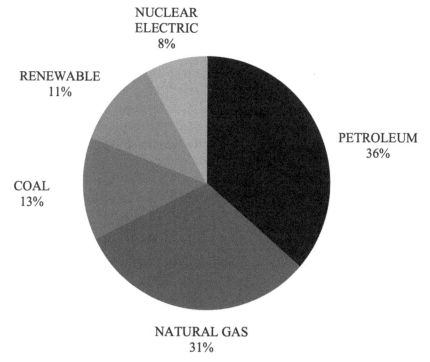

Figure 11.1. U.S. energy consumption by source, 2018
Source: U.S. Energy Information Administration

one-fourth of the world's total reserves), and the United States doubled down on this resource, building a new generation of coal-burning power plants.[3]

Remarkably, domestic oil and gas shortages disappeared, almost in the blink of an eye, near the turn of the twenty-first century. This transformation was caused by the discovery in Texas of a form of hydraulic fracturing, or "fracking," that could extract large amounts of oil and natural gas from shale, a dense sedimentary rock. In the shale fracking process, drillers send a well deep into the earth and then position it horizontally into a shale formation, often two miles or more below the surface. Once the well is in place, it is injected with massive amounts of water, combined with sand and chemicals—a mixture sometimes called "slick water." The high pressure injection causes the shale to crack, making it more permeable. When engineers remove the slick water mixture, pressure is released, and hydrocarbons begin migrating through the cracks into the well. Although the oil and gas industry had long used fracking for other purposes, the technique was not used to unlock shale until the late 1990s. No one expected it would produce such vast amounts of natural gas and oil.[4]

The United States sits on an enormous constellation of shale formations, including the Barnett, Eagle Ford, and Permian Basin in Texas, the Bakken in North Dakota, the Marcellus in Appalachia, the Niobrara near the Rocky Mountains, and many more. Some of these formations produce natural gas, others oil, and some, like the Permian Basin, large quantities of both. As shale fracking spread from Texas to other states, the United States underwent a stunning renaissance in oil and gas production. In the decade after 2008, operators drilled thousands of new wells and the United States more than doubled its oil output. By early 2020, just before the oil market crashed, the nation was producing a peak of thirteen million barrels per day, a level that surpassed the old production records set in 1970. For the first time in decades, the United States was the world's largest oil producer, beating out Saudi Arabia and Russia. Similarly, shale fracking had elevated domestic natural gas output to all-time highs and established the United States as the world's largest natural gas producer.[5]

The early stages of the shale revolution had broad, complex, and sometimes disruptive consequences. Because the revolution was concentrated in the United States (other countries with large shale deposits had not established meaningful fracking operations), it strengthened the American position in global energy markets. By 2010, the United States was sharply decreasing imports and, in 2016, began exporting oil for the first time in decades. The vast new U.S. supply drove down global prices, placing stress on other oil- and gas-producing countries. Low natural gas prices also disrupted the electricity generation industry. Gas-fired power plants now ran more cheaply than their coal and nuclear competitors, which caused many U.S. utilities to consider a switch to natural gas.

Critics attacked fracking, arguing that it produces various environmental harms; among other things, they noted that the process consumes enormous amounts of water, produces toxic wastewater, generates man-made seismicity, and can introduce toxic chemicals, oil, and gas into aquifers, especially if wells are improperly drilled and cased.[6] Activists called for strict regulations, or even a ban, on the process. Defenders countered that fracking's environmental threats have been exaggerated and that proper industry practices can mitigate these concerns.[7]

The environmentalist attack went beyond fracking to reliance on fossil fuels in any form. By the 1990s, a growing scientific consensus concluded that fossil fuels present serious threats to the planet due to their release into the atmosphere of carbon dioxide (CO_2) and other greenhouse gases (GHG). Environmentalists called for a fight against anthropogenic, or human-caused, climate change, urging governments to hasten the shift from carbon-based fuels to alternative, renewable energy sources (such as solar and wind energy) through aggressive regulation. They directed their sharpest attacks at coal, which continued to produce a majority of the world's electricity and a large share of the U.S. supply. Because coal produces more greenhouse gasses per unit of electricity than other carbon fuels—more than double the CO_2 produced by natural gas—some environmentalists believed that replacing coal with natural gas was a smart short-term strategy. Others argued that this approach was a half-measure in the war on climate change, and that the world needed to decarbonize across the board.

Ending U.S. reliance on fossil fuels would be an immense undertaking. The goal would require replacing the 80 percent share of the nation's energy portfolio derived from carbon-based sources and supplanting major elements of the American economy—the 98 percent of U.S. cars and trucks that run on gasoline or diesel, the more than 60 percent of home heating systems fueled by natural gas or heating oil, and the more than 60 percent of the nation's electricity generated by coal or natural gas.[8] A zero-emission economy would need to be run almost exclusively on electricity generated by non-carbon sources (Figure 11.2).

Where would this new, carbon-free energy come from? As of 2019, the nation's leading non-carbon electricity sources were nuclear power (19.7 percent of total electricity generation), hydroelectric (6.6 percent), wind (7.3 percent), solar (1.8 percent), and geothermal (0.4 percent). Biomass, generally considered carbon-neutral, contributed 1.4 percent.[9] To replace fossil fuels, the United States would need to develop the means to massively scale up production from a combination of these six sources (Figure 11.3).

The first option is nuclear energy. For more than half a century, the nuclear power industry has generated impressive amounts of carbon-free electricity. The United States has the world's largest nuclear generation capacity, with nearly 100 reactors producing one-fifth of the nation's electricity supply. Although stepping

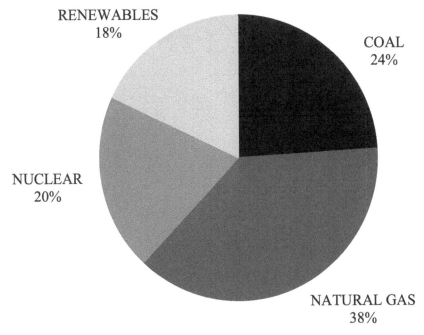

Figure 11.2. U.S. electricity generation by fuel type, 2019
Source: U.S. Energy Information Administration

up nuclear energy production could provide the most direct path to radical de-carbonization, many have flatly rejected this option. A tenacious anti-nuclear movement has long blocked the industry's development, citing concerns that range from reactor safety to the storage and disposal of radioactive waste. The 1979 reactor accident at Pennsylvania's Three Mile Island, combined with later incidents at Chernobyl in the Soviet Union (1986) and Fukushima Daiichi in Japan (2011), hardened anti-nuclear sentiment. Yet, as concerns about climate change mounted, some began to reconsider their opposition to this energy source. The Obama administration, for example, made nuclear power part of its overall energy strategy, and the industry had visions of a renaissance.[10] Most environmentalists, however, refused to get on board, unable to accept nuclear power as a major contributor to a low-carbon energy future. Moreover, before the nuclear renaissance could gain traction, the industry was hit by competition from low-cost natural gas. Citing cost factors, some utilities canceled plans for new nuclear plants, others shut down financially stressed plants before their licenses expired, and still others demanded government subsidies in order to stay in operation. As the number of reactors shrank, the prospects for a nuclear-based energy future remained dim.[11]

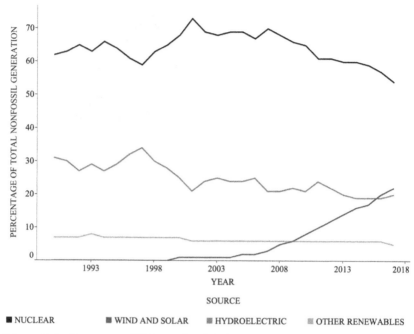

Figure 11.3. Percentage of U.S. non-fossil fuel generation by source, 1990–2018
Source: U.S. Energy Information Administration

Hydroelectricity, a second long-standing source of carbon-free energy, also faces obstacles to growth. The United States generates most of its hydroelectricity in large dams in western states, such as Grand Coulee, Hoover, Glen Canyon, Shasta, and Oroville, and environmentalists passionately oppose constructing more of their kind. Utilities may squeeze more electricity from existing dams, or create other smaller-scale hydroelectric projects, but otherwise this sector cannot be expected to expand. Similarly, geothermal power has limited growth prospects. At present, this source is available in meaningful quantities only in the western states and Hawaii; it produces less than 1 percent of the nation's energy mix. Although the earth contains essentially unlimited heat, it is difficult and expensive to capture, thus making geothermal hard to scale. By comparison, biofuels (derived from organic materials, including wood, corn, sugar, vegetable oil, grasses, and animal waste) also contribute only a small share of U.S. electricity generation and transportation fuels, but this source has the capacity to expand. Although biofuels are not carbon-free, they are renewable and are considered to have low net-carbon impact. The challenge for developing these fuels is scalability and affordability.

Many consider wind and solar the best long-term options for carbon-free power generation, because they are clean, renewable, and scalable. With the help of state and federal tax credits, subsidies, and mandates, the solar and wind industries have begun to mature in the twenty-first century—they have improved efficiency, reduced costs, and increased market share. Yet, as late as 2019, wind accounted for only 7.3 percent of U.S. electricity generation and solar less than 2 percent. To fulfill their potential, developers of these sources needed to address the problematic reality that they cannot produce around the clock—they stop generating when the sun sets or the wind stops blowing. Fully scaling wind and solar required the development of high-capacity batteries that can store energy as it is produced and release it when needed. Rapid advancements in battery performance and reductions in costs raised hopes that these sources could scale effectively, but not nearly at the rates demanded by climate change activists.

Shifting U.S. Energy and Environmental Policy

As the world struggles to determine its energy future, the United States has failed to provide consistent leadership. Indeed, the nation's energy and environmental policies have veered from right to left and back again as control in Washington, D.C., has shifted from one party to the other.

Republicans have consistently promoted full development of domestic energy resources, including fossil fuels. The party's conservative base is skeptical of climate science, believes that climate action threatens the nation's economy in exchange for uncertain benefits, and fears that ceding vast powers to environmental regulators will lead to government tyranny. Democrats, meanwhile, increasingly embrace the progressive view that climate change demands urgent action. Many have supported far-reaching environmental policies, including the "Green New Deal."[12]

When Democrats controlled the executive branch under President Obama, they advanced an ambitious environmental agenda. During these years, the Environmental Protection Agency issued a landmark "endangerment finding" that carbon emissions threaten public health, which led to new regulations limiting carbon emissions by mobile sources, and, later, by stationary sources. The Obama administration also blocked the 1,200-mile Keystone Pipeline to transport oil from Canada; handed down new, more stringent motor vehicle fuel efficiency standards; restricted drilling on federal lands and offshore tracts; and issued the Clean Power Plan to tighten CO_2 emission standards for power plants—a move critics called part of a "war on coal." In 2015, President Obama also endorsed the Paris Agreement, a pact among nearly all nations in the world to reduce carbon emissions in order to slow global warming.[13]

When Donald Trump assumed the presidency, he worked to dismantle Obama-era environmental policies and to revive federal government support for carbon-based fuels. In a flurry of early announcements, the Trump administration declared it would withdraw from the Paris Accord, greenlight the Keystone Pipeline, approve new drilling on federal lands and offshore tracts, reduce vehicle emission standards, terminate the Clean Power Plan, and more. President Trump's then–EPA administrator, Scott Pruitt, announced that "the war on coal is over." And so, too, for the moment, was the federal government's "war" on all carbon emissions.[14]

As national energy and environmental policies have whipsawed from left to right, states have pursued their own priorities. Some states have resisted the green energy movement and zealously defended fossil fuels, while others have pushed climate action beyond the most ambitious Obama-era federal regulations.[15] In the midst of this unsettled situation, Texas and California have advanced starkly contrasting visions of the nation's energy future.

Texas

Texas has secured its status as the capital of the global energy industry partly due to its vast petroleum reserves, strategic geographic location, bold entrepreneurs, ready capital, and deep technical expertise, and also due to its business-friendly political culture. For more than a century, powerful Texans in Washington have ensured that provisions of the U.S. tax code and other federal policies protect the state's oil and gas producers. Texas state government has provided additional support by authorizing drilling in every corner of the state and along its coastal tracts, licensing the large cluster of refineries and petrochemical plants along the Gulf Coast, maintaining low taxes and industry-friendly regulations, and springing to the industry's defense when either the federal government or local jurisdictions have sought to restrict its operations.

Texas views its energy resources as economic assets and has focused on maximizing their value; in recent decades, that has meant exploiting the potential of oil and gas—to be sure—but also of coal, nuclear, wind, and solar power. By building a diverse energy portfolio, Texas has far exceeded all other states in total energy production. As of 2019, Texas ranked first in crude oil, first in natural gas, first in wind, and in the top ten in solar, nuclear, and coal.[16] Texas started diversifying its energy sources in the 1970s in response to declining oil and gas production. Utilities built a new generation of coal-fired power plants throughout the state. They also opened nuclear power plants at the South Texas Project on the Gulf Coast (1988) and at the Comanche Peak Plant outside of Dallas–Fort Worth (1990). Perhaps most surprising, Texas embraced wind power in a major

way. In 1999, the Texas Legislature and Governor George W. Bush approved a renewable energy mandate as part of a landmark bill to restructure and deregulate
the state's electricity industry.[17] At the time, many Texans dismissed wind and
other renewables as a left-wing California project.[18] But as Texas leaders looked
more closely, they recognized the economic value of diversifying the state's energy portfolio, and the business community saw a chance to profit from wind
energy if a market for it could be secured. They also could see that Texas's open
expanses, steady winds, and extensive power grid made the state a prime candidate for wind generation. Large wind farms cropped up across the state, mainly
in West Texas and the Panhandle, and quickly boosted the state's overall electricity output. By 2006, Texas passed California to become the nation's largest
wind energy producer and, by 2019, wind constituted one-fifth of the state's electricity supply. At the same time, Texas's production of solar energy was rising
fast, as well.[19]

Texas policymakers have endorsed a diverse energy portfolio in part because
the state has bottomless energy needs. Texas's combination of a large and fast-
expanding population, hot summer climate, long travel distances, powerful
economy, and energy-intensive industrial sector requires far more energy than
any other state—70 percent more than runner-up California.[20] To meet this demand and keep its economy growing, the state has extracted energy from all
available sources—including oil and gas, coal, nuclear, wind, and, increasingly,
solar. Moreover, Texas believes that robust energy production from multiple
sources creates jobs and wealth both directly and indirectly through manufacturing, transportation, trade, and more. Producing more energy than any other
state has been a cornerstone of the Texas Model.

It is no surprise, then, that even as it diversified its energy sources, Texas
remained committed to fossil fuels—indeed, the Lone Star State led the shale-
based renewal of the U.S. oil and gas industry. The Texan who launched the
revolution was a Houston-based oilman named George Mitchell. In the early
1980s, Mitchell's company began drilling in the Barnett Shale, a massive 5,000-
square-mile formation that sprawls deep beneath the Dallas–Fort Worth
Metroplex and surrounding areas of North Texas. Despite industry skepticism,
Mitchell was convinced he could extract large quantities of natural gas out of
that rock. For more than a decade and a half, his engineers persisted, drilling
well after well, fracking the rock with different chemical solutions at different
pressures—without success. Finally, in the late 1990s, a young Mitchell engineer
named Nick Steinsberger solved the puzzle. By greatly expanding the volume
of water injected into the well, reducing chemicals, and increasing pressure, he
fractured the shale in just the right way to release large quantities of natural gas.[21]
Mitchell's company soon used the technique in other parts of the Barnett, and
production skyrocketed. The shale revolution was born. Instead of patenting the

technique, Mitchell believed that others should freely benefit from it. Soon, more companies employed this discovery to extract both natural gas and oil from shale formations throughout Texas and across the country.

The fracking boom has enriched many states, but none more than Texas. The Lone Star State sits above many major shale formations, including the Barnett in North Texas, Eagle Ford in South and East Texas, Haynesville in East Texas, Granite Wash in the Panhandle, and, the most important, the Permian Basin in West Texas. As the industry aggressively fracked these formations, Texas's oil and gas production rose to all-time highs. Output from the Permian Basin was the most stunning of all. By 2019, this region was yielding 4 million barrels of oil per day, one-third of all U.S. oil production. In 2018, the U.S. Geological Survey released estimates of the Permian Basin's oil and gas reserves that staggered analysts. According to the USGS report, the region contains recoverable resources of 46.3 billion barrels of oil and 281 trillion cubic feet of natural gas—raising estimates of total U.S. oil reserves by more than double, and total natural gas reserves by 65 percent. Based on these figures, the Permian Basin contains one of the largest oil and gas reserves on the planet. And, indeed, by 2019 the Permian Basin rivaled Ghawar in Saudi Arabia as the world's most productive oil field. As the state's oil and gas production surged, the industry's greatest concern was that it was creating an oversupply and that the prices of these commodities could fall below profitable levels, especially if a recession hit and global demand fell (Figure 11.4).[22]

From the start, Texas lawmakers fully embraced the shale revolution. The state established moderate safety and public notification regulations for fracking operations, but protected the industry from more far-reaching restrictions. One test came in 2014, when voters in Denton, a large suburb near Dallas and home to the University of North Texas, passed a local ballot measure banning fracking in the city. Denton sits above the Barnett Shale, not far from where George Mitchell's team first succeeded in extracting natural gas from rock. As fracking operations spread, the industry drilled and fracked more than 270 wells inside Denton city limits. Many Denton residents complained that drilling and fracking created heavy truck traffic, fumes, and noise; others argued that these operations threatened the city's water supplies. Activists formed an organization to promote a local ban on fracking. Although several cities in other states had adopted such bans, this would be the first such ordinance in Texas. In an apparent blow to the industry, Denton voters approved the fracking ban by a 59-to-41 percent margin. However, the ban never went into effect. Immediately after the election, an industry group and the Texas General Land Office challenged it in court, and, within months, the Texas Legislature passed a bill, HB 40, that prohibited all such bans and expressly pre-empted the regulation of oil and gas operations by local governments.[23]

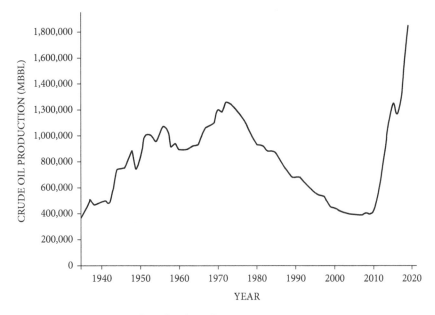

Figure 11.4. Texas annual crude oil production, 1935–2019

Sources: Texas Railroad Commission (1935–1980); U.S. Energy Information Administration (1981–2019)

At the same time Texas was blocking the local fracking ban, it was fighting a larger battle against the Obama administration over federal environmental policy. In 2009, Texas faced a harsh reality: George W. Bush, the conservative Texan and oil industry insider, had been replaced in the White House by Barack Obama, a progressive critic of the industry. During the Bush years, Texas and the federal government were closely aligned on energy and environmental policies, focusing on industry growth and moving cautiously on climate action. By contrast, President Obama came to office ready to regulate carbon-based fuels as part of an ambitious environmental program.

As the Obama team rolled out new environmental mandates, Texas rallied the resistance. Under Attorneys General Greg Abbott and Ken Paxton, Texas launched nearly thirty lawsuits against the EPA and other federal agencies. Texas built coalitions of red states and industry groups to join these cases, and often served as lead plaintiff. The litigation attacked President Obama's climate action agenda at every stage, including EPA's CO_2 endangerment finding, its "tailpipe rule" regulating carbon emissions cars and light trucks, its decision to expand these regulations to stationary sources, its rules restricting methane emissions by oil and gas producers, and its Clean Power plan. In case after case, Texas argued that the administration was overreaching—exceeding its proper authority and disregarding the damage its policies would do to the energy sector and the broader economy. Abbott charged that "EPA regulations have threatened to eliminate Texas jobs and stifle energy production, an industry at the very core of our state's economy" and that the Clean Power Plan, in particular, represented "an unprecedented meddling with Texas in order to push the Obama Administration's liberal climate change agenda." In Abbott's view, the plan would create "unprecedented control over the State's energy mix that will certainly result in higher energy prices for Texans and will threaten the reliability of Texas's electric grid."[24] Abbott further pledged that Texas would "lead the fight against an overreaching federal government that seems hell-bent on threatening the free-market principles this country was founded on."[25]

The litigation strategy had mixed success. Texas and its allies lost several battles, including their challenge to the EPA endangerment finding and the tailpipe rule, but in other cases, they defeated or delayed Obama administration environmental policies. In one important case, Texas and its allies convinced the Supreme Court to stay the implementation of the Clean Power Plan, blocking these regulations until the clock ran out on the Obama years, and the Trump administration, with Texas-friendly views, took office.[26] In federal courtrooms and elsewhere, Texas has argued that climate action must not be allowed to override other important values, including limited government, economic prosperity, and personal freedom.

California

California has struck a very different balance between energy development and environmental protection. The state's progressive political culture and sensitive ecosystems have impelled it to accept—even demand—aggressive regulation of the energy sector, even if that means leaving oil in the ground, shuttering power plants, or otherwise forgoing energy production or increasing its cost. California has chosen to build the nation's most advanced state-level environmental policy models and regulatory expertise, which, in turn, has prepared it to move to the front ranks of the global fight against climate change.

The Golden State's environmentalism has deep roots. For decades, Californians have been determined to protect the state's extraordinary coastline, mountain ranges, deserts, and forests. The Sierra Club (founded in San Francisco in 1892) and a network of other California-based organizations have reinforced this environmental commitment. Yet, at the same time, the state has sought to build an industrial economy and, to do so, it has needed to scale up energy production.

At the turn of the twentieth century, fossil fuels offered the only scalable power source, and most industrializing societies came to rely heavily on coal and oil. California had no coal, but it did possess large oil deposits. Thousands of derricks sprouted up across the southern and central parts of the state. As noted earlier, by 1910, California was producing more than seventy million barrels of oil a year, which was more than any other state, indeed more than any foreign nation.[27] This abundance of oil fueled Southern California's rapid industrial development and the birth of its world-famous car culture. But the region paid a high price for pumping exhaust into the atmosphere. Metropolitan Los Angeles sits in a large natural basin, surrounded by the ocean on one side and mountains on the other three. Within the basin, the region's mild, sunny weather creates an inversion layer—an atmospheric condition that traps and concentrates pollutants. As emissions increased, the haze thickened, and residents regularly complained of stinging eyes, shortness of breath, and other negative health effects. Los Angeles became notorious for its smog.[28]

After World War II, pressure mounted for the state to fight this plague. In 1947, Governor Earl Warren signed a bill to create the Los Angeles County Air Pollution Control District, and in 1960, Governor Pat Brown signed the Motor Vehicle Pollution Control Act, which established the nation's first statewide regulations on tailpipe emissions. The real breakthrough came in 1967. That year, Ronald Reagan signed a law establishing the California Air Resources Board (CARB), an agency with broad authority to regulate pollutants. With this regulatory system in place, California lobbied Congress for authority to set its own air quality standards above and beyond federal requirements. The auto industry strenuously objected, arguing that uniform federal standards should pre-empt state-level rules. Every member of the California congressional delegation—including all of the Republicans—fought for the proposal, and the bipartisan effort produced a landmark victory. The federal Air Quality Act of 1967 granted California sole authority to request waivers from federal law to set its own, more stringent air standards. In 1970, Congress embedded this arrangement in the federal Clean Air Act, and in 1977, it authorized other states to adopt either the California or the federal rules. In time, thirteen (blue) states and the District of Columbia adopted the stricter California standards. This two-tiered regulatory system has given California enormous power to develop air quality policy.[29]

In the first half century after the system was established, California received more than one hundred waivers, using its authority to mandate unleaded gasoline, catalytic converters, higher fuel efficiency standards, lower particulate emissions, and more. In many cases, the federal government eventually adopted the California standards for the nation as a whole.[30] California's strict air quality regulations have had remarkable success. In 1967 alone, Los Angeles had 239 Stage 1 and Stage 2 smog alerts; after 2003, it had none.[31]

Meanwhile, another plague reinforced the state's environmental commitment. On January 28, 1969, workers on an oil rig six miles off the coast of Santa Barbara were removing a pipe from a newly drilled well when oil and gas erupted through the ocean floor. Over the next eleven days, the blowout released three million gallons of crude oil into the channel. The massive slick spread to hundreds of square miles of sensitive marine habitat and thirty-five miles of shoreline, killing fish, seabirds, mammals, and other wildlife. At the time, the disaster was the largest oil spill in U.S. history.[32] The damage helped mobilize the modern global environmental movement and, in California, hardened public resistance to offshore drilling. The state established a moratorium (and, later, a ban) on new drilling off the coast, forgoing a major source of oil in order to protect the environment.

The state's environmental ethic also put it at odds with the nuclear power industry. Starting in the late 1950s, utility executives envisioned a "Super System" of nuclear power plants along the state's coastline. If built out, this network could have supplied most of the state's electricity needs for decades. However, tenacious opponents blocked nearly all of these facilities. The first fight emerged at Bodega Bay, a remote, scenic harbor and fishing village about seventy miles on the coast road north of San Francisco. The state's largest utility, Pacific Gas and Electric Company, unveiled plans for a large nuclear facility at the entrance to the bay. Local residents, anti-nuclear activists, and their progressive allies in San Francisco mobilized in opposition, arguing that the plant would destroy the area's natural beauty and pose health and safety risks. Protests increased until 1964, when the utility abandoned the project. Opponents later defeated nuclear plant construction at several other coastal locations from Point Arena in the north to Malibu near Los Angeles as well as at inland sites including Wasco in the San Joaquin Valley and Blythe on the Colorado River.[33] California eventually opened only three major nuclear facilities—at San Onofre on the south coast (1968), Rancho Seco near Sacramento (1975), and Diablo Canyon on the central coast (1985)—far fewer than the industry had hoped.[34] The state's utilities later shut down two of these plants with the third, Diablo Canyon, scheduled to close by 2025.

These fights showed that California was willing to limit energy production and consumption to achieve environmental goals. In 1974, the state's voters elected a new governor, Jerry Brown, who made this ethic of limits a centerpiece of his administration. Unlike his father, Pat, who spent his two terms as governor (1959–1967) enthusiastically building new dams, highways, aqueducts, power plants, and other large-scale projects, Jerry was convinced that the endless construction had to stop. Instead, he believed that humanity needed to reduce its material consumption and live in greater harmony with the planet. At age eighteen, Brown had entered a Catholic seminary and, after a period of training, had taken vows to become a Jesuit priest. Although he left the order, he never abandoned its asceticism, and later fused these Catholic virtues with eastern philosophies that emphasized simplicity and self-denial, as well as with the neo-Malthusian belief that humanity must limit its demands on nature.[35] As a young governor, Brown staffed his administration with environmentalists committed to implementing this ethic through policies designed to reduce energy demand and provide alternatives to fossil fuels and nuclear power.

Brown naturally aligned with the anti-nuclear movement. In 1976, he signed legislation that effectively blocked state permits for new nuclear plants, and he worked both publicly and behind the scenes to scuttle the Sundesert nuclear plant on the Colorado River, a facility designed to supply the electricity needs of the San Diego area. At a nuclear protest in 1979 headlined by activists Jane Fonda, Tom Hayden, and Ralph Nader, Brown proclaimed: "Nuclear power and its lethal impact for hundreds of thousands of years looms larger than any political personality, any political party, any country. It is a matter of the species of life that now inhabits this planet. We are living and profiting off the addiction to nuclear power. It has become a pathological addiction in that it has made many feel good, while storing up for generations to come, evils and risks that the human mind can barely grasp."[36]

Brown's primary solution to the energy problem was to reduce demand. During his first two terms, his administration set new energy efficiency standards for automobiles, buildings, and appliances, and created new business models for utilities that incentivized consumers to conserve energy. Brown also embraced alternative energy technologies, surrounding himself with scientists and futurists who were seeking to scale solar and wind energy and biofuels. In the 1970s, California became an early leader in adopting these technologies. The state's promotion of energy efficiency and alternative sources was aided by the 1973 Arab oil embargo and the fear of energy scarcity that persisted throughout the decade. In the 1980s, rising oil imports eased the energy crisis, Brown left office, and California's environmental activism waned. For the next two decades, the state remained a national leader in promoting air quality and fuel efficiency standards, but did not aggressively promote a new environmental agenda.[37]

The Golden State launched a second wave of environmental activism in the early 2000s in response to growing concerns about climate change. In 2002, California adopted a renewable portfolio standard ("RPS") requiring utilities to obtain a percentage of their electricity supply from renewable sources. (In California, "renewable" energy excluded not only fossil fuels but also nuclear energy and even hydroelectric power generated at large dams.) In 2002, the state also placed the nation's first restrictions on automobile CO_2 emissions.

In 2003, Arnold Schwarzenegger ran for governor as a moderate Republican committed to environmental protection. After he won office, he distanced himself from the George W. Bush administration and affirmed that California would lead the fight against climate change. In 2005, Schwarzenegger declared his devotion to the cause. "California will not wait for our federal government to take strong action on global warming," he proclaimed. "I say the debate is over. We know the science. We see the threat, and we know the time for action is now."[38] Schwarzenegger signed an executive order pledging California to reduce greenhouse gas emissions and then worked with the state's Democratic leaders to codify and expand this mandate through legislation titled AB 32, the Global Warming Solutions Act of 2006. Through this statute, California became the first large jurisdiction in the world to establish a comprehensive, legally binding plan to reduce greenhouse gas emissions. The act mandated an economy-wide reduction in these emissions to 1990 levels (or by approximately 30 percent) by 2020, required that one-third of the state's electricity supply come from renewable sources, and gave the California Air Resources Board authority to enforce the mandate through implementation of a state cap-and-trade program.[39]

As AB 32 was phasing in, the oil industry (led by Texas-based companies Valero and Tesoro) funded a ballot initiative to delay its implementation, claiming that the new regulations would overburden the economy and kill jobs. The campaign gathered sufficient signatures to place the measure on the November 2010 ballot. California voters were unmoved, however, by this industry-backed effort. They rejected the industry's proposal by a 62–38 percent margin, providing a popular endorsement of the state's aggressive climate policy.[40]

The cap-and-trade program became central to California's plan to combat climate change. Under the program, the state allocated to certain industries (initially, power plants and other large generators of greenhouse gases) "allowances" or "emissions credits," with the total allowances equal to the cap. The state reduced the cap by 3 percent per year between 2015 and 2020 and then by 5 percent per year through 2030. Companies that exceeded their allowances could obtain additional credits at auction or via trade and could purchase offsets through payments to fund carbon reduction projects. The state's goal was to reduce overall emissions while providing companies flexibility to manage the timing and cost of compliance. While some companies complained that cap and trade is a thinly veiled carbon tax, much of the business community accepted it as less burdensome than a direct tax or command-and-control regulation. On the left, some argued that cap and trade allowed industries in low-income areas to continue polluting at higher levels than they would under a more direct regulatory system. Over time, the environmental justice movement secured legislation targeting pollution in low-income neighborhoods and providing these communities a greater share of cap-and-trade funds. California also entered an agreement with the Canadian province of Quebec to hold joint auctions and to allow trading of allowances and offsets across jurisdictions. The state looked to enter similar agreements with other jurisdictions. In 2017, the California Legislature voted to extend the cap-and-trade program through 2030, thus ensuring a future for what had become the world's fourth-largest cap-and-trade program, trailing only the European Union, South Korea, and the Chinese Province of Guangdong.[41]

In 2011, as California's climate policies were beginning to take effect, Jerry Brown returned to the governor's office after a twenty-eight-year hiatus. During his first two terms as governor, in the 1970s and early 1980s, many had mocked his environmentalism. Three decades later, his views closely aligned with progressive Democratic thought. From 2011 through 2019, Brown worked with the state's now-heavily Democratic legislature to advance the nation's most aggressive climate policies. California developed its signature cap-and-trade program, repeatedly ratcheted up its mandates to increase alternative fuels and decrease greenhouse gas emissions, and took other specific steps to transition to a green energy economy—from mandating reductions in vehicle greenhouse gas emissions and building out a network of electric vehicle-charging stations to requiring that all new homes be constructed with solar panels.

During these years, the state also wrestled with its status as a major oil producer. As the fracking boom spread, the industry began to expand the practice in California. The largest fracking operations were near Bakersfield, in the San Joaquin Valley, which remained one of the nation's most productive oil fields. Many activists pushed for a ban on fracking in the state, with some taunting Brown: "Climate leaders don't frack!"[42] But Brown and the legislature declined to impose a ban. The reality was that Californians continued to drive about 330 billion miles per year almost exclusively in vehicles powered by gasoline and diesel. In 2018, electric vehicles, including battery electric vehicles and plug-in hybrids, still accounted for only about 8 percent of new vehicle sales in the state and a smaller percentage of all vehicles on the road.[43] Until the state could make a massive shift to electric vehicles, it would continue to require large quantities of gasoline. At the time, the state produced only one-third of the oil it consumed, and banning fracking would force it to rely even more heavily on imports. Brown argued that "as we bring down consumption, we can bring down production."[44] He signed legislation heavily regulating fracking operations, but was unwilling to go further.

Setting aside these complications, Brown embraced the role of environmental prophet and frequently used apocalyptic terms to describe the climate challenge. In 2015, he declared: "We have to realize that we are here today because of oil—oil and gas and a lesser extent, coal. What has been the source of our prosperity has become the source of our ultimate destruction if we don't get off of it."[45] Brown argued that climate change was an "existential threat" and that those who questioned the threat were "troglodytes" in deep denial.[46] He denounced resistance to climate action by red states, congressional Republicans, and, after 2016, the Trump administration.

Brown also embraced his position as a global leader in the fight. Arguing that California and other subnational governments should take independent action in reducing carbon emissions, he engaged in extensive climate diplomacy, forming agreements with blue states and foreign governments to cooperate on climate policy. Brown was hailed around the world as an environmental prophet and policy innovator.

In 2018, in one of his last acts as governor, Brown convened a major conference in San Francisco called the Global Climate Action Summit. He invited policymakers, business leaders, academics, activists, philanthropists, and celebrities from around the world to focus on practical steps that all sectors of society can take to reduce their dependence on carbon-based fuels. On the eve of the summit, Brown revealed the type of effort he had in mind. He signed a bill, SB 100, which requires California to generate all of its electricity from renewable sources by 2045. Under the mandate, the state's utilities were required to obtain 50 percent of their electricity from renewables by 2026, 60 percent by 2030, and 100 percent by 2045. Brown's signature made California the second state, after Hawaii, to set such an ambitious requirement, and by far the largest state to do so.[47]

Converting the world's fifth-largest economy completely to green electricity was already an enormous challenge. But Brown went even further. On the same day, he signed an executive order committing California to total carbon neutrality by 2045.[48] This order was truly radical—the most ambitious climate action goal ever announced by a government of its size. It expanded the commitment to decarbonization beyond electricity generation (only about 15 percent of total CO_2 emissions) to transportation, home heating, agriculture, and more—that is, to sectors that currently produce more than 80 percent of the state's carbon emissions. Brown's executive order contained no enforcement mechanisms and would require future legislation to be effective, but it established an audacious goal to inspire further policy action in the years ahead. Although many in other parts of the country considered these climate policies radical and unachievable, they represented the consensus view of California Democrats. "California is leading the world in dealing with the principal existential threat that humanity faces," Brown said. "What could be a more glorious undertaking?"[49]

During the Obama years, California worked closely with the White House and federal agencies to develop environmental policy, and it frequently intervened to oppose court challenges by Texas and other red states to federal environmental rules. When Trump won the presidency, California's relationship to Washington, D.C., radically changed. The Golden State immediately assumed Texas's former role as the leader of the resistance to federal environmental policy. It repeatedly clashed with the Trump administration on environmental issues, including offshore oil drilling, fracking, energy efficiency standards, and limits on greenhouse gas emissions. Whenever the Trump EPA, Department of Energy, or other agency rolled back an Obama-era environmental regulation or narrowly interpreted a provision of a federal environmental law, California was almost certain to sue. Like Texas before it, California often led a coalition of like-minded states and other allies to resist an administration controlled by the opposing party.

For its part, the Trump administration set its sights directly on California's progressive environmental model. It filed a lawsuit challenging the state's cap-and-trade agreement with Quebec, arguing that it exceeded constitutional limits on state powers; it sought to increase oil drilling, including fracking, within the state's boundaries; and, most consequentially, it dueled with California over motor vehicle fuel efficiency and CO_2 emissions standards.[50]

The Golden State has long sought to use its power under the Clean Air Act to limit automobile greenhouse gas emissions—a critical element in its climate policy. In 2002, the state legislature passed the nation's first bill to limit these emissions and, in 2005, the state applied for a federal waiver to implement its new rules. In 2008, the Bush administration denied the application—the first time the federal government had rejected a California waiver request.[51]

A year later, President Obama took office, and the EPA granted the waiver.[52] California regulators then worked with the EPA, the National Highway Traffic Safety Administration (NHTSA), and the auto industry to develop a set of regulations to reduce smog-causing pollutants and greenhouse gas emissions, mandate the production of more low-emission vehicles (LEVs) and zero emission vehicles (ZEVs), and increase fuel-efficiency standards in a way that harmonized California and federal rules. California and the federal agencies issued the new regulations in 2012. As part of the coordinated program, the NHTSA adopted much stricter Corporate Average Fuel Economy ("CAFE") levels through the 2017–2025 model years. The new standard was formally set at an unadjusted 54.5 miles per gallon (mpg), but with offsets and loopholes, the real figure was closer to 36 mpg. The Obama EPA estimated that the new standards would reduce CO_2 emissions by six billion metric tons over the life of the program.[53] At the same time, the program required the automobile industry to make substantial, expensive changes to its product lines at a time when many consumers preferred heavier, less fuel-efficient trucks and SUVs to lighter, more fuel-efficient vehicles.

When President Trump took office, the new leaders of the EPA declared that the agency would roll back the California-backed Obama-era requirements and instead freeze average fuel economy standards at 2020 levels. In a statement, EPA Administrator Scott Pruitt declared that the agency was "reexamining"

California's authority to set GHG emissions standards above the federal level. "Cooperative federalism doesn't mean that one state can dictate standards for the rest of the country," Pruitt said. "EPA will set a national standard for greenhouse gas emissions that allows auto manufacturers to make cars that people both want and can afford—while still expanding environmental and safety benefits of newer cars. It is in America's best interest to have a national standard."[54] Backed by a coalition of blue states, California quickly filed a lawsuit to block the Trump administration's rollback of the fuel-efficiency standards and to defend California's authority under the Clean Air Act to set GHG emissions rules.[55]

Texas opposed California, and sided with the Trump administration, in the controversy. Governor Greg Abbott wrote a letter, co-signed by the governors of seven other states, to the heads of the EPA and the Department of Transportation stating that the Obama-era rules "create[d] unrealistic fuel economy requirements that President Trump has accurately characterized as industry-killing regulations." The Trump administration policies, he wrote, would free manufacturers from spending "billions of dollars to meet onerous and unnecessary emissions standards imposed by only one of the fifty states."[56]

The conflict soon intensified. In 2019, California state officials held secret talks with representatives of several automakers and persuaded Ford, Honda, Volkswagen, and BMW to meet fuel economy standards that were less ambitious than the Obama-era regulations but more stringent than the Trump administration's proposed rules. Incensed by these back-channel negotiations, Trump and his administration convinced General Motors, Toyota, and Fiat-Chrysler to break with California and the other automakers and support the new, more lenient federal standards. Meanwhile, the administration issued a final regulation revoking California's authority to regulate GHG emissions. California immediately sued to challenge to challenge the regulation and defend its rulemaking authority. The attorneys general of nearly two dozen other states backed California in the lawsuit. Soon thereafter, California announced that it would boycott automakers that sided with the Trump administration in the dispute.[57] California and its allies were thus engaged in a fierce battle to preserve the state's progressive energy and environmental policies.

Struggle for the Nation's Energy Future

The rivals have developed radically different visions of the nation's energy future.

Texas has sought to maximize production of all energy resources and plans to continue developing fossil fuel resources for years to come. It has been especially keen to exploit the bounty of the shale revolution. Texans have taken pride in helping the United States achieve energy independence and have argued that plentiful, cheap energy promotes economic prosperity for the state, the nation, and, indeed, the entire world. By any account, the Lone Star State's high-level energy production and comparatively low energy costs have contributed to its remarkable economic growth. In Texas's view, the progressive project to decarbonize the economy is unrealistic and dangerous. The state fears that aggressive regulatory agendas such as California's climate policies or the Green New Deal would impose heavy costs on industry and consumers and, more, would place environmental regulators in charge of nearly every area of economic life. Many Texans remain unconvinced that climate challenge poses the type of urgent, existential threat that warrants high economic costs and unprecedented levels of government intervention and control. It rejects what it considers heavy-handed federal environmental rules or, worse, standards devised by regulators in California. In the face of criticism that its embrace of carbon fuels is endangering the planet, Texas points to its leadership in renewable energy and argues that the problem of climate change can be managed through market forces, new innovative technologies, and sustainable environmental improvements. In the state's view, climate policies are acceptable only if they respect business, keep costs low, and maintain individual freedom. Texas is confident that the nation's long term energy demands will allow the state to sustain its fossil fuel industry for years to come, even in the face of growing climate activism in other parts of the nation and around the world.

California, by contrast, is more fully convinced that climate change presents an existential threat, and, consistent with its progressive political orientation, has empowered government regulators to fight that threat. The Golden State has been willing to reinvent its economy to run on new energy sources, even if that transition imposes higher costs on businesses and consumers. As California has adopted a growing body of environmental regulations, its residents have been forced to pay higher prices for gasoline, electricity, new home construction, and more. Although policymakers have insisted that businesses and consumers will realize long-term savings by converting to more fuel-efficient alternatives, the short-term costs are substantial and have contributed to the state's widening economic divide. Wealthy Californians have found it easier than struggling middle-class and poor residents to absorb the costs of living in an environmentally friendly state. California has bet that its climate policies will not overly burden its economy, and indeed that its climate strategy will produce long-term economic prosperity. In this view, California's early commitment to developing a green economy will allow it to pay lower compliance costs in the future as other states struggle to catch up. Moreover, by being first movers, its green technology companies will be positioned to dominate the nation's future green economy.

Although the rivals' energy visions have overlapped in some ways, they ultimately are incompatible. Texas's plan for a robust oil- and gas-based energy future cannot survive if the nation adopts a California-style carbon-free regulatory regime, and California's aggressive effort to combat climate change will be futile if the rest of the country, indeed the world, fails to get on board. This incompatibility suggests that the two visions cannot forever coexist within the federal system, and that the outcome of their conflict ultimately depends on which side controls the federal government. The shift from the Obama to Trump administrations showed how deeply the parties have polarized on energy and environmental policies, and highlighted the stakes of federal elections for the nation's energy future. For both Texas and California, and for the nation as a whole, this struggle will help determine the character of the environment, the economy, the scope of government power, and the details of everyday life.

12

Poverty

Millions of Americans live in poverty or on the edge of it. One of the nation's most vexing questions is how best to care for this large group of dispossessed people. Most Americans would agree with the British moralist Samuel Johnson's maxim that "a decent provision for the poor is the true test of civilization" but are divided on what constitutes a decent provision, who should provide it, who should receive it, and on what terms. The debate again falls along left-right ideological lines. Progressives believe that poverty is a social injustice that requires a large-scale government response. In this view, each person is entitled to adequate nutrition, health care, housing, and income, and government should spend whatever it takes to ensure everyone possesses these goods. Conservatives, by contrast, are skeptical of government's ability to lift people from poverty through costly public welfare programs. They distinguish between the "deserving poor" (people who cannot support themselves, through no fault of their own) and those who are "undeserving" (people who can support themselves, but do not). In this view, government anti-poverty programs often perpetuate poverty by fostering dependency and sapping personal responsibility; such programs should instead promote work and assist only those who truly cannot support themselves.

Texas and California again have embodied these polarized positions. Both states are home to many poor people, but have addressed poverty in fundamentally different ways. Texas has taken the conservative approach. The Lone Star State has maintained one of the nation's leanest welfare systems and has provided its poor residents low levels of public assistance. Texas has placed greater reliance on self-help, private charity, and a comparatively low cost of living to help the poor get by. By contrast, California has pursued a progressive approach to poverty alleviation, attempting to offset its high cost of living by offering its poor residents some of the nation's most expansive government-funded health and welfare programs.

This chapter surveys the levels of poverty in Texas and California compared to the nation as a whole, the development of federal poverty alleviation policies, the various ways states can address poverty, and the polarized approaches Texas and California have staked out on these issues.

Texas vs. California. Kenneth P. Miller, Oxford University Press (2020). © Oxford University Press.
DOI: 10.1093/oso/9780190077402.001.0001.

Poverty Overview

Poverty can be defined in various ways. In the 1960s, the federal government created an official definition of poverty based on a person's or a family's ability to buy basic goods. For decades, governments at all levels have used this measure to determine eligibility for anti-poverty programs. This measure focuses on income inadequacy rather than adequacy on the view that, "if it is not possible to state unequivocally 'how much is enough,' it should be possible to assert with confidence how much, on an average, is too little."[1] The key metric is cash income: the government sets income thresholds for individuals and families of different sizes and considers those who fall below the thresholds to be in poverty. The measure excludes several other factors, however, such as taxes and tax credits, non-cash government benefits such as food stamps and housing assistance, and geographic differences in the cost of living. It also does not account for a person's net worth or access to capital, apart from income generating activities. Applying the official thresholds, in 2020, the federal poverty level for an individual was $12,760 and, for a family of four, $26,200. Between 2016 and 2018, an average of approximately thirty-nine million Americans fell below the official poverty line, a number that translated to 12.3 percent of the U.S. population.[2] The nation has never reduced the poverty rate much below that level. The percentage of Americans living in poverty fell sharply during the 1960s—from 22.4 percent in 1959 to 12.2 percent in 1969—but has plateaued ever since (Figure 12.1).[3]

According to the official measure, as of 2018, Texas and California had similar levels of poverty, and the problem was slightly more prevalent in both states than in the nation as a whole. Using three-year averages from 2016–2018, 3.8 million Texans (or 13.7 percent) and 4.9 million Californians (or 12.5 percent) fell below the official line. Of all states, Texas had the thirteenth-highest poverty rate; California was ranked eighteenth.[4]

In 2010, the federal government introduced a more sophisticated calculation called the Supplemental Poverty Measure (SPM) to account for important variations in poor people's economic circumstances. The new formula incorporated items such as tax payments and credits, non-cash government assistance, work-related expenses, child care payments, and the cost of necessities such as food, clothing, housing, and utilities. It also adjusted for geographic differences in housing costs. Although it does not determine eligibility for government assistance programs, the SPM provides a more complete picture of the economic conditions of the poor.

Applying this new poverty measure caused the nation's overall poverty rate to increase, with the number of poor rising in some states and declining in others. Under the SPM, an average of 42.3 million people were living in poverty in the United States between 2016 and 2018, or 13.1 percent of all Americans. During

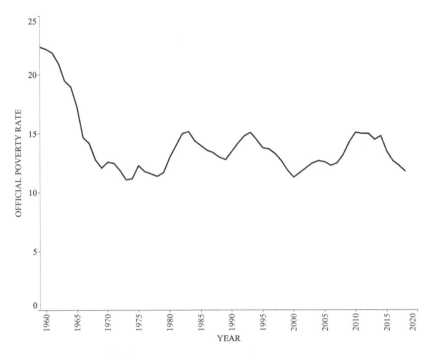

Figure 12.1. U.S. official poverty rate, 1959–2018

Source: U.S. Census Bureau

this period, the SPM caused the number of poor in Texas to rise to 4 million, or 14.2 percent of the state's population. The effect was more pronounced in California, largely due to the state's high cost of living. Based on the SPM, the number of poor Californians increased by nearly 2.2 million, to 7.1 million— which meant that 18.1 percent of the state's residents were living in poverty. According to the SPM, Texas had the eighth-highest poverty rate of any state, while California had, by a substantial margin, the highest.[5]

Another manifestation of poverty is homelessness—a sadly familiar situation in which a person "lacks a fixed, regular, and adequate nighttime residence."[6] Factors that increase the chances of homelessness include mental or physical illness, substance abuse, domestic violence, joblessness, and a shortage of affordable housing. The homeless population is often divided into two groups—the sheltered and unsheltered. Sheltered homeless people are those living in emergency shelters or transitional housing, while the unsheltered are those sleeping in places not intended for human habitation, such as cars, abandoned buildings, or the undersides of bridges. The number of homeless in the United States rose markedly in the 1980s and remains stubbornly large.[7] According to federal estimates, more than half a million Americans (about 568,000) were homeless on any given night in 2019, with more than one-third of them unsheltered.[8]

As of 2019, Texas had a substantial number of homeless people (about 26,000 on any given night), but that number was relatively small in the national context, accounting for less than 5 percent of the total U.S. homeless population. By contrast, according to official reports, more than 151,000 people were homeless in California—nearly six times the number in Texas. By almost any measure, California had the nation's most severe homeless crisis. Even as the number of homeless was declining in other parts of the country, it was increasing in California. The Golden State accounted for more than one-fourth of the nation's homeless population, and, worse, nearly half of the nation's unsheltered homeless. More than two-thirds of California's homeless residents (71.7 percent) were unsheltered, compared to less than half (43.4 percent) in Texas and only 4.4 percent in New York. The problem was particularly acute in California's urban areas, where exceptional wealth was juxtaposed with very visible destitution. According to official counts, nearly sixty thousand homeless people were living in Los Angeles County alone, and more than thirty-five thousand in the San Francisco Bay Area.[9] The state's homeless problem had persisted for years but now was becoming dire. As homelessness spread and human waste and dirty needles accumulated on the streets, public health officials compared San Francisco and Los Angeles to third world cities and issued warnings about the spread of typhus, tuberculosis, and other "medieval diseases" in encampments and shelters throughout the state.[10] Many of the causes of homelessness are present everywhere, and experts sought to explain why the problem was so much greater in California than in other parts of the nation. Some pointed to the state's temperate climate, which allowed people to live on the streets year-round. Others argued that the state's progressive tolerance for the homeless made it a magnet for that population. But most blamed the state's shortage of affordable housing, which had reached a point of crisis.

Federal Anti-Poverty Programs

For much of its history, the nation embraced the doctrine of self-help, relying primarily on a private safety net of family, churches, and charitable organizations to care for those who could not support themselves. Through the early twentieth century, public assistance was rare, flowing mainly to military veterans and indigent mothers.[11] It took the trauma of the Great Depression to persuade many Americans that self-reliance and private acts of kindness would not always suffice, and that government had a responsibility to ensure basic economic security for all. During the New Deal era, President Franklin D. Roosevelt and Congress created universal programs, such as the Social Security retirement system, to cover the vast majority of citizens, and other programs, such as Aid to the Blind (ATB) and Aid for Dependent Children (ADC) (later renamed Aid for Families with Dependent Children, or AFDC), for those with more specific needs.[12]

In the 1960s, the federal government greatly expanded aid to the poor. In his 1964 State of the Union address, President Lyndon Johnson presented an expansive vision of an "all-out war on human poverty" and called for a joint federal-state effort to "pursue poverty . . . wherever it exists," with the aim "not only to relieve the symptom of poverty, but to cure it, and above all, to prevent it."[13] Johnson aggressively waged this war. He signed legislation establishing the Office of Economic Opportunity, which administered new anti-poverty programs such as Head Start, Job Corps, and VISTA; approved a bill permanently establishing the federal food stamps program; and, most consequentially, signed legislation introducing government-run health care in the form of Medicare and Medicaid. Like Social Security, Medicare was funded largely through employee payroll deductions and employer contributions, with benefits flowing to older Americans regardless of need. Medicaid, by contrast, was a means-tested welfare program. It would provide taxpayer-funded health care to the categories of poor people many considered the most "deserving," including impoverished children and their parents, blind or disabled persons, and seniors.[14]

Other federal anti-poverty programs soon followed, including the Child Nutrition Act (1966), which expanded federal school lunch programs and launched school breakfast programs for low-income students; Supplemental Security Income (SSI) (1972), which provided additional cash assistance to low-income elderly, disabled, and blind persons; and the federal Earned Income Tax Credit (EITC) (1975), which offered cash assistance to low- and moderate-income working people. At the same time, AFDC expanded rapidly, doubling its caseload from five to ten million from 1967 to 1971. During the Great Society years, federal anti-poverty efforts received considerable bipartisan support. Congress approved the 1965 bill to establish Medicare and Medicaid, for example, by a 313–115 vote in the House of Representatives and a 68–21 vote in the Senate, with many Republicans joining the Democratic majority in launching these programs.[15]

As enthusiasm for the war on poverty faded, views of federal anti-poverty programs divided more sharply along partisan lines. During the 1980s and 1990s, Republicans became more united in their critique of these programs, with many contending that welfare often had the perverse effect of fostering dependency and thus perpetuating poverty. The GOP's main target was AFDC. In its early days, this program had supported a modest number of recipients, but over time its caseload grew dramatically. After the surge of the 1960s, it continued to expand. Between 1989 and 1994, the number of households receiving AFDC increased by one-third, and many believed that the program was out of control. Think tanks and elected officials developed various proposals to transform the existing welfare system by imposing work requirements and time limits for those receiving AFDC benefits. After Republicans gained control of Congress in 1994, they introduced legislation to dismantle AFDC and replace it with a program called Temporary Assistance for Needy Families (TANF). Among other changes, TANF required aid recipients to work within two years and placed a five-year time limit on aid. A central goal of this reform was to "end the dependence of needy parents on government benefits by promoting job preparation, work, and marriage."[16] The reform also cut off federal welfare benefits to recent immigrants. Some moderate Democrats supported the legislation, but many progressives strenuously objected, arguing that it would put vulnerable people at risk. One leading Democrat called opposition to the welfare reform bill a "crucial moral litmus test."[17] President Bill Clinton vetoed two versions of the bill, but eventually signed the Personal Responsibility and Work Opportunity Reconciliation Act in the summer of 1996.[18]

After President Obama's election in 2008, partisan division over federal anti-poverty programs deepened. The main struggle centered on the Patient Protection and Affordable Care Act of 2010, also known as the PPACA or ACA or, more commonly, "Obamacare." The ACA's central goal was to expand health care coverage to the uninsured, especially to those who could not otherwise afford it. One of the act's primary strategies for achieving that end was Medicaid expansion.

Back in the 1960s, Congress had designed Medicaid to be a hybrid federal-state program that states would be encouraged, but not required, to join. Under the system, the federal government would set minimum eligibility rules and provide half or more of the funding, depending on the state's income; states would contribute their own funds and administer the program on the ground. If a state chose to buy in, it would receive large infusions of federal money to help pay for health care for the poor, but, in return, would need to contribute a substantial amount of its own funds and abide by minimum program standards. Participating states were required to extend Medicaid coverage to those already eligible to receive public assistance—that is, poor children and families, seniors, the blind, and the disabled—but in the early years had much discretion to determine who was medically needy and the scope of their coverage. The federal matching rate, known as Federal Medical Assistance Percentage (FMAP), varied from state to state based on state personal income. Wealthier states would receive the minimum federal match of 50 percent of all costs; poorer states, a larger match, up to a maximum of 83 percent. In late 2019, the federal government set Fiscal Year 2020–2021 matching rates at the minimum 50 percent for California and at 61.81 percent for Texas (near the national median).

Although states could not reduce Medicaid coverage or benefits below the federal baseline, they could voluntarily expand them. Thus, in addition to mandated services, states could choose to cover selected optional services including dental care, prescription drugs, eyeglasses, physical therapy, and hospice care, and could expand coverage to include groups such as pregnant women, infants, and children in families with incomes above 138 percent of the federal poverty level. (Later on, some of this coverage became mandatory.) Congress placed no cap on federal Medicaid matching grants, thus giving states an incentive to increase their own Medicaid spending. The Medicaid financing plan became the nation's most generous federal matching grant program.[19]

Nearly all states signed up for the Medicaid program within four years of its enactment, with California joining in 1966 and Texas in 1967. (The last holdout, Arizona, entered the Medicaid system in 1982.) State and federal spending on Medicaid grew dramatically as Congress and some individual states gradually expanded eligibility to include new groups and as health care costs increased. In time, Medicaid bypassed Medicare as the nation's largest health care plan in terms of the number of people covered. It also became one of the largest categories of both state and federal spending and accounted for more than half of all federal transfers to the states.[20]

After Democrats gained unified control of the White House and Congress in 2009, President Obama and his Democratic congressional allies proposed the boldest expansion of Medicaid in its history. They sought to move beyond the old eligibility categories and extend Medicaid coverage to most low-income adults (those who made 138 percent of the official federal poverty line or below), regardless of whether they had dependent children or some other special need. To encourage state buy-in, the bill provided that the federal government would initially pick up 100 percent of the costs of newly eligible recipients, tapering down to 90 percent by 2020.

The Medicaid expansion plan polarized the nation. Most Democrats supported the plan because it would extend the health care safety net to large numbers of low-income people, but most Republicans rose in opposition, arguing that the plan would dangerously expand government, put it in charge of a larger share of the nation's health care system, and effectively force states to buy in. The last point galvanized red state governments. State participation in Medicaid had always been voluntary; now Congress and the president threatened to take away *all* of a state's Medicaid funding unless it signed up for expansion—a provision that the Supreme Court would later strike down.[21] In 2010, Congress approved the ACA and its Medicaid expansion plan along near-perfect party lines. Every Democratic senator and nearly all Democratic representatives supported the final version of the bill; not a single Republican in either chamber voted "aye."[22]

Soon after President Obama signed the ACA into law, California and almost every other blue state signed up for Medicaid expansion, while most red states, including Texas, declared they would seek to opt out. Over the next several years, however, eight of these states (most of which were red) decided to buy into the expansion program—between 2015 and 2019, Montana, Alaska, Louisiana, Maine, Virginia, Utah, Idaho, and Nebraska opted in. In four of these states (Maine, Idaho, Nebraska, and Utah), citizens adopted Medicaid expansion directly through their state's initiative process. As of 2019, fourteen states, again including Texas, continued to hold out.[23] Overall by 2017, 12.7 million newly eligible people enrolled in the program, and by March 2019 Medicaid covered about sixty-six million Americans, or one-fifth of the nation. In Fiscal Year 2019, the program spent approximately $613 billion in federal and state funds, excluding administrative costs (Figure 12.2).[24]

The struggle over Medicaid expansion highlighted the complexity of anti-poverty policy within the federal system. When the federal government fully funds welfare programs, such as Supplemental Security Income (SSI) and the Supplemental Nutrition Assistance Program (SNAP), benefits are distributed fairly evenly across the nation. But the scope of jointly funded federal and state welfare programs, such as Medicaid, the State Supplementary Payment (SSP), Temporary Assistance for Needy Families (TANF), and the Children's Health Insurance Program (CHIP), vary greatly from state to state.[25] Red states often

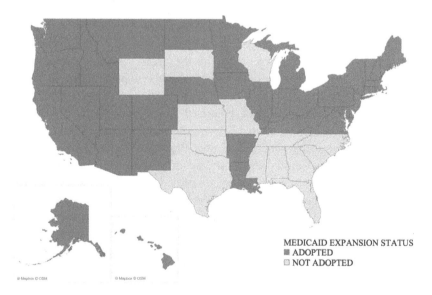

MEDICAID EXPANSION STATUS
■ ADOPTED
☐ NOT ADOPTED

Figure 12.2. State adoption of Medicaid expansion, 2019
Source: Henry J. Kaiser Family Foundation

seek to limit these programs by opting out, tightening eligibility requirements, and restricting benefits, while blue states generally opt in, loosen eligibility requirements, and expand benefits.

Texas

Texas's conservative political culture has naturally compelled the Lone Star State to lead the nation in opposing large-scale welfare programs. Many Texans believe that the best way to help the poor is by keeping the cost of living low, promoting job creation, and encouraging private charity. Public assistance programs, in this view, undermine core values of independence, self-reliance, personal responsibility, and small government. Indeed, Texas is so committed to this position that it has embedded welfare limitations in its constitution.[26] It should be noted, however, that the state's attitude toward welfare depends in part on the program's funding mechanisms. Texas is most hostile to federal programs that require it to spend its own money, on the view that federal mandates threaten the state's sovereignty and its model of low taxes and limited government. Conversely, Texas mounts little opposition when the federal government picks up the tab.

Consider SNAP, the food subsidy program. The federal government provides nearly all of the funding for this program and, without objection, Texas has distributed SNAP benefits liberally—indeed to a higher percentage of residents than has California.[27] But when a program requires substantial state contributions, Texas has dug in its heels. The Temporary Assistance for Needy Families (TANF) program provides a ready example. As a joint federal-state program that requires partial state funding, TANF budgets, coverage, and benefit levels have varied widely across the nation. Texas's TANF spending has consistently ranked near rock bottom.[28] As of Fiscal Year 2018, Texas contributed about $400 million to the program and the combined federal-state TANF outlay in Texas was just over $860 million, well below the population-adjusted spending in most other states. Moreover, the federal government has given states wide latitude in deciding how to spend federal TANF funds. Texas has distributed only about 6 percent of its TANF budget to "basic assistance"—that is, cash grants to poor families—and instead has routed most of the funds to work training programs, pre-kindergarten education, child protective services, and the like. Indeed, in 2016–2017, Texas distributed TANF cash payments to fewer than twenty-five thousand low-income families with children—that is, only about 4 percent of such families, compared with 23 percent nationally and 65 percent in California. Moreover, Texas's average benefit level was about $290 per month, again among the nation's lowest.[29]

The Lone Star State's reluctance to spend heavily on health and welfare programs can be witnessed elsewhere, especially in its long resistance to Medicaid expansion. The state's rejection of that expansion was rooted in its fear of Medicaid's long-term costs. Even without expansion, the Medicaid program was one of the largest areas of state spending. The legislature allocated about $12.6 billion per year in state funds for Medicaid for the 2020–2021 biennium—more than one-fifth of all general fund outlays, second only to public education.[30]

Some Texans have wondered whether their state would be better off exiting from Medicaid altogether and funding health care for the poor on its own. In November 2010, Governor Rick Perry floated a proposal for the state to withdraw from the Medicaid system. Doctors, hospital administrators, and others quickly objected, arguing that turning away billions of dollars each year in traditional Medicaid funding would devastate the Texas health care system. State agencies reported that withdrawing from Medicaid could cause up to 2.6 million Texans to lose health care coverage and that such a massive change would cost more than it would save.[31] Perry quickly dropped the idea of withdrawing completely from Medicaid, but he and other Texas officials refused to relent in their attack on the ACA and Medicaid expansion.

Months earlier, just hours after President Obama signed the ACA, Texas and twelve other states filed a challenge to the new law in a federal court in Florida. In time, twenty-six (mostly Republican) states joined the case, titled *Florida v. U.S. Department of Health and Human Services*, which later was consolidated with *National Federation of Independent Business (NFIB) v. Sebelius*.[32] As the fight worked its way to the U.S. Supreme Court, many blue states, including California, filed briefs defending the landmark law. Suspense built until the end of June 2012, when a divided Supreme Court announced its ruling. In a series of opinions, the Court upheld most of the ACA, but, by a 7–2 vote, sided with Florida, Texas, and the other red state parties on the Medicaid expansion issue. Chief Justice John Roberts reasoned that Congress's plan to convince states to opt in to Medicaid expansion was "much more than 'relatively mild encouragement'—it [was] a gun to the head."[33] That is, it was an unconstitutional exercise of coercive power against the states, and thus void.

Shortly after the ruling, Texas announced that it would, indeed, opt out of Medicaid expansion. In a scathing letter to HHS Secretary Kathleen Sebelius, Governor Rick Perry declared:

> Now that the "gun to the head" has been removed, please relay this message to the President: I oppose . . . the expansion of Medicaid as provided in the Patient Protection and Affordable Care Act. I stand proudly with the growing chorus of governors who reject the PPACA power grab. Thank God and our nation's founders that we have the right to do so. [The plan would] make Texas a mere

appendage of the federal government when it comes to health care.... Through its proposed expansion of Medicaid, the PPACA would simply enlarge a broken system that is already financially unsustainable. Expanding [Medicaid] would only exacerbate the failure of the current system, and would threaten even Texas with financial ruin. [The law's] unsound encroachments will find no foothold here.[34]

In the governor's view, Medicaid expansion threatened the state's sovereignty and the Texas Model itself. The day that Perry announced Texas would not participate in the program, he appeared on Fox News to defend the state's decision.

We're just not going to be a part of socializing health care in Texas.... Every Texan has healthcare in this state, from the standpoint of being able to have access to healthcare—every Texan has that. How we pay for it, and how we deliver it, should be our decision—not some bureaucrat in Washington, D.C., that may have never been to Texas a day in their life. If the federal government is serious about working with the states and finding solutions to the healthcare needs, what they would do is block grant those dollars back to the states. I can assure you that Texas and other states would find more effective, efficient ways to deliver healthcare to their citizens and do it in a way that preserves those individuals' freedom.[35]

After President Obama left office, Texas continued to attack the ACA. Texas Republicans backed the 2017 federal tax reform provision that repealed the ACA's individual mandate, and, thereafter, filed yet another lawsuit, titled *Texas v. United States*, seeking to overturn the federal health care law altogether. Led by Texas, eighteen Republican attorneys general, two governors, and private plaintiffs argued that the individual mandate was an essential element of the law, and when Congress repealed the mandate, the rest of the law became unconstitutional.[36] As the litigation worked its way through the federal courts, the rest of the ACA, including Medicaid expansion, survived—but Texas continued to refuse to buy in.

To be sure, many Texans attacked the state's position. First, critics argued that the decision to opt out of Medicaid expansion cemented Texas's dubious distinction as the nation's leader in residents with no health care coverage.[37] As of 2018, the rate of uninsured remained 17.7 percent in Texas—double the national figure of 8.9 percent.[38] All told, about five million Texas residents still lacked health care coverage, the most of any state. As Governor Perry noted, even without insurance, Texans were able to receive at least some medical care—in part because federal law required hospitals that receive Medicare funding to provide treatment to people suffering medical emergencies as well as pregnant women in labor, regardless of their ability to pay.[39] Yet the critics contended that this ad hoc system of health care was unstable and, further, that people who were forced to rely on it received little or no preventive care and thus tended to have worse health outcomes than the insured. They also argued that Texas's choice to reject Medicaid expansion left on the table billions of federal dollars that the state could have used to subsidize health care for the poor and to cover otherwise uncompensated health care costs. In this view, it made no sense for Texas to refuse a deal whereby the federal government initially paid 100 percent of the costs and 90 percent after 2020.

The state's conservative leaders continued to balk because they believed that buying in to Medicaid expansion would soon put Texas on the hook for billions of additional dollars in mandated Medicaid spending. In 2009, Governor Perry had similarly turned away the federal government's offer to send Texas more than $500 million in stimulus money to help fund unemployment insurance (UI). Perry refused because the offer would have required Texas to expand the program's eligibility and coverage. "If this money expands entitlements, we will not accept it," he said. "This is exactly how addicts get hooked on drugs."[40] He and other Texas leaders felt the same way about Medicaid expansion.

California

California has taken a radically different view of government's responsibility to the poor. The Golden State is committed to marshaling public resources to alleviate poverty, consistent with its progressive belief that government has a moral duty to care for the poor and is well positioned to do so. In the early twenty-first century, however, the challenge became more acute because the state's rising housing, utility, and other basic expenses made it hard for many to get by. California's high cost of living—40 percent higher than the national average—ate away at all residents' incomes and harmed the poor the most. For many, rent was the hardest bill to pay. By 2019, more than half of all renters in the state, or nearly three million Californians, were rent-burdened, meaning they paid more than 30 percent of their incomes toward rent, while nearly one-third were severely rent-burdened, meaning that rent ate up more than half of their incomes.[41]

Moreover, as California transitioned to the New Economy, many of its traditional blue-collar jobs disappeared, and poorly educated, low-skilled residents struggled to find work that would pay their bills. Unlike Texas, which has sought to fight poverty primarily by incentivizing work and keeping living costs low, California has compensated for its high costs by expanding government support. The state's strong coalition of social justice liberals, public sector unions, and other welfare advocates has reinforced this commitment to using government resources to provide for those in need.

California's dedication to public welfare programs has grown over time. Although the state never opposed welfare in the Texas manner, its spending on public assistance has gone through ups and downs. During the late 1960s and early 1970s, Governor Ronald Reagan advocated controversial cuts to welfare programs; in the 1990s, Governor Pete Wilson actively pursued welfare reform; and in various times of fiscal crisis, lawmakers have chosen to close budget gaps in part by reducing welfare spending. As California has shifted to the left, however, it has stepped up its commitment to government action on behalf of the poor. In his January 2019 inaugural address, Governor Gavin Newsom underscored this commitment when he compared the state to a home where everyone would be cared for. "In our home," he said,

> every child should be loved, fed, and safe. We will support parents so they can give their kids the love and care they need. . . . In our home, no one should live in constant fear of eviction or spend their whole paycheck to keep a roof overhead. We will launch a Marshall Plan for affordable housing and lift up the fight against homelessness from a local matter to a state-wide mission. In our home, every person should have access to quality, affordable health care. Faraway judges and politicians may try to turn back our progress. But we will never waver in our pursuit of guaranteed health care for all Californians.[42]

In his first budget, Newsom backed up his rhetoric by proposing large spending increases on health and welfare programs that were eagerly accepted by the legislature.

Newsom's agenda built on the state government's existing large-scale poverty alleviation efforts, which could be seen in welfare caseload and spending data. According to the U.S. Department of Health and Human Services, for example, California already had by far the nation's largest TANF caseload in both absolute and percentage terms, with approximately 700,000 individual recipients as of March 2019 (Table 12.1). To put that number in perspective, California was home to more than one-third of the nation's TANF recipients, more than *fourteen times* the number of recipients in Texas. The combined federal and state TANF spending in California was $6.6 billion—again, by far the most of any state. Measured another way, as of 2017, California provided benefits to sixty-five of every 100 low-income families with children, compared with the rate across the nation (twenty-three of 100) and in Texas (four of 100).[43] California's TANF caseload was so large in part because the state maintains comparatively liberal eligibility requirements. Unlike many other states, California often provides

Table 12.1 Number of TANF Recipients (March 2019)

State (Rank)	Number of Recipients
United States (All States)	2,008,195
California (1)	698,524
New York (2)	190,283
Texas (7)	48,077

Source: U.S. Department of Health and Human Services, Office of Family Assistance

benefits to children even after the parent or other adult caregiver fails to meet the program's work requirements or reaches the two-year time limit for cash aid.[44]

In addition to spending heavily on TANF benefits to needy families, California pursued a range of other poverty alleviation programs. Among other efforts, it adopted its own Earned Income Tax Credit (CalEITC) to supplement the federal version of this income subsidy program, extended benefits to undocumented immigrants through its CalFresh nutrition assistance program and its Cash Assistance Program for Immigrants (CAPI), and authorized billions of state and local dollars to assist its large homeless population.[45]

California's progressive approach to poverty alleviation can be seen most clearly in its efforts to provide health care for the poor. During the early 2000s, the state explored ambitious plans to expand that coverage, and when Congress enacted the ACA in 2010, the state was eager to jump on board. Even as it helped form the blue state *amicus* coalition defending the ACA in federal court, California quickly became a national leader in both establishing a state health care exchange, called Covered California, and enrolling newly eligible residents in the state's Medicaid program, known as Medi-Cal.[46] In 2011, before Medicaid expansion took effect, California was spending about $43 billion on Medi-Cal—more than $17 billion of which came from state funds. Between 2011 and 2018, the budget for the Medi-Cal program, including Medicare expansion, surged to more than $100 billion. The federal government picked up almost two-thirds of of the tab, but the state's costs were rising as well. During this brief period, Medi-Cal enrollments grew from 8.5 million to 12.9 million residents, or nearly one-third of all Californians.[47] This caseload increase exceeded most projections and highlighted the large number of Californians living in poverty. Despite the program's rapid growth, however, nearly three million Californians (7 percent of the state's residents) remained uninsured. Nearly two-thirds of them (63 percent) were Latino, nearly 40 percent were noncitizens, and about half lived in households with incomes below 200 percent of the official federal poverty line (Figure 12.3).[48]

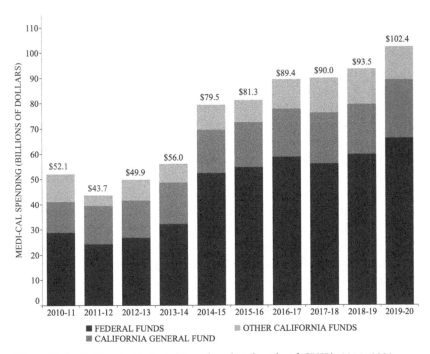

Figure 12.3. California Medi-Cal Spending (Medicaid and CHIP), 2011–2020

Sources: California State Budgets 2010–2011 through 2019–2020, California Legislative Analyst

Note: 2019–2020 projected and subject to change.

The state greatly desired to cover uninsured residents, and lawmakers recognized that achieving this goal required extending Medi-Cal to low-income immigrants regardless of their legal status. In 2015, the legislature began that process by providing full-scope Medi-Cal benefits to undocumented immigrants age 18 and under who met the program's income eligibility rules. Through this move, California became only the fifth state to provide such benefits, joining New York, Illinois, Massachusetts, and Washington as well as the District of Columbia. Because Congress does not provide Medicaid matching funds for immigrants unlawfully in the country, California had to pay the full expense of this program, a considerable sum because the state was home to the nation's largest population of young immigrants who lacked legal status.[49] Many Democrats in the legislature argued that California should extend Medi-Cal to all low-income undocumented immigrants, regardless of age—a commitment that would cost the state an additional estimated $3 billion per year. In 2019, California moved further in that direction by extending eligibility to those who are age twenty-five or under. In early 2020, Governor Newsom proposed extending Medi-Cal coverage to low-income, undocumented seniors.[50]

California's aggressive implementation of the ACA marked its short-term strategy to achieve universal coverage, but many progressives pushed for a more comprehensive, permanent solution: a single-payer system. Under the single-payer model, the state would guarantee universal health coverage for all residents; taxes would replace patient premiums, co-pays, and deductibles to cover costs; and state administrators, rather than multiple public and private insurers, would manage the entire system. In 2017, the state's most powerful and activist health care union, the California Nurses Association, backed a bill to introduce a single-payer health system in California. Fiscal analysts estimated that this program would cost $400 billion a year to operate—an eye-popping figure that was more than twice the amount of the entire state budget.[51] If California could convince the federal government to redirect all Medicare, Medicaid, and other federal health care funding to the state's single-payer program (which was far from certain), the federal subsidy would offset about one-half of the program's cost. But that would still mean the state would need to raise $200 billion per year in additional tax revenues. To put the challenge in context, the state's *total* tax revenue at the time was well below that amount.[52] Despite these daunting cost obstacles, the state senate approved the single-payer bill on a near-exact party line vote. However, the Assembly Speaker, Democrat Anthony Rendon, refused to advance the bill. Rendon argued that the single-payer bill was "woefully incomplete," in part because it did not identify taxes or other revenues that would pay for its massive costs.[53] Progressives lashed out at Rendon. The nurses union called his decision a "cowardly act," and the Progressive Caucus of the State Democratic Party called it a "clear example of moral cowardice."[54] For many California Democrats, single-payer health care had become a moral imperative and a litmus test issue—regardless of the cost.

In his 2018 campaign for governor, Gavin Newsom repeatedly endorsed a single-payer system. In a speech to fifteen hundred members of the state's nurses union, Newsom said, "There's no reason to wait around on universal healthcare and single-payer in California. . . . If we can't get it done next year, you have my firm and absolute commitment as your next governor that I will lead the effort to get it done. We will have universal health care in the state of California."[55] In January 2019, on his first day in office, Newsom issued a letter to President Trump and congressional leaders seeking the federal approvals California would need to adopt the model. "Empower States like mine to design and implement truly transformative solutions for securing affordable health care for all," Newsom wrote. "I ask that you amend federal law to enable States to apply for and receive [waivers] empowering California to truly innovate and to begin transformative reforms that provide the path to a single–payer health care system."[56] President Trump and Congress were unmoved.

Competing Poverty Policy Models

Federal statistics on total welfare spending highlight how differently the rivals address poverty. Each year, the U.S. Census Bureau publishes a comprehensive survey of the finances of every state in the Union, broken down by category. The survey's "public welfare" category captures how much each state spends on Medicaid, TANF, SSP, and other public assistance programs for low-income residents, taking into account the expenditure of both state and federal dollars. According to that measure, in 2017, the fifty state governments together spent $680 billion on public welfare. Texas spent $38 billion of state and federal money on welfare programs, while California spent $124 billion—nearly 3.3 times the expenditure of the Lone Star State.[57] Moreover, these figures may further diverge as Texas fights to limit its spending on Medicaid and other means-tested programs while California expands benefits to low-income undocumented immigrants, increases overall spending on welfare programs, and seeks to introduce health care coverage for all.

Texas has emphatically demonstrated its resistance to expanding the welfare state. In its view, government should assist the poor by fostering a robust economy that incentivizes work and keeps costs low, and should distribute public assistance sparingly, as a last resort, to those who cannot support themselves. Conversely, California increasingly has embraced large-scale welfare spending with the view that government has a moral duty to provide for the basic needs of all—even if that means its taxpayers must shoulder enormous costs.

Once again, the rivals' visions are competing for dominance in the federal system; their ultimate fates rest, in large part, on federal policy. Texas will have great difficulty maintaining a lean system of low taxes and limited government if the federal government creates mandates requiring it to spend heavily on health and welfare programs. At the same time, despite its great wealth, California cannot hope to realize its vision of a comprehensive welfare state—and especially a health care system based on the single-payer model—without the federal government's support and financial backing.

13

Social Issues

Finally, we turn to the nation's culture wars.

Many controversies have divided red and blue America, but none more profoundly than social and cultural issues. And, as we might expect, Texas and California have led the opposing sides of the struggle. Social issues have led to "war" because they tap into deeply held values. As we saw in Chapter 5, Texas and other red states have embraced conservative value systems; California and other blue states hold progressive cultural views. These different ways of seeing the world have pushed the rival camps to take opposite positions on a long list of social issues, including abortion, marriage, drugs, gun ownership, the treatment of immigrants, affirmative action, LGBT rights, and options for end-of-life care. Such issues resist political compromise because they cut to the heart of identity, religious and ethical commitments, and other core values.

Both left and right have been drawn to social issues like moths to a flame. Beginning in the 1960s, many on the left came to see politics as a means of achieving not only economic redistribution but also cultural revolution—that is, overturning traditional customs, hierarchies, and authorities and replacing them with new, more enlightened values and social arrangements. Although the left was still concerned with economic policy, it increasingly sought to use politics to advance sexual liberation, feminism, gay and lesbian rights, racial diversity, and multiculturalism, among other social goals.

As these movements gained traction, social conservatives came to believe that many of their most cherished values were under threat and needed to be defended. For the cultural right, politics was no longer merely an economic contest about "who gets what," but rather a deeper, existential conflict—a "religious war"—about "who we are," "what we believe," and "what we stand for as Americans." In short, it was a "cultural war . . . for the soul of America."[1]

Left and right have fought the culture wars on multiple fronts—in national elections, in the federal courts, and also, repeatedly, in the states. Texas and California have brought their heavy artillery to the battle. This chapter provides a conceptual overview of how both sides have engaged in this conflict by focusing on how they have framed the issues in terms of rights and have chosen different institutional venues to achieve their goals. It then discusses how Texas and California have made their divergent cultural values part of their respective governing models.

Texas vs. California. Kenneth P. Miller, Oxford University Press (2020). © Oxford University Press.
DOI: 10.1093/oso/9780190077402.001.0001.

The Power of Rights in the Culture Wars

Over the past several decades, the nation's culture wars have developed discernable patterns. Perhaps most significant, many of the battles have turned into contests over rights. Typically, activists on one side of a social policy conflict have argued that their interest should be recognized as a right, while those on the other side have resisted this definition. Usually (but not always) progressives have been the ones claiming a right.

To take one example, in the 1990s, a progressive social movement emerged to allow terminally ill persons to end their lives with a physician's assistance. Proponents of "physician-assisted death," or "aid-in-dying," argued that one has a valid interest in determining the circumstances of one's death, especially when facing a terminal illness and a painful end-of-life. At the time, the laws of every state prohibited physicians (or anyone else) from helping a person commit suicide, and no court had recognized a "right to die."[2] Proponents argued that aid-in-dying was a compassionate policy—and, more, that it was a fundamental right intimately connected to one's personal autonomy and dignity. Social conservatives resisted, arguing that creating a right to physician-assisted death would lead to coercion of the weak and, more broadly, would erode legal protection of human life—especially the lives of those who were the most socially inconvenient. As in many controversies of its type, the proponents did not confine their efforts to the legislative process, but instead turned to the courts for a ruling that death with dignity was not only an important interest, but also a protected right.

Advocates of "death with dignity" filed a case in federal court in Washington State asserting that the state's prohibition violated rights protected by the federal Constitution. The lower federal courts agreed that the Constitution protects an individual's right to assistance in hastening death.[3] After these early rounds, the proponents were on the cusp of winning a new right that would prohibit laws banning physician-assisted suicide. However, in *Washington v. Glucksberg* (1997), the U.S. Supreme Court blocked the effort by ruling that the federal Constitution does *not* protect a "right to die." Instead, the Court held that the legality of assisted death is a matter of normal politics—that is, a policy question for state lawmakers to decide.[4]

In the years that followed, several blue states—California, Colorado, Hawaii, Maine, New Jersey, Oregon, Vermont, and Washington—adopted aid-in-dying laws.[5] However, most states—including Texas and the great bloc of red states—continued to ban the practice. These divergent outcomes demonstrated the differences between red and blue state values as well as the power of rights in the development of social policy. If the U.S. Supreme Court had held that the federal Constitution protects a right to aid-in-dying, the practice would have been available everywhere in the nation. Because it did not, prohibitions remain in place in most parts of the country, most firmly in red states. It is evident, then, why adversaries in the culture wars frequently fight over the definition of rights.

Although the U.S. Supreme Court refused to recognize a "right to die," it has bestowed the status of right on other interests across a range of social policies. Most of these decisions have advanced progressive conceptions of rights, such as a right to use contraceptives, a broad right to abortion, a right of same-sex couples to marry, a right of undocumented immigrants to attend public schools, and a right of women to attend historically all-male state universities.[6] On a few occasions, the Court has advanced rights favored by social conservatives, such as a personal right to bear arms and a right to religious exemption from various legal mandates.[7]

As these examples demonstrate, state-level cultural battles are fought under two alternative conditions—either the Supreme Court has recognized a right, or it has not. The nature of the battle is quite different under the two conditions.

When the Supreme Court Has Recognized a Right

On occasions when the U.S. Supreme Court has recognized a federal constitutional right, states have reacted in a number of ways. Resistant states have sometimes taken actions that conflict with the right in order to test its scope and durability. Conversely, states that support the right have often sought to expand its reach.

The Supreme Court's decision in *Roe v. Wade* elicited both types of responses. When the Court issued the landmark decision in 1973, the nation had not yet polarized on abortion and few expected the case would become one of the most divisive in the nation's history.[8] Indeed, some hoped that the decision would settle abortion policy once and for all. To say the least, those hopes were not realized. Instead, the Court's ruling mobilized the religious right, added fuel to the culture wars, and contributed to partisan division across the nation.[9] Conservative states tested the Court's commitment to *Roe* by enacting a raft of abortion restrictions, including requirements for spousal and parental notification, informed consent rules, waiting periods, bans on government funding for abortion, and more. Progressive states countered by reinforcing and expanding *Roe*'s protections at the state level. Eventually, restrictive state laws forced the Court to reassess *Roe*. In *Planned Parenthood v. Casey* (1992), the Court held that states could regulate abortion, but only if they did not impose an "undue burden" on the woman's constitutional right.[10]

In the post-*Casey* period, conflict over abortion persisted. Texas and other red states tested *Casey*'s limits by adopting more exacting regulations on abortion, while California and other blue states rallied to defend abortion rights. In 2015, a case called *Whole Woman's Health v. Hellerstedt* reached the Supreme Court, challenging new Texas regulations on abortion providers.[11] In all, two-thirds of the states signed briefs in the case, with their positions falling almost exactly along red-blue partisan lines. Twenty-four states filed a brief backing the Texas law, while California and eleven other states urged the Court to strike it down.[12] In a 2016 decision, the Court also split along ideological lines—by a 5–3 vote, it invalidated the Texas regulations, ruling that they constituted an undue burden on a woman's right to choose.

After President Trump and the Republican Senate placed two new conservative justices, Neil Gorsuch and Brett Kavanaugh, on the Court in 2017 and 2018, a number of red states saw an opportunity to press their fight against *Roe*. In 2019, they enacted laws prohibiting abortion (with limited exceptions) at early stages of pregnancy, thus setting up further tests of the federal right to abortion.[13] By contrast, nearly all blue states had laws on the books that would protect abortion rights if *Roe* were overturned; in 2019, several of them—including Illinois, Maine, Nevada, New York, Rhode Island, and Vermont—moved to strengthen these protections.[14]

The pattern was clear—the war over abortion policy centered on the federal right established in *Roe* (as modified by *Casey*), and states sorted ideologically in the battle over that right. Red states worked to eliminate the right, while blue states tenaciously defended it.

A similar pattern could be seen on another front in the culture wars: the national struggle over gun regulations. For many decades, it was unclear, as a matter of federal constitutional interpretation, whether the Second Amendment protected an individual right to keep and bear arms—and, if so, whether that right was enforceable against state governments. The U.S. Supreme Court answered those questions in the affirmative in *District of Columbia v. Heller* (2008) and *McDonald v. Chicago* (2010).[15] In the wake of those decisions, California and other blue states tested the right by enacting new restrictions on gun ownership. By contrast, Texas and other red states countered with new laws that expanded the right at the state level.

When the Supreme Court Has Not Recognized a Right

In other situations—as in the aid-in-dying example—the U.S. Supreme Court has declined to recognize a right. Yet, because rights carry so much symbolic and legal power, activists have often persisted in their efforts to establish the right, many times by turning to the states. As Justice William Brennan observed, state constitutions can be a "font of individual liberties" that extend beyond federal constitutional protections.[16] Each state constitution has its own rights provisions, and courts can interpret those rights broadly. State courts have expanded rights in a number of areas, including public funding for abortion, equality in school funding, voting rights, free speech, and, most commonly, protections for criminal defendants.[17] Courts in California and other blue states have done so aggressively; courts in red states, including Texas, more sparingly.[18]

The states' ability to establish rights became a critical feature of one of the largest cultural clashes of the past generation—the contest over the definition of marriage. In a 1972 case called *Baker v. Nelson*, the U.S. Supreme Court considered and rejected the claim that same-sex couples have a federal constitutional right to marry.[19] The ruling remained in place for the next forty-three years. During that long period, advocates of same-sex marriage pursued a patient strategy of establishing the right to marry—or "marriage equality"—state-by-state, before bringing the issue back to the U.S. Supreme Court. The strategy focused on persuading state courts that their constitutions protected marriage rights of same-sex couples, with most of the cases filed in blue states. The strategy achieved a critical breakthrough in 2003, when the Massachusetts Supreme Judicial Court declared that the Massachusetts Constitution protected a right of same-sex couples to marry. Similar cases soon followed in other states, with some courts recognizing the right and others declining to do so. In 2008, the California Supreme Court ruled in *In re Marriage Cases* that the California Constitution guaranteed marriage rights to same-sex couples. *In re Marriage Cases* generated great controversy and, later that year, voters passed a ballot initiative, known as Proposition 8, to reverse the ruling.[20]

At that point, advocates turned to the federal courts, hoping ultimately to persuade the U.S. Supreme Court to reverse its decision in *Baker v. Nelson* and recognize marriage equality throughout the United States. The effort required multiple lawsuits and several years, but in 2015 the litigation achieved, in *Obergefell v. Hodges*, a federal right of same-sex couples to marry.[21] *Obergefell* again demonstrated the power of rights in the formation of social policy. The Court's decision brought the long struggle over the legal definition of marriage to a quick end and required all states to conform to the new rule.

Texas and California found themselves on the opposite sides of all of these controversies—aid-in-dying, abortion, guns, and marriage; indeed, for decades, they have been on the opposite side of nearly every culture war conflict.

Texas

With its traditional cultural values, Texas has taken conservative positions on most social issues. An exception occurred in 1972, when the state broke from its southern neighbors by voting to ratify the federal Equal Rights Amendment while also adopting its own state constitutional ERA.[22] As a rule, however, Texas has opposed progressive changes to the law and instead has sought to defend the state's conservative values. When the nation's culture wars intensified and Republicans gained control of Texas government, the state started to pursue a more aggressive social agenda, stepping up efforts to regulate abortion, defend the rights of gun owners, and protect religious liberty, among other goals. In time, however, Republican officials began to face cross pressures on these issues. As social conservatives sought to translate more of their values into law, moderate voters and the corporate sector pushed back.

The nature of Texas's culture war engagement can be seen by examining three fronts: abortion, guns, and LGBT rights.

Abortion

Texas's religious streak and conservative cultural views has caused it to take a restrictive stance on abortion. Like most states, Texas enacted its first criminal abortion statute in the mid-nineteenth century, and its provisions survived substantially unchanged until the 1970s. The Texas law made it a crime, punishable by two to five years in prison, to "procure" an abortion, or attempt to do so, by "any drug or medicine" or "any means externally or internally applied." The state allowed an exception only to save the life of the mother.[23] Through the mid-1960s, all states, including California, maintained similar statutes. At that point, many physicians and a legal reform group called the American Law Institute encouraged states to allow abortion in a broader range of circumstances—that is, if the pregnancy was the result of rape or incest, or if the continuance of the pregnancy would "gravely impair the physical or mental health of the mother," or if the child would be born with "grave physical or mental defect."[24] From the mid-1960s through the early 1970s, several states—including California, adopted some or all of these recommendations for reform, and four states—Hawaii, Alaska, Washington, and New York—repealed most of their prohibitions on abortion. The Texas Legislature refused to touch its abortion statutes.

In the late 1960s, the emerging feminist movement took leadership of the effort to change abortion laws. Feminists reframed the issue in terms of rights—that is, a woman's right to control over her own body and her reproductive choices. Inspired by this change, activists brought rights-based challenges to abortion laws in more than a dozen states.[25]

In Texas, Sarah Weddington, a young graduate of the University of Texas Law School, resolved to challenge the state's abortion laws. She and a small group of lawyers looked for a plaintiff and were introduced to Norma McCorvey, a pregnant woman who said she could not afford to travel out of state for a legal abortion. The lawyers drafted pleadings that identified McCorvey as "Jane Roe" and named Henry Wade, the longtime district attorney of Dallas County, as the defendant. They filed the action in federal district court in Dallas. In June 1970, a three-judge panel of that court held that the Texas criminal abortion laws violated the Ninth Amendment of the Constitution. The U.S. Supreme Court granted review.[26]

Due to her youth and inexperience, Weddington may have seemed an unlikely choice to argue what soon became one of the most consequential cases in the nation's history. Remarkably, she was only twenty-six years old and four years out of law school when she first addressed the justices.[27] Yet, many believed it was important for a woman to take the lead in a case advancing women's rights, and Weddington was a passionate and talented advocate for the cause. At the same time she was winning the *Roe* litigation, Weddington lobbied for ratification of the Equal Rights Amendment, helped to found the Texas Women's Political Caucus, and won election to the Texas Legislature (with future governor Ann Richards serving as her campaign manager).[28]

Weddington's support for an expansive right to abortion was celebrated in many parts of the country. It did not, however, reflect the opinion of most Texans. After the Supreme Court handed down *Roe*, the state spent decades pushing back against the landmark decision, repeatedly looking for ways to restrict or eliminate the right it established.

Early on, Texas found ways to limit the right to abortion. The state permitted hospitals to refuse to provide abortion services for any reason, prohibited anyone except licensed physicians from performing abortions, and restricted the use of Medicaid funds for the procedure.[29] Later, when Republicans gained unified control of Texas government, the state stepped up the attack. Beginning in 2003, and for years thereafter, the legislature enacted a broad range of abortion regulations and restrictions, including mandatory waiting periods, ultrasounds, disclosure of alternatives to abortion, and, for minors, parental notification and parental consent. Texas also funded counseling designed to dissuade women from choosing abortion. At the same time, it sought to drain the resources of abortion providers by defunding Planned Parenthood, barring most other public funding for abortions, and placing expensive requirements on abortion clinics. It also banned certain abortion procedures such as dilation and evacuation.[30] In all, Texas worked to reduce abortions—and thereby, in its view, defend the unborn—through a mix of prohibitions, persuasion, and limitation of access.

The state's anti-abortion efforts reached a peak in 2013 when the legislature enacted a bill known as HB 2. The bill shortened the allowable time for most abortions from twenty-four weeks (considered the low end of fetal viability) to twenty weeks; established new rules for administering abortion-inducing drugs; mandated that doctors performing abortions hold admitting privileges at a hospital within thirty miles of the abortion facility; and required abortion facilities to meet the standards for ambulatory surgical centers. Among other consequences, the new rules would force clinics to make costly upgrades and would reduce the number of clinics in more-remote geographic areas.[31] Governor Greg Abbott and almost all GOP lawmakers supported the measure, while most Democrats opposed it. Democratic senator Wendy Davis famously filibustered the bill, temporarily preventing its passage. However, the governor immediately called a special session, and the bill was adopted.

Critics argued that Texas had designed the new rules not to promote women's health, but rather to put abortion clinics out of business. And, indeed, many clinics did shut down after the law's enactment. A number of providers challenged the new requirements, and one of the cases, *Whole Woman's Health v. Hellerstedt*, made its way to the U.S. Supreme Court. That case dealt the antiabortion movement a setback by declaring that Texas's new rules for abortion clinics violated the *Casey* standard.[32]

Undeterred, in 2019 nine states directly challenged the *Roe/Casey* right by enacting very short time limits on abortion. Alabama's law would ban elective abortions beginning at conception. Laws in Georgia, Kentucky, Louisiana, Mississippi, Missouri, and Ohio would ban them once the fetal heartbeat could be detected (at six to eight weeks). And laws in Arkansas and Utah would ban them at the midpoint of the second trimester (approximately eighteen weeks). Texas, however, chose not to join them.

The state's lawmakers exercised caution for two reasons. First, they feared the Supreme Court's reaction to such a major limitation on abortion. To uphold a restriction of this type, the Court would need to completely overturn *Roe* and *Casey*—a move, many believed, it might be unwilling to make. Instead, many pro-life Texans concluded the Court would more likely allow an incremental restriction of the right.[33]

Second, they feared that adopting very strict regulations would alienate many Texas voters. After the difficult 2018 election, Republicans could see they were losing support among moderate suburban women, younger voters, and other segments of the electorate, and they did not want to risk further eroding that support. Although many Texas Republicans yearned to overturn *Roe*, they chose to play a patient game.[34]

Guns

Texas has taken an uncompromising stance on another controversial social policy—gun ownership. The Lone Star State's love for guns runs deep, and many Texans continue to view guns as essential to the state's identity.[35] Texas's gun policy aligns not only with the state's culture but also with a federal constitutional right—that is, the U.S. Supreme Court's interpretation of the Second Amendment's right to keep and bear arms. Texas has sought to implement, reinforce, and expand that right.

Yet the issue is fraught because the state has a long history of gun violence. In 1966, not long after the assassination of President Kennedy in Dallas, the state experienced another traumatic shooting when a gunman made his way to the University of Texas administration tower's observation deck and started spraying bullets at the people below. The shots from the tower killed fifteen people and wounded thirty-one others. This atrocity on the Austin campus was one of the nation's first mass shootings and, at the time, the deadliest. Sadly, many similar incidents followed. Half a century after the University of Texas shooting, a rash of massacres spread across the state—at a protest in Dallas (2016), a Baptist church in Sutherland Springs (2017), a high school in Santa Fe (2018), a Walmart in El Paso (2019), and on the streets of Odessa (2019). These horrific incidents deepened public anxiety about gun violence. To be sure, mass shootings were not limited to Texas, but the state led the nation in these tragedies, and its lax gun regulations became the source of intense debate.

In response to rising demands for increased gun controls, Texas instead doubled down on its commitment to gun rights. The state argued that the best defense against gun violence was not to limit access to guns, but, rather, to allow—indeed, encourage—law-abiding citizens to own and carry firearms. Far from expanding gun control, Texas chose to reduce or eliminate a number of its existing gun regulations.[36]

As a result, Texas features some of the nation's most libertarian gun laws. As of 2019, the state placed no limits on possession of high-capacity weapons such as semi-automatic rifles or .50 caliber rifles, or on handguns or ammunition. It did not require people to have a license to own a gun, or to register their guns. It imposed no limits on how many guns one could own nor how frequently one could buy them. The state also did not perform background checks for many gun purchases, including transactions between private parties and purchases at gun shows. Texas broadly allowed licensed gun owners to carry weapons in public. In 1995, it authorized "concealed carry"; in 2015, it allowed "open carry" of handguns in most public places, so long as the weapon was holstered at the shoulder or at the hip. That same year, Texas adopted a "campus carry" law that required state universities to allow open carry on campus. The campus carry law took effect on August 1, 2016, the fiftieth anniversary of the University of Texas tower shooting—underscoring the state's view that placing more guns in the hands of citizens is the best way to prevent such incidents.[37] In 2019, the legislature passed a package of bills that made it easier to possess or carry weapons in various settings, including houses of worship, school parking lots, apartments, other rental units, and foster homes. By that time, more than 1.4 million people held active conceal carry permits in Texas, compared with about 120,000 in California.[38]

In short, as the national debate on gun policy intensified, Texas continued to embrace the right to bear arms and a robust culture of gun ownership.[39]

LGBT Issues

Like many red states, Texas long resisted the LGBT rights movement. The state's conservative orientation was grounded in traditional sexual morality and understandings of marriage and family. The effort by gay, lesbian, and transgender persons to achieve acceptance of their identities and relationships challenged those moorings. Moreover, for many conservatives, marriage and sexual mores were, like abortion, not merely social issues but tenets of religious faith. To make concessions on these matters, they believed, would compromise their religious identity and conscience, and would invite broader attacks on their religious liberty.

One expression of these views could be seen in Texas's unwillingness to repeal its prohibitions on same-sex sexual relations. In 1986, the U.S. Supreme Court narrowly ruled in *Bowers v. Hardwick* that so-called sodomy laws did not violate federal constitutional rights.[40] In the years that followed, most states nevertheless chose to repeal these morals statutes. Texas did not. In 1998, sheriff deputies near Houston arrested two men engaged in private, intimate sexual conduct and charged them with violating the law. When they learned of the arrest, gay rights advocates seized the opportunity to challenge the Texas law and the *Bowers* precedent. The case, *Lawrence v. Texas*, eventually reached the U.S. Supreme Court, and in a landmark 2003 ruling, the Court declared that the state's anti-sodomy law (as well as those in other states) violated federal constitutional rights of privacy and personal autonomy.[41] Through the *Lawrence* decision, the Court again demonstrated the power of rights in determining social policy.

The struggle soon turned to the definition of marriage. As the movement for marriage equality achieved initial breakthroughs in state courts, many states responded by placing "Defense of Marriage" amendments (DOMAs) in their state constitutions. Like the federal Defense of Marriage Act, the state counterparts defined marriage as a union between a man and a woman, and some also banned legal recognition of same-sex relationships by other means, such as civil union or domestic partnership laws. Between 1998 and 2012, voters in thirty-one states approved state DOMAs. Texas adopted a "defense of marriage" statute in 2003 and a constitutional amendment in 2005.[42] The amendment defined marriage in Texas as "the union of one man and one woman" and also prohibited the state or local governments from creating any legal status that was "identical or similar to marriage." Texas voters approved the amendment by a 76–24 percent margin.[43]

As the *Obergefell* case was still pending, federal courts struck down traditional marriage laws in many states, including in Texas. In 2014, a federal judge declared that "Texas's current marriage laws deny homosexual couples the right to marry, and in so doing, demean their dignity for no legitimate reason."[44] The state was still appealing that ruling when the *Obergefell* decision brought debate on the issue to a close.

Many Americans celebrated *Obergefell* as an affirmation of the rights and dignity of gays and lesbians. At the same time, many social conservatives in Texas and elsewhere were embittered by what they considered to be the redefinition of marriage by judicial fiat. Despite their disappointment, most conservatives understood that *Obergefell* was not like *Roe*—that is, there was no reasonable prospect of reversing the decision and restoring the old definition of marriage. For a number of reasons—including the right's simplicity, its ease of administration, and, most important, its broad public acceptance—*Obergefell* was here to stay.[45] Nevertheless, activists backed by Governor Abbott, Lieutenant Governor Patrick, and Attorney General Paxton sought to limit *Obergefell's* scope by arguing that the ruling required Texas to issue marriage licenses to same-sex couples, but did not require it to confer equal benefits to same-sex married couples as it does to opposite-sex married couples. The issue arose in the context of benefit plans for spouses of public employees. The Texas courts were sympathetic to this logic, but the state's efforts to limit *Obergefell* were unlikely, ultimately, to succeed.[46] The question was no longer whether social conservatives could preserve traditional understandings of marriage and family as the dominant cultural norms. Instead, now the issue was whether they could secure, based on their religious beliefs, personal accommodations, or exemptions, from the new norms.

This search for exemption was the theme of a 2017 Texas law that would allow child welfare providers, such as adoption agencies, to decline to offer services that conflict with their sincerely held religious beliefs. Progressive critics argued the law would allow religious-based agencies to refuse to place children in the homes of gay or lesbian couples or others who did not conform to their religious views.[47] From Texas's perspective, the statute established legitimate protections for religious liberty. But others saw the matter differently, believing that the law gave agencies license to discriminate.

Finally, as discussed in Chapter 8, Texas Republicans divided on the so-called bathroom bill, which would have required transgender persons to use bathrooms in public buildings based on their biological sex. Social conservatives backed the bill, but moderates resisted—in part because large corporations increasingly supported transgender rights and opposed restrictions on those rights. In 2017, the Texas House of Representatives blocked the bathroom bill, and conservatives did not revive it in the following legislative session.

Over all, Texas has remained a leader of the conservative forces in the nation's culture wars. Although the state has chosen to pull back on some controversial issues, it has continued to advance its cultural values within the federal system across a broad range of social issues.

California

Meanwhile, by any measure, California has become the national leader of the cultural left. The Golden State has developed a comprehensive progressive agenda across all fronts of the culture wars. No social issue now escapes the state's notice or concern. California has come to view such issues as inseparable from the rest of its progressive policy model and has aggressively promoted its cultural vision both within and beyond its borders. By leveraging its enormous economic, political, and legal resources, it has led the left's resistance to cultural conservatives in Washington, D.C., and across the country.

California's full-throttle social activism is relatively new. During its long era of balanced two-party competition, the state was more closely divided between cultural left and right—between the progressivism of San Francisco, Berkeley, and west Los Angeles and the conservatism of Orange County, greater suburbia, and the rural interior. As a consequence, the state experienced an *internal* culture war. For years, Californians wrestled over women's equality, capital punishment, school busing, gay rights, immigration, bilingual education, affirmative action, and the definition of marriage. In many of these controversies, either the legislature or the state courts took the lead in advancing a progressive agenda, while the majority of the electorate pushed back by adopting ballot initiatives, and, in one case, by voting liberal justices off the state supreme court. However, as the state became more thoroughly progressive, the culture war within its own borders subsided. Without an internal conservative check, California progressives were free to pursue an ambitious social agenda both at home and at the national level. The general character of California's engagement in the nation's culture wars can be seen on the issues of abortion, guns, and LGBT rights.

Abortion

California is a national leader in providing women access to abortion. In the early 1960s, as the movement to liberalize abortion laws gained momentum, reformers focused on California, which, like other states, criminalized abortion except when needed to protect the mother's life. By 1967, the California Legislature was prepared to back a bill that would expand exceptions along the lines recommended by law reform groups—that is, if the pregnancy was the result of rape or incest, or the woman's physical or mental health would be "gravely impaired" by continuing to term, or if the child would be born with "grave physical or mental defect."[48]

The state's new governor, Ronald Reagan, was torn on the issue. After long deliberation, he agreed to sign the bill, but only after insisting that the provision allowing abortion in the case of fetal "defect" be eliminated. After the legislature amended the bill to remove that provision, Governor Reagan signed it.[49] In 1969 and 1972, the California Supreme Court issued rulings that further limited the state's restrictions and effectively established a state-level right to abortion through the twentieth week of pregnancy. The California Supreme Court's actions influenced courts in other states as well as the U.S. Supreme Court in *Roe*.[50]

In the post-*Roe* era, California expanded its abortion rights above the federal floor. For example, in 1981, a year after the U.S. Supreme Court declared that the federal Constitution does not grant women a right to a publicly funded abortion, the California Supreme Court held that the state constitution guarantees that right.[51] And after the U.S. Supreme Court decided in *Planned Parenthood v. Casey* that states may enact parental consent laws, the California Supreme Court determined that such laws were impermissible under the state's independent right to abortion.[52]

Over time, California demonstrated a foursquare commitment to abortion rights in numerous other ways. Beyond rejecting the restrictions adopted by Texas and other states—parental consent, waiting periods, ultrasounds, funding restrictions, and the like—California sought to make the abortion procedure as affordable and convenient as possible. As examples, the state required private health plans to cover abortions; authorized non-physicians, including nurse practitioners, physician assistants, and midwives, to perform the procedure; and, by a large margin, housed more abortion facilities than any other state.[53] As of 2017, California had 419 facilities that provided abortions—far more than runner-up New York (252) and more than one-fourth of the nation's total (1,587). In stark contrast, in 2017 Texas had 35 facilities that performed abortions, down from 44 in 2014. In many red states, the numbers were far lower. For example, both Kentucky and Mississippi had only three facilities that performed abortions, including one clinic in each state.[54]

California continued to look for ways to expand access. In 2019, the legislature adopted a bill called the "College Student Right to Access Act," which required all state universities to provide medical abortions—that is, early-term, drug-induced abortions—through their student health centers. The policy goal was to make abortion more accessible. The bill's author, Democratic State Senator Connie Leyva, said that "students should not have to travel off campus or miss class or work responsibilities in order to receive care that can easily be provided at a student health center"—an argument for facilitating abortions that certainly would not persuade most Texas lawmakers.[55]

In addition to expanding access to abortion services, California sought to regulate pro-life crisis pregnancy centers, religious-based organizations that encourage women to choose alternatives to terminating their pregnancies. In 2015, the legislature passed a law called the Reproductive Freedom, Accountability, Comprehensive Care, and Transparency (FACT) Act, which required pregnancy counseling centers to inform women about abortion services and to give them a number to call. The clinics challenged the law on the grounds that it violated their First Amendment rights by compelling speech and, by a 5–4 vote, the U.S. Supreme Court struck it down.[56]

Finally, California fought to defend abortion rights within the federal system. The state ramped up these efforts during the Trump presidency as it sought to block a number of administration efforts to limit abortion. For example, the state challenged an administration interim rule confirming the right of employers with religious or moral objections to omit coverage for contraception, including abortifacients, from their health plans. In this litigation, California and other blue states squared off against not only the Trump administration but also against the Little Sisters of the Poor, a Catholic order that fought for years to secure the exemption.[57] California also pushed back when the Trump administration challenged its policy requiring insurers to cover abortion services, and it sued again when the administration cut off a long-standing source of federal funds to any clinics that promoted abortion—a restriction critics called a "gag rule."[58] Through these and other actions, California made itself the leader of the nation's pro-choice forces, often in direct conflict with conservative and religious organizations, and with attorneys general in Texas and other red states.

Guns

At the same time, California became a national leader in the effort to control guns. Until the 1960s, the Golden State had relatively few gun restrictions, and one could openly carry loaded weapons in public places. In the mid-1960s, that policy became a source of controversy when heavily armed members of the Black Panther Party began patrolling the streets of Oakland. A Republican assemblyman from Oakland, Don Mulford, introduced a bill to ban the carrying of loaded weapons in urban areas. The Black Panthers, led by Huey Newton and

Bobby Seale, protested the bill. On May 2, 1967, thirty Panthers armed with loaded .357 Magnums, 12-gauge shotguns, and .45 caliber pistols, occupied the state capitol grounds in Sacramento. The militants marched into the capitol building carrying their weapons, and several of them reached the Assembly floor.[59] Police removed them from the building and there was no violence that day, but the armed occupation of the capitol motivated the legislature to enact the gun control bill—and to add an amendment prohibiting loaded firearms in the state capitol. Remarkably, from today's perspective, the National Rifle Association backed the legislation and Governor Reagan signed it. Reagan said that he saw "no reason why on the street today a citizen should be carrying loaded weapons."[60] The Mulford Act helped spur a national effort to control guns during the turbulent late 1960s, and put California on the path to enacting some of the nation's strictest gun regulations.

California's gun control policies maintained bipartisan support through the 1980s. In 1989, a gunman used a semi-automatic version of an AK-47 weapon to kill five children and wound 29 others in a schoolyard in Stockton. In the wake of the shooting, the Democratic legislature and Republican governor George Deukmejian negotiated an agreement to ban a long list of military-style semi-automatic weapons—the nation's first ban on assault weapons.[61]

Over time, however, attitudes about gun policy increasingly polarized along partisan lines. As the National Rifle Association and political conservatives pushed to establish stronger federal constitutional protections for gun ownership, progressives tested those limits. In 2019, the San Francisco Board of Supervisors demonstrated the depth of polarization on the issue by unanimously adopting a resolution declaring the National Rifle Association a "domestic terrorist organization."[62]

After the U.S. Supreme Court issued the *Heller* and *McDonald* decisions establishing an individual right to keep and bear arms, the Court avoided granting review of any further gun control cases over the following decade. During that period, California sought to limit the right by enacting many new restrictions.

In addition to banning most assault weapons and .50 caliber rifles, California has prohibited the possession and sale of large-capacity ammunition magazines. The state has also established comprehensive regulation of gun sales by requiring all gun dealers to obtain a state license; mandating that all sales be through a licensed dealer; regulating gun shows; requiring background checks and a ten-day waiting period for gun sales; establishing point-of-sale background checks for ammunition sales; and maintaining records of all gun sales. State law has required individuals to pass a written test on firearm safety before they can purchase a gun and prohibited the purchase of more than one handgun or semi-automatic rifle per month. The state has allowed residents to apply for authorization to carry concealed weapons, although local law enforcement has discretion to deny permits. In 2014, California established a "red flag" law that allows family members or police to request a court order confiscating weapons from persons who appear to be dangerous to themselves or others.[63]

Opponents have challenged several of these laws, arguing that they violate the Second Amendment.[64] The state has not only vigorously defended its existing restrictions, but has also declared its intention to expand them. One can expect California to continue to test the limits of the Second Amendment right as part of its mission to impose stronger controls on guns.

LGBT Issues

After an internal struggle, California fully established its position as the national leader of the LGBT rights movement. Californians began asserting leadership in promoting gay liberation in the mid-twentieth century, and San Francisco became a global center of gay rights activism in the 1970s. At several points, however, social conservatives in the state pushed back against this movement. One notable example occurred in the 1978, when Orange County state senator John Briggs qualified a statewide ballot initiative, Proposition 6, which would have required public school districts to fire teachers, administrators, or counselors who engaged in "public homosexual activity" or "conduct."[65] Led by San Francisco Supervisor Harvey Milk, the gay and lesbian community rallied against the Briggs Initiative and gained the support of elected officials across the political spectrum. In November 1978, voters soundly rejected the measure. Weeks after the election, Milk was shot and killed at San Francisco City Hall, but new leaders emerged and the LGBT-rights movement gained strength in the 1980s through its response to the AIDS crisis.

During the 1990s, LGBT leaders began to focus on the right of same-sex couples to marry. This choice was motivated in part by the belief that access to marriage was the surest path to social acceptance of gay and lesbian relationships. The movement divided the state, in part because many remained committed to the traditional definition of marriage. In 2000, voters approved Proposition 22, an initiative statute that banned same-sex marriage in California. Progressives looked for ways to overturn this restriction. The legislature enacted domestic partnership laws that gave same-sex couples most of the legal benefits of marriage, and in San Francisco Mayor Gavin Newsom ordered officials to issue marriage licenses to same-sex couples. In early 2004, more than four thousand gay and lesbian couples married in the city until the state supreme court shut down the ceremonies because state law did not permit them. Soon, gay and lesbian couples brought several cases in state court arguing that Proposition 22 violated their state constitutional right to marry—and in *In re Marriage Cases* (2008), the California Supreme Court agreed.[66]

By that point, nearly all of the state's political establishment, including prominent Democrats and Republican governor Arnold Schwarzenegger, supported marriage rights for same-sex couples. When California voters narrowly approved Proposition 8 to overturn *Marriage Cases* and restore the traditional definition of marriage, neither Schwarzenegger nor any other statewide elected official would defend the measure against a legal challenge in federal court. In 2010, a federal district judge declared Proposition 8 unconstitutional, and, after further litigation, the state's refusal to defend the law on appeal caused the ruling to stand.[67]

Meanwhile, California took many other actions on LGBT issues. It enacted extensive protections against discrimination on the basis of sexual orientation or gender identity in employment, housing, and public accommodations; authorized same-sex couples to adopt children; banned therapists and other mental health professionals from providing "gay conversion" therapy to minors; required all law enforcement officials to take LGBT sensitivity training; mandated that all public schools teach about the history of the LGBT community; provided for gender-neutral birth certificates and driver's licenses; paid for sex-reassignment surgery for transgender prison inmates; and required all single-occupancy bathrooms to be gender-neutral. It also authorized students to participate on sports teams and use bathrooms and locker rooms based on their gender identity rather than their biological sex at birth. Moreover, the state supreme court required that any law creating distinctions on the basis on sexual orientation be subject to strict judicial scrutiny.[68]

Finally, as California was building the nation's most expansive set of LGBT rights, it also sought to influence LGBT policies across the nation. In 2016, Assemblyman Evan Low, a Democrat from Silicon Valley, authored AB 1887, the "travel ban" to states that did not meet California's standards for LGBT rights. With some exceptions, the bill banned state-funded travel to any state that voided, repealed, or created exemptions to laws preventing discrimination on the basis of sexual orientation, gender identity, or gender expression. "By banning state-funded travel to such states," Low argued, "it sends a signal that we do not tolerate discrimination in our state and beyond our borders."[69] As of 2019, state attorney general Xavier Becerra had invoked the law to ban state-funded travel to eleven states—Alabama, Iowa, Kansas, Kentucky, Mississippi, North Carolina, Oklahoma, South Carolina, South Dakota, Tennessee, and Texas. The bans had economic repercussions for the affected states, as professional organizations canceled conventions and other events rather than lose the participation of members from California.[70]

States on the receiving end of these travel bans naturally resented them. Texas State Representative Dustin Burrows, a Republican from Lubbock, stated a common view: "I think California should be free to determine its own culture, and Texas doesn't try to influence it," he said. "This seems to be something new and different where California wants to determine our culture and our laws, and we're not going to have it."[71]

In early 2020, Texas attorney general Ken Paxton filed an action directly in the U.S. Supreme Court challenging California's travel ban policy. Paxton argued that the ban is "grounded in animus towards religion" and that it violates the U.S. Constitution's Privileges and Immunities, Commerce, and Equal Protection Clauses. The case was titled, *Texas v. California*.[72]

The Sibling Rivals in the Culture Wars

As these examples demonstrate, Texas and California have staked out leadership positions on opposite sides of the nation's culture wars. Moreover, both states view social issues as part of their broader policy models.

For years, Texas has sought to enact laws that reinforce what it considers its cultural foundations—personal responsibility, marriage, family, religion, private charity, and community involvement—partly on the view that if these cultural elements are strong, society can get by with a lean government. At the same time, the social conservative impulse has sometimes conflicted with the state's libertarian streak. As noted earlier, the Texas Republican Party has divided on how far lawmakers should go in reinforcing traditional cultural norms. Many business-oriented moderates have argued that focusing on divisive social issues, such as restrictive abortion laws and limits on the rights of LGBT persons, is bad for business and threatens the political viability of the Texas Model, especially as the state becomes more culturally diverse. Conversely, those on the right have contended that cultural conservatism is ultimately inseparable from economic conservatism and that the red state model must continue to emphasize social issues. In recent years, corporate pressure and rising Democratic electoral competition have forced even some of Texas's staunchest conservatives to moderate somewhat their positions on these issues.

By comparison, California's Democratic officials have experienced fewer internal divisions on social issues and have overwhelmingly backed progressive positions in these controversies. As California has turned deeply blue, it has become far more liberal on a range of social issues and has asserted national leadership of the cultural left. California's policy model has sought to fuse economic and social justice by overturning laws and practices that, in the progressive view, have systematically disadvantaged those at the margins—women, racial and ethnic minorities, immigrants, gays and lesbians, transgender persons, and the economically dispossessed. In addition, California has seen other policy areas—including education, criminal law, and environmental protection—as inseparable from its social and cultural concerns.

As they have polarized on social issues, both Texas and California have advanced their competing views in the national arena, through federal litigation and other means. These struggles have raised the question whether the United States should seek to establish uniform national policies on matters such as abortion, marriage, LGBT rights, drug legalization, gun regulation, end-of-life choices, and so on, or, conversely, allow state-level pluralism on these issues. As we have seen, when one side in a cultural conflict has established its interest as a federal constitutional right, the achievement has had nationalizing and standardizing effects, reducing the opportunities for state-level differences. On some questions, such as the definition of marriage, the establishment of a national standard is probably inevitable. Once same-sex couples gained marriage rights in some states, it would have been difficult if not impossible to maintain two different definitions of marriage within a highly mobile country over the long term. On other issues, however, state-level differences may be more sustainable and can be beneficial if they allow social policies to align with state-level values.

In any event, given their contrasting cultural values, Texas and California can be expected to continue to fight on opposing sides of the nation's culture wars for years to come.

PART III

POSSIBLE FUTURES

14

State of the Rivalry

This book began with a simple metaphor—Texas and California are sibling rivals. As the following pages demonstrated, the two states indeed have a sibling-like relationship. They shared a life together in New Spain and Mexico, became American at nearly the same time, grew quickly, and now lead the nation in population, diversity, and economic power. This kinship has created an inseverable bond. As members of the Union, they are forever joined together—as Gavin Newsom might say, *whether they like it or not.* In recent years, some people in both states have dreamed of separation. When Barack Obama was president, Texas governor Rick Perry flirted with talk of secession, and after Donald Trump's election, the "Cal-exit" movement had a moment of fame. Long ago, however, the Confederate surrender at Appomattox settled the question of whether states could opt out of the nation. Neither Texas nor California will be exiting this family.

Author Lawrence Wright has expanded on the sibling metaphor by describing Texas and California as "mirror image twins." Mirror image twins are identical twins who separate relatively late in the gestational process. According to Wright, "The thing about mirror image twins is that if one is left-handed, the other will be right-handed. One will have a mole on the left cheek, and the other on the right cheek. In other words, they're genetically identical, but they're physically different. And I think there is something like that in the relationship between California and Texas. These two states, they intertwine like strands of DNA; they're opposing each other, but they're also related to each other, and they're the poles around which our national politics tend to revolve."[1]

The twins' opposing features have made them antagonists. As the national family has divided into competing and often hostile factions, its most powerful members have assumed leadership of the two sides. Partisan sorting has caused both states to become more ideologically distinct. Texas has honed a conservative approach to nearly every policy question, while California has become consistently and emphatically progressive in its governance. To a large degree, both states have implemented their respective models at home, and both have fought to defend and advance these models beyond their borders.

This concluding chapter takes a broader look at the struggle between Texas and California and the directions the contest may take. The chapter briefly discusses the structure of the American federal system and considers the advantages and

Texas vs. California. Kenneth P. Miller, Oxford University Press (2020). © Oxford University Press.
DOI: 10.1093/oso/9780190077402.001.0001.

dangers of having blocs of states straining in opposite directions. Next, it assesses the rival Texas and California models and highlights their strengths and vulnerabilities. Finally, after laying out the disclaimers one should always make when speculating about future political events, especially in times of great disruption, the chapter discusses the prospects for the rivalry in the years ahead. The conclusion offers some modest suggestions for viewing the competition in a more positive way and turning it to productive ends.

One Nation, Two Systems

One of the distinctive features of American federalism is that it reserves to the states a great deal of power to develop their own policies. Ever since the nation's founding, the proper nature and scope of that authority has been a source of debate. In practice, states make a wide range of policy choices and, indeed, exercise more power than subnational governments in most other countries. This arrangement gives states the ability to develop independent policy models. As discussed in prior chapters, geographic partisan sorting has caused these models to vary radically. Red states have developed a comprehensive set of conservative policies while blue states have countered with an ambitious progressive agenda. The nation thus contains two internal, competing systems. What are we to make of this development? Is it beneficial for states to be able to divide so dramatically on major policy questions? Or is this diversity cause for concern?

U.S. Supreme Court Justice Louis Brandeis authored perhaps the most famous endorsement of state policy pluralism in a 1932 case called *New State Ice Company v. Liebmann*. The case challenged an Oklahoma law that defined the manufacture and sale of ice as a public utility and required ice-making businesses to obtain a license from the state. Invoking the dominant judicial reasoning of the day, the Court held that Oklahoma's law violated a constitutional right—that is, one's liberty under the Fourteenth Amendment's Due Process Clause to engage in ordinary business without undue interference from the state. Justice Brandeis dissented, arguing that the Constitution did not forbid states from enacting economic regulations of this type.

In his dissenting opinion, Justice Brandeis extolled the value of experimentation. "Man is weak and his judgment is at best fallible," he wrote. "Yet the advances in the exact sciences and the achievements in invention remind us that the seemingly impossible sometimes happens. . . . The discoveries in physical science, the triumphs in invention, attest the value of the process of trial and error. In large measure, these advances have been due to experimentation." Brandeis then turned to experimentation in public policy. "There must be power in the states and the nation to remould, through experimentation, our economic practices and institutions to meet changing social and economic needs," he argued. "To stay experimentation in things social and economic is a grave responsibility. Denial of the right to experiment may be fraught with serious consequences to the nation. It is one of the happy incidents of the federal system that a single courageous state may, if its citizens choose, serve as a laboratory; and try novel social and economic experiments without risk to the rest of the country."[2]

Brandeis's opinion popularized the concept of states as "laboratories."[3] The term has been invoked countless times ever since by those who embrace a robust form of federalism—one that promotes the flow of innovations from the states and provides wide latitude for state-level policy diversity and trial and error.

The development in Texas and California of radically different policy models can thus be viewed in a Brandeisian way—that is, as a beneficial consequence of the nation's constitutional design. A robust federalism allows Texas to operate a laboratory that generates conservative experiments, such as forgoing an income tax, rejecting Medicaid expansion, and promoting an all-energy policy that includes full support for both fossil fuels and renewables. At the same time, it allows California to pursue progressive experiments such as raising bountiful revenues through an income tax, expanding health care coverage by various means, and targeting carbon fuels for elimination. The proliferation of one-party-dominated states has caused this kind of experimentation and boundary testing to grow. And, in time, the thinking goes, the experiments will be put to the test; some ideas will be more broadly embraced and others cast aside.

Leaders on both sides of the nation's partisan divide have endorsed Brandeis' idea. In 2012, for example, when federal agents began a limited crackdown on marijuana dispensaries in California, Democratic governor Jerry Brown invoked the concept in defense of the state's medical marijuana policy. "We have a laboratory of democracy," Brown said. "I believe the president and the Department of Justice ought to respect the will of these sovereign states.... We are capable of self-government. We don't need some federal gendarme to come and tell us what to do."[4] On another occasion, the Republican Texas businessman Ross Perot Jr. agreed with the principle. "There are fifty labs in the United States, and you can watch the California and Texas experiment," Perot said. "That's the American way."[5]

It must be said, however, that the policy competition between Texas and California, as well as their respective allies, is no longer as benign as Justice Brandeis suggested. To be sure, on some issues, red and blue states continue to act according to the ideal by working collaboratively and drawing on best practices developed in other states regardless of their partisan orientation.[6] But in recent decades, hostile competition between rival blocs has become the more common pattern. Several reasons explain the change. After Brandeis wrote his famous opinion, the New Deal and the Great Society expanded the scope, resources, and regulatory power of government, especially at the federal level; the rights revolution gave the federal courts additional policymaking functions; polarization multiplied and deepened ideological divisions over basic policy goals; and geographic partisan realignments sorted the states into rival camps to a degree not seen since the mid-nineteenth century. Because government now exerts broader control over more areas of life, the stakes of policy debates are greater. And because the red and blue state blocs have developed comprehensive, ideologically driven, and often incompatible policy models, they are less interested in learning from the other side's experiments than in defeating them.

Thankfully, the current conflict is different from the Civil War—a division so deep, comprehensive, and irreconcilable that it could be resolved only through combat that, in the end, resulted in more casualties than nearly all of the nation's other wars combined. It is hard to imagine that the latter-day red-blue state divide would ever descend into that kind of sectional military conflict. Yet, polarization has clearly transformed the way states relate to each other and to the federal government. This new form of federalism is no longer "dual" or "cooperative," but sectional and highly confrontational.[7] These developments suggest an alternative to Brandeis's metaphor. In many ways, states are no longer laboratories so much as war rooms. The red and blue state blocs now see themselves in a long-term struggle for the nation's future as they seek to defend their respective models and extend their reach within the federal system.

The rivalry between Texas and California has become so intense and comprehensive because the two states have built their models on very different foundations. The substructure of the Texas Model is thoroughly conservative, moored to the values of individualism, personal responsibility, free market capitalism, limited government, and a resistance to outside meddling. Conversely, the California Model is anchored in contemporary progressivism, with its belief that government should use all the power at its disposal to overturn oppressive structures, redress inequality, combat discrimination in its many forms, confront the global environmental crisis, ensure public health, and more. Both states take pride in their approaches to governance; each firmly believes it has developed the superior model. As this book has tried to demonstrate, both models can claim successes—and both also suffer from various weaknesses and vulnerabilities. The following section briefly assesses the performance of the two models during the first two decades of the twenty-first century—the time when they took their current form.

Assessing the Rival Models

The Texas Model

The best argument for the Texas Model during these years was that a multitude of Americans voted for it with their feet. At the same time that California experienced a net-outmigration of more than one million residents, millions of Americans moved to the Lone Star State, especially the fast-growing metropolises within the Texas Triangle, including Dallas, Fort Worth, Houston, Austin, and San Antonio. This migration was a massive endorsement of Texas's economic opportunities and affordability. Large numbers of middle- and working-class Americans concluded that it was easier to find a job, buy a home, support a family, and build a future in Texas than in California or other blue states.

Texas's emphasis on promoting growth and keeping costs low also made it a magnet for business relocation, formation, and expansion. During the first decades of the twenty-first century, the state's urban areas hummed with new business activity.

The state's growth-oriented, light-touch regulatory system promoted economic development in numerous ways. In the energy field, the approach helped Texas re-establish its position as one of the world's greatest producers. Partly through the state's supportive regulatory policies, Texas exerted leadership in the shale revolution, which dramatically revived the nation's oil and gas output, liberated the United States from its heavy reliance on foreign oil, and generated wealth for the state and the nation. At the same time, Texas encouraged, without aggressively mandating, the development of market-based green energy sources. Private industry responded by making Texas the national leader in production of wind energy and a rising contender in solar power. The economic benefits of Texas's business-friendly, all-energy strategy spilled over into other sectors throughout the state.

The Texas Model's advantages also could be seen in housing. By placing comparatively few zoning or other restrictions on new home construction and by keeping labor and regulatory costs low, Texas expanded its housing stock to accommodate its fast-growing population. Despite rising demand for housing, this growth in supply allowed the state to keep median home prices below the national level and avoid the housing crisis that placed enormous strain on middle- and lower-income Californians.

As these and other examples indicate, Texas's disciplined focus on business-friendly tax and regulatory policies contributed to the state's long run of remarkable, broad-based economic growth.

Moreover, from a fiscal standpoint, the Texas Model was less highly leveraged than many blue states—primarily because Texans placed fewer demands on government. Unlike the federal government, states cannot spend more than they take in or borrow money to cover budget shortfalls. If a state makes outsized spending commitments, it must maintain large and steady revenues to pay for them. A state that spends lavishly in good times risks a major fiscal crisis whenever a recession hits and revenues dry up. By contrast, all else being equal, states with smaller spending obligations are less vulnerable to deep fiscal crises during economic downturns. Compared with California and other blue states, Texas kept its spending low. It paid its public employees relatively low salaries, pensions, and other benefits, and offered the poor modest social services—choices that were more defensible in light of the state's comparatively low cost of living. These choices helped Texas keep its long-term spending commitments, and thus its fiscal vulnerability, below blue state levels.[8]

At the same time, the Texas Model involved trade-offs and created its own vulnerabilities. First, Texas risked collecting too little revenue to support investments in areas of critical public need. Even in times of economic plenty, many believed that the state's tight budgets created gaps in its education, health care, and welfare systems, and allowed too many Texans to fall through a relatively thin safety net. Notably, not all such assessments came from the left. Without embracing the progressive critique of the Texas Model, some business-oriented conservatives argued that Texas's tight fiscal policies caused the state to cut corners in areas essential to its future.

In 2016, Tom Luce, a prominent Dallas lawyer and former assistant secretary of education under President George W. Bush, founded Texas 2036, a business-backed organization with a mission to identify some of the greatest threats to Texas's future and to seek solutions to those problems. At the time he founded the organization, Luce recognized that Texas faced a serious challenge educating a workforce for the twenty-first-century economy. By 2036, he noted, the state's much-expanded population would require millions of new jobs—many of which would demand high levels of education and specialized skills. For years, Texas had imported knowledge workers, including computer programmers, engineers, and other highly educated employees, from other states and foreign countries. Luce and other business leaders argued that the state should do more to prepare its own residents for these types of high-end jobs. Similarly, they contended that Texas should make more strategic investments in other areas, including infrastructure; health care access, affordability, and outcomes; resource conservation and use; and modernization of government services. In short, powerful backers of the Texas Model made the case that if that model is to succeed over the long run, it must adapt to the changing needs of a swiftly growing and diversifying society.[9]

The fact that even conservative business leaders were urging the state to spend more to address social needs underscored a central challenge to the Texas Model: most Americans across the ideological spectrum expect government to provide significant levels of public goods. The recent decisions by states such as Montana, Alaska, Louisiana, Utah, Idaho, and Nebraska to adopt Medicaid expansion further reinforced the point: the public's demand for government services was growing. Assuming this trend continued, Texas and other red state governments would find it increasingly difficult to maintain strict limits on spending—and thus on taxes.

Second, as this period progressed, the Texas Model faced the growing threat that Democrats would gain control of the state's government and dismantle its conservative policies. As the nation's only large, urban, majority-minority, red state, Texas defied expectations that demographic diversity would quickly turn the state blue. But, again, the question persisted: could Republicans maintain their dominance in Texas over the long run? The GOP's control of a majority-minority state was noteworthy, but it would have been more so if a larger share of Texans participated in the political system. By national standards, Texas residents voted at very low rates, and, in particular, turnout by Hispanics was consistently lower in Texas than in California. More generally, the composition of Texas's electorate and its state government did not reflect the increasingly diverse population.

As a rule, electorates change more slowly than the population as a whole, but eventually the gap narrows. As Texas moved deeper into the twenty-first century, its electorate was becoming more diverse, and it was clear that the only way to win elections in the long term would be to appeal to that emerging group of voters. To be sure, the state's dominant political culture remained conservative, and Hispanics as well as whites were more conservative in Texas than in California and other blue states. Many Texans across the demographic spectrum supported basic elements of the Texas Model. Yet, the GOP's hard-line messaging and close association with President Trump presented risks. These choices pleased many conservative Texans but alienated a large share of the more diverse, moderate electorate Republicans needed to attract in order to sustain their electoral majorities over the longer term. The GOP was doing little to appeal beyond its existing base and thereby attract a larger share of the state's minority, female, urban, and younger voters. Its struggle to do so imperiled the Texas Model.

Finally, these years revealed the Texas Model's vulnerability to Democratic control of the federal government. During the Obama administration, Texas learned how progressives in Washington, D.C., could threaten red state policies. The ACA's compulsory Medicaid expansion, the Clean Power Plan, and other Obama-era federal mandates would have disrupted Texas policies if the federal courts had not intervened. Based on that experience, Texans can easily imagine a scenario in which progressives gain control of the presidency, Congress, and a majority of the U.S. Supreme Court and put in place new federal laws that undermine the policy models of Texas and other red states. Defenders of the Texas Model are acutely aware of the stakes of the contest for control of the federal government.

The California Model

The best argument for the California Model during these years was that the state maintained a flourishing economy while pursuing ambitious progressive goals. In the depths of the Great Recession of 2007–2009, many concluded that California was a "failed state" because its economy was floundering and the capitol dome in Sacramento was submerged in red ink. In the decade that followed, however, the state staged a comeback.[10] The strength of the New Economy allowed California to shrug off the collapse of some of its older industries and the loss of residents and businesses to other states. In their place, California-based entrepreneurs birthed new enterprises and generated new sources of wealth.

The world's dominant technology cluster, centered in Silicon Valley, reinforced California's position as a global leader in information technology, biotech, green energy, telecommunications, entertainment, and related fields. Silicon Valley, Hollywood, and other high-flying areas of the state attracted some of the world's greatest talent as part of a larger pool of highly educated, productive workers. California's output per worker stood well above the national average and its economy secured its place in the top tier of national and global GDP rankings.

Did the state's progressive policies during this period deserve credit for the Golden State's economic vitality? One could argue that California's economy flourished not because of, but in spite of, the state's high taxes and heavy regulations. In this view, California's prosperity could be attributed to other factors, such as its favorable geography and climate, its entrepreneurial culture, and a long history of investment in institutions such as the state's world-class universities. Indeed, California's greatest economic driver was Silicon Valley, which, in turn, was nurtured by the educational and financial institutions, creative culture, and natural attractions of the San Francisco Bay Area.

On the other hand, one also could argue that California's progressive policies boosted the New Economy by helping its employers attract highly educated workers who embraced blue state social and environmental values. The relationship between these workers and the blue state model was mutually reinforcing. California's Democratic coalition leveraged support from Silicon Valley, Hollywood, and other centers of the New Economy to advance its progressive agenda. Most notably, the highly compensated members of these communities were willing to pay a lion's share of the state's steep income taxes. During these years, they transferred enormous resources to the state treasury, thereby widening the state's revenue advantage over Texas and other states. California was able to use this bounty to greatly increase its spending on a range of progressive priorities, while also balancing its budget and establishing a rainy day fund of more than $20 billion, the largest state reserve in the nation's history.

Between 2010 and 2020, as California's revenues and spending grew in tandem with its booming economy, progressive Democrats across the nation used the Golden State as evidence for the proposition that a state (or the nation as a whole) could sustain economic growth while advancing a full-throttle progressive agenda. During this period, California matched or exceeded red state growth at the same time that it was taxing the rich, providing health care coverage to the poor, fighting climate change, expanding welfare programs, increasing pay and benefits to public employees, and mandating a "living wage," among other accomplishments.

Even if they were not principally responsible for the success of the state's robust economy, California's progressive policymakers deserved credit for their ambition and moral passion. More than any other state, California was determined to confront many of the twenty-first century's most vexing challenges, from the conversion to green energy to the provision of health care to low-income residents. The state's ability to do so, while also balancing its annual budgets and setting aside additional money for the future, defied critics who said that its ambitions were too costly and unrealistic.

At the same time, California's greatest vulnerability was hubris—that is, a belief that it could pursue all of its costly progressive goals without causing serious unintended consequences. Even during the age of plenty, the state was already starting to feel those effects. California's high-cost, high-regulation, high-tax model was chasing away many businesses and residents, hollowing out the middle class, and causing its socioeconomic system to stratify. At the high end, Silicon Valley and the broader New Economy boomed. California's urban knowledge workers were living in the Shangri-La of the Pacific, enjoying high incomes and a cosmopolitan culture, all in a Mediterranean climate.[11] But for Californians who had less education, fewer skills, and, most important, lower incomes, the state was becoming a forbidding place to live. The rise of the New Economy corresponded with the collapse of the old one—as many sources of middle-class jobs moved to more business-friendly states or shuttered altogether.[12]

California's high costs—for housing, utilities, gasoline, and more—made it hard for those who stayed to pay their bills. When housing costs were factored in, California had, by a substantial margin, the nation's highest poverty rate, and the lack of affordable housing stock was at least partially responsible for the state's shocking homeless crisis, with tens of thousands living in cars, on sidewalks, and beneath bridges.

California's leaders doubled down on spending and regulations to address the gap between residents' incomes and expenses—for example, by increasing welfare payments, raising the minimum wage, imposing limits on rent increases, and funding shelters for the homeless. In addition, they urged the federal government to narrow the red state cost advantage by imposing national mandates in areas such as health and welfare, environmental protection, and worker wages and benefits. But as long as the federal government was either controlled by Republicans or evenly divided between the parties, California could not reasonably expect Washington, D.C., to provide much of that type of help.[13]

The gap between the state's outsized progressive ambitions and its capacity to afford them could be seen most clearly in the proposal to establish universal health care. As noted in Chapter 12, during his 2018 campaign for governor, Gavin Newsom pledged his "firm and absolute commitment" to lead the effort to achieve universal health care in the state—even though analysts estimated that the program would cost $400 billion per year for California to operate, an amount more than twice its annual general fund revenues.[14] Newsom and other progressives believed that California could somehow meet this expensive commitment, even with a hostile administration in the White House and even as the state increased spending on public employee pensions, education, the environment, housing, welfare, and more.

At the time Governor Newsom took office, California was in fact able to expand its spending in many areas, principally because it was taking in massive revenues from taxes on the incomes of its top 1 percent. But anyone could see that this revenue source was highly volatile and that, when the next downturn came, California would struggle mightily to meet its existing obligations, let alone the new ones progressives envisioned. In addition, California always faced the risk that its top earners would eventually tire of paying a premium to live in the state, and that these wealthy geese would take their golden eggs elsewhere.

Finally, the experience of these years showed that the California Model depends heavily on support from Washington, D.C., and thus is vulnerable to changes in federal policy. For example, during California's budget emergency following the 2008 financial meltdown, the Obama administration and the Democratic Congress sent the state a lifeline in the form of large federal transfer payments funded by the American Recovery and Reinvestment Act of 2009, also known as the "stimulus package."[15] But there was no guarantee that other congresses and administrations would be willing to bail out the state every time its spending commitments exceeded its capacity to pay. Moreover, California could never achieve its greatest aspirations, including universal health care and real progress in the fight against CO_2 emissions, without strong federal support. The stark transition from the Obama to Trump administrations made it clear to all that California, like Texas, has enormous stakes in the struggle for control of the federal government.

Looking Forward: How to View the Rivalry

Looking to the future, what can we expect of these rivals and their competition? As noted earlier, the path forward is always uncertain, and one should be cautious in making predictions about what lies ahead. This caveat is particularly necessary when considering politics, where cataclysms such as war or natural disaster—or a combination of a global pandemic and economic crisis—can change in unexpected ways how large numbers of people live, how they think, and how they vote. Although it seems as if the nation's partisan polarization is set in concrete, it may not be. Donald Trump's dominance of American political life following the 2016 presidential election, combined with the pandemic of 2020, will have disruptive consequences for years to come. These and other events could cause existing alignments to shift. Yet, while giving these uncertainties their due, one can make reasonable guesses about the rivalry's next stage.

In considering the future, we return to the fundamental question: Will the two states remain on opposite sides of the nation's partisan divide? California presents the easier case. The Golden State has become one of the nation's least likely places to change its partisan orientation, or even experience meaningful two-party competition. This is especially true as long as the Republican Party associates with Trumpism. Barring some deeper national political realignment, California should remain solidly Democratic and ideologically progressive for a long time to come.

Texas again presents the more difficult and interesting question. As discussed throughout this book, the state's rapidly changing demographics have given Democrats hope that they can turn Texas blue. Indeed, Texas Democrats made gains in the first two elections of the Trump era, winning control of several districts and narrowing the Republican advantage in a number of statewide races. It is certainly possible, even likely, that Democrats will capitalize on Texas's demographic and cultural changes and become more competitive in the years ahead.

However, Texas Democrats face a limiting factor. The state's underlying political culture remains predominantly conservative, and its economic model aligns far more closely with the GOP than with the increasingly progressive Democratic alternative. Contemporary politics are driven by the power of negative polarization—that is, many voters are primarily motivated to oppose parties or candidates they dislike.[16] As a consequence, even if they do not closely align with the GOP, many Texans are repelled by the contemporary Democratic Party, and it will be hard to convince a majority of Texas voters to give members of that party the keys to state government. Moreover, if Democrats do manage to capture the governor's office and the legislature, they will struggle to maintain control of them. A Democratic government in Texas would be torn between the progressive policy demands of the party's base (on taxes, climate action, guns, abortion, and a host of other issues) and the more conservative views of the median Texas voter.

A more likely scenario is for Texas to move into a period of two-party competition in which Democrats occasionally win elections, but Republicans remain largely in charge. This expectation is reinforced by the fact that Texas has become the essential cornerstone of the national Republican Party. The GOP will make maximum effort to defend its control of the state and, if lost, to reclaim it. To be sure, if Texas were to turn blue in an enduring way, it would shift the national partisan balance to the left—but Democrats should temper their expectations of attaining that goal without first achieving a deeper transformation of the state's political culture.

If Texas and California in fact remain on opposite sides of the nation's partisan divide, what are the prospects for their rivalry? It is safe to say that both states will continue to pursue some form of their policy models at home and advance their preferences within the federal system. One can also envision Texas moderating its model along the lines suggested by the Texas 2036 group, or in other ways. Competition from Democrats is already forcing Texas Republicans to look for ways to appeal to voters outside their conservative base. By comparison, the California electorate has shifted so far to the left that the state's Democratic leaders have little incentive to trim their progressive model—unless, perhaps, the state faces a budget crisis or other catastrophe so deep that voters demand change.

And what about other states? Will they more likely gravitate toward the Texas or the California model? As discussed in Chapter 8, most states have sorted along partisan lines and thus are naturally inclined to pursue either the red state or the blue state policy model. But states that seek to pursue the full California package will have the harder task. The nation's wealthy, progressive strongholds on either coast will have the best chance of sustaining California-style social and economic policies; most other states will struggle to do so. California has been able to finance its high-cost model because many of its residents have been willing to pay dearly for access to its New Economy clusters and its natural and cultural amenities. A few states, such as New York, Massachusetts, New Jersey, Connecticut, and Hawaii, have been able to impose similar costs on their residents. But most states would hemorrhage businesses and residents if they made the attempt. Ultimately, the high cost blue state model is hard to sustain in a nation where people, businesses, and capital can move freely across state lines to more affordable locations. States that lack exceptional economic clusters and other attractions simply cannot tax and regulate at California levels.

The blue states' best hope is for the federal government to implement a version of their model on a national scale through new federal mandates and subsidies such as a federal carbon tax, a high federal minimum wage, and Medicare for all. Nationalizing the blue state model in this manner would radically alter the competition between states by pre-empting red state policies and undermining the red state cost advantage. But national mandates of this type would certainly face fierce opposition, and unless and until the federal government puts them firmly in place, most states will likely opt for policies that resemble the Texas Model more closely than the California approach.

One might wonder whether a state can find ways to harmonize features of the competing Texas and California models. Unfortunately, a state cannot simply pick, cafeteria-style, its favorite features from each side. It cannot say, for example, that it wants to adopt Texas's low taxes while at the same time spend at California levels. The models offer no easy synthesis—they necessarily require trade-offs and the setting of priorities. Nevertheless, especially in a time of disruption, some states may seek to break out of rigid left-right categories and consider creative alternatives for addressing complex policy challenges. These solutions may involve finding compromises between strong forms of the red and blue state models.

A related question is whether the rival models can coexist in the federal system over the long run. As discussed earlier, the Brandeisian model suggests that the federal system benefits from the presence of state-level policy differences. Again, California governor Jerry Brown offered a defense of this view. The former Jesuit novice frequently extolled the virtues of "subsidiarity"—a principle of Catholic social thought that government choices should be made at the lowest level possible.[17] "There's something called subsidiarity," Brown said. "And that is moving government responsibility to the institution closest to the people. And I think that's a very important principle, consistent with fundamental human rights."[18]

A federal system committed to subsidiarity, state autonomy, and policy pluralism could find much to celebrate in the rivals' competing policy visions. As Lawrence Wright has observed, "The fact that the United States can contain such assertive contrary forces as Texas and California is a testament to our political dynamism." "But," he added, "more and more I feel that America is being compelled to make a choice between the models these states embody."[19]

That is the challenge. As the red and blue state models have become more ambitious and more polarized, they also have become more incompatible and intolerant of difference—that is, they are forcing America to make choices. The competing Texas and California approaches to energy and environmental policy offer an example. As part of its all-energy policy, Texas remains committed to developing its deep reserves of fossil fuels, while California wants to radically reduce the production and use of carbon-based energy. Unlike some preferences, these cannot easily coexist. California's expensive efforts to reduce carbon emissions will be futile unless the rest of the country—indeed, the world—follows its lead. At the same time, one of Texas's most important industries would be endangered if the nation fully adopted California's aggressive climate policies. The same can be said for many other policy areas in which the two models are diametrically opposed. Texas and California and their respective allies thus feel compelled to fight within the federal system to defend and advance their models—and to defeat the other side.

This circumstance raises an ultimate question. How should we think about our deepest political and policy differences? Many Americans lament our divisions and yearn for a time when the nation was more united. Their sense of longing is understandable. Our deep disagreements have worn on the national soul, and one can easily see how the country and its citizens would benefit from greater harmony and consensus. Yet, in a free, pluralistic, democratic society, disputes over politics and policy are natural—indeed inevitable. Americans have always engaged in a clash of competing ideas and values; as the nation has diversified and its social consensus has weakened, disagreement has become even more inescapable. The challenge of living with difference has grown.

One can have a range of attitudes about the nation's political divisions. Many Americans have not easily embraced these differences and openly dislike those with whom they disagree. In 2016, a survey by the Pew Research Center found that a majority of those who identified as either a Democrat or a Republican held deeply negative attitudes toward the other party, and the intensity of those feelings was strongest for those who were most politically engaged. Majorities of active people in both parties said that the other side made them feel "frustrated," "angry," and "afraid." Many also expressed the belief that the other party "pose[d] a threat to the nation's well-being." When asked whether they felt "warm" or "cold" toward people in the other party, respondents typically said they felt "cold."[20] The survey documented the sad reality that many Americans on both sides of the nation's partisan divide have developed animosity for the other side, viewing members of the other party not only as opponents, but as enemies. These attitudes were making the nation's political culture more toxic and caused many people to become rigid in their thinking about politics and policy. If the nation continues to move in this direction, our future will be marked by even deeper levels of division and enmity.

Yet it is possible to view the nation's differences in a more positive light—and even to see them as a source of strength. To make that shift, it helps to realize that the United States would be diminished if all of its citizens were conservative or all were progressive, or if all of its states were like Texas or all were like California. The national dialectic between right and left, red and blue, Texas and California, contributes to America's remarkable vitality. It also helps to recall that Texas and California—and, more broadly, red and blue America—are more than rivals; they are siblings, members of a common family with a shared history and future.

If I remember that those on the other side of the partisan divide are members of my family, I can more easily become curious about their experiences, values, and commitments. If I listen to them, they might be more likely to listen to me. I may never come to agree with them, but I can view them with less frustration, anger, and fear. And, I am confident, we can learn from one another.[21]

Again, one is reminded of an era of national division much deeper than our own. In an inaugural address delivered in the midst of the secession crisis, President Lincoln appealed to the states on the other side of the divide. "We are not enemies, but friends," he said. "We must not be enemies. Though passion may have strained, it must not break our bonds of affection."[22] One can hold the same hope today for Texas, California, and the states in their respective camps. In our present era of polarization, these remarkable siblings have become rivals, but they need not be enemies. Especially in light of the challenges the nation now faces, one hopes the rivals, and all of us, can compete for its future with great passion, but also with a spirit of mutual respect—and, even, with affection.

Notes

Chapter 1

1. See, generally, Bill Bishop, *The Big Sort: Why the Clustering of Like-Minded America Is Tearing Us Apart* (New York: Mariner Books, 2009); Michael S. Greve, "Federalism in a Polarized Age," in *Parchment Barriers: Political Polarization and the Limits of Constitutional Order*, ed. Zachary Courser, Eric Helland, and Kenneth P. Miller (Lawrence: University Press of Kansas, 2018), 119, 125.
2. Lawrence Wright has elaborated on the sibling analogy, calling Texas and California "mirror image twins." Michael Schaub, "Lawrence Wright Says Texas and California Are Mirror Image Twins," *Los Angeles Times*, April 12, 2018, http://www.latimes.com/books/la-ca-jc-lawrence-wright-20180412-htmlstory.html. For further discussion, see Chapter 14.
3. Maurice Chammah, "In Radio Ads, Perry Reaches Out to California Businesses," *Texas Tribune*, February 4, 2013, https://www.texastribune.org/2013/02/04/gov-perry-californians-move-texas/.
4. Lawrence Wright, "America's Future Is Texas," *New Yorker*, June 10 & 17, 2017, https://www.newyorker.com/magazine/2017/07/10/americas-future-is-texas; Jonathan Tilove, "Amid Trump-Koch Feud, Abbott Talks Texas v. California," *Austin American-Statesman*, August 4, 2018, https://www.statesman.com/news/20180804/amid-trump-koch-feud-abbott-talks-texas-v-california.
5. Adam Nagourney, "A Red Meat Rallying Cry for National Republicans: California," *New York Times*, October 22, 2018, https://www.nytimes.com/2018/10/22/us/california-gop-political-attacks.html.
6. Adam Nagourney and Charles McDermid, "California Today: 'The World Is Looking to Us,' Gavin Newsom Says," *New York Times*, June 1, 2018, https://www.nytimes.com/2018/06/01/us/california-today-gavin-newsom-speech.html.
7. Sam Roberts, "A Rank That Rankles: New York Slips to No. 3; Texas Is Now 2d Most Populous State," *New York Times*, May 19, 1994, B1. In 2014, New York fell behind Florida and now ranks fourth. US Census Bureau, "Florida Passes New York to Become the Nation's Third Most Populous State, Census Bureau Reports," December 23, 2014, https://www.census.gov/newsroom/press-releases/2014/cb14-232.html.
8. Derick Moore, "Texas Added the Most People, but California Still Most Populous," US Census Bureau, January 16, 2018, https://www.census.gov/library/stories/2018/01/state-pop-tableau.html; US Census Bureau, "The 15 Most Populous Cities, July 1, 2016," https://www.census.gov/content/dam/Census/newsroom/releases/2017/cb17-81-table3-most-populous.pdf.

9. Kieran Corcoran, "California's Economy Now the 5th Biggest in the World, and Has Overtaken the United Kingdom," *Business Insider*, May 5, 2018, https://www.businessinsider.com/california-economy-ranks-5th-in-the-world-beating-the-uk-2018-5; US Department of Commerce, Bureau of Economic Analysis, "GDP by State, Third Quarter 2019" January 10, 2020, https://www.bea.gov/data/gdp/gdp-state; International Monetary Fund, "GDP Current Prices," October 2019, https://www.imf.org/external/datamapper/NGDPD@WEO/OEMDC/ADVEC/WEOWORLD.

10. US Census Bureau, "QuickFacts: California," July 1, 2019, https://www.census.gov/quickfacts/ca; US Census Bureau, "QuickFacts: Texas," July 1, 2019, https://www.census.gov/quickfacts/tx. The other "majority-minority" states were Hawaii, New Mexico, and Nevada. Maryland had a white population of 50.5 percent, and was expected to become the sixth "majority-minority state." US Census Bureau, "QuickFacts: Maryland," July 1, 2019, https://www.census.gov/quickfacts/md.

11. American Presidency Project, "Elections," U.C. Santa Barbara, n.d., www.presidency.ucsb.edu/statistics/elections.

12. During the Depression, Texas was divided between pro– and anti–New Deal factions, but between 1935 and 1939, Governor James V Allred, a staunch supporter of Franklin D. Roosevelt, implemented New Deal programs in the state. (See Chapter 6.) Similarly, the state's long-time commitment to low taxes gave way to a series of tax increases between the late 1950s and late 1980s. (See Chapter 9.) The Texas DREAM Act was HB 1403 of 2001. The immigration debate has been waged partly over nomenclature. Some prefer terms such as "illegal" and "alien"; others, as "undocumented" or "unauthorized immigrant." This book generally uses the term "illegal" to describe actions and "undocumented" to describe persons.

13. Examples include Proposition 13 of 1978 (reducing and capping property taxes and requiring supermajority votes for future tax increases), California Secretary of State, "Voter Information Guide: Primary Election, June 6, 1978 (1978): 56–60; Proposition 184 of 1994 (enacting the "Three-Strikes-and-You're-Out" criminal sentencing law); and Proposition 187 of 1994 (restricting state benefits for immigrants not lawfully in the country and requiring reporting of suspected undocumented immigrants), California Secretary of State, "Voter Information Guide: General Election, November 8, 1994" (1994): 32–37; 50–55; and Proposition 209 of 1996 (banning race- or gender-based affirmative action in state hiring, contracting, and university admissions), California Secretary of State, "Voter Information Guide, General Election, November 5, 1996" (1996): 30–33.

14. Clinton defeated Trump in California by a popular vote margin of 8,753,788 to 4,483,810. California Secretary of State, "Statement of Vote: November 8, 2016 General Election" (2016): 17–19. Clinton's 30.1 percent margin of victory was the widest in any presidential contest in the state since the 1936 election between Franklin D. Roosevelt and Alf Landon. In that election, Roosevelt won by thirty-five points, but by fewer than one million votes. See Jeff Horseman, "November's Presidential Election Broke Records in California," *Mercury News*, December 22, 2016, https://www.mercurynews.com/2016/12/22/novembers-presidential-election-broke-records-in-california/.

15. "Election 2018: California Election Results," *New York Times*, November 19, 2018, https://www.nytimes.com/interactive/2018/11/06/us/elections/results-california-elections.html.

16. Evan Halper and Scott Martelle, "State GOP Is 'Dying at the Box Office,' Gov. Says," *Los Angeles Times*, September 8, 2007, http://articles.latimes.com/2007/sep/08/local/me-arnold8/2. After the 2018 election, former California Assembly Republican Leader Kristin Olson announced that "the California Republican Party isn't salvageable at this time. The Grand Old Party is dead—partly because it has failed to separate itself from today's toxic, national brand of Republican politics." Kristin Olson, "My Turn: GOP Is Dead in California: A New Way Must Rise," *CALmatters*, November 13, 2018, https://calmatters.org/articles/commentary/my-turn-gop-is-dead-in-california-a-new-way-must-rise/.

17. See generally John R. Knaggs, *Two Party Texas: The John Tower Era, 1961–1984* (Austin, TX: Eakin Press, 1986); Wayne Thorburn, *Red State: An Insider's Story of How the GOP Came to Dominate Texas Politics* (Austin: University of Texas Press, 2014).

18. Michael Barone and Richard E. Cohen, *The Almanac of American Politics 2006* (Washington, DC: National Journal Group, 2005), 1575–77; Thorburn, *Red State*, 135–212.

19. "Election 2018: Texas Election Results," *New York Times*, November 19, 2018, https://www.nytimes.com/interactive/2018/11/06/us/elections/results-texas-elections.html.

20. After the 2019 election, thirty-five states had "trifectas," with twenty controlled by Republicans and fifteen by Democrats. Nebraska would be considered an additional Republican trifecta state, except that its unicameral legislature is officially nonpartisan. National Conference of State Legislatures, "Post Election 2019 State & Legislative Partisan Composition," November 22, 2019, https://www.ncsl.org/Portals/1/Documents/Elections/Legis_Control_2019_Post-Election%20Nov%2022nd.pdf; Kate Rabinowitz and Ashlyn Still, "Democrats Are Dominating State-Level Races: The Party Has Gained Nine 'Trifectas' since 2016," *Washington Post*, November 17, 2019, https://www.washingtonpost.com/graphics/politics/trifecta/.

21. *New State Ice Co. v. Liebmann*, 285 US 262, 311 (1932), Brandeis, J., dissenting.

22. Abraham Lincoln, "House Divided Speech," delivered to the Illinois State Republican Convention, Springfield, Illinois, June 16, 1858, https://www.nps.gov/liho/learn/historyculture/housedivided.htm.

Chapter 2

1. Alexis de Tocqueville, *Democracy in America*, trans. George Lawrence, ed. J. P. Mayer (New York: Perennial Classics, 2000), [Book I, Chapter 2], 31. In a more recent treatment of this theme, the noted cultural geographer Wilbur Zelinsky described what he called the "Doctrine of First Effective Settlement." According to Zelinsky's theory, "Whenever an empty territory undergoes settlement, or an earlier population is

dislodged by invaders, the specific characteristics of the first group able to effect a viable, self-perpetuating society are of crucial significance for the later social and cultural geography of the area, no matter how tiny the initial band of settlers may have been." Wilbur Zelinsky, *The Cultural Geography of the United States* (Edgewood Cliffs, NJ: Prentice Hall, 1973), 13–14. See also Cal Jillson, *Lone Star Tarnished: A Critical Look at Texas Politics and Public Policy*, 3rd ed. (New York: Routledge, 2018), 5–7.

2. T. R. Fehrenbach, *Lone Star: A History of Texas and the Texans*, updated ed. (New York: Da Capo Press, 2000), 43.

3. As late as 1820, aside from Native American tribes, only about three to four thousand people resided in Texas, mostly in the San Antonio and Goliad areas, with a smaller mixed American and Mexican population at Nacogdoches, just inside the Texas border with Louisiana. Jillson, *Lone Star Tarnished*, 6.

4. Fehrenbach, *Lone Star*, 137.

5. Ibid., 165. Most early settlers to Texas were southerners of Scots-Irish descent. Michael Barone, *Shaping Our Nation: How Surges of Migration Transformed America and Its Politics* (New York: Crown Forum, 2013), 28–46. Smaller numbers came from elsewhere in the United States and other far-flung places, such as the German immigrants who settled in central Texas. See Terry G. Jordan, *German Seeds in Texas Soil: Immigrant Farmers in Nineteenth-Century Texas* (Austin: University of Texas Press, 1966).

6. Fehrenbach, *Lone Star*, 140, 145–47.

7. Ibid., 140; Andrew J. Torget, *Seeds of Empire: Cotton, Slavery, and the Transformation of the Texas Borderlands, 1800–1850* (Chapel Hill: University of North Carolina Press, 2015), 60–61.

8. Tocqueville, *Democracy in America*, [Book I, Conclusion], 409.

9. Fehrenbach, *Lone Star*, 137–38. The United States and Mexico had no agreements allowing U.S. creditors to pursue debtors who crossed the border, making Texas a safe haven where debtors could make a new start. Margaret Swett Henson, "Anglo American Colonization," Texas State Historical Association: *Handbook of Texas Online*, June 9, 2010, https://tshaonline.org/handbook/online/articles/uma01.

10. Fehrenbach, *Lone Star*, 146.

11. Tocqueville, *Democracy in America*, 409.

12. Kevin Starr, *Americans and the California Dream, 1850–1915* (New York: Oxford University Press, 1973), 34–35.

13. Ibid, 41.

14. Richard Henry Dana, Jr. *Two Years before the Mast* (1840; New York: Signet Classics, 2009), 157.

15. Ibid.

16. Hubert Howe Bancroft, *History of California, Vol. IV: 1840–1845*, in *Bancroft's Works*, Vol. XXI (San Francisco: A. L. Bancroft & Co. Publishers, 1886), 127–37; Robert Glass Cleland, *From Wilderness to Empire: A History of California* (New York: Alfred A. Knopf, 1959), 107–9.

17. Hubert Howe Bancroft, *History of California, Vol. V: 1846–1848*, in *Bancroft's Works*, Vol. XXII (San Francisco: The History Co. Publishers, 1886), 101–90; Cleland, *Wilderness to Empire*, 109–13.

18. Fehrenbach, *Lone Star*, 268–73.

19. See Neal Harlow, *California Conquered: The Annexation of a Mexican Province, 1846–1850* (Berkeley: University of California Press, 1982).

20. "Treaty of Peace, Friendship, Limits, and Settlement between the United States of America and the United Mexican States," concluded at Guadalupe Hidalgo, February 2, 1848; ratification advised by Senate, with amendments, March 10, 1848; ratified by president, March 16, 1848; ratifications exchanged at Queretaro, May 30, 1848; proclaimed July 4, 1848, http://avalon.law.yale.edu/19th_century/guadhida.asp.

21. Karl Marx and Frederick Engels, "Review: January–February 1850," *Neue Rheinische*, https://www.marxists.org/archive/marx/works/1850/01/31.htm. For a discussion, see Gordon Lloyd, "Nature and Convention in the Creation of the 1849 California Constitution," in Brian P. Janiskee and Ken Masugi, eds., *California Republic: Institutions, Statesmanship, and Policies*, 33–66 (Lanham, MD: Rowman & Littlefield, 2004), 35.

22. Austin wrote to a friend, "The principal product that will elevate us from poverty is cotton, and we cannot do this without the help of slaves." Torget, *Seeds of Empire*, 86–87. See also Randolph B. Campbell, *An Empire for Slavery: The Peculiar Institution in Texas, 1821–1865* (Baton Rouge: Louisiana State University Press, 1989).

23. Fehrenbach, *Lone Star*, 143.

24. In 1836, the year Texas won independence from Mexico, approximately four thousand *Tejanos*, thirty thousand Anglo-Texans, and five thousand slaves resided in the new Republic. Fehrenbach, *Lone Star*, 287.

25. Earl M. Maltz, "The Constitution and the Annexation of Texas," *Constitutional Commentary* 23 (2006): 381–401.

26. Randolph B. Campbell, *Gone to Texas: A History of the Lone Star State*, 3rd ed. (New York: Oxford University Press, 2018), 166–68.

27. Ibid., 168.

28. The convention was chaired by the Republic's former secretary of war, Thomas Jefferson Rusk, and included, among other prominent figures, Sam Houston; R. E. B. Baylor, co-founder of Baylor University; Hardin G. Runnels, who had served as governor of Mississippi; and Abner Smith Lipscomb, who had served as chief justice of the Alabama Supreme Court. Frederic L. Paxson, "The Constitution of Texas, 1845," *Southwestern Historical Quarterly* 18, no. 4 (April 1915): 386–98; Annie Middleton, "The Texas Convention of 1845," *Southwestern Historical Quarterly* 25, no. 1 (July 1921): 26–62.

29. Texas Constitution of 1845, Art. VIII; Paxson, "The Constitution of Texas, 1845," 388–89.

30. "Anson Jones Valedictory Speech, February 19, 1846," Texas State Library and Archives Commission, https://www.tsl.texas.gov/treasures/earlystate/nomore-3.html.

31. The Annexation Resolution provided: "New States of convenient size not exceeding four in number, in addition to said State of Texas and having sufficient population, may, hereafter by the consent of said State, be formed out of the territory thereof,

which shall be entitled to admission under the provisions of the Federal Constitution; and such states as may be formed out of the territory lying south of thirty-six degrees thirty minutes north latitude, commonly known as the Missouri Compromise Line, shall be admitted into the Union, with or without slavery, as the people of each State, asking admission shall desire; and in such State or States as shall be formed out of said territory, north of said Missouri Compromise Line, slavery, or involuntary servitude (except for crime) shall be prohibited." "Joint Resolution for Annexing Texas to the United States (March 1, 1845)," in *The Public Statutes at Large of the United States of America*, vol. 5, ed. Richard Peters (Boston: Chas. C. Little and Jas. Brown, 1850), 797–98.

32. Campbell, *Gone to Texas*, 215–16.

33. Sue Flanagan, *Sam Houston's Texas* (Austin: University of Texas Press, 1964), 122.

34. Campbell, *Gone to Texas*, 221–25.

35. Carl H. Moneyhon, *Texas after the Civil War: The Struggle of Reconstruction* (College Station: Texas A&M Press, 2004); Barry A. Crouch, *The Dance of Freedom: Texas African Americans during Reconstruction* (Austin: University of Texas Press, 2007), 134–58. Texas was readmitted to the Union on March 30, 1870.

36. Hubert Howe Bancroft, *History of California, Vol. VI: 1848–1859*, in *Bancroft's Works*, Vol. XXIII (San Francisco: The History Co. Publishers, 1888), 336–37.

37. Ibid., 282, 288. See also, Lloyd, "Nature and Convention": 39–40. Thirty of the delegates had arrived since 1846, twelve since the discovery of gold in 1848.

38. To the surprise of northern representatives, the southerners did not object to the prohibition on slavery. The clause was adopted unanimously. According to Bancroft, "the temper of the majority was understood." Indeed, most migrants to California did not want slavery introduced into the state. Bancroft cited one newcomer from the South who wanted to escape a culture where work was dishonored, and another new resident who believed that if California needed low cost labor, it could contract it from China. Bancroft, *History of California*, VI, 290.

39. Ibid., 290, 296. The delegates agreed to a compromise that set the state's eastern boundary on the 120th meridian from the Oregon line to the 39th parallel; from there, in a straight line to the Colorado River at the intersection of the 35th parallel; and finally along the Colorado River to the to the Mexican border.

40. Senator John C. Calhoun argued that "[i]f the equilibrium between North and South should be further disturbed by the admission of California as a free state, the South could no longer hope for justice in the Union." Joseph H. Parks, "John Bell and the Compromise of 1850," *Journal of Southern History* 9, no. 3 (August 1943): 343.

41. Ibid., 328–56.

42. Bancroft, *History of California*, VI, 343–345. To increase its chances of winning admission from a divided Congress, California elected as its first two Senators John C. Frémont, a hero of the conquest of California, and free-soil man, and William F. Gwin, an immigrant from Mississippi with southern sympathies.

43. Although Gwin was a man of the South, he also was committed to the preservation of the Union. See Arthur Quinn, *The Rivals: William Gwin, David Broderick, and the Birth of California* (New York: Crown Publishers, 1994), vi.

44. J. M. Guinn, "*La Estrella*: The Pioneer Newspaper of Los Angeles," *Annual Publication of the Historical Society of Southern California and Pioneer Register* (1900): 70, 72.

45. Charles S. Potts, "David S. Terry: The Romantic Story of a Great Texan," *Southwest Review* 19, no. 3 (April 1934): 295–334.

46. Quinn, *Rivals*, 168–69; 253–76. The chief justice was acquitted of murder in 1860, but soon returned to Texas where he served in the Confederate army.

47. Ibid., 282–83.

48. American Presidency Project: "Elections (1860)," University of California, Santa Barbara, n.d., https://www.presidency.ucsb.edu/statistics/elections/1860.

49. Glenna Matthews, *The Golden State in the Civil War: Thomas Starr King, the Republican Party, and the Birth of Modern California* (New York: Cambridge University Press, 2012), 155–57.

50. Lewis B. Lesley, "A Southern Transcontinental Railroad into California: Texas and Pacific versus Southern Pacific, 1865–1885," *Pacific Historical Review* 5, no. 1 (March 1936): 52–60.

51. Lewis B. Lesley, "The Entrance of the Santa Fé Railroad into California," *Pacific Historical Review* 8, no. 1 (March 1939): 89–96.

Chapter 3

1. Richard M. Scammon and Ben J. Wattenberg, *The Real Majority: An Extraordinary Examination of the American Electorate* (New York: Coward-McCann, Inc., 1970), 45–46. Scammon and Wattenberg wrote: "While it may overstate the case to paraphrase Heraclitus by saying, 'Demography is destiny,' in an electoral sense there is a good measure of truth to the phrase." (Heraclitus posits, "Character is destiny.") In recent times, political analysts seeking to draw connections between demographic and political trends have embraced Scammon and Wattenberg's adage.

2. The World Bank, "Population Growth (Annual %)" (2019), https://data.worldbank.org/indicator/SP.POP.GROW?contextual=default&locations=US-OE&name_desc=false.

3. Frank Hobbs and Nicole Stoops, "Demographic Trends in the 20th Century" (Washington, DC: U.S. Census Bureau, November 2002): 9–24; University of Virginia Weldon Cooper Center, Demographics Research Group, "National Population Projections 2018," https://demographics.coopercenter.org/national-population-projections. The Census Bureau defines mean center population as "the place where an imaginary, flat, weightless, and rigid map of the United States would balance perfectly if all residents were of identical weight." U.S. Census Bureau, "2010 Census: Center of Population," https://www.census.gov/2010census/data/center-of-population.html.

4. The Census Bureau defines urban areas based on measures of population density and defines rural areas as everything that is not urban. See Michael Ratcliffe, Charlynn Burd, Kelly Holder, and Alison Fields, "Defining Rural at the U.S. Census Bureau," ACSGEO-1, U.S. Census Bureau, Washington, DC (2016); U.S. Census Bureau, "Measuring America: Our Changing Landscape," December 8, 2016, https://www.

census.gov/content/dam/Census/library/visualizations/2016/comm/acs-rural-urban.pdf; Hobbs and Stoops, "Demographic Trends," 11, 16–18, 33; *ProQuest Statistical Abstract of the United States, 2016* (Lanham, MD: Rowman and Littlefield, 2016), 31, Table 26 "Urban and Rural Population by State, 2000 and 2010."

5. For perspectives on the problem, see, for example, Claudette Bennett, "Race: Questions and Classifications," in Margo J. Anderson, Constance F. Citro, and Joseph J. Salvo, eds., *Encyclopedia of the U.S. Census: From the Constitution to the American Community Survey* (Washington, DC: CQ Press, 2011), 352–55; William H. Frey, *Diversity Explosion: How New Racial Demographics Are Remaking America* (Washington, DC: Brookings Institution Press, 2018), 10–11.

6. Campbell Gibson and Kay Jung, "Historical Census Statistics on Population Totals by Race, 1790 to 1990, and by Hispanic Origin, 1970 to 1990, for the United States, Regions, Divisions, and States," Working Paper No. 56 (Washington, DC: U.S. Census Bureau, September 2002), 1–6, https://census.gov/content/dam/Census/library/working-papers/2002/demo/POP-twps0056.pdf.

7. The Immigration Act of 1924, also known as the Johnson-Reed Act (Pub. L. 68–139) expanded immigration restrictions adopted in 1921. Among other provisions, the 1924 act effectively banned immigration from Asia and set quotas for other countries, with the cap generally set at 2 percent of the population from those countries in the year 1890. The restrictions sharply reduced immigration into the United States, especially from disfavored countries of origin.

8. See Isabel Wilkerson, *The Warmth of Other Suns: The Epic Story of America's Great Migration* (New York: Random House, 2010).

9. This book also uses the terms "Hispanic" and "Latino" interchangeably. See U.S. Census Bureau, *Fifteenth Census of the United States, 1930*, Vol. II: 263; Gibson and Jung, "Historical Census Statistics," 1–6; Frey, *Diversity Explosion*, 10–11.

10. Gibson and Jung, "Historical Census Statistics," Table 1, with 1970 Hispanic population based on self-identification. For historical figures of U.S. population by country of origin, see Migration Policy Institute, "U.S. Immigrant Population by Country of Birth, 1960–2017," n.d., https://www.migrationpolicy.org/programs/data-hub/us-immigration-trends#source.

11. The Immigration and Nationality Act of 1965, also known as the Hart-Celler Act (Pub. L. 89–236).

12. Frey, *Diversity Explosion*, 1–5, 88. Congressional Budget Office, "Immigration Policy in the United States," February 2006, https://www.cbo.gov/sites/default/files/109th-congress-2005-2006/reports/02-28-immigration.pdf.

13. Frey, *Diversity Explosion*, 132–33.

14. Hobbs and Stoops, "Demographic Trends," 24.

15. Office of the Historian, U.S. House of Representatives, "Representatives Apportioned to Each State (1st to 23rd Census, 1790–2010)," https://history.house.gov/.

16. Brian Uhler and Justin Garosi, "California Losing Residents via Domestic Migration," California Legislative Analyst's Office, February 21, 2018; Mark DiCamillo, "Leaving California: Half of the State's Voters Have Been Considering This; Republicans and Conservatives Three Times as Likely as Democrats and Liberals to Be Giving Serious

Consideration to Leaving the State," Release # 2019-08, U.C. Berkeley IGS Poll, September 27, 2019, https://escholarship.org/uc/item/96j2704t.

17. California Department of Finance, "State's Population Increases by 141,300 While Rate of Growth Continues to Decline," December 20, 2019, https://capsweb.org/wp-content/uploads/2019/12/population-estimate.pdf; Joe Mathews, "California's Population to Hit 40 Million—and About to Fall," *Orange County Register*, July 15, 2018, https://www.ocregister.com/2018/07/15/californias-population-to-hit-40-million-and-about-to-fall/.

18. Gibson and Jung, "Historical Census Statistics," Tables 19 and 58; U.S. Census Bureau, American Factfinder for Texas and California, 2000 and 2010; California Department of Finance, "P-1: State Population Projections (2010–2060): Total Population by Race/Ethnicity: Hispanic Combined," last modified May 2019, http://www.dof.ca.gov/Forecasting/Demographics/projections/; Texas Demographic Center, "Age, Sex, and Race/Ethnicity (ASRE) Population, by Age Group for 2010–2050 in 1 year Increments," last modified January 2020, https://demographics.texas.gov/Data/TPEPP/Projections/. Figures 3.1 and 3.3 use the California Department of Finance's and the Texas Demographic Center's population projections for 2020. The U.S. Census Bureau often disagrees with California Department of Finance in their respective estimates of California's population. For example, in 2019 the Census Bureau estimated that California's population was 39.56 million, while the Department of Finance estimated it to be 39.96 million. That year, the Department of Finance projected that California's population would reach 40.12 million in 2020, but if the Census Bureau's population estimates were correct, the number would likely be lower. For a discussion, see Dan Walters, "The Politics of Slow Population Growth," *CalMatters*, January 12, 2020, https://calmatters.org/commentary/census-population-congressional-slow/. The Texas Demographic Center has also estimated the state's population at levels higher than Census Bureau estimates, although the gap is not as large as in California. In 2019, the Texas Demographic Center estimated that the state's population was 29.19 million, while the Census Bureau estimated it was 29.0 million.

19. Historical population data for U.S. cities compiled by the U.S. Census Bureau and published at www.biggestuscities.com. For urban density in California, see U.S. Census Bureau, "Urban/Rural and Metropolitan/Nonmetropolitan Population: 2000—State—Urban/Rural and Inside/Outside Metropolitan Area," https://factfinder.census.gov/faces/tableservices/jsf/pages/productview.xhtml?pid=DEC_00_SF1_GCTP1.ST93&prodType=table.

20. Ibid.

21. Gibson and Jung, "Historical Census Statistics," Table 58. According to historian T. R. Fehrenbach, as of 1900, 70,000 ethnic Mexicans lived in Texas, or less than 5 percent of the total population. ; T. R. Fehrenbach, *Lone Star: A History of Texas and the Texans*, updated ed. (New York: Da Capo Press, 2000), 687.

22. Nelson W. Polsby, *How Congress Evolves: Social Bases of Institutional Change* (New York: Oxford University Press, 2012), 80–88; Raymond Arsenault, "The End of the Long Hot Summer: The Air Conditioner in Southern Culture," *Journal of Southern History* 50, no. 4 (November 1984): 597–628.

23. Texas Demographic Center, "Population Projections for the State of Texas (2010–2050)," State_of_Texas.csv. (2018), https://demographics.texas.gov/Data/TPEPP/Projections/.

24. By the 1870s, 10 percent of San Francisco's population was Jewish. Hubert Howe Bancroft, cited in Joel Kotkin, "California and the Jews," *Forbes*, November 22, 2008, https://www.forbes.com/2008/11/22/cities-jews-blacks-oped-cx_jk_1124kotkin.html#6bd500156877, U.S. Census Bureau, "Statistical Abstract of the United States, 2012: Population," https://www.census.gov/library/publications/2011/compendia/statab/131ed/population.html.

25. Kevin Starr, *Inventing the Dream: California through the Progressive Era* (New York: Oxford University Press, 1986), 236–39; George E. Mowry, *The California Progressives* (Berkeley and Los Angeles: University of California Press, 1951), 7–8.

26. James N. Gregory, *American Exodus: The Dust Bowl Migration and Okie Culture in California* (New York: Oxford, 1989), 36–77.

27. U.S. Census Bureau, Statistical Abstract of the United States, 2012: Table 77: "Christian Church Adherents and Jewish Population, States," https://www2.census.gov/library/publications/2011/compendia/statab/131ed/tables/pop.pdf; Ira M. Sheskin and Arnold Dashefsky, eds. "Jewish Population in the United States, 2014," in *American Jewish Yearbook* (Dordrecht: Springer, 2014), 220–223.

28. Arnold Dashefsky and Ira M. Sheskin, eds., *American Jewish Year Book 2018: The Annual Record of the North American Jewish Communities since 1899*, vol. 118 (Springer International Publishing, 2019), 264–65.

29. Gibson and Jung, "Historical Census Statistics," Table 19, using Census Bureau's self-reporting measure for Hispanics in 1970 (5 percent sample). As noted earlier, in 1970, the Census Bureau used a range of methods to estimate the Hispanic population. The different methods produced different estimates of the Hispanic population in California (between 2.4 and 2.7 million). These differences also affected the Census's estimate of the non-Hispanic white population, which in California ranged from 76.3 to 78 percent.

30. Ibid.; U.S. Census Bureau, "Quickfacts: California" (2019), https://www.census.gov/quickfacts/CA. The decline of the white percentage in California was steep: 66.6 percent in 1980, 57.2 percent in 1990, 46.7 in 2000, 40.1 in 2010.

31. Gibson and Jung, "Historical Census Statistics," Table 58. According to Census figures, the black population of Texas was 182,921 in 1860 (30.27 percent of the state's population); by 1870, it had risen to 253,475 (30.97 percent).

32. Major General Gordon Granger announced: "The people of Texas are informed that, in accordance with a proclamation from the Executive of the United States, all slaves are free. This involves an absolute equality of personal rights and rights of property between former masters and slaves, and the connection heretofore existing between them becomes that between employer and hired labor." Gordon Granger, General Order No. 3, June 19, 1865, available at https://tshaonline.org/handbook/online/articles/lkj01.

33. Carl H. Moneyhon, *Texas after the Civil War: The Struggle of Reconstruction* (College Station: Texas A&M Press, 2004), 188–205.

34. Marvin Dulaney, "African Americans," Texas State Historical Association, July 25, 2016, https://tshaonline.org/handbook/online/articles/pkaan; Gibson and Jung, "Historical Census Statistics," Table 58; Fehrenbach, *Lone Star*, 683.

35. V. O. Key Jr., *Southern Politics in State and Nation* (New York: A. A. Knopf, 1949), 254.

36. For a discussion of how Texas featured in prominently in civil rights and voting rights litigation, see Lucas A. Powe Jr. *America's Lone Star Constitution: How Cases from Texas Shape the Nation* (Oakland: University of California Press, 2018), 15–27, 45–55.

37. U.S. Census Bureau, "ACS Demographic and Housing Estimates, 2018 5-year ACS Data Profiles (Texas)," https://www.census.gov/acs/www/data/data-tables-and-tools/data-profiles/; U.S. Census Bureau, American Community Survey, Estimates of Black Alone Population (2017), https://factfinder.census.gov/faces/tableservices/jsf/pages/productview.xhtml?pid=ACS_17_1YR_B02001&prodType=table. According to Census Bureau estimates, approximately 1.19 million African Americans lived in the Houston Metro area and 1.16 million in the Dallas–Ft. Worth Metro area, which together made up more than 68 percent of the state's black population.

38. Gibson and Jung, "Historical Census Statistics."

39. The development of a black middle class translated into political influence. Los Angeles produced the first African American state legislator on the West Coast in 1918 when it elected Frederick Madison Roberts to the Assembly. Roberts was a newspaper editor and business owner, as well as a great-grandson of Thomas Jefferson and Sally Hemings. He represented his Los Angeles district in the legislature for sixteen years and paved the way for the election of other black representatives in the state. See Delilah L Beasley, *Negro Trailblazers in California* (1919; repr. Whitefish, MT: Kessinger Legacy Reprints, 2010), 137–215.

40. Gibson and Jung, "Historical Census Statistics," Tables 19 and 58; Sonya Rastogi, Tallese D. Johnson, Elizabeth M. Hoeffel, and Malcolm J. Drewery, Jr., "The Black Population: 2010," U.S. Census Bureau, September 2011, Table 5. www.census.gov/prod/cen2010/briefs/c2010br-06.pdf.

41. Carey McWilliams, *North from Mexico: The Spanish-Speaking People of the United States*, 3rd ed., updated by Alma M. Garcia (Santa Barbara, CA: Praeger, 2016), 67.

42. U.S. Census Bureau, *Fourteenth Census of the United States, 1920*, Vol. II, Table 11: "Distribution, by State of Residence, of Population Born in the Principal Foreign Countries: 1920, 1910, and 1900," 727; U.S. Census Bureau, *Fifteenth Census of the United States, 1930*, Vol. II, Table 11: "Color or Race and Nativity, by Divisions and States: 1930," 35. See also Will J. French, "Mexicans in California: Report of Governor C. C. Young's Mexican Fact-Finding Committee" (Sacramento: California State Printing Office, 1930), 3; McWilliams, *North from Mexico*, 128.

43. Office of the Historian, U.S. Department of State, Bureau of Public Affairs, "The Immigration Act of 1924 (The Johnson-Reed Act)," https://history.state.gov/milestones/1921-1936/immigration-act.

44. See, generally, Edna E. Kelley, "The Mexicans Go Home," *Southwest Review* 17 (April 1932); Robert R. McKay, "Mexican Repatriation from Texas during the Great Depression," *Journal of South Texas* 3 (Spring 1990); David E. Hayes-Bautista, *La Nueva California: Latinos from Pioneers to Post-Millennials* (Oakland: University of California Press, 2017), 20–21.

45. See Kelly Lytle Hernández, "The Crimes and Consequences of Illegal Immigration: A Cross-Border Examination of Operation Wetback, 1943–1954," *Western Historical Quarterly* 37 (Winter 2006): 421–44; Hayes-Bautista: *La Nueva California*, 37.

46. The Immigration Reform and Control Act of 1986 (P.L. 99-603). Estimates of the number who received amnesty under the law vary, but the consensus figure is approximately 2.7 million. Muzaffar Chishti, Doris Meissner, and Claire Bergeron, "At Its 25th Anniversary, IRCA's Legacy Lives On," Migration Policy Institute, November 16, 2011, https://www.migrationpolicy.org/article/its-25th-anniversary-ircas-legacy-lives.

47. Gibson and Jung, "Historical Census Statistics," Tables 19 and 58; U.S. Census Bureau, American Factfinder for Texas and California, 2000 and 2010; California Department of Finance, "P-1: State Population Projections (2010–2060): Total Population by Race/Ethnicity: Hispanic Combined," last modified May 2019, http://www.dof.ca.gov/Forecasting/Demographics/projections/; Texas Demographic Center, "Age, Sex, and Race/Ethnicity (ASRE) Population, by Age Group for 2010–2050 in 1 year increments," last modified 2018, https://demographics.texas.gov/Data/TPEPP/Projections/.

48. Pew Research Center, "Hispanic Trends: Hispanic Population and Origin in Select U.S. Metropolitan Areas, 2014," September 6, 2016, http://www.pewhispanic.org/interactives/hispanic-population-in-select-u-s-metropolitan-areas/. As of 2014, the nation's top ten metropolitan areas based on Mexican-origin population were as follows: Los Angeles–Long Beach–Anaheim (CA) 4,696,000; Riverside–San Bernardino–Ontario (CA) 1,920,000; Houston–The Woodlands–Sugar Land (TX) 1,767,000; Chicago-Naperville-Elgin (IL-IN-WI) 1,652,000; Dallas–Fort Worth–Arlington (TX) 1,638,000; Phoenix-Mesa-Scottsdale (AZ) 1,199,000; San Antonio–New Braunfels (TX) 1,128,000; San Diego–Carlsbad (CA) 974,000; McAllen-Edinburg-Mission (TX) 738,000; San Francisco–Oakland–Hayward (CA) 702,000. Ibid.

49. Gibson and Jung, "Historical Census Statistics," Table 19.

50. Elmer Clarence Sandmeyer, *The Anti-Chinese Movement in California* (1939; repr. Urbana and Chicago: University of Illinois Press, 1991), 12.

51. Starr, *Inventing the Dream*, 172.

52. Henry George, *Our Land and Land Policy, National and State.* Pamphlet (San Francisco: White and Bauer, 1871); Kevin Starr, *Americans and the California Dream, 1850–1915* (New York: Oxford University Press, 1973), 136–38.

53. In 1879, California adopted a new constitution, which included Article XIX titled "Chinese." Section 4 of that article states: "Asiatic coolieism is a form of human slavery, and is forever prohibited in this State, and all contracts for coolie labour shall be void." In 1875, Congress adopted the Page Act (P.L. 43-141), which restricted immigration by Chinese women, followed in 1882 by the Chinese Exclusion Act (P.L. 47-126), which placed broader limitations on the number of Chinese allowed to enter the United States. Congress renewed the Chinese immigration restrictions in 1892 and 1902 and did not repeal them until 1943. See Kevin Starr, *Endangered Dreams: The Great Depression in California* (New York: Oxford University Press, 1996), 5–17, 62–63.

54. The Asian share of California's population hit a historic low in 1950 at 1.7 percent. Gibson and Jung, "Historical Census Statistics," Table 19. For accounts of this history, see Edwin E. Ferguson, "The California Alien Land Law and the Fourteenth Amendment," *California Law Review* 35, no. 1 (1947): 61–90; Richard Reeves, *Infamy: The Shocking Story of the Japanese-American Internment in World War II* (New York: Henry Holt and Co., 2015).

55. U.S. Census Bureau, American Factfinder: Demographic and Housing Estimates, 2013–2017 American Community Survey, 5-Year Estimates, https://factfinder. census.gov/faces/tableservices/jsf/pages/productview.xhtml?pid=ACS_17_5YR_ DP05&prodType=table.

56. Ibid. In Los Angeles County, cities with majority Asian populations as of 2017 included (with percentages in parentheses): Monterey Park (67), Walnut (64), Arcadia (62), Cerritos (62), Rosemead (62), Temple City (62), San Gabriel (61), Rowland Heights (61), Diamond Bar (55), San Marino (54), and Alhambra (51). In the San Francisco Bay Area, the cities were Milpitas (67), Cupertino (67), Fremont (58), Daly City (57), and Union City (55). These percentages do not include the Pacific Islander populations in these jurisdictions.

57. Bruce A. Glasrud, "Asians in Texas: An Overview, 1870–1990," *East Texas Historical Journal* 39, no. 2 (2001).

58. Texans of Asian descent comprised 5.2 percent of the state's population as of July 2019. U.S. Census Bureau, "Quickfacts: Texas" (2019)." For data on the Asian population by national origin, see U.S. Census, "Asian Alone by Selected Groups: Universe: Total Asian Alone: 2013–2017 American Community Survey 5-Year Estimates (Texas)," https://factfinder.census.gov/faces/tableservices/jsf/pages/productview.xhtml?pid= ACS_17_5YR_B02015&prodType=table.

59. U.S. Census Bureau, "Quickfacts" by city, n.d., https://www.census.gov/quickfacts/.

60. See, for example, Matt A. Barreto, Tyler Reny, and Bryan Wilcox-Archuleta, "Survey Methodology and the Latino/a Vote: Why a Bilingual, Bicultural, Latino-Centered Approach Matters," *Aztlán: A Journal of Chicano Studies* 42, no. 2 (Fall 2017): 211–27.

61. For an analysis of the contested 2004 polling data, see Roberto Suro, Richard Fry, and Jeffrey Passel, "Hispanics and the 2004 Election: Population, Electorate, and Voters: How Latinos Voted in 2004." Washington, DC: Pew Hispanic Center (June 27, 2005).

62. Again, critics contested the 2016 exit poll estimates of the Latino vote. See Gabriel Sanchez and Matt A. Barreto, "In Record Numbers, Latinos Voted Overwhelmingly against Trump," *Washington Post,* November 11, 2016, citing a Latino Decisions pre-election poll that indicated only 18 percent of Latinos supported Trump over Clinton, far below the 29 percent reported by the national exit poll. https://www. washingtonpost.com/news/monkey-cage/wp/2016/11/11/in-record-numbers- latinos-voted-overwhelmingly-against-trump-we-did-the-research/. The Latino Decisions election eve poll also reported that Latinos in Texas supported Clinton over Trump by 80 to 16 percent, the same percentage as in California. While acknowledging the methodological limitations of the exit poll, some also questioned the Latino Decisions findings. See, for example, Harry Enton, "Trump Probably Did

Better with Latino Voters Than Romney Did," *FiveThirtyEight*, November 18, 2018, https://fivethirtyeight.com/features/trump-probably-did-better-with-latino-voters-than-romney-did/.

63. U.S. Census Bureau, "Voting and Registration Tables (2006–2018)," https://www.census.gov/topics/public-sector/voting/data/tables.All.html.

64. Karthick Ramakrishnan, "How Asians Became Democrats," *The American Prospect*, July 26, 2016, https://prospect.org/article/how-asian-americans-became-democrats-0.

Chapter 4

1. Although Texas had a larger total gross domestic product than New York, it still trailed the Empire State in per capita GDP.

2. International Monetary Fund, "GDP Current Prices," October 2019, https://www.imf.org/external/datamapper/NGDPD@WEO/OEMDC/ADVEC/WEOWORLD; US Department of Commerce, Bureau of Economic Analysis, "GDP by State, Third Quarter 2019" January 10, 2020, https://www.bea.gov/data/gdp/gdp-state; California Department of Finance, "Gross State Product Comparison to Other U.S. States: Annual Since 1987," http://www.dof.ca.gov/Forecasting/Economics/Indicators/Gross_State_Product/.

3. International Monetary Fund, "GDP Current Prices."

4. For a discussion of the factors that lead people to migrate to new locations, see Michael Storper and Allen J. Scott, "Rethinking Human Capital, Creativity, and Urban Growth," *Journal of Economic Geography* 9 (2009): 147–67.

5. Harvard Business School professor Michael Porter developed the theory of clusters and demonstrated their importance to the economic development and competitiveness of a region, state, or nation. Michael E. Porter, "Clusters and the New Economics of Competition," *Harvard Business Review* (November–December 1998). Porter more fully developed the concept in Michael E. Porter, *The Competitive Advantage of Nations* (New York: The Free Press, 1990). See also Stefano Breschi and Franco Malerba, *Clusters, Networks, and Innovation* (New York: Oxford University Press, 2005).

6. Richard Florida, "The Winners and Losers of Economic Clustering," *Citylab*, January 6, 2016, https://www.citylab.com/life/2016/01/creativity-clustering-us-cities/422718/; Roger Martin, Richard Florida, Melissa Pogue, and Charlotta Mellander, "Creativity, Clusters, and the Competitive Advantage of Cities," *Competiveness Review* 25, no. 5 (2015): 482–96; Joel Kotkin, *The New Class Conflict* (Candor, NY: Telos Press Publishing, 2014); Michael Storper, Thomas Kemeny, Naji P. Makarem, and Taner Osman, *The Rise and Fall of Urban Economies: Lessons from San Francisco and Los Angeles* (Stanford, CA: Stanford Business Books, 2015), 20–34.

7. T. R. Fehrenbach, *Lone Star: A History of Texas and the Texans* (Cambridge, MA: Da Capo Press, 2000), 633.

8. Karen Gerhardt Britton, Fred C. Elliott, and E. A. Miller, "Cotton Culture," Texas State Historical Association, June 12, 2010, https://tshaonline.org/handbook/online/articles/afc03.

9. Robert S. Maxwell, "Lumber Industry," Texas State Historical Association, February 21, 2012, https://tshaonline.org/handbook/online/articles/drl02.

10. Daniel Yergin, *The Prize: The Epic Quest for Oil, Money, and Power* (New York: Touchstone, 1992), 82–86; Lawrence Wright, "The Dark Bounty of Texas Oil," *The New Yorker*, December 25, 2017, https://www.newyorker.com/magazine/2018/01/01/the-dark-bounty-of-texas-oil.

11. Yergin, *Prize*, 244–48.

12. For a discussion of the pipeline construction and the importance of Texas oil to the war effort, see Harold L. Ickes, *Fightin' Oil* (New York: Alfred A. Knopf, 1943). See also Yergin, *Prize*, 379; Keith Martin, "The Big Inch: Fueling America's World War II War Effort," National Institute of Standards and Technology: Taking Measure, March 26, 2018, https://www.nist.gov/blogs/taking-measure/big-inch-fueling- americas-wwii-war-effort.

13. "Fortune 500 (2019)," *Fortune*, May 16, 2019, https://fortune.com/fortune500/2019/search/?hqstate=TX. In 2019, Occidental Petroleum announced the acquisition of Anadarko (ranked 237), an oil and gas exploration and production company headquartered in the Houston area, for $57 billion, defeating Chevron in a bidding war for the firm.

14. Pablo Pinto and Ryan Kennedy, "No More Business as Usual for Oil and Gas Companies," Forbes.com, June 28, 2019, https://www.forbes.com/sites/uhenergy/2019/06/28/no-more-business-as-usual-for-oil-and-gas-companies/#737373616794.

15. Ariel Cohen, "America's Oil and Gas Reserves Double with Massive New Permian Discovery," *Forbes*, December 21, 2018, https://www.forbes.com/sites/arielcohen/2018/12/21/americas-oil-and-gas-reserves-double-with-massive-new-permian-discovery/.

16. Railroad Commission of Texas, "Crude Oil Production and Well Counts (since 1935): History of Texas Initial Crude Oil, Annual Production, and Producing Wells," July 25, 2019, https://www.rrc.state.tx.us/oil-gas/research-and-statistics/production-data/historical-production-data/crude-oil-production-and-well-counts-since-1935/; U.S. Energy Information Administration, "Texas State Energy Profile," March 19, 2020, https://www.eia.gov/state/print.php?sid=TX#37.

17. Theodore R. Eck, "The Growth of the Southwestern Petrochemical Industry," *Business Review* 45, no. 6 (June 1960): 1–5.

18. Susan Belkin, "Now, It's Remember the Oil Bust!" *New York Times*, August 22, 1989, https://www.nytimes.com/1989/08/22/business/now-it-s-remember-the-oil-bust.html; Wright, "Dark Bounty."

19. Houston, known as "Space City," has served as mission control for the nation's manned spaceflight program, including for the Mercury, Gemini, Apollo, Skylab, Space Shuttle, and International Space Station missions. It is also the training center and home for the nation's astronaut corps. The city was immortalized on July 20,

1969, when Apollo 11 Commander Neil Armstrong spoke the first words from the moon: "Houston, Tranquility Base here. The Eagle has landed." John Noble Wilford, "Men Walk on Moon," *New York Times*, July 21, 1969, A–1.

20. See Laila Assanie, Kristin E. Davis, Pia Orrenius, and Michael Weiss, "At the Heart of Texas: Cities' Industry Clusters Drive Growth, Second Edition," Dallas, TX: Federal Reserve Bank of Dallas (2018): 4–9; Mike W. Thomas, "Texas Takes the Lead in Technology Exports," *San Antonio Business Journal*, February 11, 2014, https://www.bizjournals.com/sanantonio/blog/2014/02/texas-takes-the-lead-in-technology-exports.html.

21. See Assanie, Davis, Orrenius, and Weiss, "Heart of Texas," 4.

22. Jared Walczak, Scott Drenkard, and Joseph Bishop-Henchman, "2019 State Business Climate Index," The Tax Foundation, September 26, 2018, https://taxfoundation.org/publications/state-business-tax-climate-index/; Alexandra Suich Bass, "California and Texas Are Both Failing Their Neediest Citizens," *The Economist*, June 20, 2019, https://www.economist.com/special-report/2019/06/20/california-and-texas-are-both-failing-their-neediest-citizens.

23. Patrick Clark, "Texas Is a Homebuilding Machine. And the Rest of the U.S.?" *Bloomberg*, August 15, 2017, https://www.bloomberg.com/news/articles/2017-08-16/texas-leads-the-u-s-in-new-home-construction-and-california.

24. See, for example, Scott Cohn, "Texas Is CNBC's Top State for Business this Year," CNBC.com, June 10, 2018, https://www.cnbc.com/2018/06/29/texas-rebounds-to-become-americas-top-state-for-business-in-2018.html.

25. Although some of California's most productive agricultural lands have yielded to urbanization, in a state of about one hundred million total acres, forty-three million acres remain agricultural, with sixteen million devoted to grazing and twenty-seven million to crops. California has become the nation's most productive agricultural state by a large margin, the leading producer of a cornucopia of fruits, vegetables, and other agricultural products. No other place in the world has such a rich and diverse agricultural bounty. Edward J. Thompson Jr., "California Agricultural Land Loss & Conservation: The Basic Facts," American Farmland Trust, 2009, https://4aa2dc132bb150caf1aa-7bb737f4349b47aa42dce777a72d5264.ssl.cf5.rackcdn.com/aft-ca-agricultural-land-loss-basic-facts_11-23-09.pdf; California Department of Agriculture, "California Agricultural Statistics Review, 2017–2018, n.d., https://www.cdfa.ca.gov/statistics/PDFs/2017-18AgReport.pdf.

26. Yergin, *Prize*, 81–82; Margaret Leslie Davis, *Dark Side of Fortune: Triumph and Scandal in the Life of Oil Tycoon Edward L. Doheny* (Berkeley: University of California Press, 1998).

27. Allen J. Scott, *Technopolis: High-Technology Industry and Regional Development in Southern California* (Berkeley: University of California Press, 1993); Jacob Vander Meulen, "West Coast Labor and the Military Aircraft Industry, 1935–1941," *Pacific Northwest Quarterly* 88, no. 2 (Spring 1997): 82–92. See also Roger W. Lotchin, *Fortress California: From Warfare to Welfare* (New York: Oxford University Press, 1992).

28. Lotchin, *Fortress*, 178. See also Vander Meulen, *West Coast Labor,* 91, citing U.S. Military Aircraft Acceptances, 1940–1945; Storper, Kemeny, Makarem, and Osman, *Rise and Fall,* 77–80; Peter J. Westwick, quoted in "Blue Sky Metropolis: The Aerospace Industry in California," kcetlink, 2019. https://www.pbssocal.org/programs/blue-sky-metropolis/.

29. Dan Walters, "How the New Los Angeles Has Reshaped California Politics," in *The New Political Geography of California*, ed. Frederick Douzet, Thad Kousser, and Kenneth P. Miller (Berkeley, CA: Berkeley Public Policy Press, 2008), 201–205. Jerry Nickelsburg, "Where Does Southern California Aerospace Go from Here?" UCLA Anderson Forecast, September 15, 2006; Hans P. Johnson, "Movin' Out: Domestic Migration to and from California in the 1990s," in *California Counts: Population Trends and Problems* 2, no. 1 (Public Policy Institute of California, August 2000); Jerry Nickelsburg, "Richer and Poorer: Income Inequality in Los Angeles," UCLA Anderson Forecast, March 2007.

30. Christine Cooper, Shannon Sedgwick, and Wesley DeWitt, "The Changing Face of Aerospace in Southern California," Los Angeles Economic Development Corporation Institute for Applied Economics, March 2016, https://laedc.org/wp-content/uploads/2016/03/Dr-Cooper-on-SoCal-Aerospace-Deck-2.1.16.pdf.

31. Kevin Starr, *Inventing the Dream: California through the Progressive Era* (New York: Oxford University Press, 1985), 287; Allen J. Scott, *On Hollywood* (Princeton, NJ: Princeton University Press (2005), 12–25.

32. Starr, *Inventing the Dream*, 317.

33. Ibid., 334–37.

34. Ibid., 313.

35. *U.S. v. Paramount Pictures*, 334 U.S. 131 (1948). In 2019, the U.S. Department of Justice announced it would seek to terminate the *Paramount* consent decrees on the grounds that changes in the industry had made them obsolete.

36. Storper, Kemeny, Makarem, and Osman, *Rise and Fall*, 98–102.

37. Ibid., 57, 98–102.

38. Timothy J. Sturgeon, "How Silicon Valley Came to Be," in *Understanding Silicon Valley: The Anatomy of an Entrepreneurial Region*, ed. Martin Kenney (Stanford, CA: Stanford University Press, 2000), 39–47; Storper, Kemeny, Makarem, and Osman, *Rise and Fall*, 80–81; Annalee Saxenian, *Regional Advantage: Culture and Competition in Silicon Valley and Route 128* (Cambridge, MA: Harvard University Press, 1994), 20–24.

39. Saxenian, *Regional Advantage*, 25–27, 179, n.6.

40. Homa Bahrami and Stuart Evans, "Flexible Recycling and High-Technology Entrepreneurship," in *Understanding Silicon Valley*, 165–89; Storper, Kemeny, Makarem, and Osman, *Rise and Fall*, 198.

41. Storper, Kemeny, Makarem, and Osman, *Rise and Fall*, 57; Arden Pennell, "Facebook to Move to Stanford Research Park: Some Employees May Remain in Downtown Palo Alto—Neighborhood Part of Firm's 'DNA,'" *Palo Alto Weekly*, August 8, 2008, https://www.paloaltoonline.com/news/2008/08/18/facebook-to-move-to-stanford-research-park.

42. "Fortune 500 (2019)," *Fortune*, May 16, 2019, https://fortune.com/fortune500/2019/ search/?hqstate=CA; in December 2019, Saudi Aramco's initial public offering caused it to surpass Apple in the top spot. See Aya Batrawy, "Aramco IPO Makes It Most Valuable Company, Edging Out Apple," *San Francisco Chronicle*, December 11, 2019, https://www.sfchronicle.com/business/article/Aramco-IPO-makes-it-world-s-most-valuable-14900184.php#.

43. Despite this success, even some technology firms were struggling with California's high costs. See Alexandra Suich Bass, "Peak Valley: Silicon Valley Will Lose Some of Its Lustre," The World in 2019, *The Economist,* https://worldin2019.economist.com/ siliconvalleylosesitsshine.

44. Walters, "How the New Los Angeles," 205.

45. The management expert Peter Drucker coined the term "knowledge worker" in the late 1950s. Peter Ferdinand Drucker, *The Landmarks of Tomorrow: A Report on the New Postmodern World* (New York: Harper 1959).

46. Joel Kotkin and Marshall Toplansky, "Research Brief: California Feudalism: The Squeeze on the Middle Class," Center for Demographics and Policy, Chapman University, October 19, 2018: 13, https://www.newgeography.com/content/006117-california-feudalism-the-squeeze-middle-class, citing Liana Fox, "The Supplemental Poverty Measure: 2017," U.S. Census Bureau, September 12, 2018; Suich Bass, "California and Texas Are Both Failing."

47. Mac Taylor, "California's High Housing Costs: Causes and Consequences," Legislative Analyst's Office (March 17, 2015): 10–20, https://lao.ca.gov/reports/2015/finance/ housing-costs/housing-costs.pdf.

48. According to the Zillow Home Value Index, the median home value in California in December 2019 was $556,815, compared to $244,054 in the nation as a whole and $207,829 in Texas. "Zillow Home Value Index," Zillow.com (2019), https://www. zillow.com/home-values/.

49. Alexandra Suich Bass, "Many People Are Moving from California to Texas: The Cost of Living, as Well as High Taxes and Red Tape, are Precipitating the Push," *The Economist*, June 20, 2019, https://www.economist.com/special-report/2019/06/20/ many-people-are-moving-from-california-to-texas.

50. Alan Brinklow, "Housing Crisis: San Francisco's Median Market Rent Hits New All-time Highs," *Curbed San Francisco*, June 13, 2019, https://sf.curbed.com/2019/ 6/13/18663215/san-franciso-rent-numbers-record-prices-median-graphs; Mark Baldassare, Dean Bonner, David Kordus, and Lunna Lopes, "Californians and Housing Affordability," San Francisco, CA: Public Policy Institute of California (September 2017), https://www.ppic.org/publication/californians-and-housing-affordability/.

51. Brian Womack, "Charles Schwab to Move HQ to DFW from San Francisco after TD Ameritrade Acquisition," *Dallas Business Journal*, November 25, 2019, https://www. bizjournals.com/dallas/news/2019/11/25/charles-schwab-dfw-td-ameritrade.html; Roland Li, "McKesson, Biggest U.S. Drug Distributor, to Move from SF to Texas," *San Francisco Chronicle*, December 1, 2018, https://www.sfchronicle.com/busi-ness/article/McKesson-biggest-U-S-drug-distributor-to-move-13435748.php; Lori

Weisberg and Jonathan Horn, "Another SD Firm Moving to Texas," *San Diego Union-Tribune*, July 18, 2014, https://www.sandiegouniontribune.com/business/economy/sdut-rick-perry-omnitracs-texas-enterprise-fund-jobs-2014jul18-story.html.

52. "Why Start-ups are Leaving Silicon Valley," *The Economist*, August 30, 2018, https://www.economist.com/leaders/2018/08/30/why-startups-are-leaving-silicon-valley.

53. Antonio García Martínez, "In Texas, Techies Are Trying to Turn the Red State Blue," *Wired* October 23, 2018, https://www.wired.com/story/flipping-texas-elections-voter-registration-tech/; Susan Milligan, "Could Changing Demographics Turn Texas Politically Purple?" *U.S. News & World Report*, October 11, 2018, https://www.usnews.com/news/best-states/articles/2018-10-11/in-texas-changing-demographics-cold-have-political-implications.

54. Walters, "How the New Los Angeles," 205.

55. See Steven J. Ross, *Hollywood Left and Right: How Movie Stars Shaped American Politics* (New York: Oxford University Press, 2011); David Broockman, Greg F. Ferenstein, and Neil Malhotra, "The Political Behavior of Wealthy Americans: Evidence from Technology Entrepreneurs," Stanford Graduate School of Business Working Paper No. 3581, December 9, 2017.

Chapter 5

1. Erica Greider, *Big, Hot, Cheap, and Right: What America Can Learn from the Strange Genius of Texas* (New York: Public Affairs, 2013): 229–31. Manny Fernandez, "What Makes Texas Texas," *New York Times*, May 7, 2016, https://www.nytimes.com/2016/05/08/us/what-makes-texas-texas.html.

2. John Steinbeck, *Travels with Charley in Search of America* (1961; repr. New York: Penguin, 2017), 165. Citations refer to the Penguin edition.

3. Wallace Stegner, "California: The Experimental Society," *Saturday Review*, September 23, 1967, 28.

4. Darren Dochuk, *From Bible Belt to Sunbelt: Plain Folk Religion, Grassroots Politics, and the Rise of Evangelical Conservatism* (New York: W. W. Norton, 2011): 1–26.

5. James Davison Hunter, *Culture Wars: The Struggle to Define America* (New York: Basic Books, 1991), 280–81.

6. *Cambridge Dictionary* (Cambridge: Cambridge University Press, 2019), s.v. "culture," https://dictionary.cambridge.org/us/dictionary/english/culture.

7. Wilbur Zelinsky, *The Cultural Geography of the United States*, rev. ed. (Edgewood Cliffs, NJ: Prentice Hall, 1992), 38.

8. Ibid., 35.

9. Ibid., 110.

10. Ibid., 110–22. For analysis of the nation's cultural regions, see also Joel Garreau, *The Nine Nations of North America* (New York: Avon Books, 1982), and Colin Woodard, *American Nations: A History of the Eleven Rival Regional Cultures of North America* (New York: Penguin, 2011).

11. Daniel J. Elazar, *American Federalism: A View from the States*, 2nd ed. (New York: Thomas Y. Crowell Company, 1972), 93–102. Elazar defined "political

culture" as "the particular pattern of political action in which each political system is embedded" (84–85).

12. Ibid., 107, 117–18.

13. Elazar's categories of political culture do not align perfectly with the nation's partisan geography. The closest match is his category of states with traditionalistic political cultures. Almost all of these states were in the South and almost all later became solidly Republican. By comparison, several states with dominant moralistic political cultures (such as California, Oregon, Washington, Vermont, and Maine) became solidly Democratic, but others in that category did not. For example, Utah had a moralistic political culture, but remains one of the nation's reddest states. For a complete geography of state political cultures, see Elazar, *American Federalism*, 106–07.

14. Pew Research Center, "Religious Landscape Study (2014)," May 12, 2015, https://www.pewforum.org/religious-landscape-study/. The study was based on interviews with more than 35,000 Americans from all 50 states.

15. Ibid.

16. Ibid.

17. Ibid.

18. Ibid.

19. See Geoffrey Layman, *The Great Divide: Religious and Cultural Conflict in American Party Politics* (New York: Columbia University Press, 2001), 168–204.

20. Pew Research Center, "Religious Landscape Study (2014)."

21. "President: Full Results," CNN, December 12, 2012, http://www.cnn.com/election/2012/results/race/president/#exit-polls; "Exit Polls 2016," CNN, November 23, 2016, https://www.cnn.com/election/2016/results/exit-polls.

22. Zelinsky, *Cultural Geography*, 119.

23. Cal Jillson, *Lone Star Tarnished: A Critical Look at Texas Politics and Policy*, 3rd ed. (New York: Routledge, 2018), 24.

24. Light Townsend Cummins, "History, Memory, and Rebranding Texas as Western for the 1936 Centennial," in *This Corner of Canaan: Essays on Texas in Honor of Randolph B. Campbell*, ed. Richard B. McCaslin, Donald E. Chipman, and Andrew J. Torget (Denton: University of North Texas Press, 2013), 37–57.

25. Texas Historical Commission, "1936 Texas Centennial Markers," n.d., http://www.thc.texas.gov./preserve/projects-and-programs/state-historical-markers/1936-texas-centennial-markers.

26. Cummins, "History, Memory, and Rebranding," 49; Kenneth B. Ragsdale, *Centennial '36: The Year America Discovered Texas* (College Station: Texas A&M Press, 1987), 13–154, 246–47, 254. According to Dallas-based retail magnate Stanley Marcus, "Modern Texas history started with the celebration of the Texas Centennial, because it was in 1936 . . . that the rest of America discovered Texas" (xix).

27. Cummins, "History, Memory, and Rebranding," 52.

28. V. O. Key Jr., *Southern Politics in State and Nation* (New York: Alfred A. Knopf, 1949), 254–55.

29. Walter L. Buenger and Robert S. Calvert, eds., *Texas through Time: Evolving Interpretations* (College Station: Texas A&M University Press, 1991), xv; Jillson, *Lone Star Tarnished*, 5–9, 23–32.

30. In the early 1840s, only about 15 percent of Anglo Texans attended church. William Ransom Hogan, *The Texas Republic: A Social and Economic History* (Norman: University of Oklahoma Press, 1946), 223.

31. Robert Wuthnow, *Rough Country: How Texas Became America's Most Powerful Bible-Belt State* (Princeton, NJ: Princeton University Press, 2014), 63–67.

32. James L. Haley, *Passionate Nation: The Epic History of Texas* (New York: Free Press, 2006), 85, 425–29; Wuthnow, *Rough Country*, 229–36.

33. "Religious Affiliation in Texas: Texas's Largest Religious Bodies," *Texas Almanac*, https://texasalmanac.com/topics/religion/religious-affiliation-texas.

34. Pew Research Center, "Religious Landscape Study."

35. As of 2019, Texas's megachurches included Lakewood Church (Houston), the nation's largest, pastored by Joel Osteen; Potters House (Dallas), pastored by T. D. Jakes; Fellowship Church (Grapevine), pastored by Ed Young; Cornerstone (San Antonio), pastored by John Hagee; Prestonwood Baptist Church (Plano), pastored by Jack Graham; Gateway Church (Southlake), pastored by Robert Morris; Woodlands Church (Houston), pastored by Kerry Shook; Second Baptist Church (Houston), pastored by Edwin Young; Stonebriar Community Church (Frisco), pastored by Chuck Swindoll; First Baptist Church (Dallas), pastored by Robert Jeffress; Watermark Community Church (Dallas), pastored by Todd Wagner; and Oak Cliff Bible Fellowship (Dallas), pastored by Tony Evans. Hartford Seminary, "Database of Megachurches in the United States," n.d., http://hirr.hartsem.edu/megachurch/database.html.

36. Daniel K. Williams, *God's Own Party: The Making of the Christian Right* (New York: Oxford University Press, 2010), 1–9; Layman, *Great Divide*, 40–50.

37. Wuthnow, *Rough Country*, 325–68.

38. See, generally, Daniel D. Arreola, *Tejano South Texas: A Mexican American Cultural Province* (Austin: University of Texas Press, 2012). South Texas is usually distinguished from the borderlands of West Texas, which are sparsely populated except for the large city of El Paso, at the state's far southwestern corner. Latinos constitute the large majority of many South Texas cities, including, in 2018, approximately 95 percent of Laredo, 94 percent of Brownsville, 85 percent of McAllen, 84 percent of Del Rio, 64 percent of San Antonio, and 62 percent of Corpus Christi (U.S. Census Quickfacts 2019 for these cities). Joel Garreau includes South Texas as part of a larger area straddling northern Mexico and the American Southwest he calls "Mex-America." Garreau, *The Nine Nations*, 167–244. Similarly, Colin Woodard makes the case for understanding South Texas as part of a broader "nation" on both sides of the U.S.-Mexico border he calls "El Norte." Woodard, *American Nations*, 23–33.

39. Milligan, "Could Changing Demographics."

40. See David McRaney, "How Your Address Changes Your Politics," *Politico Magazine*, August 2, 2015, https://www.politico.com/magazine/story/2015/08/how-your-address-changes-your-politics-120899.

41. Albert Morales, quoted in Ashley Lopez, "In Trump Era, Republicans Are Split on Whether to Court Hispanic Voters," KUT News, August 30, 2018, https://www.kut.org/post/trump-era-texas-republicans-are-split-whether-court-hispanic-voters;

See also Peter Skerry, *Mexican Americans: The Ambivalent Minority* (Cambridge, MA: Harvard University Press (1995), 59–60, describing the stronger religious culture among Latinos in San Antonio than in Los Angeles.

42. John Daniel Davidson, "Austin Votes to Keep the Books Closed," *Wall Street Journal*, November 30, 2018, https://www.wsj.com/articles/austin-votes-to-keep-the-books-closed-1543620879; Lawrence Wright, *God Save Texas: A Journey into the Soul of the Lone Star State* (New York: Knopf, 2018), 237. The city's unofficial motto is "Keep Austin weird."

43. Lomi Kriel, "Just How Diverse Is Houston? 145 Languages Spoken Here," *Houston Chronicle*, November 5, 2015, https://www.houstonchronicle.com/news/houston-texas/article/Houstonians-speak-at-least-145-languages-at-home-6613182.php.

44. Melissa Repko, "Video: Check Out D-FW's Pitch to Bring Amazon's HQ2 to Texas, and See If It Impresses You," *Dallas Morning News*, October 19, 2017, https://www.dallasnews.com/business/technology/2017/10/19/watch-video-dfw-sent-pitch-amazon-actually-reallygood/. Dallas was eventually the runner-up in the competition.

45. The pledge reads as follows: "Honor the Texas flag. I pledge allegiance to thee, Texas, one state under God, one and indivisible." Texas Government Code Title 11, Section 3100.101. See Sean P. Cunningham, *Cowboy Conservatism: Texas and the Rise of the Modern Right* (Lexington: The University Press of Kentucky, 2010), 12–13.

46. Zelinsky, *Cultural Geography*, 35, 110; Stegner, "California," 28.

47. Kevin Starr, *Americans and the California Dream, 1850–1915* (New York: Oxford University Press, 1973), 85–109.

48. Ibid.,108, 241.

49. Ibid., 69–89, 307–38.

50. Ibid., 189–90. The Sierra Club's longtime executive director, David Brower of Berkeley, founded Friends of the Earth, the League of Conservation Voters, and the Earth Island Institute. The Sierra Club also spun off its legal defense fund into a new organization called EarthJustice. At the same time, other independent environmental groups, including the Rainforest Action Network, Save the Bay, the Greenbelt Alliance, among many others, emerged in the Bay Area. This cluster of organizations has helped make Northern California a global center for environmental advocacy.

51. George E. Mowry, *The California Progressives* (Berkeley: University of California Press, 1951), 8; Starr, *Inventing the Dream*, 235–39.

52. Kevin Starr, *Golden Dreams: California in an Age of Abundance* (New York: Oxford University Press, 2009), 285–351.

53. Manuel Castells, "Cultural Identity, Sexual Liberation, and Urban Structure: The Gay Community in San Francisco," in *The City and the Grassroots: A Cross-Cultural Theory of Urban Social Movements* (Berkeley: University of California Press, 1983), 142–43; Lillian Faderman, *The Gay Revolution: The Story of the Struggle* (New York: Simon and Schuster, 2015), 74–90.

54. W. J. Rorabaugh, *Berkeley at War: The 1960s* (New York: Oxford University Press, 1989), 8–47; Terry F. Lunsford, "The Free Speech Crisis at Berkeley, 1964–1965: Some Issues for Social and Legal Research," Berkeley, CA: Center for Study of Law and Society, University of California at Berkeley (December 1965): 4–16.

55. Ethan Rarick, *California Rising: The Life and Times of Pat Brown* (Berkeley and Los Angeles: University of California Press, 2005), 325; see, generally, W. J. Rorabaugh, *American Hippies* (New York: Cambridge University Press, 2015).

56. Rorabaugh, *American Hippies*, 11, 24.

57. Pew Research Center, "Religious Landscape."

58. Stewart Brand, *Whole Earth Catalog*, Fall 1968: 2; Anna Wiener, "The Complicated Legacy of Stewart Brand's 'Whole Earth Catalog,'" *New Yorker*, November 16, 2018, https://www.newyorker.com/news/letter-from-silicon-valley/the-complicated-legacy-of-stewart-brands-whole-earth-catalog.

59. Ibid. See also Fred Turner, *From Counterculture to Cyberculture: Stewart Brand, the Whole Earth Network, and the Rise of Digital Utopianism* (Chicago: The University of Chicago Press, 2006), 1–9; Steve Jobs, "Stay Hungry, Stay Foolish," Commencement Address at Stanford University, June 14, 2005, https://news.stanford.edu/2005/06/14/jobs-061505/.

60. Carey McWilliams, *Southern California: An Island on the Land* (1946; repr. Layton, UT: Gibbs Smith, 1973), 3–8. McWilliams credits the author Helen Hunt Jackson as first describing Southern California as "sort of an island on the land" (5).

61. Mowry, *California Progressives*, 7.

62. Ibid., 38.

63. Zelinsky, *Cultural Geography*, 135.

64. McWilliams describes the Archipelago of Los Angeles and the Island of Hollywood. See McWilliams, *Southern California*, 315–29; 331–49.

65. Lisa McGirr, *Suburban Warriors: The Origins of the New American Right* (Princeton, NJ: Princeton University Press, 2001), 20–53, 98–110.

66. Ibid., 259–61; Dochuk, *From Bible Belt*, xv–xviii, 341–42.

67. Dochuk, *From Bible Belt*, 406; William Lobdell and Mitchell Landsberg, "Robert F. Schuller, Who Built Crystal Cathedral, Dies at 88," *Los Angeles Times*, April 2, 2015, http://www.latimes.com/local/obituaries/la-me-robert-schuller-20150403-story.html. As of 2019, the new Catholic Cathedral, now known as Christ Cathedral, conducted masses each week in English, Spanish, Vietnamese, and Mandarin Chinese. Diocese of Orange, "Christ Cathedral: Mass Times," https://parish.christcathedralcalifornia.org/mass-times/.

68. McWilliams, *Southern California*, 330–45. The geography of Hollywood is, indeed, nebulous. The neighborhood known as "Hollywood" was briefly incorporated as a municipality in 1903, then consolidated with the City of Los Angeles in 1910. The nearby community of West Hollywood, formerly an unincorporated area of Los Angeles County, became an independent city in 1984. The community known as North Hollywood is part of the City of Los Angeles, located over the Hollywood Hills in the San Fernando Valley.

69. Kevin Starr, *Coast of Dreams: California on the Edge* (New York: Alfred A. Knopf, 2004), 42.

70. See, generally, Donald T. Critchlow, *When Hollywood Was Right: How Movie Stars, Studio Moguls, and Big Business Remade American Politics* (New York: Cambridge University Press, 2013).

71. Neil Gross, "Why Is Hollywood So Liberal?" *New York Times*, January 27, 2018, https://www.nytimes.com/2018/01/27/opinion/sunday/hollywood-liberal.html; Ross, *Hollywood*, 3–10.

72. George L. Pla and David R. Ayón, *Power Shift: How Latinos in California Transformed Politics in America* (Berkeley, CA: Berkeley Public Policy Press, 2018), 262.

73. Stegner, "California," 28.

Chapter 6

1. Everett Carll Ladd Jr. and Charles D. Hadley, *Transformations of the American Party System: Political Coalitions from the New Deal to the 1970s*, 2nd ed. (New York: W. W. Norton, 1978), 31–87.

2. V. O. Key Jr., *Southern Politics in State and Nation* (New York: A. A. Knopf, 1949), 277. On the GOP's history as a sectional party, see Earl Black and Merle Black, *The Rise of Southern Republicans* (Cambridge, MA: Belknap Press of Harvard University Press, 2002), 13–16.

3. Howard Raines, "George Wallace, Segregation Symbol, Dies at 79," *New York Times*, September 14, 1998, https://www.nytimes.com/1998/09/14/us/george-wallace-segregation-symbol-dies-at-79.ht. See, generally, James Patterson, *Congressional Conservatism and the New Deal: The Growth of the Conservative Coalition in Congress, 1933–1939* (Lexington: University of Kentucky Press, 1967).

4. Evron M. Kirkpatrick, "Toward a More Responsible Two-Party System: A Report of the Committee on Political Parties," Supplement, *American Political Science Review* 44, no. 3, Part 2 (September 1950): 965–90.

5. American Presidency Project, "Elections," U.C. Santa Barbara, n.d., https://www.presidency.ucsb.edu/statistics/elections.

6. Roscoe C. Martin, *The People's Party in Texas: A Study in Third Party Politics* (1933; repr., Austin: University of Texas Press, 1970), 16.

7. Wayne Thorburn, *Red State: An Insider's Story of How the GOP Came to Dominate Texas Politics* (Austin: University of Texas Press, 2014), 47.

8. Ibid., 52–53.

9. Gregg Cantrell, "'A Host of Sturdy Patriots': The Texas Populists" in *The Texas Left: The Radical Roots of Lone Star Liberalism*, ed. David O'Donald Cullen and Kyle Wilkinson (College Station: Texas A&M Press, 2010), 53–73.

10. Ibid., 53–55.

11. Chandler Davidson, *Race and Class in Texas Politics* (Princeton, NJ: Princeton University Press, 1990), 20; Key, *Southern Politics*, 533–34.

12. Martin, *People's Party*, 210–11; Cantrell, "'A Host of Sturdy Patriots,'" 66–69.

13. Key, *Southern Politics*, 533–54.

14. Ibid., 521. The Texas poll tax amendment was proposed by Acts 1901, 27th Leg., 322–23, S.J.R. No. 3 and adopted at the November 4, 1902, election. See Davidson, *Race and Class*, 19–23. In addition, at least some local officials prohibited Mexican immigrants with indigenous ancestry from voting. Bernard L. Fraga, *The Turnout Gap: Race,*

Ethnicity, and Political Inequality in a Diversifying America (New York: Cambridge University Press, 2018), 25, http://www.lrl.texas.gov/scanned/sessionLaws/ 27-0/SJR_3.pdf. See also Texas Legislative Council, "Amendments to the Texas Constitution Since 1876," Austin, TX: Texas Legislative Council (May 2018): 76, http://www.tlc.state.tx.us/docs/amendments/Constamend1876.pdf.   The   Terrell Election Law was first enacted in 1903 and amended in 1905.

15. Davidson, *Race and Class*, 21.

16. "Voter Participation in Texas," *Texas Almanac*, n.d., www.texasalmanac.com/sites/ default/files/images/topics/prezturnout.pdf; see also Key, *Southern Politics*, 533–34.

17. General Laws, 1923, 74, cited in Robert Wendell Hainsworth, "The Negro and the Texas Primaries," *Journal of Negro History* 18, no. 4 (October 1933): 426–50.

18. The U.S. Supreme Court struck down Texas's 1923 white primary statute in *Nixon v. Herndon* (1927), on the grounds that the state-mandated, race-based restriction on voting violated the Fourteenth Amendment's Equal Protection Clause. The Texas Legislature responded by passing a new statute that authorized, but did not require, party officials to restrict access to primary elections on the basis of race. The Court struck down that statute in *Nixon v. Condon* (1932), holding that the state authorization of the race-based restriction violated the Equal Protection Clause. In response, the Texas Democratic Party independently passed a resolution banning blacks from voting in party primaries. In *Grovey v. Townsend* (1935), the Supreme Court upheld this latest ban on the grounds that the party was a private organization that could lawfully establish restrictions on the basis of race. Nearly a decade later, however, Lonnie Smith again challenged the state's white primary, and a reconstituted Supreme Court held in *Smith v. Allwright*, 321 U.S. 649 (1944), that race-based restrictions were unconstitutional.

19. *United States v. Texas*, 252 F. Supp. 234 (W.D. Tex. 1966).

20. With few exceptions, the state's only meaningful electoral competition occurred within Democratic primaries. In non-presidential years, the Democratic primary routinely drew more than twice as many voters as the general election. Thorburn, *Red State*, 52.

21. Key, *Southern Politics*, 318.

22. Four other "peripheral" southern states—Florida, North Carolina, Tennessee, and Virginia—also voted for Hoover over Smith in 1928. Ibid., 317–29.

23. Robert A. Caro, *The Years of Lyndon Johnson: The Path to Power* (New York: Knopf, 1982), 417.

24. Keith Volanto, "The Far Right in Texas Politics during the Roosevelt Era," in *The Texas Right: The Radical Roots of Lone Star Conservatism*, ed. David O'Donald Cullen and Kyle G. Wilkison (College Station: Texas A&M Press, 2014), 68–86.

25. Ibid., 71–78. A 1940 *Time Magazine* profile of Garner described the vice president and his native state as follows: "Cactus Jack is 71, sound in wind & limb, a hickory conservative who does not represent the Old South of magnolias, hoopskirts, pillared verandas, but the New South: moneymaking, industrial, hardboiled, still expanding too rapidly to brood over social problems. He stands for oil derricks, sheriffs who use airplanes, prairie skyscrapers, mechanized farms, $100 Stetson hats. Conservative

John Garner appeals to many a conservative voter." "National Affairs: Men Aplenty," *Time Magazine*, April 15, 1940.

26. George Norris Green, *The Establishment in Texas Politics: The Primitive Years, 1938–1957* (Norman: University of Oklahoma Press, 1979), 49–52.

27. Key, *Southern Politics*, 259. See also Davidson, *Race and Class,* 11–15.

28. Thorburn, *Red State*, 53.

29. Shivers endorsed Eisenhower in part because the general supported Texas's claim to oil-rich tidelands in the Gulf of Mexico, while Stevenson sided with the federal government in the dispute. Texas eventually won its claim. See *U.S. v. Louisiana*, 363 U.S. 1 (1960).

30. John R. Knaggs, *Two Party Texas: The John Tower Era, 1961–1984* (Austin, TX: Eakin Press 1986), 33–34.

31. Bill Porterfield, "H. L. Hunt's Long Goodbye," *Texas Monthly*, March 1975, https://www.texasmonthly.com/articles/h-l-hunts-long-goodbye/.

32. Knaggs, *Two Party Texas,* 1–15.

33. Ibid., 33–35.

34. Ibid.

35. Ibid., 38–39; Cunningham, *Cowboy Conservatism*, 54–56.

36. Knaggs, *Two Party Texas*, 53–55.

37. For examples of the conventional view that the Civil Rights Act of 1964 was the pivotal event in the realignment of the South, see, for example, "The Long Goodbye," *The Economist,* November 11, 2010, https://www.economist.com/united-states/2010/11/11/the-long-goodbye; Kevin Drum, "Why Did Democrats Lose the White South?" *Mother Jones*, November 25, 2015, https://www.motherjones.com/kevin-drum/2015/11/why-did-democrats-lose-white-south/.

38. Bernard Cosman, *Five States for Goldwater: Continuity and Change in Southern Presidential Voting Patterns* (Tuscaloosa: University of Alabama Press, 1966), 104–105; Andrew E. Busch, *Reagan's Victory: The Presidential Election of 1980 and the Rise of the Right* (Lawrence: University Press of Kansas, 2005), 15–20.

39. Cunningham, *Cowboy Conservatism*, 134–41.

40. Thorburn, *Red State*, 151–53; Daniel K. Williams, *God's Own Party: The Making of the Christian Right* (New York: Oxford University Press, 2010), 93–94.

41. Reagan made similar remarks in many settings. The quotation comes from a campaign speech in 1988. Ronald Reagan, *Public Papers of the President of the United States: Ronald Reagan, 1988–1989*, Book 2 (Washington, DC: Office of the Federal Register, 1991), 1460.

42. Thorburn, *Red State*, 126–34.

43. James P. Sterba, "Democratic Vote Propels Reagan to Texas Sweep," *New York Times*, May 3, 1976, A-1; Roger Olien, *From Token to Triumph: The Texas Republicans Since 1920* (Dallas: SMU Press, 1982), 236–42.

44. American Presidency Project, "Elections"; Thorburn, *Red State*, 126–34; Lawrence Wright, "America's Future Is Texas," *New Yorker*, July 3, 2017, https://www.newyorker.com/magazine/2017/07/10/americas-future-is-texas.

45. Knaggs, *Two Party Texas*, 201–31. Connally would later convert to the GOP and run for president as a Republican. See also Kenneth Bridges, *Twilight of the Texas Democrats: The 1978 Governor's Race* (College Station: Texas A&M University Press, 2008).

46. Carolyn Barta, "Why Bill Clements Mattered," *Texas Tribune*, May 30, 2011, https://www.texastribune.org/2011/05/30/guest-column-why-bill-clements-mattered/.

47. Ibid.; Thorburn, *Red State*, 120–26.

48. Quoted in Wright, "America's Future."

49. Thorburn, *Red State*, 166–87.

50. Michael Barone and Richard E. Cohen, *The Almanac of American Politics 2006* (Washington, DC: National Journal Group, 2005), 1575–77. The U.S. Supreme Court upheld all but one of the new districts in *League of United Latin American Citizens v. Perry*, 548 U.S. 399 (2006).

51. Christopher Hooks, "Losing Ground," *Texas Observer*, December 30, 2014, https://www.texasobserver.org/losing-ground-battleground-texas-democratic-party/.

52. Ibid; Mary Beth Rogers, *Turning Texas Blue: What It Will Take to Break the GOP Grip on America's Reddest State* (New York: St. Martin's Press, 2016), 29–42.

53. American Presidency Project, "Elections." For a discussion of Democrats' hopes in 2016, see, for example, Clare Foran, "Can Hillary Clinton Win Texas?" *The Atlantic*, September 8, 2016, https://www.theatlantic.com/politics/archive/2016/09/clinton-texas-trump/499097/.

54. Texas Office of the Secretary of State, "Race Summary Report, 2018 General Election, November 6, 2018," https://elections.sos.state.tx.us/elchist331_state.htm; Kirk Goldsberry, "What Really Happened in Texas," *FiveThirtyEight*, November 14, 2018, https://fivethirtyeight.com/features/how-beto-orourke-shifted-the-map-in-texas/.

55. Following the U.S. Supreme Court's decision in *Rucho v. Common Cause*, 588 U.S. __ (2019), Texas Democrats will be barred from bringing federal constitutional challenges against Republican districting plans on the basis that they dilute Democrats' voting strength. Adam Liptak, "Supreme Court Bars Challenges to Partisan Gerrymandering," *New York Times*, June 27, 2019, https://www.nytimes.com/2019/06/27/us/politics/supreme-court-gerrymandering.html.

56. A 2018 study ranked the difficulty of registering and voting in all fifty states using a measure it called the "cost of voting index." The index included factors such as availability of online registration, procedures for early voting, presence or absence of voter-identification requirements, and the like. According to the study, Texas was among the five states where it was hardest to vote, along with Mississippi, Virginia, Tennessee, and Indiana. Quan Li, Michael J. Pomante II, and Scot Schraufnagel, "Cost of Voting in the American States," *Election Law Journal: Rules, Politics, and Policy* 17, no. 3. (September 18, 2018): 234–47, https://doi.org/10.1089/elj.2017.0478.

Chapter 7

1. Rick Perlstein, *Before the Storm: Barry Goldwater and the Unmaking of the American Consensus* (New York: Hill and Wang, 2001), 27, 348–49. Goldwater backer Phyllis Schlafly used the term "a choice not an echo" in her bestselling 1964 book by that title. See Phyllis Schlafly, *A Choice Not an Echo: The Inside Story of How American Presidents Are Chosen* (Alton, IL: Pere Marquette Press, 1964).

2. Perlstein, *Before the Storm*, 374.

3. Patrick J. Buchanan, "Address to the Republican National Convention," August 17, 1992, https://voicesofdemocracy.umd.edu/buchanan-culture-war-speech-speech-text/.

4. Gerhard Peters and John T. Woolley, "American Presidency Project: Elections," Online resource: University of California at Santa Barbara, https://www.presidency.ucsb.edu/statistics/elections; Dave Leip, "Atlas of U.S. Presidential Elections," https://uselectionatlas.org/.

5. "List of California Governors," California State Library, https://governors.library.ca.gov/list.html; Leip, "Atlas."

6. John R. Haynes, "Birth of Democracy in California," Manuscript, Haynes Foundation, Los Angeles, cited in George E. Mowry, *The California Progressives* (Berkeley: University of California Press, 1951; Chicago: Encounter, 1963), 16. Citations refer to the University of California Press edition. See also Frank Norris, *The Octopus: A Story of California* (1901; repr., New York: Penguin Twentieth Century Classics, 1994).

7. Mowry, *The California Progressives*, 70.

8. Ibid., 88–89, 93. Kevin Starr, *Inventing the Dream: California through the Progressive Era* (New York: Oxford University Press, 1985), 236–37. Although these reformers pursued a "moralistic" agenda, they also had moral blind spots. Many Progressives held nativist views, believing that the nation's progress depended on maintaining its white Anglo-Saxon character. As a consequence, they tended to favor immigration policies that excluded immigrants from non-European countries, especially from Asia. Moreover, some prominent Progressives openly embraced eugenics, including involuntary sterilizations, as a means to improve the human race. See Alexandra Minna Stern, *Eugenic Nation: Faults and Frontiers of Better Breeding in Modern America* (Berkeley: University of California Press, 2005), 85–86.

9. Starr, *Inventing the Dream*, 237, 242–44.

10. California Secretary of State, Voter Information Guide for 1911 General Election (1911), http://repository.uchastings.edu/ca_ballot_props/24.

11. In the 1912 presidential election in California, Socialist Eugene Debs finished third with nearly 12 percent of the vote. President Taft did not even appear on the California ballot and received write-ins totaling less than 1 percent. American Presidency Project, "Elections." See also Mowry, *California Progressives*, 159–89.

12. Kevin Starr, *Endangered Dreams: The Great Depression in California* (New York: Oxford University Press, 1996), 197. Hoover moved to California in 1891 to enroll in Stanford University's inaugural class. At Stanford, he studied to be an engineer and embraced many of California's emerging Progressive ideals. In the years surrounding World War I, he earned a reputation as a humanitarian and expert government administrator. That reputation was overshadowed during his presidency, however, when he was blamed for an inadequate response to the Great Depression. Kevin Starr, *Americans and the California Dream, 1850–1915* (New York: Oxford University Press, 1973), 338–44.

13. In one consequential conversion, future governor Edmund G. "Pat" Brown changed his registration from Republican to Democrat in the months leading up to the

1936 election. Ethan Rarick, *California Rising: The Life and Times of Pat Brown* (Berkeley: University of California Press, 2005), 25, 394, n. 13.

14. That election was held during a turbulent year in the state's history. In Long Beach, a physician named Francis Everett Townsend sparked a national movement demanding a federal pension for the elderly, while in San Francisco a longshoremen's strike turned bloody and workers in the city engaged in a five-day general strike. The left was on the march and conditions seemed ripe for Democrats to gain control of state government in California. Starr, *Endangered Dreams*, 84–120, 133–37; Frances Perkins, *The Roosevelt I Knew* (New York: Harper & Row, 1964), 294.

15. Upton Sinclair, "Immediate EPIC: The Final Statement of the Plan," SSA History Archives, https://www.ssa.gov/history/epic.html; James N. Gregory, "Introduction," in Upton Sinclair, *I, Candidate for Governor, and How I Got Licked* (Berkeley: University of California Press, 1994), iii–viii; Starr, *Endangered Dreams*, 138, 155; Greg Mitchell, *The Campaign of the Century: Upton Sinclair's Race for Governor of California and the Birth of Media Politics* (New York: Random House, 1992).

16. A firm called Campaigns, Inc., founded and managed by the team of Clem Whitaker and Leone Baxter, introduced new campaign techniques including direct mail and attack ads. The team worked with Hollywood's leading Republican, Louis B. Mayer, to produce newsreels assaulting Sinclair and distribute them to movie theaters across the state. Many of these films disseminated false information—or what would later be called "fake news." Mitchell, *Campaign*, 83–85, 128–30, 499–501.

17. Although the incumbent Republican governor, Frank Merriam, was held to under 50 percent of the vote, voters who wanted change were divided between Sinclair (38 percent) and Raymond Haight, a more moderate candidate (13 percent). Starr, *Endangered Dreams*, 137–55; Mitchell, *Campaign*, 523–50.

18. Starr, *Endangered Dreams*, 154–55; Mitchell, *Campaign*, 577–78.

19. Olson's most enduring legacy was his appointment to the California Supreme Court four justices—Jesse W. Carter, Phil S. Gibson, Roger J. Traynor, and B. Rey Schauer— who transformed the court into a national model of progressive state jurisprudence. See Charles J. McClain, "The Gibson Era: 1940–1964," in *Constitutional Governance and Judicial Power: The History of the California Supreme Court*, ed. Harry N. Scheiber (Berkeley, CA: Berkeley Public Policy Press, 2016); Ben Field, *Activism in Pursuit of the Public Interest: The Jurisprudence of Chief Justice Roger J. Traynor* (Berkeley, CA: Institute of Governmental Studies Press, 2003), xiii.

20. G. Edward White, *Earl Warren: A Public Life* (New York: Oxford University Press, 1982), 17–18.

21. Kevin Starr, *Golden Dreams: California in an Age of Abundance, 1950–1963* (New York: Oxford University Press, 2009), 193.

22. Ibid., 192–94.

23. In 1946, the young Nixon challenged five-term incumbent Democratic Congressman Jerry Voorhis for a Southern California congressional seat. Nixon attacked Voorhis for his former membership in the Socialist party and his left-wing voting record in Congress. In 1948, Nixon cross-filed and won the nomination of both parties for

re-election to Congress. In 1950, he defeated the actress Helen Gahagan Douglas for a U.S. Senate seat, setting himself up for his selection in 1952 as Dwight D. Eisenhower's running mate. Although his early career is known for its tough anti-communist rhetoric, Nixon also followed the California Republican playbook of centrism on domestic issues—an orientation that would define his later campaigns and, eventually, his administration's domestic policy agenda. For a discussion of Nixon's Progressive orientation, see John J. Pitney Jr., "Nixon, California, and American Politics," in *The California Republic: Institutions, Statesmanship, and Policies*, ed. Brian P. Janiskee and Ken Masugi (Lanham, MD: Rowman & Littlefield, 2004), 219–27. See also Starr, *Golden Dreams*, 203–6.

24. Starr, *Golden Dreams*, 191–216.

25. Jonathan Bell, *California Crucible: The Forging of Modern American Liberalism* (Philadelphia: University of Pennsylvania Press, 2012), 84–90. In a study of Democratic clubs in Los Angeles County, political scientist James Q. Wilson noted that they tended to attract college-educated professionals devoted to political reform and a liberal policy agenda. James Q. Wilson, *The Amateur Democrat: Club Politics in Three Cities* (Chicago: University of Chicago Press, 1962), 16, 126–53.

26. Bell, *California Crucible*, 90.

27. Ibid., 127–39; Rarick, *California Rising*, 102.

28. Starr, *Golden Dreams*, 212–16.

29. Rarick, *California Rising*, 25–27, 34–38, 59–65, 87–110.

30. Totton J. Anderson, "The 1958 Election in California," *Western Political Quarterly* 12, no. 1, Part 2 (March 1959): 276–300; Bell, *California Crucible*, 151–53; Starr, *Golden Dreams*, 215–16.

31. Starr, *Golden Dreams*, 212.

32. See, generally, Miriam Pawel, *The Browns of California: The Family Dynasty That Transformed a State and Shaped a Nation* (New York: Bloomsbury, 2018).

33. Bell, *California Crucible*, 143–44. During this era, California produced a number of powerful liberal politicians, including Phil Burton, who represented San Francisco in the state assembly from 1957 to 1964 and in Congress from 1964 until his death in 1983, and Alan Cranston, a founder of the California Democratic Council, who served as state controller from 1959–1967 and U.S. senator from 1969–1993. One of the state Democratic Party's few conservative elected officials was Sam Yorty, a who served as mayor of Los Angeles from 1961 to 1973. Yorty eventually switched to the Republican Party.

34. The contest sharply divided Republicans in the state and highlighted the era's ideological division between Northern and Southern California, with Rockefeller winning two-thirds of the primary vote in the San Francisco, but barely 40 percent in Los Angeles. Totton J. Anderson and Eugene C. Lee, "The 1964 Election in California," *Western Political Quarterly* 18, no. 2, Part 2 (June 1, 1965): 451–71, 461; Matthew Dallek, *The Right Moment: Ronald Reagan's First Victory and the Decisive Turning Point in American Politics* (New York: Oxford University Press, 2000), 212.

35. Henry Olsen, *The Working Class Republican: Ronald Reagan and the Return of Blue Collar Conservatism* (New York: Broadside Books, 2017), 99–128.

36. Republicans won majorities in both houses in the 1969–1970 session, the two parties were evenly divided in the state senate in 1968 and 1973–1974, and Republicans held an unstable majority in the assembly in 1995–1996; otherwise, Democrats have maintained a firm grip on the legislative branch.

37. See, generally, James Richardson, *Willie Brown: A Biography* (Berkeley: University of California Press, 1996) and Bill Boyarsky, *Big Daddy: Jesse Unruh and the Art of Power Politics* (Berkeley: University of California Press, 2007).

38. Harry N. Scheiber, "The Liberal Court: Ascendancy and Crisis," in *Constitutional Governance*; Kenneth P. Miller, "The California Supreme Court and the Popular Will," *Chapman Law Review* 19, no. 1 (Winter 2016): 151–98 [153–65].

39. During the first decades of the twentieth century, many states in the upper Midwest and the West with progressive political cultures adopted the initiative process, whereas the South (including Texas) rejected that device and other forms of direct democracy. See Nathaniel A. Persily, "The Peculiar Geography of Direct Democracy: Why the Initiative, Referendum, and Recall Developed in the American West," *Michigan Law and Policy Review* 2 (1997): 11–42.

40. Daniel A. Smith, *Tax Crusaders and the Politics of Direct Democracy* (New York: Routledge, 1998), 52–84; Peter Schrag, *Paradise Lost: California's Experience, America's Future* (Berkeley: University of California Press, 2004), 129–54.

41. For a comprehensive summary of California statewide voter-approved initiatives, see Rose Institute of State and Local Government, "Miller-Rose Institute Initiative Database: California," http://roseinstitute.org/initiatives/california/.

42. Scheiber, "The Liberal Court," 479–86.

43. Brian Uhler and Justin Garosi, "California Losing Residents via Domestic Migration," California Legislative Analyst's Office, February 21, 2018, https://lao.ca.gov/laoecontax/article/detail/265.

44. Gerald C. Lubenow, ed. *California Votes—The 1994 Governor's Race: An Inside Look at the Candidates and Their Campaigns by the People Who Managed Them* (Berkeley: Institute of Governmental Studies Press, 1995), viii, 116–18. A May 1993 poll by the Field Organization showed Brown had a 23-point lead over Wilson. See "Vote for Governor: Wilson vs. Kathleen Brown," California Poll 93-02: May 14-1993–May 22, 1993.

45. Under Proposition 184 of 1994, the "Three-Strikes-and-You're-Out" initiative, a court could sentence a defendant with two prior serious or violent felonies to twenty-five-years-to-life for the third offense, even if that offense was only a misdemeanor. California Secretary of State, "Voter Information Guide for 1994 General Election, November 8, 1994": 32–37, 64–65. https://elections.cdn.sos.ca.gov/sov/1994-general/sov-complete.pdf. Later ballot measures repealed various provisions of Proposition 184.

46. Governor Pete Wilson Committee, "Vote Yes on Proposition 187," https://www.youtube.com/watch?v=lLIzzs2HHgY.

47. John S. W. Park, "Race Discourse and Proposition 187," *Michigan Journal of Race and Law* 2, no. 1 (1996): 175, 179–85; "SOS Initiative: Costly, Mean, and Wrong," *San Francisco Chronicle*, October 16, 1994.

48. *League of United Latin American Citizens v. Wilson*, 1998 U.S. Dist. LEXIS 3372 (U.S.D.C. C.D. Cal. 1998).

49. Lubenow, ed., *California Votes—the 1994 Governor's Race*, 118–19. In 1994, a "Republican wave" crossed the nation. The GOP picked up fifty-four House seats to secure a House majority for the first time since 1954. Republicans also netted eight seats in the Senate to regain control of that chamber. In addition, the GOP gained ten governorships, which gave them a majority of those offices, as well. Gary C. Jacobsen, The 1994 House Elections in Perspective," in *Midterm: The Elections of 1994 in Context*, ed. Philip A. Klinkner (Boulder, CO: Westview Press, 1996).

50. California Secretary of State, "Statement of Vote, November 8, 1994," 1–66.

51. Iris Hui and David O. Sears, "Reexamining the Effect of Racial Propositions on Latinos' Partisanship in California," *Political Behavior* 40 (2018): 149–74 (150–56).

52. Dan Walters, "How the New Los Angeles Has Reshaped California Politics," in *The New Political Geography of California*, ed. Frédérick Douzet, Thad Kousser, and Kenneth P. Miller (Berkeley, CA: Berkeley Public Policy Press, 2008), 208–10; Aurelio Rojas, "Labor Leader Left Band of Loyalists: State's Democrats Were Shaped by L.A.'s Miguel Contreras," *Sacramento Bee*, May 11, 2005.

53. Hui and Sears, "Reexamining the Effect," 150–56.

54. Evan Halper and Scott Martelle, "State GOP Is 'Dying at the Box Office,' Gov Says: Schwarzenegger Blames Republicans' Declining Fortunes on the Party's Failure to Reach Out to Independent and Moderate Voters," *Los Angeles Times*, September 8, 2008, http://articles.latimes.com/2007/sep/08/local/me-arnold8. For an account of the 2003 recall election, Schwarzenegger's victory and his first term in office, see Joe Mathews, *The People's Machine: Arnold Schwarzenegger and the Rise of Blockbuster Democracy* (New York: Public Affairs, 2006).

55. The final tally in California's 2016 presidential contest was 8,753,788 for Clinton, 4,483,810 for Trump—a margin of 4,269,978 votes. Overall, Clinton won the national popular vote by fewer than three million votes. Peters and Woolley, "American Presidency Project."

56. See U.S. Archives and Records Administration, "U.S. Electoral College: Historical Election Results," https://www.archives.gov/federal-register/electoral-college/votes/votes_by_state.html. The home states of presidential or vice-presidential nominees refer to their residence at the time they ran for office. Some Democratic nominees lived briefly in California before moving to the states where they launched their political careers. For example, Adlai Stevenson was born in Los Angeles before moving to Illinois, and Barack Obama was born in Hawaii and attended college in California before moving east and, eventually, to Illinois, to begin his career in politics.

Chapter 8

1. Michael S. Greve, "Federalism in a Polarized Age," in *Parchment Barriers: Political Polarization and the Limits of Constitutional Order*, ed. Zachary Courser, Eric Helland, and Kenneth P. Miller (Lawrence: University Press of Kansas, 2018), 119–20.

2. National Conference of State Legislatures, "Partisan Composition of State Legislatures, 1990–2000," http://www.ncsl.org/documents/statevote/legiscontrol_1990_2000.pdf; National Conference of State Legislatures, "Post Election 2019 State & Legislative Partisan Composition," November 22, 2019, https://www.ncsl.org/Portals/1/Documents/Elections/Legis_Control_2019_Post-Election%20Nov%2022nd.pdf. After the 2019 election, one party controlled both houses of the legislature in every state except Minnesota, where Democrats controlled the House of Representatives and Republicans the Senate, and Nebraska, with its unicameral, nonpartisan legislature. In other states with divided government, different parties controlled the legislature and the governor's office.

3. National Conference of State Legislatures, "Post Election 2019."

4. To see how moving from divided government to unified party control helped Democrats pursue their agenda in California, see Thad Kousser, "Partisan Polarization and Policy Gridlock: Does One Lead to the Other?" in Ethan Rarick, ed. *Governing California: Politics, Government, and Public Policy in the Golden State* (Berkeley, CA: Berkeley Public Policy Press, 2013), 277–98. Political scientist Matt Grossman has shown that unified state governments have not always changed policies as dramatically as one might expect. See Matt Grossman, *Red State Blues: How the Conservative Revolution Stalled in the States* (New York: Cambridge University Press, 2019). Yet, especially in a polarized era, significant policy change is more likely when government is united than when it is divided.

5. See, generally, Richard Briffault, "The Challenge of the New Preemption," *Stanford Law Review* 70, no. 5 (May 2018): 1997–2027.

6. Paul Nolette, *Federalism on Trial: State Attorneys General and National Policymaking in Contemporary America* (Lawrence: University Press of Kansas, 2015), 34, 187–92.

7. See *Florida v. Department of Health and Human Services*, 648 F.3d 1235 (11th Cir. 2011), decided with *NFIB v. Sebelius*, 567 U.S. 519 (2012), challenging provisions of the Affordable Care Act; *West Virginia v. Environmental Protection Agency,* 577 U.S. __ (2016), challenging the "Clean Power Plan"; *Texas v. United States*, 579 U.S. __ (2016), challenging the Obama Department of Homeland Security's Deferred Action for Parents of Americans (DAPA) program.

8. Nolette, *Federalism on Trial,* 187–90; Neena Satija, Lindsay Carbonell, and Ryan McCrimmon, "Texas vs. the Feds—A Look at the Lawsuits," *Texas Tribune,* January 17, 2017, https://www.texastribune.org/2017/01/17/texas-federal-government-lawsuits/.

9. Elbert Lin, "States Suing the Federal Government: Protecting Liberty or Playing Politics?" *University of Richmond Law Review* 52, no. 3 (March 2018): 633–52; Don Thompson, "California Attorney General Leads Trump Resistance into 2019," *AP News,* January 4, 2019, https://www.apnews.com/2a41bfdffd344b3a954a98bd44bd9ac9.

10. Greve, "Federalism," 126; Timothy J. Conlan and Paul L. Posner, "American Federalism in an Era of Partisan Polarization: The Intergovernmental Paradox of Obama's 'New Nationalism,'" *Publius: The Journal of Federalism* 46, no. 3 (2016): 299.

11. The Texas House of Representatives has 150 members; the Texas Senate, 31. For details of constitutional provisions for the Texas Legislature, see Texas Constitution,

Article III. For comparative data on legislative sessions, staffing, and salaries, see The Council of State Governments, *The Book of the States, 2018* (Lexington, KY: The Council of State Governments, 2018), 26–31, 48–52; National Conference of State Legislatures, "2018 Legislator Compensation Information," April 16, 2018, http:// www.ncsl.org/research/about-state-legislatures/legislator-compensation-2018.aspx.

12. The constitutional spending limits include Texas Constitution Article III, section 49a ("pay as you go" limit); Article VIII, section 22 (spending limit); Article III, section 49-j (debt limit); and Article III, section 51-a (welfare spending limit). See Texas Legislative Budget Board, "Constitutional Limitations on Spending," presented to the House Appropriations Committee, January 2019, https://www.lbb.state.tx.us/ Documents/Publications/Presentation/5671_spen.pdf. In 2019, voters amended the constitution to replace the existing restrictions on income taxes with a more explicit ban. Now, any income tax would require two-thirds approval of both houses of the legislature, plus majority approval by the electorate. Texas Constitution, Article VIII, section 24-a. For a discussion of Texas' approach to limited government, see Chuck DeVore, *The Texas Model: Prosperity in the Lone Star State and Lessons for America.* (Austin, TX: Texas Public Policy Foundation, 2014).

13. Social conservatives have outsized influence in the state Republican Party. Their social agenda appears prominently in the state party platform. See Republican Party of Texas, "2018 Republican Party of Texas Platform," n.d., https://www.texasgop.org/ platform/.

14. The Obama administration initiated the bathroom controversy in 2016 when it issued guidance requiring the nation's public schools to allow students access to bathrooms in accordance with their gender identity. Texas and other states immediately challenged the federal policy. In early 2017, President Trump rescinded the order but action did not settle the issue in Texas. SB 6 of 2017 would have required persons to use bathrooms in public schools, government buildings, and public universities based on "biological sex," defined as the sex listed on one's birth certificate. Texas Legislature Online: History, "SB 6: 85th Texas Legislature Regular Session" (2017), https://capitol.texas.gov/billlookup/History. aspx?LegSess=85R&Bill=SB6.

15. See letter to Governor Greg Abbott dated May 27, 2017, published in Anthony Cuthbertson, "Apple, Facebook, Google and Other Tech Firms Oppose 'Bathroom Bill' Transgender Discrimination in Texas," *Newsweek*, April 30, 2017, https://www. newsweek.com/tech-firms-oppose-transgender-discrimination-617293.

16. Lauren McGaughy and Melissa Repko, "Tech Firms Helped Knock Down Texas's Bathroom Bill. Is Apple's $1B Campus the Fatal Blow?" *Dallas Morning News*, December 13, 2018, https://www.dallasnews.com/news/politics/2018/12/13/tech-firms-helped-knock-texas-bathroom-bill-apples-1b-campus-fatal-blow.

17. Marc Ramirez, "State Republicans Vote to Censure House Speaker Joe Straus," *Dallas Morning News*, January 27, 2018, https://www.dallasnews.com/news/texas-politics/ 2018/01/27/state-republicans-vote-censure-house-speaker-joe-straus.

18. Robert T. Garrett, Terri Langford, and Stephanie Lamm, "Fracking Billionaires Pump Millions into Texas Races, Pushing State GOP Even Further to the Right," *Dallas Morning News*, February 22, 2018, https://www.dallasnews.com/news/

2018-elections/2018/02/22/fracking-billionaires-pump-millions-texas-races-pushing-state-gop-even-right. The more conservative candidates were backed by groups including Empower Texans, Texas Right to Life, Texas Eagle Forum, and Texans for Fiscal Responsibility; more moderate, pro-business candidates were backed by groups including the Texas Association of Business (TAB). See also Alex Samuels, "Lt. Gov. Dan Patrick on Outgoing House Speaker Joe Straus: 'He's Not Much of a Republican,'" *Texas Tribune*, November 8, 2018, https://www.texastribune.org/2018/11/08/texas-senate-lieutenant-governor-dan-patrick-joe-straus-midterms/.

19. Sean Collins Walsh, "After Standing Up Biz Group, Lt Gov Dan Patrick Lobs Bombs Their Way," *Austin American-Statesman*, February 9, 2018, https://www.mystatesman.com/news/state--regional-govt--politics/after-standing-biz-group-gov-dan-patrick-lobs-bombs-their-way/q91CYJvGjAPL3zj4MJl9rM/.

20. "Political Competition Is Moderating Texas Republicans," *The Economist*, March 7, 2019, https://www.economist.com/united-states/2019/03/07/political-competition-is-moderating-texas-republicans.

21. Manny Fernandez, "Texas Banned Sanctuary Cities. Some Police Departments Didn't Get the Memo," *New York Times*, March 15, 2018, https://www.nytimes.com/2018/03/15/us/texas-sanctuary-sb4-immigration.html.

22. Jonathan Tilove, "Gov-elect Abbott: End Ban on Bags, Fracking, Tree Cutting," *Austin American-Statesman*, September 24, 2016, https://www.statesman.com/news/20160924/gov-elect-abbott-end-local-bans-on-bags-fracking-tree-cutting.

23. See, for example, Jim Malewitz, "Curbing Local Control, Abbott Signs 'Denton Fracking Bill,'" *Texas Tribune*, May 28, 2015, https://www.texastribune.org/2015/05/18/abbott-signs-denton-fracking-bill/. Gov. Abbott raised the idea of banning local regulations across the board—also known as "nuclear preemption." Briffault, "Challenge of the New Preemption," 2007–8.

24. Satija, Carbonell, and McCrimmon, "Texas vs. the Feds."

25. Wayne Slater, "Atty Gen Greg Abbott Says His Job Is Simple: Sue the Federal Government, Then Go Home," *Dallas Morning News*, June 6, 2012, https://www.dallasnews.com/news/politics/2012/06/07/atty-gen-greg-abbott-says-his-job-is-simple-sue-the-federal-government-then-go-home.

26. See *Texas v. United States*, Case No. 19-10011 (5th Cir. 2019), challenging constitutional validity of Affordable Care Act; *Texas v. Nielsen*, Civil Action No. 1:18 CV 00068 (S.D. Tex.), challenging the constitutional validity of the Deferred Action for Childhood Arrivals (DACA) program.

27. The 2010 election was a "wave" year for Republicans across the United States, but not in California. In the nation as a whole, Democrats lost six seats in the U.S. Senate, sixty-four seats in the House of Representatives, six governorships, and about seven hundred seats in state legislatures. Yet, in California, Democrats held all thirty-four of their House seats, returned Barbara Boxer to the Senate, won all races for state-wide office, maintained their margin in the state senate, and increased their advantage in the state assembly. Commentators said that the national Republican wave stopped at the Sierra Nevada. James E. Campbell, "The Midterm Landslide of 2010: A Triple Wave Election," *The Forum* 8, no. 4, Article 3 (January 10, 2011); Casey B. K. Dominguez, "Boxer vs. Fiorina in California's Senate Race: The Wave Stopped at the

Sierra Nevada," in Randall E. Adkins and David A. Dulio, eds., *Cases in Congressional Campaigns: Riding the Wave*, 2nd ed. (New York: Routledge, 2012), 78–96. The ballot measure that changed the vote requirement for the budget bill was Proposition 25. California Secretary of State, "Official Voter Information Guide, General Election, November 2, 2010," 52–55.

28. Ballot measures that added conservative provisions to the California Constitution included Proposition 13 of 1978 (restrictions on taxing power); Proposition 140 of 1990 (term limits on state-elected officials); Proposition 209 of 1996 (ban on affirmative action); Proposition 8 of 1982 and Proposition 115 of 1990 (restrictions on rights of criminal defendants); Proposition 1 of 1979 (limit on busing for integration); and Proposition 63 of 1986 (English-only requirement). All of these measures were citizen-initiated except the 1979 busing amendment, which was placed on the ballot by the legislature. For full text, see U.C. Hastings Law Library—California Ballot Measures Database, https://www.uchastings.edu/academics/library/ca-ballots/.

29. The constitutional amendment that created the full-time legislature was Proposition 1a of 1966. See California Secretary of State, "Voter Information Guide for 1966 General Election," Part I, 1–2; Part II, 1–27; the California Legislature has eighty assembly members who serve two-year terms and forty senators who serve four-year terms. Under the state's current term-limit provisions, individuals may serve only twelve years in the legislature. See Council of State Governments, *The Book of the States, 2018*, 26–31, 48–52; National Conference of State Legislatures, "2018 Legislator Compensation"; California State Assembly, "Salaries and Expenditures," January 9, 2019, https://www.assembly.ca.gov/salariesandexpenditures.

30. See Chapter 11 for more detail. For an additional overview, see David Vogel, *California Greenin': How the Golden State Became an Environmental Leader* (Princeton, NJ: Princeton University Press, 2018).

31. See Chapter 12 for more detail.

32. Melanie Mason, "California Gives Immigrants Unprecedented Rights and Benefits," *Governing*, August 12, 2015, https://www.governing.com/topics/politics/tns-california-immigration-alien.html; Robert Suro, "California Dreaming: The New Dynamism in Immigration Federalism and Opportunities for Inclusion on a Variegated Landscape," *Journal on Migration and Human Security* 3, no. 1 (2015): 1–25.

33. California Assembly Bill 1887 (2016); Government Code section 11139.8, subd. (a)(5).

34. Melanie Mason, "Business-friendly Democrats Pick New Leaders for Informal, but Powerful Sacramento Caucus," *Los Angeles Times*, December 9, 2015, https://www.latimes.com/politics/la-pol-sac-moderate-democrats-leaders-20151209-story.html.

35. According to a 2017 survey by researchers at Stanford Graduate School of Business, 74 percent of technology entrepreneur respondents reported that they would like to see labor union influence decrease. By contrast, only 18 percent of Democratic donors and 33 percent of Democratic citizens held that view. David Broockman, Greg F. Ferenstein, and Neil Malhotra, "The Political Behavior of Wealthy Americans: Evidence from Technology Entrepreneurs," Stanford Graduate School

of Business Working Paper No. 3581, December 9, 2017, 28; Martin Gelin, "Silicon Valley's Libertarians Are Trading Blows with California Democrats in a Fight for the Left," *Quartz*, March 1, 2018, https://qz.com/1219254/california-democrats-are-trading-blows-with-silicon-valleys-libertarians-in-a-fight-for-the-left/.

36. AB 5 of 2019 codified and expanded significantly upon a decision by the California Supreme Court in *Dynamex Operations West, Inc. v. Superior Court*, 4 Cal. 5th 903 (2018) that required employers to treat a larger class of workers as employees rather than as independent contractors. In 2019, Uber and other companies filed a lawsuit in federal court challenging AB 5, and also prepared a ballot initiative to overturn parts of the law. The case was *Olson v. California*, U.S.D.C. C.D. Cal. Case No. 2:19-cv-10956.

37. The struggle between education reformers and teachers' unions was one of the deepest divisions within the California Democratic Party. See, for example, Joel Warner, "Reed Hastings: Netflix CEO Goes Nuclear on Public Schools," *Capital and Main*, November 1, 2018, https://capitalandmain.com/reed-hastings-the-disrupter-1101.

38. The sanctuary state bill was SB 54 of 2017. The federal challenge to SB 54 was *United States v. California*, 921 F.3d 865 (9th Cir., 2019). In this case, United States sought an injunction against SB 54 as well as two other California statutes, AB 103 of 2017, which imposed inspection requirements for federal immigrant detention facilities, and AB 450 of 2017, which, among other provisions, required employers to notify employees of federal immigration inspections. The housing mandate was SB 35 of 2017. Many local governments opposed the law as a usurpation of local zoning authority, and the City of Huntington Beach sued to block it. *City of Huntington Beach v. State of California*, Case No. 30-201-01044945-CU-WM-CJC.

39. For texts and analyses of these measures, see U.C. Hastings Law Library—California Ballot Measures Database, https://www.uchastings.edu/academics/library/ca-ballots/.

40. Anthony Rendon and Kevin de León, "Joint Statement from California Legislative Leaders on Result of Presidential Election," November 9, 2016, https://calnonprofits. org/publications/article-archive/514-a-joint-statement-from-our-california-legislative-leaders-on-the-result-of-the-presidential-election.

41. For discussion of Brown's climate activism, see Chapter 11. The DACA case was *State of California, et al. v. U.S. Dep't of Homeland Security, et al.*, No. 3:17-cv-05235, consolidated with *Regents of the University of California v. Department of Homeland Security*, 908 F.3d 476 (9th Cir. 2018); on California's activism on health care policy, see Victoria Colliver, "California Goes Even Bigger on Obamacare," *Politico*, June 16, 2019, https://www.politico.com/story/2019/06/16/california-obamacare-health-care-1530461; on California's negotiations with the auto industry, see Ben Foldy and Mike Colias, "Trump-California Showdown on Fuel Economy Rules Divides Automakers," *Wall Street Journal*, August 21, 2019, https://www.wsj.com/articles/car-makers-follow-divergent-paths-on-fuel-efficiency-regulations-11566404594?mod=searchresults&page=1&pos=2.

42. Paul Nolette, "State Attorneys General Data: Multistate Litigation Database," https://attorneysgeneral.org/multistate-lawsuits-vs-the-federal-government/list-of-lawsuits-1980-present/.

Chapter 9

1. U.S. Census Bureau, "2018 Annual Survey of State Tax Collections," June 11, 2019, https://www.census.gov/data/tables/2018/econ/stc/2018-annual.html. These data did not include property, sales, and other taxes collected by local governments.

2. In 2017, California collected $3,936 per resident in state taxes while Texas collected $1,894, or less than half as much. By further comparison, the State of New York, with 8.5 million fewer residents than Texas, collected $79.7 billion in revenue, exceeding Texas by $26 billion—that worked out to $4,014 in state taxes per New York resident, exceeding even California's receipts. U.S. Census Bureau, "Annual Survey."

3. For a discussion of the enactment of the first federal income tax in 1861 and repeal in 1872, see John F. Witte, *The Politics and Development of the Federal Income Tax*, rev. ed. (Madison: University of Wisconsin Press, 1986), 67–70.

4. John O. Stark, "The Establishment of Wisconsin's Income Tax," *Wisconsin Magazine of History* 71, no. 1 (Autumn 1987): 27–45. Congress adopted a federal income tax in 1894, but the Supreme Court declared the law unconstitutional a year later in *Pollock v. Farmers' Loan and Trust Co.*, 157 U.S. 429 (1895). Congress sent the Sixteenth Amendment to the states in 1909. By 1913, the amendment received support from enough states for ratification.

5. Alaska, Florida, Nevada, South Dakota, Texas, Washington, and Wyoming have no state income tax. In addition to these seven states, New Hampshire and Tennessee assess no tax on earned income, but do impose a 5 percent income tax on interest and dividends. Tennessee has enacted legislation to eliminate its income tax in 2021. See Meg Wiehe et al., "Who Pays?: A Distributional Analysis of the Tax Systems in All 50 States," 6th ed. (Washington, DC: Institute on Taxation and Economic Policy [ITEP], October 2018): 8, https://itep.org/wp-content/uploads/whopays-ITEP-2018.pdf.

6. The nine states with a flat income tax are Colorado, Illinois, Indiana, Kentucky, Massachusetts, Michigan, North Carolina, Pennsylvania, and Utah. See Wiehe et al., "Who Pays?" 14. In 2019, Illinois governor J. B. Pritzker and the state legislature proposed for voter approval a constitutional amendment allowing a progressive income tax. For California's income tax brackets, see California Revenue and Tax Code sec. 17041.

7. The first state general sales taxes were adopted in the following years: Mississippi (1930); Arizona, California, Illinois, Indiana, Iowa, Michigan, New Mexico, North Carolina, Oklahoma, South Dakota, Utah, Washington, and West Virginia (1933); Missouri and Ohio (1934); Arkansas, Colorado, Hawaii, North Dakota, and Wyoming (1935); Alabama (1936); Kansas (1937); Louisiana (1938). U.S. Advisory Commission on Intergovernmental Relations, "Significant Features of Fiscal Federalism, Vol. I: Budget Processes and Tax Systems" (1993), 34.

8. Services range from access to the Internet, phone, and cable or satellite television; home remodeling; appliance repair; yard maintenance; entertainment (tickets to movies, concerts, or sporting events); personal services such as dry cleaning and barbering; and more. Digital products include digital music, photographs, movies, podcasts, and books.

9. Elizabeth Malm and Ellen Kant, "The Sources of State and Local Tax Revenues," Tax Foundation, January 29, 2013, https://files.taxfoundation.org/legacy/docs/ff354.pdf.

10. School districts, fire prevention districts, and various other local jurisdictions may tack additional levies on property. Some states make distinctions between the taxes assessed on residential and commercial properties and some allow for adjustments or abatements for particular groups of property owners, such as seniors.

11. Janelle Cammenga, "To What Extent Does Your State Rely on Property Taxes?" Tax Foundation, May 1, 2019, https://taxfoundation.org/state-and-local-property-tax-reliance-2019/.

12. Tax Foundation, "Facts and Figures: How Does Your State Compare?" (2019): Table 34, https://files.taxfoundation.org/20190715165329/Facts-Figures-2019-How-Does-Your-State-Compare.pdf. Among other provisions, California Proposition 13 of 1978 capped the ad valorem tax on real property to 1 percent of the property's value and limited increases in a property's taxable value to no more than 2 percent per year until the property is sold. See California Constitution Article XIIIA.

13. Tax Foundation, "Facts and Figures:" Table 35.

14. See T. R. Fehrenbach, *Lone Star: A History of Texas and the Texans*, 2nd ed. (New York: Da Capo Press, 2000), 278 (quoting Texas historian Rupert Richardson); Cal Jillson, *Lone Star Tarnished: A Critical Look at Texas Politics and Public Policy*, 3rd ed. (New York: Routledge, 2018), 251.

15. E. T. Miller, "The State Finances of Texas during the Civil War," *The Quarterly of the Texas State Historical Association* 14, no. 1 (July 1910): 1–23, 6–10, https://www.jstor.org/stable/pdf/30242999.

16. Fehrenbach, *Lone Star*, 433.

17. Ibid., 435; Texas Constitution of 1876, Article VIII, sections 1, 9.

18. Jillson, *Lone Star Tarnished*, 253–54.

19. Ibid., 253.

20. Ibid., 254–58.

21. Glen Hegar, "A Field Guide to the Taxes of Texas," Austin: Texas Comptroller of Public Accounts (January 2020): 2. https://comptroller.texas.gov/transparency/revenue/docs/96-1774.pdf. HB 3 of 2005 eliminated the capital and earned surplus bases for calculating the franchise tax and replaced them with a firm's "taxable margin," defined as "total revenue less the greater of: cost of goods sold, or total compensation." The tax rate on margin apportioned to Texas was set at 1 percent for most taxable businesses, with a 0.5 percent rate applicable to businesses in retail or wholesale trade.

22. Ibid, 14–17. This trend is due partly to flat rates (no increase since 1951) and to expanding exemptions.

23. For a time, Texas assessed a statewide property tax in addition to local property taxes, but it abolished the state property tax in 1980. Hegar, "Field Guide," 20.

24. The bill was SB 2 (Bettencourt). Riane Roldan and Shannon Najmabadi, "Gov. Greg Abbott Signs Bill Designed to Limit Property Tax Growth, *Texas Tribune*, June 12, 2019. See also Hegar, "A Field Guide," 20.

25. Dave McNeeley and Jim Henderson, *Bob Bullock: God Bless Texas* (Austin: University of Texas Press, 2008), 216–18.

26. Ibid., 216–18. See Texas Constitution, Article VIII, sec. 24, added November 2, 1993, replaced by Article III, section 24-a, added November 5, 2019.

27. Ballotpedia, "Texas Income Tax, Proposition 4 (1993)," https://ballotpedia.org/Texas_Income_Tax,_Proposition_4_(1993).

28. Christian Britschgi, "Texas Voters Ban State Income Taxes. Again." Reason, November 6, 2019. https://reason.com/2019/11/06/texas-voters-ban-state-income-taxes-again/.

29. Marvel M. Stockwell, "The Income Tax in California," *Bulletin National Tax Association* 31, no. 9 (June 1946): 257, 271–83, citing *Report of the State Tax Commission of the State of California* (Sacramento, 1917): 110–20.

30. James E. Hartley, Steven M. Sheffrin, and J. David Vasche, "Reform during Crisis: The Transformation of California's Fiscal System during the Great Depression," *Journal of Economic History* 56, no. 3 (September 1996): 657–78; Roger John Traynor and Frank M. Keesling, "The Scope and Nature of the California Income Tax," *California Law Review* 24, no. 5 (July 1936): 493–11.

31. Associated Press, "Tax Drives Hearst Out of California," *New York Times*, October 23, 1935, 1.

32. Ibid.

33. California Secretary of State, *Voter Information Guide, 1936 General Election*, "Proposition 2."

34. The vote was 737,629 Yes, 1,193,225 No. See California Secretary of State, Statement of the Vote, 1936 General Election. In 1942, critics of the income tax qualified another ballot measure to repeal the tax. That measure came closer than the 1936 effort, but also failed, by a 54–46 percent vote. See California Secretary of State, Statement of the Vote, 1942 General Election.

35. Jim Newton, *Justice for All: Earl Warren and the Nation He Made* (New York: Riverhead, 2006), 175–76.

36. Rarick, *California Rising*, 120–21; Lou Cannon, *Governor Reagan: His Rise to Power* (New York: Public Affairs, 2003), 194–201; Jean Ross, "The Largest Tax Increase in History?" California Budget and Policy Center, March 29, 2011, https://calbudgetcenter.org/blog/the-largest-tax-state-increase-in-history/.

37. Cannon, *Governor Reagan*, 199.

38. Henry Olsen, *The Working Class Republican: Ronald Reagan and the Return of Blue Collar Conservatism* (New York: Broadside Books, 2017), 99–109.

39. In 1989, Governor Deukmejian and the legislature agreed to a temporary quarter-cent increase in the sales tax to fund emergency repairs following the state's Loma Prieta earthquake. The temporary increase expired the following year. See George Skelton and Douglas P. Shuit, "Sales Tax Sought for Quake Relief: Deukmejian and Legislative Leaders Agree on a Proposal for a Quarter-cent Increase for 13 Months," *Los Angeles Times*, October 31, 1989, http://articles.latimes.com/1989-10-31/news/mn-284_1_sales-tax-increase.

40. For text and analysis of Proposition 13, see California Secretary of State, *California Voters Pamphlet*, Primary Election, June 6, 1978: 56–60. See also David O. Sears and Jack Citrin, *Tax Revolt: Something for Nothing in California*, enl. ed. (Cambridge, MA: Harvard University Press, 1985), 19–31. Jarvis's account can be found in Howard Jarvis with Robert Pack, *I'm Mad as Hell* (New York: Times Books, 1979).

41. California State Controller, "Property Tax Financial Data (2019) https://propertytax.bythenumbers.sco.ca.gov/#!/year/default; Tax Policy Center, "Property Tax Revenue," https://www.taxpolicycenter.org/statistics/property-tax-revenue.

42. Gavin Newsom, "Governor's Budget Summary 2020–2021, Sacramento: California Department of Finance, January 10, 2020, http://www.ebudget.ca.gov/budget/2020-21/. The sales tax also contributes to non–general fund spending, including transfers to local governments. See also Ryan Miller and Vu Chu, "California's Tax System: A Visual Guide," Sacramento: California Legislative Analyst's Office (2018), 34–36, https://lao.ca.gov/reports/2018/3805/ca-tax-system-041218.pdf. The relative decline in sales tax revenues can be attributed in part to the declining share of taxable goods in the modern economy. For years, sales of services and non-tangible goods have grown faster than sales of tangible goods, but the sales tax largely fails to capture them. Some tax reformers have urged the state to extend sales taxes into these higher growth areas. For example, Senator Robert Hertzberg (D–Los Angeles) has made repeated efforts to expand taxes on services. See Liam Dillon, "California Lawmaker Tries Again to Increase Taxes on Legal, Accounting, and Other Services," *Los Angeles Times*, February 5, 2018, http://www.latimes.com/politics/essential/la-pol-ca-essential-politics-updates-california-lawmaker-tries-again-to-1517862729-htmlstory.html.

43. Judy Lin, "The Open Secret about California Taxes," *CALmatters*, May 8, 2018, https://calmatters.org/articles/the-open-secret-about-california-taxes/; California Legislative Analyst's Office, "The 2012–13 Budget: Economic and Revenue Update," February 27, 2012, http://www.lao.ca.gov/analysis/2012/update/economic-revenue-update-022712.aspx.

44. Proposition 30 also included a temporary increase in the state sales tax from 7.25 to 7.5 percent. That additional increment was allowed to expire in 2016.

45. See Carl Davis et al., *Who Pays? A Distributional Analysis of the Tax Systems in All 50 States*, 5th ed. (Washington, DC: The Institute on Taxation and Economic Policy, 2015), 4.

46. Joshua Rauh and Ryan Shyu, "Behavioral Responses to State Income Taxation of High Earners: Evidence from California," Stanford Graduate School of Business, Working Paper No. 3835, October 8, 2019.

47. Cristobal Young, Charles Varner, Ithai Z. Lurie, and Richard Prisinzano, "Millionaire Migration and Taxation of the Elite: Evidence from Administrative Data," *American Sociological Review* 81, no. 3 (2016): 421–46; Charles Varner and Cristobal Young, "Millionaire Migration in California: The Impact of Top Tax Rates," Working Paper, Stanford University Center on Poverty and Inequality, Stanford, CA (2012).

48. The ACA's Medicaid expansion payment provisions were codified as 42 U.S.C. sec. 1396d(y)(1). The provision authorizing the Secretary of Health and Human

Services to determine that "further payments will not be made to the State" is at 42 U.S.C. sec. 1396c.

49. Chuck Lindell, "Perry: Texas Will Opt Out of Medicare Expansion, Insurance Exchange," *Austin American-Statesman,* September 1, 2012, https://www.statesman.com/news/20120901/perry-texas-will-opt-out-of-medicaid-expansion-insurance-exchange.

50. *National Federation of Independent Business v. Sebelius,* 567 U.S. 519, 581 (2012), consolidated with *Florida v. Department of Health and Human Services.*

51. Lindell, "Perry."

52. Kathleen Pender, "Governors Howl: Why Tax Plan Would Hammer Blue States," *San Francisco Chronicle,* December 4, 2017, https://www.sfchronicle.com/business/article/Governors-howl-Why-tax-plan-would-hammer-blue-12405179.php.

Chapter 10

1. The Labor Management Relations Act of 1935 ("Wagner Act"), 29 U.S.C. sec. 151-169, Pub. L. 74-198 (49 Stat. 449) enacted July 5, 1935. The Wagner Act excluded several types of workers, including federal, state, and local government workers, agricultural workers, domestic workers, and independent contractors.

2. The Supreme Court narrowly upheld the NRLA against constitutional attack in *NLRB v. Jones & Laughlin Steel Corp.,* 301 U.S. 1 (1937).

3. Marc Dixon, "Limiting Labor: Business Political Mobilization and Union Setback in the States," *Journal of Policy History* 19, no. 3 (2007): 313; Elizabeth Tandy Shermer, "Counter-Organizing the Sunbelt: Right-to-Work Campaigns and Anti-Union Conservatism, 1943–1958," *Pacific Historical Review* 78, no. 1 (2009): 81–118; Melvin W. Reder, "The Rise and Fall of Unions: The Public Sector and the Private," *Journal of Economic Perspectives* 2, no. 2 (Spring 1988): 89–110 (91). In 1919–1920, union membership temporarily peaked at about 5 million, and then fell to 3 million in early 1933. From that low point, it rose to 9 million at the beginning of World War II, and then to 17 million by the early 1950s.

4. Conservative groups active in this countermovement included the U.S. Chamber of Commerce, the American Farm Bureau Federation, the Southern States Industrial Council, the Christian American Association, and the National Association of Manufacturers. Dixon, "Limiting Labor," 316.

5. The Labor Management Relations Act of 1947 ("Taft-Hartley Act"), 29 U.S.C. sec. 141-197 (80 H.R. 3020, Pub. L. 80-101), enacted June 23, 1947. The final House vote to enact Taft-Hartley over President Truman's veto was 331–83. Representatives from Texas voted 15-3-2 for the override while representatives from California supported the override by a 16–7 margin. The final Senate vote was 68–25 for the override. Both Texas senators (Tom Connally and Pappy O'Daniel) voted to override Truman, while California's senators split, with Republican William Knowland supporting the override and Democrat Sheridan Downey voting to sustain Truman's veto. CQ Researcher, "Record Votes in 80th Congress (January–July, 1947)," https://library.cqpress.com/cqresearcher/document.php?id=cqresrre1947073000.

6. Agency fees are generally enforced through "security clauses" in union contracts, and states that allow these agreements are sometimes called "union security states."

7. Other provisions of Taft-Hartley banned direct contributions by unions and corporations to federal political campaigns; required union officers to sign non-communist affidavits with the government; and authorized the executive branch of the federal government to obtain injunctions to break strikes if an impending or current strike imperiled the national health or safety. See 29 U.S.C. sec. 141–197.

8. Various sources assign different dates to the adoption of right-to-work laws in a number of states. The variance is sometimes attributable to the difference between the date the law was enacted and the date it became effective. For example, some sources say Michigan became a right-to-work state in 2012 (the date the statute was enacted); others say 2013 (the law's effective date). Table 10.1 relies on the National Right to Work Committee's timeline. Many states, including Texas, adopted right-to-work laws by 1947, but the validity of these laws remained uncertain until Congress settled the question. Several states have adopted and later repealed right-to-work laws. Marc Dixon notes, for example, that Delaware and New Hampshire adopted right-to-work laws in 1947 and repealed them in 1949; Louisiana adopted a right-to-work law in 1954, repealed it in 1956, and readopted it in 1976; Indiana adopted a right-to-work law in 1957, repealed it in 1965, and readopted in 2012. Most recently, the Missouri Legislature adopted a right-to-work statute in 2017 but in 2018 voters repealed it through a citizen referendum by a 67.5 percent vote. Dixon, "Limiting Labor," 319; National Right to Work Committee, "Right to Work States Timeline," n.d., https://nrtwc.org/facts/state-right-to-work-timeline-2016/.

9. U.S. Department of Labor, Bureau of Labor Statistics, "Economic News Release: Union Members Summary," January 18, 2019, https://www.bls.gov/news.release/union2.nr0.htm. For presentation of the data, see Barry T. Hirsch and David A. Macpherson, "Union Membership, Coverage, Density, and Employment by State" for the years 1983–2018, available at www.unionstats.com.

10. See, for example, William Moore, "The Determinants and Effects of Right-to-Work Laws: A Review of the Recent Literature," *Journal of Labor Research* 19, no. 3 (1998) 445–469; Richard C. Kearney and Patrice Mareschal, *Labor Relations in the Public Sector*, 5th ed. (Boca Raton, FL: CRC Press, 2014), 4–13.

11. George Norris Green with Michael R. Botson Jr., "Looking for Lefty: Liberal/Left Activism and Texas Labor, 1920s–1960s," in *The Texas Left: The Radical Roots of Lone Star Liberalism*, edited by David O'Donald Cullen and Kyle G. Wilkison (College Station: Texas A&M Press, 2010), 113–117.

12. Dixon, "Limiting Labor," 324.

13. "Magna Carta," *Dallas Morning News*, September 1, 1941, Sec. II, p. 4.

14. See, for example, George Gresham, "Call It 'Right-to-Work-for-Less,' Not Right-to-Work," *New York Times Room for Debate*, March 12, 2015, https://www.nytimes.com/roomfordebate/2015/03/12/scott-walker-right-to-work-and-labors-waning-power/call-it-right-to-work-for-less-not-right-to-work.

15. George and Botson, "Looking for Lefty," 123. See also William P. Barnes, "The Mass Picketing and Closed Shop Statutes of 1947," *Southwestern Law Journal* 2, no. 79 (1948).

16. George E. Mowry, *The California Progressives* (Berkeley: University of California Press, 1951), 24; Kevin Starr, *Endangered Dreams: The Great Depression in California* (New York: Oxford University Press, 1996), 7–14.

17. Mowry, *California Progressives*, 49; Kevin Starr, *Americans and the California Dream, 1850–1915* (New York: Oxford University Press, 1973), 203; Kevin Starr, *Inventing the Dream: Americans through the Progressive Era* (New York: Oxford University Press, 1985), 74.

18. For text of Proposition 12 of 1944 and arguments for and against the measure, see California Secretary of State, *Voter Information Guide for 1944, General Election* (1944), 13–14; appendix 14. Voters defeated Proposition 12 by a 59.2–40.8 margin. Max Radin, "Popular Legislation in California: 1936–1946," *California Law Review* 35, no. 171 (1947): 180.

19. For text of Proposition 18 of 1958 and arguments for and against the measure, see California Secretary of State, "Voter Information Guide for 1958, General Election" (1958), 24–26; appendix 20–21. California voters defeated Proposition 18 of 1958 by a 59.6–41.4 percent margin, nearly identical to the 1944 results. Totton J. Anderson, "The 1958 Election in California," *Western Political Quarterly* 12, no. 1, Part 2 (March 1959): 276–300.

20. The new organization was originally named the National Farm Workers Association (NFWA); in 1966, the NFWA merged with the AFL-CIO's Agricultural Workers' Organizing Committee (AWOC) to form the United Farm Worker's Organizing Committee (UFWOC), renamed in 1970 the United Farm Workers of America. Fred B. Glass, *From Mission to Microchip: A History of the California Labor Movement* (Oakland: University of California Press, 2016), 334–46.

21. Glass, *From Mission to Microchip*, 348–58.

22. Ibid, 412–413.

23. Hirsch and Macpherson, "Union Membership."

24. Steven Greenhouse, "Most U.S. Union Members Are Working for the Government, New Data Shows," *New York Times*, January 22, 2010, B-1.

25. *Janus v. American Federation of State, County, and Municipal Employees, Council 31, et al.*, 588 U.S. __ (2018). California has sought to blunt Janus's effects. In 2018, the legislature enacted SB 866 which prohibits public officials from saying anything that might "deter or discourage" government workers from joining a union.

26. President Franklin D. Roosevelt, "Letter to Mr. Luther C. Steward, President, National Federation of Federal Employees," August 16, 1937, http://www.presidency.ucsb.edu/ws/?pid=15445.

27. Wisconsin Bill 309-A, codified as chap. 509 of the Laws of 1959, effective date Oct. 3, 1959.

28. President John F. Kennedy, "Executive Order 10988—Employee-Management Cooperation in the Federal Service," January 17, 1962, http://www.presidency.ucsb.edu/ws/?pid=58926.

29. Hirsch and Macpherson, "Union Membership."

30. Tex. Rev. Civ. Stat. Ann. art. 5154c (current version at Tex. Gov't Code Ann. secs. 617.001–.005 (West 2004)); Act of April 29, 1947, 50th Leg., R.S., ch. 135, 1947 Tex. Gen. Laws 231, 231–32.

31. Fire and Police Employee Relations Act, Tex. Local Gov't Code sec. 174 (1973). The act states that a local jurisdiction can engage in collective bargaining with fire and police unions only if local voters adopt section 174's collective bargaining provisions through a special referendum. Tex. Local Gov't Code sec. 174.051. Stanley Greer, "State Labor-Management Policy and the Texas Model," Austin: Texas Public Policy Foundation (February 2015), 11.

32. Tex. Local Gov. Code sec. 146.001–146.017, added by Acts 2005, 79th Leg., Ch. 1144 (H.B. 2866), Sec. 2, effective September 1, 2005.

33. Association of Texas Professional Educators, "Collective Bargaining, Exclusive Consultation, and the Right to Work," n.d., https://www.atpe.org/en/Advocacy/ Issues/Collective-Bargaining.

34. Amber M. Winkler, Janie Scull, and Dara Zeehandelaar, "How Strong Are U.S. Teachers Unions?: A State-by-State Comparison," Thomas B. Fordham Institute, October 2012, https://files.eric.ed.gov/fulltext/ED537563.pdf; NEA Research, "Ranking of the States 2017 and Estimates of School Statistics 2018" (Washington, DC: National Education Association, April 2018), http://www.nea.org/assets/docs/ 180413-Rankings_And_Estimates_Report_2018.pdf.

35. Glass, *From Mission to Microchip*, 354.

36. Ibid, 366.

37. The Meyers-Milias-Brown Act, Gov't Code secs. 3500–3511, added by Stats. 1968, Ch. 1390.

38. The Educational Employment Relations Act (EERA), Cal. Gov't Code secs. 3540– 3549, added by Stats. 1975, Ch. 961, known as the Rodda Act, was signed by Governor Jerry Brown in 1975, and became effective in 1976. The Rodda Act extended collective bargaining rights to employees in public K–12 schools and community colleges. The State Employer-Employee Relations Act, Gov't Code secs. 3512–3524 added by Stats. 1977, Ch. 1159, also known as the Ralph C. Dills Act, became effective in 1978. The Dills Act established collective bargaining for state employees. The Higher Education Employer-Employee Relations Act of 1979 (HEERA), Gov't Code secs. 3560–3599, added by Stats. 1978, Ch. 744, extended this right to employees of the University of California and the California State University systems. These laws, combined with the 1968 Meyers-Milias-Brown Act, covered most state and local public employees.

39. The legislature established the Educational Employment Relations Board as part of the Rodda Act (effective 1976) and renamed it Public Employment Relations Board as part of the Dills Act expansion of public sector collective bargaining in the state (effective 1978).

40. *Janus v. AFSCME*, 588 U.S. __ (2018).

41. Winkler et al., "How Strong." In 2019, the California Faculty Association disaffiliated from the CTA, contributing to a reduction in the CTA's membership to approximately 310,000 members. Figure 10.2 developed by Wesley Whitaker using U.S.

Census Bureau Current Population Survey data compiled by Barry T. Hirsch and David A. Macpherson, "Union Membership, Coverage, Density, and Employment by State and Sector" for years 1983–2018, available at www.unionstats.com.

42. The Fair Labor Standards Act is codified at 29 U.S.C. sec. 206; Occupational Safety and Health Act, 29 U.S.C. sec. 15; and Family and Medical Leave Act, 29 U.S.C. sec. 2601.

43. Texas Labor Code sec. 62.001 et seq.

44. Texas Labor Code sec. 62.0515.

45. In 1913, the California Legislature passed the state's first minimum wage law for women and children workers. The law established the Industrial Welfare Commission and delegated it power to establish a minimum wage for all industries employing women, and to regulate hours and working conditions. In 1914, California voters approved a state constitutional amendment confirming the legislature's power to enact a minimum wage law. See Norris C. Hundley Jr., "Katherine Philips Edson and the Fight for the California Minimum Wage, 1912–1923," *Pacific Historical Review* 29, no. 3 (August 1960): 271–85. Massachusetts adopted the nation's first state-level minimum wage in 1912; California was one of eight states to adopt a minimum wage law in 1913. The others were Colorado, Minnesota, Nebraska, Oregon, Utah, Washington, and Wisconsin. Arthur F. Lucas, "The Legal Minimum Wage in Massachusetts," *Annals of the American Academy of Political and Social Science* 130, Suppl. (March 1927): i–iv; 1–84.

46. The California law gave smaller employers (25 or fewer employees) until 2023 to meet the $15 per hour minimum wage standard. Many of the state's local jurisdictions put the $15 per hour wage requirement in place before the state rule went into effect.

47. Christine Mai-Duc, "On Minimum Wage, De León Says, California Is 'First . . . Period.'" *Los Angeles Times*, April 4, 2016, http://www.latimes.com/la-pol-sac-essential-poli-on-minimum-wage-de-leon-says-california-is-firs-1459790713-htmlstory.html.

48. Jon Ortiz, "How the $15 Minimum Wage Will Affect California State Workers," *Sacramento Bee*, April 5, 2016, https://www.sacbee.com/article70139177.html.

49. See California Labor Code Section 2698–2699.5.

50. For an overview of organized labor's recent policy agenda and successes in California, see the California Labor Federation's legislative reports. California Labor Federation, "Legislation," n.d., https://calaborfed.org/issuetypes/legislation/.

51. George I. Long, "Differences between Union and Non-union Pay," *Monthly Labor Review*, U.S. Bureau of Labor Statistics (April 2013), https://www.bls.gov/opub/mlr/2013/04/art2full.pdf.

52. U.S. Department of Labor, Bureau of Labor Statistics, U.S. Department of Labor, Bureau of Labor Statistics, "Characteristics of Minimum Wage Workers, 2018," March 2019, https://www.bls.gov/opub/reports/minimum-wage/2018/pdf/home.pdf.

53. In 2018, California's median hourly wage for all occupations was $20.40; in Texas, it was $17.84. U.S. Department of Labor Bureau of Labor Statistics, "May 2018 State Occupational Employment and Wage Estimates, California and Texas, April 2, 2019," (California: https://www.bls.gov/oes/current/oes_ca.htm. Texas: https://www.bls.gov/oes/current/oes_tx.htm#00-0000).

54. U.S. Department of Labor, Bureau of Labor Statistics, "Quarterly Census of Employment and Wages: State Government: All States and U.S., 2018 Annual Average," last updated January 2, 2020, https://data.bls.gov/cew/apps/table_maker/v4/table_maker.htm#type=0&year=2018&qtr=A&own=2&ind=10&supp=0; NEA Research, "Ranking of the States 2018 and Estimates of School Statistics 2019," Washington, DC: National Education Association, April 2019: 49 (Table E-7: Average Salaries of Public School Teachers), http://www.nea.org/assets/docs/2019%20Rankings%20and%20Estimates%20Report.pdf. The teacher salary data are projections based on reports by state departments of education. The California data do not include charter school teachers and exclude some forms of compensation. Ibid. at 5, 83.

55. U.S. Department of Labor, Bureau of Labor Statistics, "Quarterly Census;" NEA Research, "Ranking of the States," 49.

56. SB 400, 1999–2000 Reg. Sess., Stats. 1999, Ch. 555.

57. City of Stockton, No. 12-32118, Bankr. E.D. Cal., Dkt. 1134; City of San Bernardino, No. 6:12-bk-28006-MJ, Bankr. C.D. Cal., Dkt. 1504.

58. Liz Farmer, "How Are Pensions Protected, State-by-State?" *Governing*, January 28, 2014, http://www.governing.com/finance101/gov-pension-protections-state-by-state.html.

59. Public Employees' Pension Reform Act, Stats. 2012, Ch. 296 (AB 340), effective January 1, 2013. Some public unions resisted these relatively modest reforms. After the bill was signed, for example, firefighter unions challenged the new law in court, alleging that the elimination of certain practices that allowed employees to manipulate pension benefit formulas violated the California Rule. See *Cal Fire Local 2881 v. CalPERS,* California Supreme Court, Case No. S239958. The court ruled against the unions, but in a way that did not resolve the future of the California Rule.

60. The Stanford Institute for Economic Policy Research maintains a "California Pension Tracker" at http://www.pensiontracker.org/ that analyzes the financial condition of public employee pension systems in cities, counties, and special districts. The institute calculates pension debt—that is, total pension fund assets minus liabilities—using both actuarial and market bases. The actuarial basis, favored by most pension funds, uses a discount rate of 7 percent based on anticipated investment return on assets and conversion of future liabilities to current dollars. Under that formula, California's state and local pension debt in 2019 was approximately $311 billion. However, under the market basis, which uses a smaller discount rate, California's state and local pension debt as of 2019 was a staggering *$1.1 trillion.* See Joe Nation, "California Pension Debt Climbs despite Strong Economy," *Mercury News*, October 6, 2019, https://www.mercurynews.com/2019/10/06/opinion-california-pension-debt-climbs-despite-decade-of-soaring-stocks/.

61. U.S. Census Bureau, "2018 Annual Survey of Public Pensions: State and Local Tables," June 16, 2019, https://www.census.gov/data/tables/2018/econ/aspp/aspp-historical-tables.html. The Texas Constitution caps the state's pension contributions at 10 percent of the employee's salary and for years the state has provided even less.

62. Farmer, "How Are Pensions Protected."

63. Mary Williams Walsh, "In Texas, Some Rare Good News about Cities with Pension Woes," *New York Times*, June 1, 2017, www.nytimes.com/2017/06/01/business/dealbook/municipal-pensions-dallas-houston-bankruptcy.html.

64. See, for example, the proposed Raise the Wage Act of 2017, H.R. 15 (115th Congress 2017–2018), which would have incrementally increased the federal minimum wage to $15 per hour by 2024.

65. See Brief of Amici Curiae State of Michigan and 18 Other States in Support of Petitioner, *Janus v. AFSCME, Council 31, et al.*, No. 16-1466 (July 2017), http://www.scotusblog.com/wp-content/uploads/2017/07/16-1466-cert-tsac-michigan.pdf.

Chapter 11

1. Russell Gold, *The Boom: How Fracking Ignited the American Energy Revolution and Changed the World* (New York: Simon and Schuster, 2014), 58–59. In 2018, petroleum provided about 92 percent of the nation's transportation fuel; natural gas and coal generated more than 60 percent of its electricity. See U.S. Energy Information Administration, "U.S. Energy Facts Explained," August 28, 2019, https://www.eia.gov/energyexplained/us-energy-facts/; U.S. Energy Information Administration, "What Is U.S. Electricity Generation by Source?" October 25, 2019, https://www.eia.gov/tools/faqs/faq.php?id=427&t=3.

2. Gold, *The Boom*, 78; U.S. Energy Information Administration, "U.S. Field Production of Crude Oil," February 28, 2019, www.eia.gov/dnav/pet/hist/LeafHandler.ashx?n=pet&s=mcrfpus1&f=a.

3. Gold, *The Boom,* 225; The Powerplant and Industrial Fuel Use Act of 1978. Pub. L. 95–620, https://www.congress.gov/bill/95th-congress/house-bill/5146.

4. Gold, *The Boom*, 8.

5. Candace Dunn and Tim Hess, "The United States Is Now the Largest Global Crude Oil Producer," U.S. Energy Information Administration: September 12, 2018, https://www.eia.gov/todayinenergy/detail.php?id=37053; Jordan Blum, "U.S. Oil Production Hits Estimated Record 13 Million Barrels per Day," *Houston Chronicle*, January 15, 2020. https://www.chron.com/business/energy/article/U-S-oil-production-hits-estimated-record-13-14977192.php.

6. Gold, *The Boom*, 30–33.

7. See, for example, Seth Whitehead, "Fracking, 10 Years Later: Its Benefits Far Outweigh Its Risks," *Washington Examiner*, August 28, 2018, https://www.washingtonexaminer.com/opinion/op-eds/fracking-ten-years-later-its-benefits-far-outweigh-its-risks.

8. U.S. Energy Information Administration, "Annual Energy Outlook, 2019: Table 40: Light Duty Vehicle Stock by Technology Type," January 24, 2019, https://www.eia.gov/outlooks/aeo/pdf/aeo2019.pdf; Rebecca Bellan, "The Grim State of Electric Vehicle Adoption in the U.S.," Citylab, October 15, 2018, https://www.citylab.com/transportation/2018/10/where-americas-charge-towards-electric-vehicles-stands-today/572857/; Chrishelle Lawrence and Chip Berry, "U.S. Households' Heating Equipment Choices Are Diverse and Vary by Climate

Region," U.S. Energy Information Administration, April 6, 2017, https://www.eia.gov/todayinenergy/detail.php?id=30672; U.S. Energy Information Administration, "What Is U.S. Electricity Generation."

9. "What Is U.S. Electricity Generation by Energy Source?" U.S. Energy Information Administration, October 25, 2019, https://www.eia.gov/tools/faqs/faq.php?id=427&t=3.

10. In 2010, President Obama said, "Even though we have not broken ground on a new nuclear plant in nearly 30 years, nuclear energy remains our largest source of fuel that produces no carbon emissions. To meet our growing energy needs and prevent the worst consequences of climate change, we'll need to increase our supply of nuclear power. It's that simple." Suzanne Goldenberg, "Barack Obama Gives Green Light to New Wave of Nuclear Reactors," *The Guardian*, February 16, 2010, https://www.theguardian.com/environment/2010/feb/16/barack-obama-nuclear-reactors.

11. Brad Plummer, "How Retiring Nuclear Power Plants May Undercut U.S. Climate Goals," *New York Times*, June 13, 2017, https://www.nytimes.com/2017/06/13/climate/nuclear-power-retirements-us-climate-goals.html?module=inline.   Despite the nuclear power industry's decline, interest in this source persisted, based in part on advancements in small nuclear reactor design and waste handling and storage. See Leigh Phillips, "The New, Safer Nuclear Reactors That Might Help Stop Climate Change," *MIT Technology Review*, February 27, 2019, https://www.technologyreview.com/s/612940/the-new-safer-nuclear-reactors-that-might-help-stop-climate-change/.

12. For survey data highlighting the national partisan divide on climate issues, see Pew Research Center, "The Politics of Climate," October 4, 2016, http://www.pewresearch.org/science/2016/10/04/the-politics-of-climate/.

13. See David M. Konisky and Neal D. Woods, "Environmental Policy, Federalism, and the Obama Presidency," *Publius: The Journal of Federalism* 46, no. 3 (July 1, 2016): 366–91.

14. Lisa Friedman and Brad Plumer, "E.P.A. Announces Repeal of Major Obama-Era Carbon Emissions Rule," *New York Times*, October 9, 2017, https://www.nytimes.com/2017/10/09/climate/clean-power-plan.html.

15. In 2015, for example, West Virginia repealed a state law requiring utilities to produce 25 percent of the state's electricity supply from alternative or renewable sources, instead deciding to rely on coal-fired plants to continue to generate more than 90 percent of the state's electricity. West Virginia lawmakers concluded that switching to renewable sources would destroy coal industry jobs and increase electricity costs. See National Conference of State Legislatures, "State Renewable Portfolio Standards and Goals," February 1, 2019, http://www.ncsl.org/research/energy/renewable-portfolio-standards.aspx; John Eich, "West Virginia Becomes First State to Repeal RPS," American Legislative Exchange Council ("ALEC") February 4, 2015, https://www.alec.org/article/west-virginia-becomes-first-state-repeal-rps/. Similarly, most oil- and gas-producing states have promoted full development of those resources and have resisted attempts to restrict them.

16. U.S. Energy Information Administration, "Texas: State Profile and Energy Estimates," n.d., https://www.eia.gov/state/?sid=TX#tabs-4.

17. Public Utility Regulatory Act (PURA), as amended by Senate Bill 7, Act of May 21, 1999, 76th Legislature, Regular Session, Chapter 405. Among other provisions, SB 7 required the state's utilities to develop 2,000 megawatts of new renewable energy sources by 2009—a goal it met by 2005. In 2005, the legislature required an additional 5,880 megawatts of renewable energy sources be built by 2015 and 10,000 by 2025, with 500 megawatts coming from sources other than wind.

18. Kate Galbraith and Asher Price, *The Great Texas Wind Rush: How George W. Bush, Ann Richards, and a Bunch of Tinkerers Helped the Oil and Gas State Win the Race to Wind Power* (Austin: University of Texas Press, 2013), 123.

19. Galbraith and Price, *Great Texas Wind Rush*, 113–152; Robert Fares, "Texas Got 18 Percent of Its Energy from Wind and Solar Last Year," *Scientific American*, January 29, 2018, https://blogs.scientificamerican.com/plugged-in/texas-got-18-percent-of-its-energy-from-wind-and-solar-last-year/; David A. Todd and Jonathan Ogren, *The Texas Landscape Project: Nature and People* (College Station: Texas A&M Press, 2016), 353–58.

20. U.S. Energy Information Administration, "State Energy Consumption Estimates: 1960–2017," June 2019: 3, https://www.eia.gov/state/seds/archive/seds2017.pdf.

21. Gold, *The Boom,* 8, 120–122.

22. Stephanie B. Gaswirth et al., "Fact Sheet 2018–3073: Assessment of Undiscovered Continuous Oil and Gas Resources in the Wolfcamp Shale and Bone Spring Formation of the Delaware Basin, Permian Basin Province, New Mexico and Texas, 2018" (Washington, DC: U.S. Geological Survey, 2018), https://pubs.er.usgs.gov/publication/fs20183073; Ariel Cohen, "America's Oil and Gas Reserves Double with Massive New Permian Discovery," *Forbes*, December 21, 2018, https://www.forbes.com/sites/arielcohen/2018/12/21/americas-oil-and-gas-reserves-double-with-massive-new-permian-discovery/. According to the U.S. Energy Information Administration, Texas's oil production peaked at 1.8 billion barrels per year in 2019. U.S. Energy Information Administration, "Texas State Energy Profile," March 19, 2020, https://www.eia.gov/state/print.php?sid=TX#37.

23. Marissa Barnett, "Fracking Returns to Denton after State Outlaws Local Hydraulic Fracturing Bans," *Dallas Morning News*, May 22, 2015, www.dallasnews.com/news/politics/2015/05/22/fracking-returns-to-denton-after-state-outlaws-local-hydraulic-fracturing-bans; Ballotpedia, "City of Denton Fracking Ban Initiative (2014)," https://ballotpedia.org/City_of_Denton_Fracking_Ban_Initiative_(November_2014); Texas House Bill 40, effective May 18, 2015, codified in Texas Nat. Res. Code § 81.0523.

24. Greg Abbott, "Defending Texas Energy and Jobs," news release, June 2, 2014, https://www.gregabbott.com/greg-abbott-defending-texas-energy-jobs/; Greg Abbott, "Governor Abbott Meets with Senators McConnell, Cornyn and Cruz to Discuss Texas Response to EPA," news release, May 7, 2015, https://gov.texas.gov/news/post/governor_abbott_meets_with_senators_mcconnell_cornyn_and_cruz_to_discuss_te .

25. Greg Abbott, "Governor Abbott Statement on President Obama's Environmental Proposal," news release, August 3, 2015. Office of the Texas Governor, https://gov.

texas.gov/news/post/governor_abbott_statement_on_president_obamas_environ-mental_proposal.

26. See, for example, *Coalition for Responsible Regulation, Inc. v. Environmental Protection Agency*, 684 F.3d 102 (D.C. Cir. 2012), cert. denied, Case No. 12-1253 (2013) (failed challenge to endangerment finding and tailpipe rule); *Utility Air Regulatory Group v. Environmental Protection Agency*, 573 U.S. 302 (2014) (lim-iting EPA authority to regulate CO_2 emissions from some stationary sources); *West Virginia, et al. v. EPA*, D.C. Cir., 15–1363. (winning stay of implementation of the Clean Power Plan).

27. Daniel Yergin, *The Prize: The Epic Quest for Oil, Money, and Power* (New York: Free Press, 1991), 81–82.

28. David Vogel, *California Greenin': How the Golden State Became an Environmental Leader* (Princeton, NJ: Princeton University Press, 2018), 156–58.

29. The Mulford-Carrell Air Resources Act established the California Air Resources Board. Stats. 1967, Ch. 1545. Health and Safety Code 39000–39570. The California waiver provision of the Federal Air Quality Act of 1967, 42 U.S.C. 7543(b) states:

    (1) The Administrator shall, after notice and opportunity for public hearing, waive application of this section to any State which has adopted standards . . . for the control of emissions from new motor vehicles or new motor vehicle engines prior to March 30, 1966, if the State determines that the State standards will be, in the aggregate, at least as protective of public health and welfare as applicable Federal standards. No such waiver shall be granted if the Administrator finds that—

    (A) the determination of the State is arbitrary and capricious,

    (B) such State does not need such State standards to meet compelling and extraordinary conditions, or

    (C) such State standards and accompanying enforcement procedures are not consistent with section 7521(a) of this title.

    See Vogel, *California Greenin'*, 161–78.

30. Vogel, *California Greenin'*, 187–88.

31. The government issues a Stage 1 smog alert when ozone levels reach 0.20 parts per million (PPM) and a Stage 2 smog alert when ozone levels reach 0.35 PPM. California Air Resources Board, "Fact Sheet: Reducing Emissions From California Vehicles," https://ww2.arb.ca.gov.

32. Kate Wheeling and Max Ufberg, "The Ocean Is Boiling: The Complete Oral History of the 1969 Santa Barbara Oil Spill," *The Pacific Standard*, April 18, 2017, https://psmag.com/news/the-ocean-is-boiling-the-complete-oral-history-of-the-1969-santa-barbara-oil-spill. See also Rosanna Xia, "Coastal Commission on Trump's Offshore Drilling Plan: Ain't Gonna Happen," *Los Angeles Times*, February 8, 2018, https://www.latimes.com/local/lanow/la-me-california-offshore-drilling-20180208-story.html. The Santa Barbara disaster was later exceeded by the Exxon Valdez tanker spill off the coast of Alaska (1989) and the Deepwater Horizon platform spill in the Gulf of Mexico (2010).

33. Thomas Raymond Wellock, *Critical Masses: Opposition to Nuclear Power in California, 1958–1978* (Madison: University of Wisconsin Press, 1998), 17–67.

34. California was also the site of three much smaller, now-decommissioned nuclear plants: Santa Susanna (Ventura County) (1957–1964); Vallecitos (Contra Costa County) 1957–1967; and Humboldt Bay (Humboldt County) (1963–1976). California Energy Commission, "Nuclear Energy," n.d., https://www.energy.ca.gov/nuclear/california.html.
35. Pawel, *Browns of California*, 75–82; Wellock, *Critical Masses*, 186–87.
36. Wellock, *Critical Masses*, 186–205; Jerry Brown, speech to anti-nuclear rally in Washington, D.C., May 6, 1979, quoted in Pawel, *Browns of California*, 275–76.
37. Vogel, *California Greenin'*, 189–98; Pawel, *Browns of California*, 248–56.
38. Carolyn Marshall, "Schwarzenegger Issues Plan to Reduce Greenhouse Gases," *New York Times*, June 2, 2005; Vogel, *California Greenin'*, 205–10.
39. California Assembly Bill 32 of 2006, codified as Health and Safety Code Section 38500 et seq. For a summary, see California Air Resources Board, "Assembly Bill 32 Overview," August 5, 2014, https://www.arb.ca.gov/cc/ab32/ab32.htm.
40. Eric Biber, "Cultivating a Green Political Landscape: Lessons for Climate Change Policy from the Defeat of California's Proposition 23," 66 *Vanderbilt Law Review* 399 (2013): 400–11.
41. Ann E. Carlson, "Regulatory Capacity and State Environmental Leadership: California's Climate Policy," 24 *Fordham Environmental Law Review* 63, 70–75 (2017); California Environmental Protection Agency, Air Resources Board "California's Cap and Trade Program: Fuel Facts," December 2014, https://www.arb.ca.gov/cc/capandtrade/guidance/facts_fuels_under_the_cap.pdf.
42. John Wildermuth, "Gov. Brown Clashes with Environmentalists over Fracking," *San Francisco Chronicle*, May 16, 2017, https://www.sfchronicle.com/science/article/Gov-Brown-clashes-with-environmentalists-over-11151180.php.
43. California Senate Transportation Committee, "Governor Brown's Transportation Funding Plan," September 3, 2015: 8, https://stran.senate.ca.gov/sites/senate.ca.gov/files/governor_brown_transportation_funding_plan.pdf; EVAdoption, "EV Marketshare—California," n.d., evadoption.com/ev-market-share/ev-market-share-california/.
44. Wildermuth, "Gov. Brown Clashes."
45. David R. Baker, "Brown Signs Climate Law Mandating 50% Renewable Power by 2030," *SF Gate*, October 7, 2015.
46. David Siders, "Jerry Brown's Climate Warning: 'We are Talking about Extinction,'" *Sacramento Bee*, July 21, 2015, https://www.sacbee.com/news/politics-government/capitol-alert/article27998554.html.
47. California SB 100 (De León), "The 100 Percent Clean Energy Act of 2018," https://leginfo.legislature.ca.gov/faces/billNavClient.xhtml?bill_id=201720180SB100.
48. Edmund G. Brown Jr., Executive Order B-55-18, September 9, 2018, https://www.gov.ca.gov/wp-content/uploads/2018/09/9.10.18-Executive-Order.pdf.
49. Chris Magerian, "Governor Jerry Brown Signs Law to Extend Cap and Trade, Securing the Future of California's Key Climate Program," *Los Angeles Times*, July 25, 2017, https://www.latimes.com/politics/la-pol-ca-jerry-brown-climate-change-law-20170725-story.html.

50. See *United States v. California*, Case No. 2:19-at-01013, U.S.D.C. E.D. Cal. October 13, 2019, https://www.justice.gov/opa/press-release/file/1212416/download; Phil Willon, "To Stop Trump Fracking Plans, California Is Going to Court," *Los Angeles Times*, January 17, 2020, https://www.latimes.com/california/story/2020-01-17/california-heads-to-court-to-block-trump-efforts-new-fracking. The standards for fuel efficiency and emissions are closely related because vehicles emit carbon dioxide in direct relation to the amount of carbon fuel they burn—electric plug-ins and hybrids have the best fuel economy and produce the least carbon emissions; heavy, gasoline- or diesel-powered SUVs and trucks burn more fuel and emit more carbon. California has no authority to set fuel economy standards, but it has sought to do so indirectly by invoking its power under the Clean Air Act to set emission rules.

51. U.S. Environmental Protection Agency, "California State Motor Vehicle Pollution Control Standards; Notice of Decision Denying a Waiver of Clean Air Act Preemption for California's 2009 and Subsequent Model Year Greenhouse Gas Emission Standards for New Motor Vehicles," *Federal Register* 73, no. 45 (March 6, 2008): 12156–69.

52. U.S. Environmental Protection Agency, "California State Motor Vehicle Pollution Control Standards; Notice of Decision Granting a Waiver of Clean Air Act Preemption for California's 2009 and Subsequent Model Year Greenhouse Gas Emission Standards for New Motor Vehicles," *Federal Register* 74, no. 129 (July 8, 2009): 32743–84.

53. Environmental Protection Agency and National Highway Traffic Safety Administration, "2017 and Later Model Year Light-Duty Vehicle Greenhouse Gas Emissions and Corporate Average Fuel Economy Standards," *Federal Register* 77, no. 199 (October 15, 2012): 62624–63200.

54. U.S. Environmental Protection Agency, "EPA Administrator Pruitt: GHG Emissions Standards for Cars and Light Trucks Should Be Revised," April 2, 2018, https://www.epa.gov/newsreleases/epa-administrator-pruitt-ghg-emissions-standards-cars-and-light-trucks-should-be.

55. *State of California v. Environmental Protection Agency*, U.S. Court of Appeals, District of Columbia Circuit (Case No. 18-1114, May 1, 2018). California was joined by sixteen other states (Connecticut, Delaware, Illinois, Iowa, Maine, Maryland, Massachusetts, Minnesota, New Jersey, New York, Oregon, Pennsylvania, Rhode Island, Vermont, Virginia, and Washington) and the District of Columbia in challenging the Trump administration's rollback of the federal emission standards.

56. Greg Abbott, Letter to Secretary of Transportation Elaine L. Chao and Acting EPA Administrator Andrew Wheeler, October 27, 2018, https://www.regulations.gov/document?D=NHTSA-2018-0067-11935. The governors of Kansas, Kentucky, Maine, Mississippi, Nebraska, North Dakota, and Oklahoma also signed the letter.

57. *California v. Chao*, U.S.D.C., D.C. Case No. 1:19-cv-02826, filed September 20, 2019; Coral Davenport and Hiroko Tabuchi, "Automakers, Rejecting Trump Pollution Rule, Strike a Deal with California," *New York Times*, July 25, 2019, https://www.nytimes.com/2019/07/25/climate/automakers-rejecting-trump-pollution-rule-strike-a-deal-with-california.html?module=inline; Coral Davenport, "California to Stop Buying from Automakers That Backed Trump on Emissions," *New York Times*,

November 18, 2019, https://www.nytimes.com/2019/11/18/climate/california-automakers-trump.html.

Chapter 12

1. Mollie Orshansky, "Counting the Poor: Another Look at the Poverty Profile," *Social Security Bulletin*, January 1965, https://www.ssa.gov/policy/docs/ssb/v28n1/v28n1p3.pdf. See also Gordon M. Fisher, "The Development and History of the U.S. Poverty Thresholds—A Brief Overview," U.S. Department of Health and Human Services, January 1, 1997, https://aspe.hhs.gov/history-poverty-thresholds.

2. U.S. Department of Health and Human Services, "Annual Update of the HHS Poverty Guidelines," *Federal Register* 85, no. 12 (January 17, 2020): 3060, https://www.govinfo.gov/content/pkg/FR-2020-01-17/pdf/2020-00858.pdf; Jessica Semega, Melissa Kollar, John Creamer, and Abinash Mohanty, "Income and Poverty in the United States: 2018," U.S. Census Bureau, September 2019, https://www.census.gov/content/dam/Census/library/publications/2019/demo/p60-266.pdf. The figure of 38 million Americans below the poverty line in 2018 represented an improvement from 2014, when a record 46.7 million Americans fell below this line.

3. Ajay Chaudry, Christopher Eimer, Suzanne Macartney, Lauren Frohlich, Colin Campbell, Kendall Swenson, Don Oellerich, and Susan Hauan, "Poverty in the United States: Fifty Year Trends and Safety Net Impacts," U.S. Department of Health and Human Services, March 2016, www.aspe.hhs.gov/system/files/pdf.

4. Liana Fox, "The Supplemental Poverty Measure: 2018," U.S. Census Bureau, October 7, 2019, https://www.census.gov/library/publications/2019/demo/p60-268.html, Table A-5: "Number and Percentage of People in Poverty by State Using 3-Year Average Over: 2016, 2017, and 2018."

5. Ibid. The Public Policy Institute of California and the Stanford Center for Poverty and Inequality have developed a "California Poverty Measure" that accounts for the cost of living as well as government benefits. According to that measure, in 2017, approximately 17.8 percent of Californians lacked enough resources to meet basic needs. Marybeth Mattingly, Sarah Bohn, Caroline Danielson, Sara Kimberlin, and Christopher Wimer, "Poverty Declines in California, but More Than 1 in 3 Are Poor or Nearly Poor," Public Policy Institute of California, October 2019, https://inequality.stanford.edu/sites/default/files/california_poverty_measure_2017.pdf.

6. Meghan Henry, Rian Watt, Anna Mahathey, Jillian Ouellette, and Aubrey Sitler, "The 2019 Annual Homeless Assessment Report (AHAR) to Congress" (Washington, DC: U.S. Department of Housing and Urban Development, January 2020): 2, https://files.hudexchange.info/resources/documents/2019-AHAR-Part-1.pdf.

7. Jennifer Wolch and Michael Dear, *Malign Neglect: Homelessness in an American City* (San Francisco: Jossey-Bass, 1993).

8. Henry et al., "2019 Annual Homeless": 1.

9. Ibid., 83, 96; Los Angeles Homeless Services Authority, "2019 Greater Los Angeles Homeless Count—Los Angeles County," September 5, 2019, https://www.lahsa.org/

documents?id=3423-2019-greater-los-angeles-homeless-count-los-angeles-county. pdf; Kate Eby, "History of How Many People Are Homeless in the Bay Area," ABC7 News, July 5, 2019, https://abc7news.com/society/homeless-population-history-in- bay-area/5260657/; Laura Petry et al., "San Francisco Homeless Count & Survey 2019," Applied Survey Research, http://hsh.sfgov.org/wp-content/uploads/FINAL-PIT-Report-2019-San- Francisco.pdf.

10. Anna Gorman and Kaiser Health News, "Medieval Diseases Are Infecting California's Homeless: Typhus, Tuberculosis, and Other Illnesses Are Spreading Quickly through Camps and Shelters," *The Atlantic*, March 8, 2019, https://www.theatlantic.com/health/archive/2019/03/typhus-tuberculosis-medieval-diseases-spreading-homeless/584380/.

11. Theda Skocpol, *Protecting Soldiers and Mothers: The Political Origins of Social Policy in the United States* (Cambridge, MA: Belknap Press, 1995), 65–66. Shanna Rose, *Financing Medicaid: Federalism and the Growth of America's Health Care Safety Net* (Ann Arbor: University of Michigan Press, 2013), 33.

12. Rose, *Financing Medicaid*, 33.

13. Lyndon B. Johnson, "State of the Union," January 8, 1964, University of Virginia Miller Center, https://millercenter.org/the-presidency/presidential-speeches/january-8-1964-state-union.

14. The Medicaid program was established through Title XIX of the Social Security Act Amendments of 1965. As Shanna Rose notes, in 1965 Medicaid was considered an afterthought to the 1965 bill, yet it has become the nation's largest health care plan in terms of the number of people covered. Rose, *Financing Medicaid*, 2–4, 46–47.

15. "Vote Tallies for Passage of Medicare in 1965," Social Security Administration, https://www.ssa.gov/history/tally65.html; Jillson, *Lone Star Tarnished*, 168.

16. H.R. 3734 Section 401.

17. Peter T. Kilborn and Sam Howe Verhovek, "Clinton's Welfare Shift Ends Tortuous Journey," *New York Times*, August 2, 1996, A1. Marian Wright Edelman, founder of the Children's Defense Fund and a close Clinton ally, invoked the term "crucial moral litmus test." After President Clinton signed the welfare reform bill, Peter Edelman and two other senior administration officials resigned in protest. Alison Mitchell, "Two Clinton Aides Resign to Protest New Welfare Law," *New York Times*, September 12, 1996, A1.

18. Pub. L. 104–193. The final vote on welfare reform united Republicans and divided Democrats. In the House of Representatives, Republicans supported the bill, 230–2; Democrats split 98–98. In the Senate, all 53 Republicans voted for passage; Democrats voted 25 yea and 21 no, with one not voting. In the House, one independent voted no.

19. Rose, *Financing Medicaid*, 1–11, 46–50. As of Fiscal Year 2020–2021, California was one of thirteen states that paid the maximum 50 percent share of its Medicaid costs; Mississippi paid the lowest share—just over 20 percent. The federal government's payment of 68.81 percent of Texas's Medicaid costs was near the national median. U.S. Department of Health and Human Services, "Federal Financial Participation in State Assistance Programs," *Federal Register* 84, no. 232 (December 3, 2019): 66204.

20. Robin Rudowitz, Elizabeth Hinton, and Larisa Antonisse, "Medicaid Enrollment and Spending Growth: FY 2018 and 2019," Henry J. Kaiser Family Foundation, October 2018, http://files.kff.org/attachment/Issue-Brief-Medicaid-Enrollment-and-Spending-Growth-FY-2018-2019.

21. See The Patient Protection and Affordable Care Act, Pub. L. 111–148, 124 Stat. 119–1024 (2010). *NFIB v. Sebelius,* 567 U.S. 519 (2012), held that the ACA's threat to withdraw all Medicaid funding for states that opted out of the expansion plan unconstitutionally coerced the states into compliance.

22. Final vote on passage of the ACA was 60–39 in the Senate and 219–212 in the House to agree to Senate amendments. "Roll Call Vote 111th Congress—1st Session—On Passage of the Bill (H.R. 3590 As Amended)," https://www.senate.gov/legislative/LIS/roll_call_lists/roll_call_vote_cfm.cfm?congress=111&session=1&vote=00396; "Final Vote Results for Roll Call 165," U.S. Congress, http://clerk.house.gov/evs/2010/roll165.xml.

23. As of 2019, states besides Texas opting out of Medicaid expansion were Alabama, Florida, Georgia, Kansas, Missouri, Mississippi, North Carolina, Oklahoma, South Carolina, South Dakota, Tennessee, Wisconsin, and Wyoming. See "Status of State Medicaid Expansion Decisions," Henry J. Kaiser Family Foundation, May 13, 2019, https://www.kff.org/medicaid/issue-brief/status-of-state-medicaid-expansion-decisions-interactive-map/. For information on citizen initiatives that expanded Medicaid, see Miller-Rose Institute Initiative Database, http://roseinstitute.org/initiatives/.

24. "Medicaid Expansion Enrollment," n.d., Henry J. Kaiser Family Foundation, n.d., https://www.kff.org/health-reform/state-indicator/medicaid-expansion-enrollment/?currentTimeframe=0&sortModel=%7B%22colId%22:%22Expansion%20Group%20Enrollment%22,%22sort%22:%22desc%22%7D; "March 2019 Medicaid & CHIP Enrollment," Centers for Medicare and Medicaid Services, n.d., https://www.medicaid.gov/medicaid/program-information/medicaid-and-chip-enrollment-data/report-highlights/index.html; National Association of State Budget Officers, "2019 State Expenditure Report," November 21, 2019: 51–58, https://www.nasbo.org/reports-data/state-expenditure-report.

25. CHIP is a joint federal-state program that provides health insurance coverage to children in low-income families that have incomes too high to qualify for Medicaid. The federal government historically has contributed an average of 71 percent of the program's funding, states 29 percent; the ACA temporarily increased the federal contribution to 93 percent. Data available at https://www.medicaid.gov/chip/financing/index.html.

26. Texas Constitution, Article III, section 51-a (b) provides that "the amount paid from state funds to or on behalf of needy dependent children and their caretakers shall not exceed one percent of the state budget in any biennium." The following subsection provides, however, that if this restriction on state welfare spending conflicts with federal law in a way that prevents the state from receiving federal matching funds, the legislature is authorized to make necessary adjustments in order that "such federal matching money will be available for assistance and/or medical care for or on behalf of needy persons." Texas Constitution, Article III, section 51-a(c).

27. According to the Food Research and Action Center, based on a five-year average from 2014–2018, 12.2 percent of Texans received SNAP benefits, compared to 9.1 percent of Californians. Food Research and Action Center, "State Data for Households Participating in SNAP," n.d., http://www.frac.org/maps/snap-state-map/snap-states.html#pdflist. Measured another way, in 2017, 73 percent of Texans eligible for SNAP benefits participated in the program, compared with 72 percent in California. U.S. Department of Agriculture Food and Nutrition Service, "Supplemental Nutrition Assistance Program (SNAP): SNAP Community Characteristics," August 20, 2019, https://www.fns.usda.gov/ops/snap-community-characteristics.

28. Jillson, *Lone Star Tarnished*, 167–70.

29. U.S. Department of Health and Human Services, Office of Family Assistance, "TANF and MOE Spending and Transfers by Activity, FY 2017 (Contains National & State Pie Charts)," February 6, 2019, https://www.acf.hhs.gov/sites/default/files/ofa/fy2017_tanf_and_moe_state_piechart_508.pdf; Center for Budget and Policy Priorities, "Chart Book: Temporary Assistance for Needy Families," August 21, 2018, https://www.cbpp.org/research/family-income-support/chart-book-temporary-assistance-for-needy-families; Ife Floyd, Ashley Burnside, and Liz Schott, "TANF Reaching Few Poor Families," Center for Budget and Policy Priorities, November 28, 2018: 11–19, https://www.cbpp.org/sites/default/files/atoms/files/6-16-15tanf.pdf; Alexa Ura, "How Texas Killed Welfare: 'We Spend Our Dollars on Anything but Poor Families," *The Guardian*, November 30, 2017, https://www.theguardian.com/us-news/2017/nov/30/texas-welfare-spending-poor-families.

30. Texas Legislative Budget Board, "Summary of Legislative Budget Estimates, 2020–2021 Biennium: House," (January 2019): 56–58, http://www.lbb.state.tx.us/Documents/Appropriations_Bills/86/LBB_Recommended_House/5492_House_LBE_Bill_Summary.pdf. These figures were subject to supplemental spending adjustments.

31. Emily Ramshaw and Marilyn Serafini, "Battle Lines Drawn over Medicaid in Texas," *New York Times*, November 11, 2010, 'https://www.nytimes.com/2010/11/12/us/politics/12ttmedicaid.html; Rose, *Financing Medicaid*, 241–43.

32. The twenty-six-state suit was titled *Florida v. U.S. Department of Health & Human Services,* 648 F.3d 1235 (11th Cir. 2011).

33. *National Federation of Independent Business v. Sebelius*, 567 U.S. 519, 581 (2012).

34. Governor Rick Perry, "Letter to Kathleen Sebelius, Secretary of the U.S. Department of Health and Human Services, July 9, 2012," https://www.governing.com/news/state/mct-texas-rick-perry-rejects-medicaid-expansion-state-health-exchange.html.

35. Kristin Brown, "Rick Perry: Texas Won't Implement Obamacare," Fox News, July 9, 2012, https://www.foxnews.com/politics/rick-perry-texas-wont-implement-obamacare.

36. The U.S. Court of Appeals for the Fifth Circuit heard the case in July 2019. The federal government changed its position to side with the plaintiffs, pitting it against the California-led coalition of twenty-one states that intervened to defend the ACA. *Texas, et al. v. United States, et al.; California, et al., Intervenors-Defendants*, U.S.D.C. N.D. Tex. Civil Action No. 4:18-cv-00167-O, December 14, 2018, https://oag.ca.gov/system/files/attachments/press-docs/

211-texas-order-granting-plaintiffs-partial-summary-judgment.pdf;   MaryBeth
Musumeci, "Explaining *Texas v. U.S.*: A Guide to the 5th Circuit Appeal in the Case
Challenging the ACA," Kaiser Family Foundation, July 3, 2019, https://www.kff.
org/health-reform/issue-brief/explaining-texas-v-u-s-a-guide-to-the-5th-circuit-
appeal-in-the-case-challenging-the-aca/.

37. See, for example, Senator Rodney Ellis, "Let's Take Full Advantage of Affordable
Care Act," *Houston Chronicle*, July 27, 2012, https://www.chron.com/opinion/out-
look/article/Let-s-take-full-advantage-of-Affordable-Care-Act-3741457.php;
Kristine Lykens, "The Right Thing to Do," *Fort Worth Star-Telegram*, April 26, 2014,
https://www.star-telegram.com/opinion/editorials/article3855213.html;   "Refusing
Medicaid Expansion Has Consequences," *Houston Chronicle*, June 4, 2015, https://
www.chron.com/opinion/editorials/article/Refusing-Medicaid-expansion-has-
consequences-6308050.php.

38. Edward R. Berchick, Emily Hood, and Jessica C. Barnett, "Health Care Coverage in
the United States: 2018," U.S. Census Bureau, November 2019, Table 6, https://www.
census.gov/content/dam/Census/library/publications/2019/demo/p60-267.pdf. The
percentage of uninsured in Texas dropped from 22.1 percent in 2013 to 17.3 percent
in 2017, then rose to 17.7 percent in 2018. At 17.7 percent, Texas had the highest rate
of uninsured residents in the nation (next highest was Oklahoma, at 14.2 percent).
The national uninsured rate was 8.9 percent—less than half the Texas percentage.

39. See the Emergency Medical Treatment and Labor Act (EMTALA) of 1986, 42 U.S.
Code sec. 1395dd.

40. Governor Rick Perry Letter to President Barack Obama, cited in "Review and
Outlook: Governors vs. Congress: The Stimulus Bill Sets a Long-term Trap for
the States," *Wall Street Journal*, February 23, 2009, https://www.wsj.com/articles/
SB123535040968044863. Perry echoed the sentiments of Bill Hammond, the president of the Texas Association of Business. When the federal government offered
Texas more than $550 million in stimulus funds on the condition that it expanded un-
employment insurance eligibility, Hammond said, "It's like a drug dealer. The dealer
gives you your first hit for free to get you hooked, and then you are addicted and are
paying the consequences for a long, long time." Lee Nichols, "One Pol's Stimulus Is
Another's Crack Cocaine," *Austin Chronicle*, March 6, 2009: 22.

41. Alissa Anderson and Sara Kimberlin, "New Census Figures Show That 1 in 5
Californians Struggle to Get By," California Budget and Policy Center, September 2017,
https://calbudgetcenter.org/resources/new-census-figures-show-1-5-californians-
struggle-get/. See also "Curbing Runaway Rents: Assessing the Impact of a Rent Cap,"
Terner Center for Housing Innovation, U.C. Berkeley (July 2019), https://ternercenter.
berkeley.edu/curbing-runaway-rents: "Currently over 3 million households in
California (more than half of all renter households) pay more than 30 percent of their
income in rent. The challenge is significantly greater for low-income renters; among
renters with incomes below $25,000, fully 92 percent are rent-burdened."

42. Gavin Newsom, "Inaugural Address: A California for All," January 7, 2019, https://
www.gov.ca.gov/2019/01/07/newsom-inaugural-address/.

43. U.S. Department of Health and Human Services, "TANF and MOE Spending and Transfers," https://www.acf.hhs.gov/sites/default/files/ofa/fy2017_tanf_and_moe_state_piechart_508.pdf; Center for Budget and Policy Priorities, "Chart Book."

44. "The CalWORKS Program," Public Policy Institute of California, n.d., https://www.ppic.org/publication/the-calworks-program/.

45. The CalFresh program provides immigrant residents of California a substitute for the SNAP benefits denied to them under federal law; CAPI provides them a substitute for SSI/SSP assistance. "Cash Assistance Program for Immigrants (CAPI)," California Department of Social Services, n.d., http://www.cdss.ca.gov/CAPI. Local measures included San Francisco Measure C of 2018 ($300 million per year through a tax on large businesses to fund homeless programs in the City), "San Francisco Proposition C, Gross Receipts Tax for Homelessness Services (November 2018)," Ballotpedia, n.d., https://ballotpedia.org/San_Francisco,_California,_Proposition_C,_Gross_Receipts_Tax_for_Homelessness_Services_(November_2018); LA County Measure HHH of 2016 (a $1.2 billion bond to fund low-income housing in the county), "Los Angeles, California, Homelessness Reduction and Prevention Housing, and Facilities Bond Issue, Measure HHH (November 2016)," Ballotpedia, n.d., https://ballotpedia.org/Los_Angeles,_California,_Homelessness_Reduction_and_Prevention_Housing,_and_Facilities_Bond_Issue,_Measure_HHH_(November_2016); and Los Angeles County Measure H of 2017 (a one-quarter cent sales tax increase to raise $355 million per year for support for the homeless in the County), "Los Angeles County, California, Sales Tax for Homeless Services and Prevention, Measure H (March 2017)," Ballotpedia, n.d., https://ballotpedia.org/Los_Angeles_County,_California,_Sales_Tax_for_Homeless_Services_and_Prevention,_Measure_H_.

46. See Brief of the States of Oregon, Vermont, California, Connecticut, Delaware, Hawaii, Illinois, Iowa, Maryland, Massachusetts, New Mexico, and New York, and the Governor of Washington as Amici Curiae in Support of Respondents (Addressing Medicaid Expansion), *State of Florida, et al. v. Department of Health and Human Services, et al.* (No. 11-400). Medi-Cal also administers the Children's Health Insurance Program (CHIP).

47. Edmund G. Brown Jr., "California State Budget, 2018–2019: Budget Summary" (2018), 46, http://www.ebudget.ca.gov/2018-19/pdf/Enacted/BudgetSummary/HealthandHumanServices.pdf.

48. Paulette Cha, Shannon McConville, and Daniel Tan, "California Is Looking to Protect and Expand Health Care Coverage Gains," Public Policy Institute of California, January 2020, https://www.ppic.org/wp-content/uploads/californias-future-health-care-january-2020.pdf.

49. SB 75 of 2015, Stats. 2015, Ch. 18, extended Medi-Cal coverage to income-eligible undocumented immigrants under age nineteen. The governor's 2019–2020 budget set aside $260 million ($196.5 million from the General Fund) to extend that coverage to those aged nineteen through twenty-five. The state expected this additional expansion to provide full Med-Cal coverage to approximately 138,000 undocumented adults in the first year. See Gavin Newsom, "Governor's Budget Summary 2019–2020," January 10, 2019, http://www.ebudget.ca.gov/budget/2019-20/#/

BudgetSummary, 64–65; Gavin Newsom, "Governor's Budget Summary 2020–2021," January 10, 2020, http://www.ebudget.ca.gov/2020-21/pdf/BudgetSummary/FullBudgetSummary.pdf, 34. See Rachel Fabi and Brendan Saloner, "Covering Undocumented Immigrants—State Innovation in California," *New England Journal of Medicine* 375 (November 17, 2016): 1913–15, https://www-nejm-org.ccl.idm.oclc.org/doi/full/10.1056/NEJMp1609468; Shannon McConville, Laura Hill, Iwunze Ugo, and Joseph Hayes, "Health Care Coverage for Undocumented Immigrants," Public Policy Institute of California: November 2015, https://www.ppic.org/content/pubs/report/R_1115SMR.pdf.

50. Sophia Bollag and Adam Ashton, "Undocumented Immigrants to Get Healthcare in Gavin Newsom's California Budget Deal," *Sacramento Bee*, June 9, 2019, https://www.sacbee.com/news/politics-government/capitol-alert/article231310348.html.

51. See Scott Bain, California Senate Rules Committee, Office of Senate Floor Analyses, "Third Reading: SB 562 (Lara and Atkins)," June 1, 2017, 10–11.

52. "2017 State Government Tax Tables," U.S. Census Bureau, last revised June 19, 2019, https://www.census.gov/data/tables/2017/econ/stc/2017-annual.html.

53. Anthony Rendon, "Speaker Rendon Statement on Health Care," June 23, 2017, https://speaker.asmdc.org/press-releases/speaker-rendon-statement-health-care.

54. George Skelton, "In Blocking a Bad Single-Payer Bill, Assembly Speaker Anthony Rendon Was Not 'Cowardly'—Quite the Opposite," *Los Angeles Times*, June 29, 2017, https://www.latimes.com/politics/la-pol-sac-skelton-anthony-rendon-single-payer-obamacare-20170629-story.html.

55. Melanie Mason, "We Will Have Universal Health Care in California,' Gavin Newsom Promises Single-Payer Advocates," *Los Angeles Times*, September 22, 2017, https://www.latimes.com/politics/essential/la-pol-ca-essential-politics-updates-in-speech-to-single-payer-advocates-1506103477-htmlstory.html.

56. Governor Gavin Newsom, "Letter to President Donald J. Trump, Senate Majority Leader Mitch McConnell, Senate Minority Leader Charles E. Schumer, House Speaker Nancy Pelosi, and House Minority Leader Kevin McCarthy," January 7, 2019, https://www.gov.ca.gov/wp-content/uploads/2019/01/1.7.19-Letter-to-the-White-House-and-Congress.pdf.

57. U.S. Census Bureau, "2017 Annual Survey of State Government Finances" (ASFIN 2017), https://www.census.gov/data/tables/2017/econ/state/historical-tables.html; U.S. Census Bureau, *Government Finance and Employment Classification Manual* (2006), 5–60 through 5–67, https://www2.census.gov/govs/pubs/classification/2006_classification_manual.pdf.

Chapter 13

1. Patrick J. Buchanan, "Address to the Republican National Convention," August 17, 1992, https://voicesofdemocracy.umd.edu/buchanan-culture-war-speech-speech-text/.

2. In *Cruzan v. Director, Missouri Department of Health*, 497 U.S. 261 (1990), the Court held that the Constitution did not prevent states from refusing to withhold medical

treatment from a patient in a persistent vegetative state where there was no "clear and convincing evidence" that the person would wish to end treatment. The Court found that competent individuals have a right to refuse medical treatment. This right was distinguished from an asserted right to take action to end one's life. In 1994, voters in Oregon approved the nation's first "aid-in-dying" law through a ballot measure called the "Death with Dignity Act," but a federal court challenge blocked the law's implementation until 1997. See *Lee v. Oregon*, 107 F.3d 1382 (9th Cir. 1997).

3. *Compassion in Dying v. Washington*, 850 F. Supp. 1454 (W.D. Wash. 1994), affirmed by *Compassion in Dying v. Washington*, 79 F.3d 790 1994 (9th Cir. 1996) (en banc).

4. *Washington v. Glucksberg*, 521 U.S. 702 (1997).

5. In addition, the Montana Supreme Court issued a ruling shielding physicians from prosecution if they assist a patient in dying. The state has not legislated on the issue. *Baxter v. Montana*, 354 Mont. 234 (2009). The California statute was AB 15 of 2015, adopted during a special session of the legislature, https://leginfo.legislature.ca.gov/faces/billTextClient.xhtml?bill_id=201520162AB15. See Bob Egelko, "Right-to-Die Law Upheld by California Appeals Court after Lower Judge Blocked It," *Governing*, November 28, 2018, https://www.governing.com/topics/health-human-services/tns-right-to-die-california-appeal.html.

6. *Griswold v. Connecticut*, 381 U.S. 479 (1965) (right of married couples to use contraception); *Eisenstadt v. Baird*, 405 U.S. 438 (1972) (right of unmarried persons to use contraception); *Roe v. Wade*, 410 U.S. 113 (1973) (right to abortion); *Obergefell v. Hodges*, 576 U.S. __ (2015) (right of same-sex couples to marry); *Plyler v. Doe*, 457 U.S. 202 (1982) (right of undocumented children to attend public school); *United States v. Virginia*, 518 U.S. 515 (1996) (right of women to attend all-male public university). Note that Congress can create rights as well, although the rights are statutory and not constitutional. Examples include the Civil Rights Act of 1964 and the Voting Rights Act of 1965. As the nation has become more polarized, however, Congress has had difficulty resolving contested social questions and has taken a lesser role in the formation of rights.

7. *District of Columbia v. Heller*, 554 U.S. 570 (2008) (recognizing personal right to bear arms); and *McDonald v. Chicago*, 561 U.S. 742 (2010) (enforcing Second Amendment right against local government through the Fourteenth Amendment); *Burwell v. Hobby Lobby Stores, Inc.*, 573 U.S. 682 (2014) (enforcing religious exemption from federal contraceptive mandate pursuant to Religious Freedom Restoration Act).

8. *Roe v. Wade*, 410 U.S. 113 (1973). The Court itself reflected the lack of partisan polarization on the issue at the time. Five of the seven justices who formed the *Roe* majority, including the opinion's author, Justice Harry Blackmun, had been placed on the Court by Republican presidents; one of the two dissenters, Justice Byron White, was a Democrat nominated by John F. Kennedy.

9. Gerald N. Rosenberg, *The Hollow Hope: Can Courts Bring About Social Change?* (Chicago: University of Chicago Press, 1991), 175–201. Opposition to abortion rights formed before *Roe* but intensified after the ruling. Daniel K. Williams, *Defenders of the Unborn: The Pro-life Movement before Roe v. Wade* (New York: Oxford University Press, 2016), 205–42. Examples of polarization over abortion at the national level include Supreme Court confirmation hearings, which have often turned on the

nominee's view of *Roe*, and the Mexico City Policy, a federal rule first instated by President Reagan in 1984 that blocks federal funds to non-governmental organizations operating in foreign countries that advocate or counsel in favor of abortion. The policy has been rescinded by every Democratic president and reinstated by every Republican president. See, for example, Donald J. Trump, "The Mexico City Policy," *Federal Register* 82, no. 15 (January 25, 2017): 8495, https://www.federalregister.gov/documents/2017/01/25/2017-01843/the-mexico-city-policy.

10. *Planned Parenthood of Southeastern Pennsylvania v. Casey*, 505 U.S. 833 (1992).

11. *Whole Woman's Health v. Hellerstedt*, 579 U.S. __ (2016).

12. Ibid. The coalition supporting the Texas abortion law included Arizona, Arkansas, Florida, Georgia, Idaho, Indiana, Kansas, Louisiana, Michigan, Mississippi, Montana, Nebraska, Nevada, North Dakota, Ohio, Oklahoma, South Carolina, South Dakota, Tennessee, Utah, West Virginia, Wisconsin, and Wyoming. The coalition opposing the law consisted of California, Connecticut, Hawaii, Illinois, Maine, Maryland, Massachusetts, New York, Oregon, Vermont, Virginia, and Washington, as well as the District of Columbia.

13. In 2019, nine states—Alabama, Arkansas, Georgia, Kentucky, Louisiana, Missouri, Mississippi, Ohio, and Utah—enacted early pregnancy prohibitions on abortion (with various exceptions). Alabama's law was the most restrictive, banning abortions at any stage of the pregnancy except to prevent a serious health risk for the mother. The bill did not take immediate effect. Rebecca Lai, "Abortion Bans: 9 States Have Passed Bills to Limit the Procedure This Year," *New York Times*. May 15, 2019, https://www.nytimes.com/interactive/2019/us/abortion-laws-states.html. "Alabama House Bill 314," *LegiScan*, May 15, 2019.

14. Elizabeth Nash, Lizamarie Mohammed, Olivia Cappello, Sophia Naide, and Zohra Ansari-Thomas, "State Policy Trends at Mid-Year 2019: States Race to Ban or Protect Abortion," Guttmacher Institute, July 1, 2019, https://www.guttmacher.org/article/2019/07/state-policy-trends-mid-year-2019-states-race-ban-or-protect-abortion.

15. *District of Columbia v. Heller*, 554 U.S. 570 (2008); *McDonald v. Chicago*, 561 U.S. 742 (2010). *See also* note 7.

16. William J. Brennan Jr., "State Constitutions and the Protection of Individual Rights," *Harvard Law Review* 90, no. 3 (January 1977): 489–504 (at 491).

17. Kenneth P. Miller, "Defining Rights in the States: Judicial Activism and Popular Response," *Albany Law Review* 76, no. 4 (2012/2013): 2061–78. For a discussion of state supreme courts' expansion of rights, see Robert F. Williams, *The Law of American State Constitutions* (New York: Oxford University Press, 2009), 111–34.

18. Miller, "Defining Rights," 2065–69.

19. *Baker v. Nelson*, 409 U.S. 810 (1972).

20. The cases in both Massachusetts and California were decided by 4–3 votes. *Goodridge v. Department of Public Health*, 440 Mass. 309 (2003); *In re Marriage Cases*, 43 Cal.4th 757 (2008). Proposition 8 of 2008 overturned the central holding of *In re Marriage Cases*. See California Secretary of State, "Voter Information Guide for 2008 General Election," November 4, 2008, https://repository.uchastings.edu/cgi/viewcontent.cgi?article=2265&context=ca_ballot_props.

21. *Obergefell v. Hodges*, 576 U.S. __ (2015).

22. Texas Constitution Art. I, Sec. 3a provides that "equality under the law shall not be denied or abridged because of sex, race, color, creed, or national origin." Dallas attorney Hermine Tobolowsky led the effort to secure this amendment and Representative Frances Farenthold and Senator Barbara Jordan cosponsored the measure in the legislature. Voters approved it in November 1972 by a 2,156,536 to 548,422 vote. The Texas Legislature voted to ratify the federal Equal Rights Amendment in a special session in March 1972. Wolfgang P. Hirczy de Mino, "Does an Equal Rights Amendment Make a Difference?" *Albany Law Review* 60 (1997): 1581–1610.

23. See Texas Laws of 1854, chapter 49; Texas Penal Code of 1857, chapter 7, Articles 531–536. The statutes challenged in *Roe v. Wade* were Texas Penal Code (1961), Articles 1191–94 and 1196.

24. American Law Institute, Model Penal Code, section 230.3 (2) (Proposed Official Draft, 1962).

25. Lucas A. Powe Jr., *America's Lone Star Constitution: How Supreme Court Cases from Texas Shape the Nation* (Berkeley: University of California Press, 2018), 175–76.

26. Ibid., 179.

27. The Court heard argument in *Roe v. Wade* on December 13, 1971, and reargument on October 11, 1972. *Roe*, 410 U.S. at 113; David J. Garrow, "She Put the Roe in Roe v. Wade," *New York Times*, September 27, 1992, https://www.nytimes.com/1992/09/27/books/she-put-the-v-in-roe-v-wade.html.

28. Powe, *America's Lone Star Constitution*, 180, 85.

29. See Texas Occupations Code sec. 103.001–.004; and Health & Safety Code sec. 245.010(b); Texas Health & Safety Code sec. 32.005.

30. For a summary of the pro-life movement's success in enacting policies restricting abortion in Texas, see Texas Right to Life, "Active State Laws," https://www.texasrighttolife.com/active-state-laws/.

31. HB 2 of 2013. See Texas Health & Safety Code sec. 171.0031, 171.041–064.

32. *Whole Woman's Health v. Hellerstedt*, 579 U.S. __ (2016).

33. Stephen Young, "Texas Lawmakers Leading the Anti-Abortion Effort Take a Gentler, More Tactical Approach," *Texas Observer*, May 22, 2019, https://www.dallasobserver.com/news/texas-lawmakers-arent-going-soft-on-abortion-theyre-going-tactical-11669327.

34. Ibid.

35. Erica Greider, *Big, Hot, Cheap, and Right: What America Can Learn from the Strange Genius of Texas* (New York: Public Affairs, 2013), 62.

36. For a full defense of this position, see John R. Lott Jr., *More Guns, Less Crime: Understanding Crime and Gun Control Laws*, 3rd ed. (Chicago: University of Chicago Press, 2010).

37. SB 11 of 2015. See Texas State Law Library, "Gun Laws," https://guides.sll.texas.gov/gun-laws.

38. Ibid. The package included SB 535 (allowing concealed carry in churches and other places of worship unless the organization prohibits firearms and posts signs); HB 302

(preventing landlords from banning tenants and their guests from carrying firearms); SB 741 (preventing homeowner associations from banning storage of guns); HB 1143 (limiting school districts discretion in restricting storage of guns and ammunition in school parking lots).

39. David Tarrant and María Méndez, "What Are the Gun Laws in Texas, and What's Changing Sept. 1?" *Dallas Morning News*, August 9, 2019, https://www. dallasnews.com/news/2019/08/09/what-are-the-gun-laws-in-texas-and-what-s-changing-sept-1/; Patrick J. Charles, "The Second Amendment in the Twenty-First Century: What Hath *Heller* Wrought?" *William and Mary Bill of Rights Journal* 23 (May 2015): 1143–83.

40. *Bowers v. Hardwick*, 478 U.S. 186 (1986).

41. *Lawrence v. Texas*, 539 U.S. 558 (2003).

42. Texas Family Code Section 6.204; Texas Constitution, Article I, section 32.

43. Texas Constitution, Article I, section 32; Texas Office of the Secretary of State, "Race Summary Report: 2005 Constitutional Amendment Election" (2005), http://elections.sos.state.tx.us/elchist117_state.htm.

44. *DeLeon v. Perry*, 975 F. Supp. 2d 632, 639–640 (W.D. Texas 2014) *aff'd sub nom. De Leon v. Abbott*, 791 F.3d 619 (5th Cir., 2015).

45. Walter Olson, "Gay Marriage Is Here to Stay, Even with a Conservative Court," *Wall Street Journal*, July 8, 2018, https://www.wsj.com/articles/gay-marriage-is-here-to-stay-even-with-a-conservative-court-1531074136.

46. In *Pidgeon v. Turner*, the Texas Supreme Court remanded for further proceedings a case seeking to narrow the right to same-sex marriage on the grounds that the *Obergefell* decision does not require the City of Houston or other employers to take steps beyond the bare recognition of same-sex marriage—"steps like subsidizing same-sex marriages (through the allocation of employee benefits) on the same terms as traditional marriages." *Pidgeon v. Turner*, 538 S.W.3d 73 (Tex. 2017). At that stage of the litigation, the U.S. Supreme Court denied Turner's petition for certiorari. Turner v. Pidgeon, No. 17-424 (December 4, 2017).

47. Texas HB 3859 of 2017.

48. American Law Institute, Model Penal Code, section 230.3 (2) (Proposed Official Draft, 1962).

49. The bill was SB 462 of 1967 (Beilenson). In a crucial showdown in the Senate Judiciary Committee, Republicans cast several of the votes that sent the abortion liberalization bill to the floor, and throughout the legislative process, numerous Democrats opposed the bill. Lou Cannon, *Ronnie and Jesse: A Political Odyssey* (New York: Doubleday, 1969), 179–82; Arthur G. Scotland, "The Landmark Abortion Decisions: Justifiable Termination or Miscarriage of Justice?—Proposals for Legislative Response," *Pacific Law Journal* 4 (1973): 821, 823–27; Zad Leavy and Alan F. Charles, "California's New Therapeutic Abortion Act: An Analysis and Guide to Medical and Legal Procedure," *UCLA Law Review* 15, no. 1 (November 1967): 1–31.

50. *People v. Belous*, 71 Cal. 2d 954 (1969); *People v. Barksdale*, 8 Cal. 3d 321 (1972). See Scotland, "The Landmark Abortion Decisions," 833.

51. *Harris v. McRae,* 448 U.S. 297, 309–16 (1980); *Committee to Defend Reproductive Rights v. Myers,* 29 Cal.3d 252 (1981).

52. *Planned Parenthood v. Casey,* 505 U.S. 833, 872 (1992); *American Academy of Pediatrics v. Lungren,* 16 Cal.4th 307 (1997). California's parental consent law was enacted in 1987 through AB 2274, Stats. 1987, Ch. 1237 (amending California Civil Code section 34.5 and adding California Health and Safety Code section 25958). The law was challenged immediately after its adoption and its enforcement was stayed pending the outcome of the litigation. It was never enforced.

53. For a summary of California's expansive abortion rights, see NARAL Pro-choice America, "State Laws: California," https://www.prochoiceamerica.org/state-law/california/.

54. Rachel K. Jones, Elizabeth Witwer, and Jenna Jerman, "Abortion Incidence and Service Availability in the United States, 2017," https://www.guttmacher.org/sites/default/files/report_pdf/abortion-incidence-service-availability-us-2017.pdf.

55. The bill was SB 24 of 2019.

56. The FACT Act was AB 775 of 2015, Cal. Health & Safety Code sec. 123470 et seq., invalidated in *National Institute of Family and Life Advocates (NIFLA) v. Becerra,* 585 U.S. __ (2018).

57. *Federal Register* 82, no. 197 (October 13, 2017): 47792; *California v. Azar (California v. The Little Sisters of the Poor Jeanne Jugan Residence, Defendant Intervenors),* 911 F.3d 558 (9th Cir., 2018).

58. *California v. Azar,* 927 F.3d 1068 (9th Cir., 2019). As the litigation was pending, Planned Parenthood refused funding rather than comply with the rule. Pam Belluck, "Planned Parenthood Refuses Federal Funds over Abortion Restriction," *New York Times,* August 19, 2019, https://www.nytimes.com/2019/08/19/health/planned-parenthood-title-x.html.

59. Adam Winkler, "The Secret History of Guns," *The Atlantic,* September 2011, https://www.theatlantic.com/magazine/archive/2011/09/the-secret-history-of-guns/308608/. See also Cynthia Deitle Leonardatos, "California's Attempts to Disarm the Black Panthers," *San Diego Law Review* 36, no. 4 (Fall 1999): 947–96.

60. Winkler, "Secret History."

61. The bill was SB 292 of 1989 (Roberti), Stats. 1989, Ch. 18. Carl Ingram, "Assault Gun Ban Wins Final Vote: Deukmejian's Promised Approval Would Make It 1st Such U.S. Law," *Los Angeles Times,* May 19, 1989, https://www.latimes.com/archives/la-xpm-1989-05-19-mn-112-story.html.

62. San Francisco Board of Supervisors, "Resolution Declaring the National Rifle Association as a Domestic Terrorist Organization," September 3, 2019, https://sfgov.legistar.com/View.ashx?M=F&ID=7568748&GUID=DF64490F-D8BC-4BF7-A43D-287F02BECCCA.

63. Giffords Law Center, "California: State Law Background," n.d., https://lawcenter.giffords.org/gun-laws/state-law/california/.

64. Ben Christopher, "As Gun Control Efforts Advance in California Capitol, Opponents Bank on the Courts," *CalMatters,* August 21, 2019, https://calmatters.org/justice/2019/08/gun-control-california-legislature-courts-push-back-second-amendment/.

65. California Secretary of State, *Voter Information Guide for 1978 General Election, November 7, 1978*, 28–31, 41. Voters defeated Proposition 6 by a 58–42 percent margin.

66. *In re Marriage Cases*, 43 Cal.4th 757 (2008).

67. *Hollingsworth v. Perry*, 570 U.S. 693 (2013).

68. For a summary of the LGBT rights movement's accomplishments in California, see Movement Advancement Project, "California's Equality Profile." http://www.lgbtmap.org/equality-maps/profile_state/CA. The California Supreme Court established the strict scrutiny rule in *In re Marriage Cases*, 43 Cal.4th 757, 833-857 (2008).

69. Felipe Lopez, "Senate Floor Analysis, AB 1887: Third Reading," August 3, 2016, http://www.leginfo.ca.gov/pub/15-16/bill/asm/ab_1851-1900/ab_1887_cfa_20160816_175754_sen_floor.html.

70. Attorney General Xavier Becerra, "Prohibition on State-Funded and State-Sponsored Travel to States with Discriminatory Laws (Assembly Bill No. 1887)," n.d., https://oag.ca.gov/ab1887. This kind of ban became an increasingly common blue-state practice, with Connecticut, New York, Minnesota, Oregon, Vermont, and Washington issuing similar sanctions. Alan Blinder, "Travel to Texas? Not on California's Dime, You Don't," *New York Times*, July 19, 2017, https://www.nytimes.com/2017/07/19/us/public-employee-travel.html.

71. Blinder, "Travel to Texas?"

72. *Texas v. California*, No. 153, Original, "Motion for Leave to File a Bill of Complaint," (February 10, 2020), https://www.texasattorneygeneral.gov/sites/default/files/images/admin/2020/Press/Texas%20v.%20California%20-%20filed.pdf. Nineteen red states signed an amicus brief supporting Texas's motion.

Chapter 14

1. Michael Schaub, "Lawrence Wright Says Texas and California are Mirror Image Twins," *Los Angeles Times*, April 12, 2018, http://www.latimes.com/books/la-ca-jc-lawrence-wright-20180412-htmlstory.html.

2. *New State Ice Co. v. Liebmann*, 285 U.S. 262, 310–311 (1932), Brandeis, J., dissenting. For a critical analysis of Brandeis's use of the metaphor, see G. Alan Tarr, "Laboratories of Democracy?: Brandeis, Federalism, and Scientific Management," *Publius* 31, no. 1 (Winter 2001): 37–46; Michael S. Greve, "Laboratories of Democracy: Anatomy of a Metaphor," *Federalist Outlook* (American Enterprise Institute: March 31, 2001), http://www.aei.org/publication/laboratories-of-democracy/.

3. Brandeis was not the first to use the metaphor. Two decades earlier, in 1912, Theodore Roosevelt used it to refer to the state of Wisconsin under the leadership of Progressive governor Robert La Follette. Roosevelt said, "Wisconsin . . . has become literally a laboratory for wise experimental legislation, aiming to secure the social and political betterment of the people as a whole." James K. Conant, *Wisconsin Politics and Government: America's Laboratory of Democracy* (Lincoln: University of Nebraska Press, 2006), 318.

4. Edmund G. Brown Jr., "CNN Transcript: State of the Union with Candy Crowley," CNN November 11, 2012, http://edition.cnn.com/TRANSCRIPTS/1211/11/sotu.01. html.

5. Alexandra Suich Bass, "California and Texas Have Different Visions for America's Future," *The Economist*, June 20, 2019, https://www.economist.com/ technology-quarterly/2019/06/20/california-and-texas-have-different-visions-for-americas-future.

6. For examples of how states have historically acted as laboratories to spread policy innovations, see Jack L. Walker, "The Diffusion of Innovation among the American States," *American Political Science Review* 63 (September 1969): 880–89; Virginia Gray, "Competition, Emulation, and Policy Innovation," in *New Perspectives on American Politics*, ed. Lawrence C. Dodd and Calvin Jillson, 230–48 (Washington, DC: CQ Press, 1994).

7. Michael S. Greve, "Federalism in a Polarized Age," in *Parchment Barriers: Political Polarization and the Limits of Constitutional Order*, ed. Zachary Courser, Eric Helland, and Kenneth P. Miller (Lawrence: University Press of Kansas, 2018), 119.

8. For a comparison, see U.S. Census Bureau, "2017 Annual Survey of State Government Finances," October 31, 2019, https://www.census.gov/data/tables/2017/econ/state/ historical-tables.html.

9. "Red Flags Ahead," Texas 2036, https://texas2036.org/red-flags.

10. For a book on this theme, see Narda Zacchino, *California Comeback: How a "Failed State" Became a Model for the Nation*. (New York: St. Martin's Press, 2016).

11. Sarah Burd-Sharps and Kristen Lewis, "Well-Being in the Golden State: The Five Californias of the Human Development Index," in *Governing California: Politics, Government, and Policy in the Golden State*, ed. Ethan Rarick, 3–26 (Berkeley, CA: Berkeley Public Policy Press, 2013).

12. Brian Uhler and Justin Garosi. "California Losing Residents via Domestic Migration," California Legislative Analyst's Office, February 21, 2018.

13. Greve, "Federalism in a Polarized Age," 119–20.

14. Melanie Mason, "'We Will Have Universal Health Care in California,' Gavin Newsom Promises Single-Payer Advocates," *Los Angeles Times*, September 22, 2017, https:// www.latimes.com/politics/essential/la-pol-ca-essential-politics-updates-in-speech-to-single-payer-advocates-1506103477-htmlstory.html; Scott Bain, California Senate Rules Committee, Office of Senate Floor Analyses, "Third Reading: SB 562 (Lara and Atkins)," June 1, 2017, 10–11.

15. Greve, "Federalism in a Polarized Age," 145.

16. Pew Research Center, "Partisanship and Political Animosity in 2016," June 22, 2016, https://www.people-press.org/2016/06/22/partisanship-and-political-animosity-in-2016/.

17. Dan Walters, "Jerry Brown Honors the Principle of Subsidiarity Sometimes," *Sacramento Bee*, October 5, 2014, https://www.sacbee.com/news/politics-government/politics-columns-blogs/dan-walters/article2620620.html.

18. Brown, "CNN Transcript: State of the Union."

19. Lawrence Wright, *God Save Texas: A Journey into the Soul of the Lone Star State* (New York: Knopf, 2018), 202.

20. Pew Research Center, "Partisanship and Political Animosity."

21. For further reflections on this theme, see John Inazu, *Confident Pluralism: Surviving and Thriving through Deep Difference* (Chicago: University of Chicago Press, 2016); Arthur C. Brooks, *Love Your Enemies: How Decent People Can Save America from the Culture of Contempt* (New York: Broadside Books, 2019).

22. Abraham Lincoln, "First Inaugural Address," March 4, 1861, https://www.presidency. ucsb.edu/documents/inaugural-address-34.

References

Abbott, Greg. "Defending Texas Energy and Jobs." News release, June 2, 2014, https://www.gregabbott.com/greg-abbott-defending-texas-energy-jobs/.

Abbott, Greg. "Governor Abbott Meets with Senators McConnell, Cornyn and Cruz to Discuss Texas Response to EPA," news release, May 7, 2015, https://gov.texas.gov/news/post/governor_abbott_meets_with_senators_mcconnell_cornyn_and_cruz_to_discuss_te.

Abbott, Greg. "Governor Abbott Statement on President Obama's Environmental Proposal." News release, August 3, 2015. Office of the Texas Governor, https://gov.texas.gov/news/post/governor_abbott_statement_on_president_obamas_environmental_proposal.

Abbott, Greg. Letter to Secretary of Transportation Elaine L. Chao and Acting EPA Administrator Andrew Wheeler. October 27, 2018, https://www.regulations.gov/document?D=NHTSA-2018-0067-11935.

American Presidency Project. "Elections." U.C. Santa Barbara, n.d., https://www.presidency.ucsb.edu/statistics/elections.

Anderson, Alissa, and Sara Kimberlin. "New Census Figures Show That 1 in 5 Californians Struggle to Get By." California Budget and Policy Center, September 2017, https://calbudgetcenter.org/resources/new-census-figures-show-1-5-californians-struggle-get/.

Anderson, Totton J. "The 1958 Election in California." *Western Political Quarterly* 12, no. 1, Part 2 (March 1959): 276–300.

Anderson, Totton J., and Eugene C. Lee. "The 1964 Election in California." *Western Political Quarterly* 18, no. 2, Part 2 (June 1, 1965): 451–71.

Arreola, Daniel D. *Tejano South Texas: A Mexican American Cultural Province.* Austin: University of Texas Press, 2012.

Arsenault, Raymond. "The End of the Long Hot Summer: The Air Conditioner in Southern Culture." *Journal of Southern History* 50, no. 4 (November 1984): 597–628.

Assanie, Laila, Kristin E. Davis, Pia Orrenius, and Michael Weiss. "At the Heart of Texas: Cities' Industry Clusters Drive Growth, Second Edition." Dallas, TX: Federal Reserve Bank of Dallas, 2018.

Associated Press. "Tax Drives Hearst Out of California." *New York Times*, October 23, 1935, 1.

Association of Texas Professional Educators. "Collective Bargaining, Exclusive Consultation, and the Right to Work," n.d., https://www.atpe.org/en/Advocacy/Issues/Collective-Bargaining.

Bahrami, Homa, and Stuart Evans. "Flexible Recycling and High-Technology Entrepreneurship." In *Understanding Silicon Valley: The Anatomy of an Entrepreneurial Region*, edited by Martin Kenney and Richard Florida, 165–89. Stanford, CA: Stanford University Press, 2000.

Bain, Scott. California Senate Rules Committee, Office of Senate Floor Analyses. "Third Reading: SB 562 (Lara and Atkins)," June 1, 2017, 10–11.

Baker, David R. "Brown Signs Climate Law Mandating 50% Renewable Power by 2030." *SF Gate*, October 7, 2015.

Baldassare, Mark, Dean Bonner, David Kordus, and Lunna Lopes. "Californians and Housing Affordability." San Francisco, CA: Public Policy Institute of California (September 2017).

Bancroft, Hubert Howe. *History of California, Vol. IV: 1840–1845.* In *Bancroft's Works,* Vol. XXI. San Francisco: A. L. Bancroft & Co. Publishers, 1886.

Bancroft, Hubert Howe. *History of California, Vol. V: 1846–1848.* In *Bancroft's Works,* Vol. XXII. San Francisco: The History Co. Publishers, 1886.

Bancroft, Hubert Howe. *History of California, Vol. VI: 1848–1859.* In *Bancroft's Works,* Vol. XXIII. San Francisco: The History Co. Publishers, 1888.

Barnes, William P. "The Mass Picketing and Closed Shop Statutes of 1947." *Southwestern Law Journal* 2, no. 79 (1948): 79–93.

Barnett, Marissa. "Fracking Returns to Denton after State Outlaws Local Hydraulic Fracturing Bans." *Dallas Morning News,* May 22, 2015, www.dallasnews.com/news/politics/2015/05/22/fracking-returns-to-denton-after-state-outlaws-local-hydraulic-fracturing-bans.

Barone, Michael. *Shaping Our Nation: How Surges of Migration Transformed America and Its Politics.* New York: Crown Forum, 2013.

Barone, Michael, and Richard E. Cohen. *The Almanac of American Politics 2006.* Washington, DC: National Journal Group, 2005.

Barone, Michael, and Grant Ujifusa. *The Almanac of American Politics 1990.* Washington, DC: National Journal Group, 1990.

Barreto, Matt A., Tyler Reny, and Bryan Wilcox-Archuleta. "Survey Methodology and the Latino/a Vote: Why a Bilingual, Bicultural, Latino-Centered Approach Matters." *Aztlán: A Journal of Chicano Studies* 42, no. 2 (Fall 2017): 211–27.

Barta, Carolyn. "Why Bill Clements Mattered." *Texas Tribune,* May 30, 2011, https://www.texastribune.org/2011/05/30/guest-column-why-bill-clements-mattered/.

Batrawy, Aya. "Aramco IPO Makes It Most Valuable Company, Edging Out Apple." *San Francisco Chronicle,* December 11, 2019, https://www.sfchronicle.com/business/article/Aramco-IPO-makes-it-world-s-most-valuable-14900184.php#.

Beasley, Delilah L. *Negro Trailblazers in California.* 2019; repr. Whitefish MT: Kessinger Legacy Reprints, 2010.

Becerra, Xavier. "Prohibition on State-Funded and State-Sponsored Travel to States with Discriminatory Laws (Assembly Bill No. 1887)," n.d., https://oag.ca.gov/ab1887.

Belkin, Susan. "Now, It's Remember the Oil Bust!" *New York Times,* August 22, 1989, https://www.nytimes.com/1989/08/22/business/now-it-s-remember-the-oil-bust.html.

Bell, Jonathan. *California Crucible: The Forging of Modern American Liberalism.* Philadelphia: University of Pennsylvania Press, 2012.

Belluck, Pam. "Planned Parenthood Refuses Federal Funds over Abortion Restriction." *New York Times,* August 19, 2019, https://www.nytimes.com/2019/08/19/health/planned-parenthood-title-x.html.

Bennett, Claudette. "Race: Questions and Classifications." In *Encyclopedia of the U.S. Census: From the Constitution to the American Community Survey,* edited by Margo J. Anderson, Constance F. Citro, and Joseph J. Salvo, 313–17. Washington, DC: CQ Press, 2011.

Berchick, Edward R., Emily Hood, and Jessica C. Barnett. "Health Care Coverage in the United States: 2018." U.S. Census Bureau, November 2019, https://www.census.gov/content/dam/Census/library/publications/2019/demo/p60-267.pdf.

Biber, Eric. "Cultivating a Green Political Landscape: Lessons for Climate Change Policy from the Defeat of California's Proposition 23." 66 *Vanderbilt Law Review* 399 (2013): 400–11.

Bishop, Bill. *The Big Sort: Why the Clustering of Like-Minded America Is Tearing Us Apart.* New York: Mariner Books, 2009.

Black, Earl, and Merle Black. *The Rise of Southern Republicans.* Cambridge, MA: Belknap Press of Harvard University Press, 2002.

Blinder, Alan. "Travel to Texas? Not on California's Dime, You Don't." *New York Times,* July 19, 2017, https://www.nytimes.com/2017/07/19/us/public-employee-travel.html.

"Blue Sky Metropolis: The Aerospace Industry in California." Kcetlink, 2019, https://www.pbssocal.org/programs/blue-sky-metropolis/.

Blum, Jordan. "U.S. Oil Production Hits Estimated Record 13 Million Barrels per Day." *Houston Chronicle,* January 15, 2020, https://www.chron.com/business/energy/article/U-S-oil-production-hits-estimated-record-13-14977192.php.

Bollag, Sophia, and Adam Ashton. "Undocumented Immigrants to Get Healthcare in Gavin Newsom's California Budget Deal." *Sacramento Bee,* June 9, 2019, https://www.sacbee.com/news/politics-government/capitol-alert/article231310348.html.

Boyarsky, Bill. *Big Daddy: Jesse Unruh and the Art of Power Politics.* Berkeley: University of California Press, 2007.

Brand, Stewart. *Whole Earth Catalog,* Fall 1968.

Brennan, William J., Jr. "State Constitutions and the Protection of Individual Rights," *Harvard Law Review* 90, no. 3 (January 1977): 489–504.

Breschi, Stefano, and Franco Malerba. *Clusters, Networks, and Innovation.* New York: Oxford University Press, 2005.

Bridges, Kenneth. *Twilight of the Texas Democrats: The 1978 Governor's Race.* College Station: Texas A&M University Press, 2008.

Briffault, Richard. "The Challenge of the New Preemption." *Stanford Law Review* 70, no. 5 (May 2018): 1997–2027.

Brinklow, Alan. "Housing Crisis: San Francisco's Median Market Rent Hits New All-time Highs." *Curbed San Francisco,* June 13, 2019, https://sf.curbed.com/2019/6/13/18663215/san-franciso-rent-numbers-record-prices-median-graphs.

Britschgi, Christian. "Texas Voters Ban State Income Taxes. Again." *Reason,* November 6, 2019, https://reason.com/2019/11/06/texas-voters-ban-state-income-taxes-again/.

Britton, Karen Gerhardt, Fred C. Elliott, and E. A. Miller. "Cotton Culture." Texas State Historical Association, June 12, 2010, https://tshaonline.org/handbook/online/articles/afc03.

Broockman, David, Greg F. Ferenstein, and Neil Malhotra. "The Political Behavior of Wealthy Americans: Evidence from Technology Entrepreneurs." Stanford Graduate School of Business Working Paper No. 3581, December 9, 2017.

Brooks, Arthur. *Love Your Enemies: How Decent People Can Save America from the Culture of Contempt.* New York: Broadside Press, 2019.

Brown, Edmund G., Jr. "CNN Transcript: State of the Union with Candy Crowley." CNN November 11, 2012, http://edition.cnn.com/TRANSCRIPTS/1211/11/sotu.01.html.

Brown, Edmund G., Jr. Executive Order B-55-18, September 9, 2018.

Brown, Edmund G., Jr. "Governor's Budget Summary 2018–2019, Sacramento: California Department of Finance (January 10, 2018), 156; Appendix 7 "Comparative Yield of State Taxes, 1970–71 through 2018–19."

Brown, Kristin. "Rick Perry: Texas Won't Implement Obamacare." Fox News, July 9, 2012, https://www.foxnews.com/politics/rick-perry-texas-wont-implement-obamacare.

Buchanan, Patrick J. "Address to the Republican National Convention." August 17, 1992, https://voicesofdemocracy.umd.edu/buchanan-culture-war-speech-speech-text/.

Buenger, Walter L., and Robert S. Calvert, eds. *Texas through Time: Evolving Interpretations.* College Station: Texas A&M University Press, 1991.

Burd-Sharps, Sarah, and Kristen Lewis. "Well-Being in the Golden State: The Five Californias of the Human Development Index." In *Governing California: Politics, Government, and Policy in the Golden State,* edited by Ethan Rarick, 3–26. Berkeley, CA: Berkeley Public Policy Press, 2013.

Busch, Andrew E. *Reagan's Victory: The Presidential Election of 1980 and the Rise of the Right.* Lawrence: University Press of Kansas, 2005.

California Air Resources Board. "Assembly Bill 32 Overview," August 5, 2014, https://www.arb.ca.gov/cc/ab32/ab32.htm.

California Air Resources Board. "Fact Sheet: Reducing Emissions from California Vehicles," n.d., https://ww2.arb.ca.gov.

California Department of Agriculture. "California Agricultural Statistics Review, 2017–2018," n.d., https://www.cdfa.ca.gov/statistics/PDFs/2017-18AgReport.pdf.

California Department of Finance. Gross State Product Comparison to Other U.S. States: Annual since 1987," n.d., http://www.dof.ca.gov/Forecasting/Economics/Indicators/Gross_State_Product/.

California Department of Finance. "P-1: State Population Projections (2010–2060): Total Population by Race/Ethnicity: Hispanic Combined," May 2019, http://www.dof.ca.gov/Forecasting/Demographics/projections/.

California Department of Finance. "State's Population Increases by 141,300 While Rate of Growth Continues to Decline," December 20, 2019, https://capsweb.org/wp-content/uploads/2019/12/population-estimate.pdf.

California Energy Commission. "Nuclear Energy," n.d., https://www.energy.ca.gov/nuclear/california.html.

California Environmental Protection Agency. Air Resources Board. "California's Cap and Trade Program: Fuel Facts," December 2014, https://www.arb.ca.gov/cc/capandtrade/guidance/facts_fuels_under_the_cap.pdf.

California Labor Federation. "Legislation," n.d., https://calaborfed.org/issuetypes/legislation/.

California Legislative Analyst's Office. "The 2012–13 Budget: Economic and Revenue Update," February 27, 2012.

California Secretary of State. "Statement of Vote," General Elections of 1936, 1942, 1994, 2016. Sacramento, CA: Office of the Secretary of State.

California Secretary of State. "Voter Information Guide," General Elections of 1911, 1936, 1944, 1958, 1966, 1978, 1994, 1996, 2008, and 2010, and for Primary Election of 1978, available at U.C. Hastings Ballot Measures Database, https://www.uchastings.edu/academics/library/ca-ballots/.

California Senate Transportation Committee. "Governor Brown's Transportation Funding Plan," September 3, 2015, https://stran.senate.ca.gov/sites/senate.ca.gov/files/governor_brown_transportation_funding_plan.pdf.

California State Assembly. "Salaries and Expenditures," January 9, 2019, https://www.assembly.ca.gov/salariesandexpenditures.

"The CalWORKS Program," Public Policy Institute of California, n.d., https://www.ppic.org/publication/the-calworks-program/.

Cambridge Dictionary. Cambridge: Cambridge University Press, 2019, s.v. "culture," https://dictionary.cambridge.org/us/dictionary/english/culture.

Cammenga, Janelle. "To What Extent Does Your State Rely on Property Taxes?" Tax Foundation, May 1, 2019, https://taxfoundation.org/state-and-local-property-tax-reliance-2019/.

Campbell, James E. "The Midterm Landslide of 2010: A Triple Wave Election," *The Forum* 8, no. 4, Article 3 (January 10, 2011).

Campbell, Randolph B. *An Empire for Slavery: The Peculiar Institution in Texas, 1821–1865*. Baton Rouge: Louisiana State University Press, 1989.

Campbell, Randolph B. *Gone to Texas: A History of the Lone Star State*, 3rd ed. New York: Oxford University Press, 2018.

Cannon, Lou. *Governor Reagan: His Rise to Power*. New York: Public Affairs, 2003.

Cantrell, Gregg. "'A Host of Sturdy Patriots': The Texas Populists." In *The Texas Left: The Radical Roots of Lone Star Liberalism*, edited by David O'Donald Cullen and Kyle Wilkinson, 53–73. College Station: Texas A&M Press, 2010.

Carlson, Ann E. "Regulatory Capacity and State Environmental Leadership: California's Climate Policy," 24 *Fordham Environmental Law Review* 63 (2012): 70–75

Caro, Robert A. *The Years of Lyndon Johnson: The Path to Power*. New York: Knopf, 1982.

Castells, Manuel. "Cultural Identity, Sexual Liberation, and Urban Structure: The Gay Community in San Francisco." In Manuel Castells, *The City and the Grassroots: A Cross-Cultural Theory of Urban Social Movements*. Berkeley: University of California Press, 1983.

Center for Budget and Policy Priorities. "Chart Book: Temporary Assistance for Needy Families," August 21, 2018, https://www.cbpp.org/research/family-income-support/chart-book-temporary-assistance-for-needy-families.

Centers for Medicare and Medicaid Services. "March 2019 Medicaid & CHIP Enrollment," n.d., https://www.medicaid.gov/medicaid/program-information/medicaid-and-chip-enrollment-data/report-highlights/index.html.

Cha, Paulette, Shannon McConville, and Daniel Tan. "California Is Looking to Protect and Expand Health Care Coverage Gains." Public Policy Institute of California, January 2020.

Chammah, Maurice. "In Radio Ads, Perry Reaches Out to California Businesses." *Texas Tribune*, February 4, 2013, https://www.texastribune.org/2013/02/04/gov-perry-californians-move-texas/.

Charles, Patrick J. "The Second Amendment in the Twenty-First Century: What Hath *Heller* Wrought?" *William and Mary Bill of Rights Journal* 23 (May 2015): 1143–83.

Chaudry, Ajay, Christopher Eimer, Suzanne Macartney, Lauren Frohlich, Colin Campbell, Kendall Swenson, Don Oellerich, and Susan Hauan. "Poverty in the United States: Fifty Year Trends and Safety Net Impacts." U.S. Department of Health and Human Services, March 2016.

Chishti, Muzaffar, Doris Meissner, and Claire Bergeron. "At Its 25th Anniversary, IRCA's Legacy Lives On." Migration Policy Institute, November 16, 2011.

Christopher, Ben. "As Gun Control Efforts Advance in California Capitol, Opponents Bank on the Courts." *CalMatters*, August 21, 2019, https://calmatters.org/justice/2019/08/gun-control-california-legislature-courts-push-back-second-amendment/.

"City of Denton Fracking Ban Initiative (2014)," Ballotpedia, n.d., https://ballotpedia.org/City_of_Denton_Fracking_Ban_Initiative_(November_2014).

Clark, Patrick. "Texas Is a Homebuilding Machine. And the Rest of the U.S.?" *Bloomberg*, August 15, 2017, https://www.bloomberg.com/news/articles/2017-08-16/texas-leads-the-u-s-in-new-home-construction-and-california.

Cleland, Robert Glass. *From Wilderness to Empire: A History of California.* New York: Alfred A. Knopf, 1959.

Cohen, Ariel. "America's Oil and Gas Reserves Double with Massive New Permian Discovery." *Forbes*, December 21, 2018, https://www.forbes.com/sites/arielcohen/2018/12/21/americas-oil-and-gas-reserves-double-with-massive-new-permian-discovery/.

Cohn, Scott. "Texas Is CNBC's Top State for Business this Year." CNBC.com, June 10, 2018. https://www.cnbc.com/2018/06/29/texas-rebounds-to-become-americas-top-state-for-business-in-2018.html.

Colliver, Victoria. "California Goes Even Bigger on Obamacare." *Politico*, June 16, 2019, https://www.politico.com/story/2019/06/16/california-obamacare-health-care-1530461.

Conant, James K. *Wisconsin Politics and Government: America's Laboratory of Democracy.* Lincoln: University of Nebraska Press, 2006.

Congressional Budget Office. "Immigration Policy in the United States," February 2006, https://www.cbo.gov/sites/default/files/109th-congress-2005-2006/reports/02-28-immigration.pdf.

Conlan, Timothy J., and Paul L. Posner. "American Federalism in an Era of Partisan Polarization: The Intergovernmental Paradox of Obama's 'New Nationalism.'" *Publius: The Journal of Federalism* 46, no. 3 (2016): 299.

Cooper, Christine, Shannon Sedgwick, and Wesley DeWitt. "The Changing Face of Aerospace in Southern California." Los Angeles Economic Development Corporation Institute for Applied Economics, March 2016.

Corcoran, Kieran. "California's Economy Now the 5th Biggest in the World, and Has Overtaken the United Kingdom." *Business Insider*, May 5, 2018, https://www.businessinsider.com/california-economy-ranks-5th-in-the-world-beating-the-uk-2018-5.

Cosman, Bernard. *Five States for Goldwater: Continuity and Change in Southern Presidential Voting Patterns.* Tuscaloosa: University of Alabama Press, 1966.

The Council of State Governments. *The Book of the States, 2018.* Lexington, KY: The Council of State Governments, 2018.

CQ Researcher. "Record Votes in 80th Congress (January–July, 1947)," https://library.cqpress.com/cqresearcher/document.php?id=cqresrre1947073000.

Critchlow, Donald T. *When Hollywood Was Right: How Movie Stars, Studio Moguls, and Big Business Remade American Politics.* New York: Cambridge University Press, 2013.

Crouch, Barry A. *The Dance of Freedom: Texas African Americans during Reconstruction.* Austin: University of Texas Press, 2007.

Cummins, Light Townsend. "History, Memory, and Rebranding Texas as Western for the 1936 Centennial." In *This Corner of Canaan: Essays on Texas in Honor of Randolph B. Campbell*, edited by Richard B. McCaslin, Donald E. Chipman, and Andrew J. Torget, 37–57. Denton: University of North Texas Press, 2013.

Cunningham, Sean P. *Cowboy Conservatism: Texas and the Rise of the Modern Right.* Lexington: The University Press of Kentucky, 2010.

Cuthbertson, Anthony. "Apple, Facebook, Google and Other Tech Firms Oppose 'Bathroom Bill' Transgender Discrimination in Texas." *Newsweek*, April 30, 2017, https://www.newsweek.com/tech-firms-oppose-transgender-discrimination-617293.

Dallek, Matthew. *The Right Moment: Ronald Reagan's First Victory and the Decisive Turning Point in American Politics*. New York: Oxford University Press, 2000.

Dana, Richard Henry, Jr. *Two Years before the Mast*. 1840; New York: Signet Classics, 2009.

Dashefsky, Arnold, and Ira M. Sheskin, eds. *American Jewish Year Book 2018: The Annual Record of the North American Jewish Communities since 1899*, vol. 118. Cham, Switzerland: Springer International Publishing, 2019.

Davidson, Chandler. *Race and Class in Texas Politics*. Princeton, NJ: Princeton University Press, 1990.

Davidson, John Daniel. "Austin Votes to Keep the Books Closed." *Wall Street Journal*, November 30, 2018, https://www.wsj.com/articles/austin-votes-to-keep-the-books-closed-1543620879.

Davis, Carl, et al. *Who Pays? A Distributional Analysis of the Tax Systems in All 50 States*, 5th ed. Washington, DC: The Institute on Taxation and Economic Policy, 2015.

Davis, Margaret Leslie. *Dark Side of Fortune: Triumph and Scandal in the Life of Oil Tycoon Edward L. Doheny*. Berkeley: University of California Press, 1998.

DeVore, Chuck. *The Texas Model: Prosperity in the Lone Star State and Lessons for America*. Austin, TX: Texas Public Policy Foundation, 2014.

DiCamillo, Mark. "Leaving California: Half of the State's Voters Have Been Considering This; Republicans and Conservatives Three Times as Likely as Democrats and Liberals to Be Giving Serious Consideration to Leaving the State." Release # 2019-08, U.C. Berkeley IGS Poll, September 27, 2019, https://escholarship.org/uc/item/96j2704t.

Dillon, Liam. "California Lawmaker Tries Again to Increase Taxes on Legal, Accounting, and Other Services." *Los Angeles Times*, February 5, 2018, http://www.latimes.com/politics/essential/la-pol-ca-essential-politics-updates-california-lawmaker-tries-again-to-1517862729-htmlstory.html.

Dixon, Marc. "Limiting Labor: Business Political·Mobilization and Union Setback in the States." *Journal of Policy History* 19, no. 3 (2007): 313.

Diocese of Orange. "Christ Cathedral: Mass Times," https://parish.christcathedralcalifornia.org/mass-times/.

Dochuk, Darren. *From Bible Belt to Sunbelt: Plain Folk Religion, Grassroots Politics, and the Rise of Evangelical Conservatism*. New York: W. W. Norton, 2011.

Dominguez, Casey B. K. "Boxer vs. Fiorina in California's Senate Race: The Wave Stopped at the Sierra Nevada." In *Cases in Congressional Campaigns: Riding the Wave*, 2nd ed, edited by Randall E. Adkins and David A. Dulio, 78–96. New York: Routledge, 2012.

Drucker, Peter Ferdinand. *The Landmarks of Tomorrow: A Report on the New Postmodern World*. New York: Harper, 1959.

Drum, Kevin. "Why Did Democrats Lose the White South?" *Mother Jones*, November 25, 2015, https://www.motherjones.com/kevin-drum/2015/11/why-did-democrats-lose-white-south/.

Dulaney, Marvin. "African Americans." Texas State Historical Association, July 25, 2016, https://tshaonline.org/handbook/online/articles/pkaan.

Dunn, Candace, and Tim Hess. "The United States Is Now the Largest Global Crude Oil Producer." U.S. Energy Information Administration, September 12, 2018, https://www.eia.gov/todayinenergy/detail.php?id=37053.

Eby, Kate. "History of How Many People Are Homeless in the Bay Area." *ABC7 News*, July 5, 2019, https://abc7news.com/society/homeless-population-history-in-bay-area/5260657/.

Eck, Theodore R. "The Growth of the Southwestern Petrochemical Industry." *Business Review* 45, no. 6 (June 1960): 1–5.

Egelko, Bob. "Right-to-Die Law Upheld by California Appeals Court after Lower Judge Blocked It." *Governing*, November 28, 2018, https://www.governing.com/topics/health-human-services/tns-right-to-die-california-appeal.html.

Eich, John. "West Virginia Becomes First State to Repeal RPS." American Legislative Exchange Council ("ALEC"), February 4, 2015.

Elazar, Daniel J. *American Federalism: A View from the States,* 2nd ed. New York: Thomas Y. Crowell Company, 1972.

"Election 2018: California Election Results." *New York Times*, November 19, 2018, https://www.nytimes.com/interactive/2018/11/06/us/elections/results-california-elections.html.

"Election 2018: Texas Election Results." *New York Times*, November 19, 2018, https://www.nytimes.com/interactive/2018/11/06/us/elections/results-texas-elections.html.

Ellis, Rodney. "Let's Take Full Advantage of Affordable Care Act." *Houston Chronicle*, July 27, 2012, https://www.chron.com/opinion/outlook/article/Let-s-take-full-advantage-of-Affordable-Care-Act-3741457.php.

Enton, Harry. "Trump Probably Did Better with Latino Voters Than Romney Did." *FiveThirtyEight*, November 18, 2018, https://fivethirtyeight.com/features/trump-probably-did-better-with-latino-voters-than-romney-did/.

"Exit Polls 2016." CNN, November 23, 2016, https://www.cnn.com/election/2016/results/exit-polls.

Fabi, Rachel, and Brendan Saloner. "Covering Undocumented Immigrants—State Innovation in California." *New England Journal of Medicine* 375 (November 17, 2016): 1913–15.

Faderman, Lillian. *The Gay Revolution: The Story of the Struggle.* New York: Simon and Schuster, 2015.

Fares, Robert. "Texas Got 18 Percent of Its Energy from Wind and Solar Last Year." *Scientific American*, January 29, 2018, https://blogs.scientificamerican.com/plugged-in/texas-got-18-percent-of-its-energy-from-wind-and-solar-last-year/.

Farmer, Liz. "How Are Pensions Protected, State-by-State?" *Governing*, January 28, 2014, http://www.governing.com/finance101/gov-pension-protections-state-by-state.html.

Fehrenbach, T. R. *Lone Star: A History of Texas and the Texans*, updated ed. New York: Da Capo Press, 2000.

Ferguson, Edwin E. "The California Alien Land Law and the Fourteenth Amendment." *California Law Review* 35, no. 1 (1947).

Fernandez, Manny. "Texas Banned Sanctuary Cities. Some Police Departments Didn't Get the Memo." *New York Times*, March 15, 2018, https://www.nytimes.com/2018/03/15/us/texas-sanctuary-sb4-immigration.html.

Fernandez, Manny. "What Makes Texas Texas." *New York Times*, May 7, 2016, https://www.nytimes.com/2016/05/08/us/what-makes-texas-texas.html.

Field, Ben. *Activism in Pursuit of the Public Interest: The Jurisprudence of Chief Justice Roger J. Traynor.* Berkeley, CA: Institute of Governmental Studies Press, 2003.

Fisher, Gordon M. "The Development and History of the U.S. Poverty Thresholds—A Brief Overview." U.S. Department of Health and Human Services, January 1, 1997.

Flanagan, Sue. *Sam Houston's Texas.* Austin: University of Texas Press, 1964.

Florida, Richard. "The Winners and Losers of Economic Clustering." *Citylab*, January 6, 2016, https://www.citylab.com/life/2016/01/creativity-clustering-us-cities/422718/.

Floyd, Ife, Ashley Burnside, and Liz Schott. "TANF Reaching Few Poor Families." Center for Budget and Policy Priorities, November 28, 2018: 11–19, https://www.cbpp.org/sites/default/files/atoms/files/6-16-15tanf.pdf.

Foldy, Ben, and Mike Colias. "Trump-California Showdown on Fuel Economy Rules Divides Automakers." *Wall Street Journal*, August 21, 2019, https://www.wsj.com/articles/carmakers-follow-divergent-paths-on-fuel-efficiency-regulations-11566404594?mod=searchresults&page=1&pos=2.

Food Research and Action Center. "State Data for Households Participating in SNAP," n.d., http://www.frac.org/maps/snap-state-map/snap-states.html#pdflist.

Foran, Clare. "Can Hillary Clinton Win Texas?" *The Atlantic*, September 8, 2016, https://www.theatlantic.com/politics/archive/2016/09/clinton-texas-trump/499097/.

"Fortune 500 (2019)." *Fortune*, May 16, 2019, https://fortune.com/fortune500/2019/.

Fox, Liana. "The Supplemental Poverty Measure 2018." U.S. Census Bureau, October 7, 2019, https://www.census.gov/content/census/en/library/publications/2018/demo/p60-265.html.

Fraga, Bernard L. *The Turnout Gap: Race, Ethnicity, and Political Inequality in a Diversifying America*. New York: Cambridge University Press, 2018.

French, Will J. "Mexicans in California: Report of Governor C. C. Young's Mexican Fact Finding Committee." Sacramento: California State Printing Office, 1930.

Frey, William H. *Diversity Explosion: How New Racial Demographics Are Remaking America*. Washington, DC: Brookings Institution Press, 2018.

Friedman, Lisa, and Brad Plumer. "E.P.A. Announces Repeal of Major Obama-Era Carbon Emissions Rule." *New York Times*, October 9, 2017, https://www.nytimes.com/2017/10/09/climate/clean-power-plan.html.

Galbraith, Kate, and Asher Price. *The Great Texas Wind Rush: How George W. Bush, Ann Richards, and a Bunch of Tinkerers Helped the Oil and Gas State Win the Race to Wind Power*. Austin: University of Texas Press, 2013.

García Martínez, Antonio. "In Texas, Techies Are Trying to Turn the Red State Blue." *Wired*, October 23, 2018, https://www.wired.com/story/flipping-texas-elections-voter-registration-tech/.

Garreau, Joel. *The Nine Nations of North America*. New York: Avon Books, 1982.

Garrett, Robert T., Terri Langford, and Stephanie Lamm. "Fracking Billionaires Pump Millions into Texas Races, Pushing State GOP Even Further to the Right." *Dallas Morning News*, February 22, 2018, https://www.dallasnews.com/news/2018-elections/2018/02/22/fracking-billionaires-pump-millions-texas-races-pushing-state-gop-even-right.

Garrow, David J. "She Put the Roe in Roe v. Wade." *New York Times*, September 27, 1992, https://www.nytimes.com/1992/09/27/books/she-put-the-v-in-roe-v-wade.html.

Gaswirth, Stephanie B., et al. "Fact Sheet 2018–3073: Assessment of Undiscovered Continuous Oil and Gas Resources in the Wolfcamp Shale and Bone Spring Formation of the Delaware Basin, Permian Basin Province, New Mexico and Texas, 2018." Washington, DC: U.S. Geological Survey (2018), https://pubs.er.usgs.gov/publication/fs20183073.

Gelin, Martin. "Silicon Valley's Libertarians Are Trading Blows with California Democrats in a Fight for the Left." *Quartz*, March 1, 2018, https://qz.com/1219254/california-democrats-are-trading-blows-with-silicon-valleys-libertarians-in-a-fight-for-the-left/.

George, Henry. *Our Land and Land Policy, National and State*. Pamphlet. San Francisco: White and Bauer, 1871.

Gibson, Campbell, and Kay Jung. "Historical Census Statistics on Population Totals by Race, 1790 to 1990, and by Hispanic Origin, 1970 to 1990, for the United States, Regions, Divisions, and States." Working Paper No. 56. Washington, DC: U.S. Census Bureau, September 2002, https://census.gov/content/dam/Census/library/working-papers/2002/demo/POP-twps0056.pdf.

Giffords Law Center. "California: State Law Background," n.d., https://lawcenter.giffords.org/gun-laws/state-law/california/.

Glasrud, Bruce A. "Asians in Texas: An Overview, 1870–1990." *East Texas Historical Journal* 39, no. 2 (2001), https://scholarworks.sfasu.edu/cgi/viewcontent.cgi?article=2329&context=ethj.

Glass, Fred B. *From Mission to Microchip: A History of the California Labor Movement*. Oakland: University of California Press, 2016.

Gold, Russell. *The Boom: How Fracking Ignited the American Energy Revolution and Changed the World*. New York: Simon and Schuster, 2014.

Goldenberg, Suzanne. "Barack Obama Gives Green Light to New Wave of Nuclear Reactors." *The Guardian*, February 16, 2010, https://www.theguardian.com/environment/2010/feb/16/barack-obama-nuclear-reactors.

Goldsberry, Kirk. "What Really Happened in Texas." *FiveThirtyEight*, November 14, 2018, https://fivethirtyeight.com/features/how-beto-orourke-shifted-the-map-in-texas/.

Gorman, Anna, and Kaiser Health News. "Medieval Diseases Are Infecting California's Homeless: Typhus, Tuberculosis, and Other Illnesses Are Spreading Quickly through Camps and Shelters." *The Atlantic*, March 8, 2019, https://www.theatlantic.com/health/archive/2019/03/typhus-tuberculosis-medieval-diseases-spreading-homeless/584380/.

Governor Pete Wilson Committee. "Vote Yes on Proposition 187," https://www.youtube.com/watch?v=lLIzzs2HHgY.

Granger, Gordon. General Order No. 3, June 19, 1865, available at https://tshaonline.org/handbook/online/articles/lkj01.

Gray, Virginia. "Competition, Emulation, and Policy Innovation." In *New Perspectives on American Politics*, edited by Lawrence C. Dodd and Calvin Jillson, 230–48. Washington, DC: CQ Press, 1994.

Green, George Norris. *The Establishment in Texas Politics: The Primitive Years, 1938–1957*. Norman: University of Oklahoma Press, 1979.

Green, George Norris, with Michael R. Botson Jr. "Looking for Lefty: Liberal/Left Activism and Texas Labor, 1920s–1960s." In *The Texas Left: The Radical Roots of Lone Star Liberalism*, edited by David O'Donald Cullen and Kyle G. Wilkison, 112–32. College Station: Texas A&M Press, 2010.

Greenblatt, Alan. "All or Nothing: In Most States These Days, One Party Controls All the Levers of Power. And Once They Get It, They Are Keeping It." *Governing*, January 2019, https://www.governing.com/topics/politics/gov-state-politics-governors-2019.html.

Greenhouse, Steven. "Most U.S. Union Members Are Working for the Government, New Data Shows." *New York Times*, January 22, 2010, B-1.

Greer, Stanley. "State Labor-Management Policy and the Texas Model." Austin: Texas Public Policy Foundation, February 2015.

Gregory, James N. *American Exodus: The Dust Bowl Migration and Okie Culture in California*. New York: Oxford University Press, 1989.

Gregory, James N. "Introduction." In Upton Sinclair, *I, Candidate for Governor, and How I Got Licked*. Berkeley: University of California Press, 1994.

Greider, Erica. *Big, Hot, Cheap, and Right: What America Can Learn from the Strange Genius of Texas*. New York: Public Affairs, 2013.

Gresham, George. "Call It 'Right-to-Work-for-Less,' Not Right-to-Work." *New York Times Room for Debate*, March 12, 2015, https://www.nytimes.com/roomfordebate/2015/03/12/scott-walker-right-to-work-and-labors-waning-power/call-it-right-to-work-for-less-not-right-to-work.

Greve, Michael S. "Federalism in a Polarized Age." In *Parchment Barriers: Political Polarization and the Limits of Constitutional Order*, edited by Zachary Courser, Eric Helland, and Kenneth P. Miller, 119–56. Lawrence: University Press of Kansas, 2018.

Greve, Michael S. "Laboratories of Democracy: Anatomy of a Metaphor." *Federalist Outlook* (American Enterprise Institute: March 31, 2001), http://www.aei.org/publication/laboratories-of-democracy/.

Gross, Neil. "Why Is Hollywood So Liberal?" *New York Times*, January 27, 2018, https://www.nytimes.com/2018/01/27/opinion/sunday/hollywood-liberal.html.

Grossman, Matt. *Red State Blues: How the Conservative Revolution Stalled in the States*. New York: Cambridge University Press, 2019.

Guinn, J. M. "*La Estrella*: The Pioneer Newspaper of Los Angeles." *Annual Publication of the Historical Society of Southern California and Pioneer Register* (1900).

Hainsworth, Robert Wendell. "The Negro and the Texas Primaries." *Journal of Negro History* 18, no. 4 (October 1933): 426–50.

Haley, James L. *Passionate Nation: The Epic History of Texas*. New York: Free Press, 2006.

Halper, Evan, and Scott Martelle. "State GOP Is 'Dying at the Box Office,' Gov Says: Schwarzenegger Blames Republicans' Declining Fortunes on the Party's Failure to Reach Out to Independent and Moderate Voters." *Los Angeles Times*, September 8, 2008, http://articles.latimes.com/2007/sep/08/local/me-arnold8.

Harlow, Neal. *California Conquered: The Annexation of a Mexican Province, 1846–1850*. Berkeley: University of California Press, 1982.

Hartford Seminary. "Database of Megachurches in the United States." n.d., http://hirr.hartsem.edu/megachurch/database.html.

Hartley, James E., Steven M. Sheffrin, and J. David Vasche. "Reform During Crisis: The Transformation of California's Fiscal System during the Great Depression." *Journal of Economic History* 56, no. 3 (September 1996): 657–78.

Hayes-Bautista, David E. *La Nueva California: Latinos from Pioneers to Post-Millennials*. Oakland: University of California Press, 2017.

Haynes, John R. "Birth of Democracy in California." Manuscript, Haynes Foundation, Los Angeles.

Hegar, Glen. "A Field Guide to the Taxes of Texas." Austin: Texas Comptroller of Public Accounts (December 2017).

Henry, Meghan, Rian Watt, Anna Mahathey, Jillian Ouellette, and Aubrey Sitler. "The 2019 Annual Homeless Assessment Report (AHAR) to Congress." Washington, DC: U.S. Department of Housing and Urban Development, January 2020, https://files.hudexchange.info/resources/documents/2019-AHAR-Part-1.pdf.

Henry J. Kaiser Family Foundation. "Federal Medicaid Assistance Percentage," n.d., https://www.kff.org/medicaid/state-indicator/federal-matching-rate-and-multiplier/view/.

Henry J. Kaiser Family Foundation. "Medicaid Expansion Enrollment," n.d., https://www.kff.org/health-reform/state-indicator/medicaid-expansion-enrollment/?currentTimeframe=0&sortModel=%7B%22colId%22:%22Expansion%20Group%20Enrollment%22,%22sort%22:%22desc%22%7D.

Henson, Margaret Swett. "Anglo American Colonization." Texas State Historical Association: *Handbook of Texas Online*, June 9, 2010, https:// tshaonline.org/ handbook/ online/ articles/ uma01.

Hernández, Kelly Lytle. "The Crimes and Consequences of Illegal Immigration: A Cross-Border Examination of Operation Wetback, 1943–1954." *Western Historical Quarterly* 37 (Winter 2006): 421–44.

Hirczy de Mino, Wolfgang P. "Does an Equal Rights Amendment Make a Difference?" *Albany Law Review* 60 (1997): 1581–610.

Hirsch, Barry T., and David A. Macpherson. "Union Membership, Coverage, Density, and Employment by State and Sector" for years 1983–2018, www.unionstats.com.

Hobbs, Frank, and Nicole Stoops. "Demographic Trends in the 20th Century." Washington, DC: U.S. Census Bureau, November 2002.

Hogan, William Ransom. *The Texas Republic: A Social and Economic History*. Norman: University of Oklahoma Press, 1946.

Hooks, Christopher. "Losing Ground." *Texas Observer*, December 30, 2014, https://www.texasobserver.org/losing-ground-battleground-texas-democratic-party/.

Horseman, Jeff. "November's Presidential Election Broke Records in California." *Mercury News*, December 22, 2016, https://www.mercurynews.com/2016/12/22/novembers-presidential-election-broke-records-in-california/.

Hui, Iris, and David O. Sears. "Reexamining the Effect of Racial Propositions on Latinos' Partisanship in California." *Political Behavior* 40 (2018): 149–74.

Hundley, Norris C., Jr. "Katherine Philips Edson and the Fight for the California Minimum Wage, 1912–1923." *Pacific Historical Review* 29, no. 3 (August 1960): 271–85.

Hunter, James Davison. *Culture Wars: The Struggle to Define America*. New York: Basic Books, 1991.

Ickes, Harold L. *Fightin' Oil*. New York: Alfred A. Knopf, 1943.

Inazu, John. *Confident Pluralism: Surviving and Thriving through Deep Difference*. Chicago: University of Chicago Press, 2016.

Ingram, Carl. "Assault Gun Ban Wins Final Vote: Deukmejian's Promised Approval Would Make It 1st Such U.S. Law." *Los Angeles Times*, May 19, 1989, https://www.latimes.com/archives/la-xpm-1989-05-19-mn-112-story.html.

International Monetary Fund. "GDP Current Prices," October 2019, https://www.imf.org/external/datamapper/NGDPD@WEO/OEMDC/ADVEC/WEOWORLD.

Jacobsen, Gary C. "The 1994 House Elections in Perspective." In *Midterm: The Elections of 1994 in Context*, edited by Philip A. Klinkner, 203–23. Boulder, CO: Westview Press, 1996.

Jarvis, Howard, with Robert Pack. *I'm Mad as Hell*. New York: Times Books, 1979.

Jillson, Cal. *Lone Star Tarnished: A Critical Look at Texas Politics and Public Policy*, 3rd ed. New York: Routledge, 2018.

Jobs, Steve. "Stay Hungry, Stay Foolish." Commencement Address at Stanford University, June 14, 2005, https://news.stanford.edu/2005/06/14/jobs-061505/.

Johnson, Hans P. "Movin' Out: Domestic Migration to and from California in the 1990s." *California Counts: Population Trends and Problems* 2, no. 1 (Public Policy Institute of California, August 2000).

Johnson, Lyndon B. "State of the Union," January 8, 1964. University of Virginia Miller Center, https://millercenter.org/the-presidency/presidential-speeches/january-8-1964-state-union.

"Joint Resolution for Annexing Texas to the United States (March 1, 1845)." In *The Public Statutes at Large of the United States of America*, vol. 5, edited by Richard Peters, 797–98. Boston: Chas. C. Little and Jas. Brown, 1850, https://www.tsl.texas.gov/ref/abouttx/annexation/march1845.html.

Jones, Anson. "Anson Jones Valedictory Speech, February 19, 1846." Texas State Library and Archives Commission, https://www.tsl.texas.gov/treasures/earlystate/nomore-3.html.

Jones, Rachel K. and Jenna Jerman. "Abortion Incidence and Service Availability in the United States, 2014." *Perspectives on Sexual and Reproductive Health* 49, no. 1 (March 2017), https://www.guttmacher.org/sites/default/files/article_files/abortion-incidence-us.pdf.

Jordan, Terry G. *German Seeds in Texas Soil: Immigrant Farmers in Nineteenth Century Texas.* Austin: University of Texas Press, 1966.

Kearney, Richard C., and Patrice Mareschal. *Labor Relations in the Public Sector*, 5th ed. Boca Raton, FL: CRC Press, 2014.

Kelley, Edna E. "The Mexicans Go Home." *Southwest Review* 17 (April 1932).

Kennedy, John F. "Executive Order 10988—Employee-Management Cooperation in the Federal Service," January 17, 1962, http://www.presidency.ucsb.edu/ws/?pid=58926.

Key, V. O., Jr. *Southern Politics in State and Nation.* New York: A. A. Knopf, 1949.

Kilborn, Peter T., and Sam Howe Verhovek. "Clinton's Welfare Shift Ends Tortuous Journey." *New York Times*, August 2, 1996, A1.

Kirkpatrick, Evron M. "Toward a More Responsible Two-Party System: A Report of the Committee on Political Parties." Supplement, *American Political Science Review* 44, no. 3, Part 2 (September 1950): 965–90.

Knaggs, John R. *Two Party Texas: The John Tower Era, 1961–1984.* Austin, TX: Eakin Press, 1986.

Konisky, David M., and Neal D. Woods. "Environmental Policy, Federalism, and the Obama Presidency." *Publius: The Journal of Federalism* 46, no. 3 (July 1, 2016): 366–91.

Kotkin, Joel. "California and the Jews." *Forbes*, November 22, 2008, https://www.forbes.com/2008/11/22/cities-jews-blacks-oped-cx_jk_1124kotkin.html#6bd500156877.

Kotkin, Joel. *The New Class Conflict.* Candor, NY: Telos Press Publishing, 2014.

Kotkin, Joel, and Marshall Toplansky. "Research Brief: California Feudalism: The Squeeze on the Middle Class." Center for Demographics and Policy, Chapman University, October 19, 2018, https://www.newgeography.com/content/006117-california-feudalism-the-squeeze-middle-class.

Kousser, Thad. "Partisan Polarization and Policy Gridlock: Does One Lead to the Other?" In *Governing California: Politics, Government, and Public Policy in the Golden State*, edited by Ethan Rarick, 277–298. Berkeley, CA: Berkeley Public Policy Press, 2013.

Kriel, Lomi. "Just How Diverse Is Houston? 145 Languages Spoken Here." *Houston Chronicle*, November 5, 2015, https://www.houstonchronicle.com/news/houston-texas/article/Houstonians-speak-at-least-145-languages-at-home-6613182.php.

Ladd, Everett Carll, Jr., and Charles D. Hadley. *Transformations of the American Party System: Political Coalitions from the New Deal to the 1970s.* 2nd. ed. New York: W. W. Norton, 1978.

Lai, Rebecca. "Abortion Bans: 9 States Have Passed Bills to Limit the Procedure This Year." *New York Times*, May 15, 2019, https://www.nytimes.com/interactive/2019/us/abortion-laws-states.html.

Lawrence, Chrishelle, and Chip Berry. "U.S. Households' Heating Equipment Choices are Diverse and Vary by Climate Region." U.S. Energy Information Administration, April 6, 2017, https://www.eia.gov/todayinenergy/detail.php?id=30672.

Layman, Geoffrey. *The Great Divide: Religious and Cultural Conflict in American Party Politics.* New York: Columbia University Press, 2001.

Leavy, Zad, and Alan F. Charles. "California's New Therapeutic Abortion Act: An Analysis and Guide to Medical and Legal Procedure." *UCLA Law Review* 15, no. 1 (November 1967): 1–31.

Leip, Dave. "Atlas of U.S. Presidential Elections," https://uselectionatlas.org/.

Leonardatos, Cynthia Deitle. "California's Attempts to Disarm the Black Panthers." *San Diego Law Review* 36, no. 4 (Fall 1999): 947–96.

Lesley, Lewis B. "The Entrance of the Santa Fé Railroad into California." *Pacific Historical Review* 8, no. 1 (March 1939): 89–96.

Lesley, Lewis B. "A Southern Transcontinental Railroad into California: Texas and Pacific versus Southern Pacific, 1865–1885." *Pacific Historical Review* 5, no. 1 (March 1936): 52–60.

Li, Quan, Michael J. Pomante II, and Scot Schraufnagel. "Cost of Voting in the American States." *Election Law Journal: Rules, Politics, and Policy* 17, no. 3 (September 18, 2018): 234–47, https://doi.org/10.1089/elj.2017.0478.

Li, Roland. "McKesson, Biggest U.S. Drug Distributor, to Move from SF to Texas." *San Francisco Chronicle*, December 1, 2018, https://www.sfchronicle.com/business/article/McKesson-biggest-U-S-drug-distributor-to-move-13435748.php.

Lin, Elbert. "States Suing the Federal Government: Protecting Liberty or Playing Politics?" *University of Richmond Law Review* 52, no. 3 (March 2018): 633–52.

Lin, Judy. "The Open Secret about California Taxes." *CALmatters*, May 8, 2018, https://calmatters.org/articles/the-open-secret-about-california-taxes/.

Lincoln, Abraham. "First Inaugural Address," March 4, 1861, https://www.presidency.ucsb.edu/documents/inaugural-address-34.

Lincoln, Abraham. "House Divided Speech." Delivered to the Illinois State Republican Convention, Springfield, Illinois, June 16, 1858, https://www.nps.gov/liho/learn/historyculture/housedivided.htm.

Lindell, Chuck. "Perry: Texas Will Opt Out of Medicare Expansion, Insurance Exchange." *Austin American-Statesman*, September 1, 2012, https://www.statesman.com/news/20120901/perry-texas-will- opt-out-of-medicaid-expansion-insurance-exchange.

Liptak, Adam. "Supreme Court Bars Challenges to Partisan Gerrymandering." *New York Times*, June 27, 2019, https://www.nytimes.com/2019/06/27/us/politics/supreme-court-gerrymandering.html.

"List of California Governors." The California State Library, https://governors.library.ca.gov/list.html.

Lloyd, Gordon. "Nature and Convention in the Creation of the 1849 California Constitution." In *California Republic: Institutions, Statesmanship, and Policies*, edited by Brian P. Janiskee and Ken Masugi, 33–66. Lanham, MD: Rowman & Littlefield, 2004.

Lobdell, William, and Mitchell Landsberg. "Robert F. Schuller, Who Built Crystal Cathedral, Dies at 88." *Los Angeles Times*, April 2, 2015, http://www.latimes.com/local/obituaries/la-me-robert-schuller-20150403-story.html.

Long, George I. "Differences between Union and Non-union Pay." *Monthly Labor Review,* U.S. Bureau of Labor Statistics (April 2013), https://www.bls.gov/opub/mlr/2013/04/art2full.pdf.

"The Long Goodbye." *The Economist,* November 11, 2010, https://www.economist.com/united-states/2010/11/11/the-long-goodbye.

Lopez, Ashley. "In Trump Era, Republicans Are Split on Whether to Court Hispanic Voters." KUT News, August 30, 2018, https://www.kut.org/post/trump-era-texas-republicans-are-split-whether-court-hispanic-voters.

Lopez, Felipe. "Senate Floor Analysis, AB 1887: Third Reading," August 3, 2016, http://www.leginfo.ca.gov/pub/15-16/bill/asm/ab_1851-1900/ab_1887_cfa_20160816_175754_sen_floor.html.

"Los Angeles, California, Homelessness Reduction and Prevention Housing, and Facilities Bond Issue, Measure HHH (November 2016)." Ballotpedia, n.d., https://ballotpedia.org/Los_Angeles,_California,_Homelessness_Reduction_and_Prevention_Housing,_and_Facilities_Bond_Issue,_Measure_HHH_(November_2016).

"Los Angeles County, California, Sales Tax for Homeless Services and Prevention, Measure H (March 2017)." Ballotpedia, n.d., https://ballotpedia.org/Los_Angeles_County,_California,_Sales_Tax_for_Homeless_Services_and_Prevention,_Measure_H_.

Los Angeles Homeless Services Authority. "2019 Greater Los Angeles Homeless Count— Los Angeles County." September 5, 2019, https://www.lahsa.org/documents?id=3423-2019-greater-los-angeles-homeless-count-los-angeles-county.pdf.

Lotchin, Roger W. *Fortress California: From Warfare to Welfare.* New York: Oxford University Press, 1992.

Lott, John R., Jr. *More Guns, Less Crime: Understanding Crime and Gun Control Laws,* 3rd ed. Chicago: University of Chicago Press, 2010.

Lubenow, Gerald C., ed. *California Votes—The 1994 Governor's Race: An Inside Look at the Candidates and Their Campaigns by the People Who Managed Them.* Berkeley: Institute of Governmental Studies Press, 1995.

Lucas, Arthur F. "The Legal Minimum Wage in Massachusetts." *Annals of the American Academy of Political and Social Science* 130, Suppl. (March 1927), https://www.jstor.org/stable/1016389.

Lunsford, Terry F. "The Free Speech Crisis at Berkeley, 1964–1965: Some Issues for Social and Legal Research." Berkeley, CA: Center for Study of Law and Society, University of California at Berkeley (December 1965): 4–16, https://oac.cdlib.org/view?docId=kt9r2 9p975&query=&brand=oac4.

Lykens, Kristine. "The Right Thing to Do." *Fort Worth Star-Telegram,* April 26, 2014, https://www.star-telegram.com/opinion/editorials/article3855213.html.

"Magna Carta." *Dallas Morning News,* September 1, 1941, Sec. II, 4.

Mai-Duc, Christine. "On Minimum Wage, De León Says, California is 'First . . . Period.'" *Los Angeles Times,* April 4, 2016, http://www.latimes.com/la-pol-sac-essential-poli-on-minimum-wage-de-leon-says-california-is-firs-1459790713-htmlstory.html.

Malewitz, Jim. "Curbing Local Control, Abbott Signs 'Denton Fracking Bill.'" *Texas Tribune,* May 28, 2015, https://www.texastribune.org/2015/05/18/abbott-signs-denton-fracking-bill/.

Malm, Elizabeth, and Ellen Kant. "The Sources of State and Local Tax Revenues." Tax Foundation, January 29, 2013, https://files.taxfoundation.org/legacy/docs/ff354.pdf.

Maltz, Earl M. "The Constitution and the Annexation of Texas." *Constitutional Commentary* 23 (2006): 381–401.

Marshall, Carolyn. "Schwarzenegger Issues Plan to Reduce Greenhouse Gases." *New York Times*, June 2, 2005.

Martin, Keith. "The Big Inch: Fueling America's World War II War Effort." National Institute of Standards and Technology: Taking Measure, March 26, 2018, https://www.nist.gov/blogs/taking-measure/big-inch-fueling-americas-wwii-war-effort.

Martin, Roger, Richard Florida, Melissa Pogue, and Charlotta Mellander. "Creativity, Clusters, and the Competitive Advantage of Cities." *Competiveness Review* 25, no. 5 (2015): 482–96, http://doi.org/10.1108/CR-07-2015-0069.

Martin, Roscoe C. *The People's Party in Texas: A Study in Third Party Politics.* 1933; repr., Austin: University of Texas Press, 1970.

Marx, Karl, and Frederick Engels. "Review: January–February 1850." *Neue Rheinische*, https://www.marxists.org/archive/marx/works/1850/01/31.htm.

Mason, Melanie. "Business-friendly Democrats Pick New Leaders for Informal, but Powerful Sacramento Caucus." *Los Angeles Times*, December 9, 2015, https://www.latimes.com/politics/la-pol-sac-moderate-democrats-leaders-20151209-story.html.

Mason, Melanie. "California Gives Immigrants Unprecedented Rights and Benefits." *Governing*, August 12, 2015, https://www.governing.com/topics/politics/tns-california-immigration-alien.html.

Mason, Melanie. "'We Will Have Universal Health Care in California,' Gavin Newsom Promises Single-Payer Advocates." *Los Angeles Times*, September 22, 2017, https://www.latimes.com/politics/essential/la-pol-ca-essential-politics-updates-in-speech-to-single-payer-advocates-1506103477-htmlstory.html.

Matthews, Glenna. *The Golden State in the Civil War: Thomas Starr King, the Republican Party, and the Birth of Modern California.* New York: Cambridge University Press, 2012.

Mathews, Joe. "California's Population to Hit 40 Million—and About to Fall." *Orange County Register*, July 15, 2018, https://www.ocregister.com/2018/07/15/californias-population-to-hit-40-million-and-about-to-fall/.

Mathews, Joe. *The People's Machine: Arnold Schwarzenegger and the Rise of Blockbuster Democracy.* New York: Public Affairs, 2006.

Mattingly, Marybeth, Sarah Bohn, Caroline Danielson, Sara Kimberlin, and Christopher Wimer. "Poverty Declines in California, but More Than 1 in 3 Are Poor or Nearly Poor." Public Policy Institute of California, October 2019, https://inequality.stanford.edu/sites/default/files/california_poverty_measure_2017.pdf.

Maxwell, Robert S. "Lumber Industry." Texas State Historical Association, February 21, 2012, https://tshaonline.org/handbook/online/articles/drl02.

McClain, Charles J. "The Gibson Era: 1940–1964." In *Constitutional Governance and Judicial Power: The History of the California Supreme Court*, edited by Harry N. Scheiber, 245–325. Berkeley, CA: Berkeley Public Policy Press, 2016.

McConville, Shannon, Laura Hill, Iwunze Ugo, and Joseph Hayes. "Health Care Coverage for Undocumented Immigrants." Public Policy Institute of California: November 2015, https://www.ppic.org/content/pubs/report/R_1115SMR.pdf.

McGaughy, Lauren, and Melissa Repko. "Tech Firms Helped Knock Down Texas's Bathroom Bill. Is Apple's $1B Campus the Fatal Blow?" *Dallas Morning News*, December 13, 2018, https://www.dallasnews.com/news/politics/2018/12/13/tech-firms-helped-knock-texas-bathroom-bill-apples-1b-campus-fatal-blow.

McGirr, Lisa. *Suburban Warriors: The Origins of the New American Right.* Princeton, NJ: Princeton University Press, 2001.

McKay, Robert R. "Mexican Repatriation from Texas during the Great Depression." *Journal of South Texas* 3 (Spring 1990).

McNeeley, Dave, and Jim Henderson. *Bob Bullock: God Bless Texas.* Austin: University of Texas Press, 2008.

McRaney, David. "How Your Address Changes Your Politics." *Politico Magazine*, August 2, 2015, https://www.politico.com/magazine/story/2015/08/how-your-address-changes-your-politics-120899.

McWilliams, Carey. *North from Mexico: The Spanish Speaking People of the United States.* 1948; 3rd ed. updated by Alma M. Garcia. Santa Barbara, CA: Praeger, 2016.

McWilliams, Carey. *Southern California: An Island on the Land.* 1946; repr. Layton, UT: Gibbs Smith, 1973.

Middleton, Annie. "The Texas Convention of 1845." *Southwestern Historical Quarterly* 25, no. 1 (July 1921): 26–62.

Migration Policy Institute. "U.S. Immigrant Population by Country of Birth, 1960–2017." https://www.migrationpolicy.org/programs/data-hub/us-immigration-trends#source.

Miller, E. T. "The State Finances of Texas during the Civil War." *Quarterly of the Texas State Historical Association* 14, no. 1 (July 1910): 1–23, https://www.jstor.org/stable/pdf/30242999.pdf?refreqid=excelsior%3Ab967fa0b5e13709756383921817a1e88.

Miller, Kenneth P. "The California Supreme Court and the Popular Will." *Chapman Law Review* 19, no. 1 (Winter 2016): 151–98.

Miller, Kenneth P. "Defining Rights in the States: Judicial Activism and Popular Response." *Albany Law Review* 76, no. 4 (2012/2013): 2061–78.

Miller, Ryan, and Vu Chu. "California's Tax System: A Visual Guide." California Legislative Analyst's Office, 2018, https://lao.ca.gov/reports/2018/3805/ca-tax-system-041218.pdf.

Milligan, Susan. "Could Changing Demographics Turn Texas Politically Purple?" *U.S. News & World Report*, October 11, 2018, https://www.usnews.com/news/best-states/articles/2018-10-11/in-texas-changing-demographics-could-have-political-implications.

Mitchell, Alison. "Two Clinton Aides Resign to Protest New Welfare Law," *New York Times*, September 12, 1996, A1.

Mitchell, Greg. *The Campaign of the Century: Upton Sinclair's Race for Governor of California and the Birth of Media Politics.* New York: Random House, 1992.

Moneyhon, Carl H. *Texas After the Civil War: The Struggle of Reconstruction.* College Station: Texas A&M Press, 2004.

Moore, Derick. "Texas Added the Most People, but California Still Most Populous." U.S. Census Bureau, January 16, 2018, https://www.census.gov/library/stories/2018/01/state-pop-tableau.html.

Moore, William. "The Determinants and Effects of Right-to-Work Laws: A Review of the Recent Literature." *Journal of Labor Research* 19, no. 3 (1998): 445–69.

Movement Advancement Project. "California's Equality Profile," http://www.lgbtmap.org/equality-maps/profile_state/CA.

Mowry, George E. *The California Progressives.* Berkeley and Los Angeles: University of California Press, 1951.

Musumeci, MaryBeth. "Explaining Texas v. U.S.: A Guide to the 5th Circuit Appeal in the Case Challenging the ACA." Kaiser Family Foundation, July 3, 2019, https://www.kff.org/health-reform/issue-brief/explaining-texas-v-u-s-a-guide-to-the-5th-circuit-appeal-in-the-case-challenging-the-aca/.

Nagourney, Adam. "A Red Meat Rallying Cry for National Republicans: California." *New York Times*, October 22, 2018, https://www.nytimes.com/2018/10/22/us/california-gop-political-attacks.html.

Nagourney, Adam, and Charles McDermid. "California Today: 'The World Is Looking to Us,' Gavin Newsom Says." *New York Times*, June 1, 2018, https://www.nytimes.com/2018 /06/01/us/california-today-gavin-newsom-Ipeech.html.

NARAL Pro-choice America. "State Laws: California," https://www.prochoiceamerica.org/state-law/california/.

Nash, Elizabeth, Lizamarie Mohammed, Olivia Cappello, Sophia Naide, and Zohra Ansari-Thomas. "State Policy Trends at Mid-Year 2019: States Race to Ban or Protect Abortion." Guttmacher Institute, July 1, 2019, https://www.guttmacher.org/article/2019/07/state-policy-trends-mid-year-2019-states-race-ban-or-protect-abortion.

Nation, Joe. "California Pension Debt Climbs Despite Strong Economy." *Mercury News*, October 6, 2019. https://www.mercurynews.com/2019/10/06/opinion-california-pension-debt-climbs-despite-decade-of-soaring-stocks/.

"National Affairs: Men Aplenty." *Time Magazine*, April 15, 1940.

National Association of State Budget Officers. "2019 State Expenditure Report," November 21, 2019, https://www.nasbo.org/reports-data/state-expenditure-report.

National Conference of State Legislatures. "2018 Legislator Compensation Information," April 16, 2018, http://www.ncsl.org/research/about-state-legislatures/legislator-compensation-2018.aspx.

National Conference of State Legislatures. "Partisan Composition of State Legislatures, 1990–2000," http://www.ncsl.org/documents/statevote/legiscontrol_1990_2000.pdf .

National Conference of State Legislatures. "Post Election 2019 State & Legislative Partisan Composition," November 22, 2019, https://www.ncsl.org/Portals/1/Documents/Elections/Legis_Control_2019_Post-Election%20Nov%2022nd.pdf.

National Conference of State Legislatures. "Right to Work States," n.d., http://www.ncsl.org/research/labor-and-employment/right-to-work-laws-and-bills.aspx.

National Conference of State Legislatures. "State Renewable Portfolio Standards and Goals," February 1, 2019, http://www.ncsl.org/research/energy/renewable-portfolio-standards.aspx.

NEA Research. "Ranking of the States 2018 and Estimates of School Statistics 2019." Washington, DC: National Education Association, April 2019: 49, http://www.nea.org/assets/docs/2019%20Rankings%20and%20Estimates%20Report.pdf.

Newsom, Gavin. "Governor's Budget Summary 2019–2020," January 10, 2019, http://www.ebudget.ca.gov/budget/2019-20/#/BudgetSummary.

Newsom, Gavin. "Governor's Budget Summary 2020–2021," January 10, 2020, http://www.ebudget.ca.gov/2020-21/pdf/BudgetSummary/FullBudgetSummary.pdf.

Newsom, Gavin. "Inaugural Address: A California for All," January 7, 2019, https://www.gov.ca.gov/2019/01/07/newsom-inaugural-address/.

Newsom, Gavin. "Letter to President Donald J. Trump, Senate Majority Leader Mitch McConnell, Senate Minority Leader Charles E. Schumer, House Speaker Nancy Pelosi, and House Minority Leader Kevin McCarthy," January 7, 2019, https://www.gov.ca.gov/wp-content/uploads/2019/01/1.7.19-Letter-to-the-White-House-and-Congress.pdf.

Newton, Jim. *Justice for All: Earl Warren and the Nation He Made*. New York: Riverhead, 2006.

Nichols, Lee. "One Pol's Stimulus Is Another's Crack Cocaine." *Austin Chronicle*, March 6, 2009: 22.

Nickelsburg, Jerry. "Richer and Poorer: Income Inequality in Los Angeles." UCLA Anderson Forecast, March 2007.

Nickelsburg, Jerry. "Where Does Southern California Aerospace Go from Here?" UCLA Anderson Forecast, September 15, 2006.

Nolette, Paul. *Federalism on Trial: State Attorneys General and National Policymaking in Contemporary America.* Lawrence: University Press of Kansas, 2015.

Nolette, Paul. "State Attorneys General Data: Multistate Litigation Database," n.d., https://attorneysgeneral.org/multistate-lawsuits-vs-the-federal-government/list-of-lawsuits-1980-present/.

Norris, Frank. *The Octopus: A Story of California.* 1901; repr., New York: Penguin Twentieth Century Classics, 1994.

Office of the Historian, U.S. Department of State, Bureau of Public Affairs. "The Immigration Act of 1924 (The Johnson-Reed Act)," https://history.state.gov/milestones/1921-1936/immigration-act.

Office of the Historian, U.S. House of Representatives. "Representatives Apportioned to Each State (1st to 23rd Census, 1790–2010)," https://history.house.gov/.

Olien, Roger. *From Token to Triumph: The Texas Republicans since 1920.* Dallas: SMU Press, 1982.

Olsen, Henry. *The Working Class Republican: Ronald Reagan and the Return of Blue Collar Conservatism.* New York: Broadside Books, 2017.

Olson, Kristin. "My Turn: GOP Is Dead in California. A New Way Must Rise." *CALmatters,* November 13, 2018, https://calmatters.org/articles/commentary/my-turn-gop-is-dead-in-california-a-new-way-must-rise/.

Olson, Walter. "Gay Marriage Is Here to Stay, Even with a Conservative Court." *Wall Street Journal,* July 8, 2018, https://www.wsj.com/articles/gay-marriage-is-here-to-stay-even-with-a-conservative-court-1531074136.

Orshansky, Mollie. "Counting the Poor: Another Look at the Poverty Profile." *Social Security Bulletin,* January 1965, https://www.ssa.gov/policy/docs/ssb/v28n1/v28n1p3.pdf.

Ortiz, Jon. "How the $15 Minimum Wage Will Affect California State Workers." *Sacramento Bee,* April 5, 2016, https://www.sacbee.com/article70139177.html.

Park, John S. W. "Race Discourse and Proposition 187." *Michigan Journal of Race and Law* 2, no. 1 (1996).

Patterson, James. *Congressional Conservatism and the New Deal: The Growth of the Conservative Coalition in Congress, 1933–1939.* Lexington: University of Kentucky Press, 1967.

Pawel, Miriam. *The Browns of California: The Family Dynasty That Transformed a State and Shaped a Nation.* New York: Bloomsbury, 2018.

Paxson, Frederic L. "The Constitution of Texas, 1845." *Southwestern Historical Quarterly* 18, no. 4 (April 1915): 386–98.

Pender, Kathleen. "Governors Howl: Why Tax Plan Would Hammer Blue States." *San Francisco Chronicle,* December 4, 2017, https://www.sfchronicle.com/business/article/Governors-howl-Why-tax-plan-would-hammer-blue-12405179.php.

Pennell, Arden. "Facebook to Move to Stanford Research Park: Some Employees May Remain in Downtown Palo Alto—Neighborhood Part of Firm's 'DNA.'" *Palo Alto Weekly,* August 8, 2008, https://www.paloaltoonline.com/news/2008/08/18/facebook-to-move-to-stanford-research-park.

Perkins, Frances. *The Roosevelt I Knew.* New York: Harper & Row, 1964.

Perlstein, Rick. *Before the Storm: Barry Goldwater and the Unmaking of the American Consensus.* New York: Hill and Wang, 2001.

Perry, Rick. "Letter to Kathleen Sebelius, Secretary of the U.S. Department of Health and Human Services, July 9, 2012," https://www.governing.com/news/state/mct-texas-rick-perry-rejects-medicaid-expansion-state-health-exchange.html.

Persily, Nathaniel A. "The Peculiar Geography of Direct Democracy: Why the Initiative, Referendum, and Recall Developed in the American West." *Michigan Law and Policy Review* 2 (1997): 11–42.

Peters, Gerhard, and John T. Woolley. "American Presidency Project: Elections." Online resource: University of California at Santa Barbara, https://www.presidency.ucsb.edu/statistics/elections.

Petry, Laura, et al. "San Francisco Homeless Count & Survey 2019." Applied Survey Research, http://hsh.sfgov.org/wp-content/uploads/FINAL-PIT-Report-2019-San-Francisco.pdf.

Pew Research Center. "Hispanic Trends: Hispanic Population and Origin in Select U.S. Metropolitan Areas, 2014," September 6, 2016, http://www.pewhispanic.org/interactives/hispanic-population-in-select-u-s-metropolitan-areas/.

Pew Research Center. "Partisanship and Political Animosity in 2016," June 22, 2016, https://www.people-press.org/2016/06/22/partisanship-and-political-animosity-in-2016/.

Pew Research Center. "The Politics of Climate," October 4, 2016, http://www.pewresearch.org/science/2016/10/04/the-politics-of-climate/.

Pew Research Center. "Religious Landscape Study (2014)," May 12, 2015, https://www.pewforum.org/religious-landscape-study/.

Phillips, Leigh. "The New, Safer Nuclear Reactors That Might Help Stop Climate Change." *MIT Technology Review*, February 27, 2019, https://www.technologyreview.com/s/612940/the-new-safer-nuclear-reactors-that-might-help-stop-climate-change/.

Pinto, Pablo, and Ryan Kennedy. "No More Business as Usual for Oil and Gas Companies." Forbes.com, June 28, 2019, https://www.forbes.com/sites/uhenergy/2019/06/28/no-more-business-as-usual-for-oil-and-gas-companies/#737373616794.

Pitney, John J., Jr. "Nixon, California, and American Politics." In *The California Republic: Institutions, Statesmanship, and Policies*, edited by Brian P. Janiskee and Ken Masugi, 219–35. Lanham, MD: Rowman & Littlefield, 2004.

Pla, George L., and David R. Ayón. *Power Shift: How Latinos in California Transformed Politics in America*. Berkeley, CA: Berkeley Public Policy Press, 2018.

Plummer, Brad. "How Retiring Nuclear Power Plants May Undercut U.S. Climate Goals." *New York Times*, June 13, 2017, https://www.nytimes.com/2017/06/13/climate/nuclear-power-retirements-us-climate-goals.html?module=inline.

"Political Competition Is Moderating Texas Republicans." *The Economist*, March 7, 2019, https://www.economist.com/united-states/2019/03/07/political-competition-is-moderating-texas-republicans.

Polsby, Nelson W. *How Congress Evolves: Social Bases of Institutional Change*. New York: Oxford University Press, 2012.

Porter, Michael E. "Clusters and the New Economics of Competition." *Harvard Business Review* (November–December 1998), https://hbr.org/1998/11/clusters-and-the-new-economics-of-competition.

Porter, Michael E. *The Competitive Advantage of Nations*. New York: Free Press, 1990.

Porterfield, Bill. "H. L. Hunt's Long Goodbye." *Texas Monthly*, March 1975, https://www.texasmonthly.com/articles/h-l-hunts-long-goodbye/.

Potts, Charles S. "David S. Terry: The Romantic Story of a Great Texan." *Southwest Review* 19, no. 3 (April 1934): 295–334.

Powe, Lucas A., Jr. *America's Lone Star Constitution: How Cases from Texas Shape the Nation.* Oakland: University of California Press, 2018.

"President: Full Results." CNN, December 12, 2012, http://www.cnn.com/election/2012/results/race/president/#exit-polls.

ProQuest Statistical Abstract of the United States, 2016. Lanham, MD: Rowman and Littlefield, 2016.

Quinn, Arthur. *The Rivals: William Gwin, David Broderick, and the Birth of California.* New York: Crown Publishers, 1994.

Rabinowitz, Kate, and Ashlyn Still. "Democrats Are Dominating State-Level Races: The Party Has Gained Nine 'Trifectas' since 2016." *Washington Post*, November 17, 2019. https://www.washingtonpost.com/graphics/politics/trifecta/.

Radin, Max. "Popular Legislation in California: 1936–1946." *California Law Review* 35, no. 171 (1947): 180.

Ragsdale, Kenneth B. *Centennial '36: The Year America Discovered Texas.* College Station: Texas A&M Press, 1987.

Railroad Commission of Texas. "Crude Oil Production and Well Counts (since 1935): History of Texas Initial Crude Oil, Annual Production, and Producing Wells," July 25, 2019, https://www.rrc.state.tx.us/oil-gas/research-and-statistics/production-data/historical-production-data/crude-oil-production-and-well-counts-since-1935/.

Raines, Howard. "George Wallace, Segregation Symbol, Dies at 79." *New York Times*, September 14, 1998, https://www.nytimes.com/1998/09/14/us/george-wallace-segregation-symbol-dies-at-79.ht.

Ramakrishnan, Karthick. "How Asians Became Democrats." *The American Prospect*, July 26, 2016, https://prospect.org/article/how-asian-americans-became-democrats-0.

Ramirez, Marc. "State Republicans Vote to Censure House Speaker Joe Straus." *Dallas Morning News*, January 27, 2018, https://www.dallasnews.com/news/texas-politics/2018/01/27/state-republicans-vote-censure-house-speaker-joe-straus.

Ramshaw, Emily, and Marilyn Serafini. "Battle Lines Drawn Over Medicaid in Texas." *New York Times*, November 11, 2010, https://www.nytimes.com/2010/11/12/us/politics/12ttmedicaid.html.

Rarick, Ethan. *California Rising: The Life and Times of Pat Brown.* Berkeley and Los Angeles: University of California Press, 2005.

Ratcliffe, Michael, Charlynn Burd, Kelly Holder, and Alison Fields. "Defining Rural at the U.S. Census Bureau." Washington, DC: ACSGEO-1, U.S. Census Bureau, 2016.

Reagan, Ronald. *Public Papers of the President of the United States: Ronald Reagan, 1988–1989.* Book 2. Washington, DC: Office of the Federal Register, 1991.

"Red Flags Ahead." Texas 2036, https://texas2036.org/red-flags/.

Reder, Melvin W. "The Rise and Fall of Unions: The Public Sector and the Private." *Journal of Economic Perspectives* 2, no. 2 (Spring 1988): 89–110 (91).

Reeves, Richard. *Infamy: The Shocking Story of the Japanese-American Internment in World War II.* New York: Henry Holt and Co., 2015.

"Refusing Medicaid Expansion Has Consequences." *Houston Chronicle*, June 4, 2015, https://www.chron.com/opinion/editorials/article/Refusing-Medicaid-expansion-has-consequences-6308050.php.

"Religious Affiliation in Texas: Texas' Largest Religious Bodies." *Texas Almanac.* https://texasalmanac.com/topics/religion/religious-affiliation-texas.

Rendon, Anthony. "Speaker Rendon Statement on Health Care," June 23, 2017, https://speaker.asmdc.org/press-releases/speaker-rendon-statement-health-care.

Rendon, Anthony, and Kevin de León. "Joint Statement from California Legislative Leaders on Result of Presidential Election," November 9, 2016, https://calnonprofits.org/publications/article-archive/514-a-joint-statement-from-our-california-legislative-leaders-on-the-result-of-the-presidential-election.

Repko, Melissa. "Video: Check Out D-FW's Pitch to Bring Amazon's HQ2 to Texas, and See If It Impresses You." *Dallas Morning News*, October 19, 2017, https://www.dallasnews.com/business/technology/2017/10/19/watch-video-dfw-sent-pitch-amazon-actually-reallygood./.

Republican Party of Texas. "2018 Republican Party of Texas Platform," n.d., https://www.texasgop.org/platform/.

"Review and Outlook: Governors vs. Congress: The Stimulus Bill Sets a Long-term Trap for the States." *Wall Street Journal*, February 23, 2009, https://www.wsj.com/articles/SB123535040968044863.

Richardson, James. *Willie Brown: A Biography*. Berkeley: University of California Press, 1996.

Roberts, Sam. "A Rank That Rankles: New York Slips to No. 3; Texas Is Now 2d Most Populous State." *New York Times*, May 19, 1994, B1.

Rogers, Mary Beth. *Turning Texas Blue: What It Will Take to Break the GOP Grip on America's Reddest State*. New York: St. Martin's Press, 2016.

Rojas, Aurelio. "Labor Leader Left Band of Loyalists: State's Democrats Were Shaped by L.A.'s Miguel Contreras." *Sacramento Bee*, May 11, 2005.

Roldan, Riane, and Shannon Najmabadi. "Gov. Greg Abbott Signs Bill Designed to Limit Property Tax Growth." *Texas Tribune*, June 12, 2019.

Roosevelt, Franklin D. "Letter to Mr. Luther C. Steward, President, National Federation of Federal Employees," August 16, 1937, http://www.presidency.ucsb.edu/ws/?pid=15445.

Rorabaugh, W. J. *American Hippies*. New York: Cambridge University Press, 2015.

Rorabaugh, W. J. *Berkeley at War: The 1960s*. New York: Oxford University Press, 1989.

Rose, Shanna. *Financing Medicaid: Federalism and the Growth of America's Health Care Safety Net*. Ann Arbor: University of Michigan Press, 2013.

Rose Institute of State and Local Government. "Miller-Rose Institute Initiative Database: California," http://roseinstitute.org/initiatives/california/.

Rosenberg, Gerald N. *The Hollow Hope: Can Courts Bring About Social Change?* Chicago: University of Chicago Press, 1991.

Ross, Jean. "The Largest Tax Increase in History?" California Budget and Policy Center, March 29, 2011, https://calbudgetcenter.org/blog/the-largest-tax-state-increase-in-history/.

Ross, Steven J. *Hollywood Left and Right: How Movie Stars Shaped American Politics*. New York: Oxford University Press, 2011.

Rudowitz, Robin, Elizabeth Hinton, and Larisa Antonisse. "Medicaid Enrollment and Spending Growth: FY 2018 and 2019." Henry J. Kaiser Family Foundation, October 2018, http://files.kff.org/attachment/Issue-Brief-Medicaid-Enrollment-and-Spending-Growth-FY-2018-2019.

Samuels, Alex. "Lt. Gov. Dan Patrick on Outgoing House Speaker Joe Straus: 'He's Not Much of a Republican.'" *Texas Tribune*, November 8, 2018, https://www.texastribune.org/2018/11/08/texas-senate-lieutenant-governor-dan-patrick-joe-straus-midterms/.

Sanchez, Gabriel, and Matt A. Barreto. "In Record Numbers, Latinos Voted Overwhelmingly against Trump." *Washington Post*, November 11, 2016, https://www.washingtonpost.com/news/monkey-cage/wp/2016/11/11/in-record-numbers-latinos-voted-overwhelmingly-against-trump-we-did-the-research/.

Sandmeyer, Elmer Clarence. *The Anti-Chinese Movement in California.* 1939; repr. Urbana and Chicago: University of Illinois Press, 1991.

San Francisco Board of Supervisors. "Resolution Declaring the National Rifle Association as a Domestic Terrorist Organization," September 3, 2019, https://sfgov.legistar.com/View.ashx?M=F&ID=7568748&GUID=DF64490F-D8BC-4BF7-A43D-287F02BECCCA.

"San Francisco Proposition C, Gross Receipts Tax for Homelessness Services (November 2018)." Ballotpedia, n.d., https://ballotpedia.org/San_Francisco,_California,_Proposition_C,_Gross_Receipts_Tax_for_Homelessness_Services_(November_2018).

Satija, Neena, Lindsay Carbonell, and Ryan McCrimmon. "Texas vs. the Feds—A Look at the Lawsuits." *Texas Tribune*, January 17, 2017, https://www.texastribune.org/2017/01/17/texas-federal-government-lawsuits/.

Saxenian, Annalee. *Regional Advantage: Culture and Competition in Silicon Valley and Route 128.* Cambridge, MA: Harvard University Press, 1994.

Scammon, Richard M., and Ben J. Wattenberg. *The Real Majority: An Extraordinary Examination of the American Electorate.* New York: Coward-McCann, Inc., 1970.

Scheiber, Harry N. "The Liberal Court: Ascendancy and Crisis." In *Constitutional Governance and Judicial Power: The History of the California Supreme Court*, edited by Harry N. Scheiber, 327–513. Berkeley, CA: Berkeley Public Policy Press, 2016.

Schaub, Michael. "Lawrence Wright Says Texas and California Are Mirror Image Twins." *Los Angeles Times*, April 12, 2018, http://www.latimes.com/books/la-ca-jc-lawrence-wright-20180412-htmlstory.html.

Schlafly, Phyllis. *A Choice Not an Echo: The Inside Story of How Americans Are Chosen.* Alton, IL: Pere Marquette Press, 1964.

Schrag, Peter. *Paradise Lost: California's Experience, America's Future.* Berkeley: University of California Press, 2004.

Scotland, Arthur G. "The Landmark Abortion Decisions: Justifiable Termination or Miscarriage of Justice?—Proposals for Legislative Response." *Pacific Law Journal* 4 (1973): 821.

Scott, Allen J. *On Hollywood.* Princeton, NJ: Princeton University Press, 2005.

Scott, Allen J. *Technopolis: High-Technology Industry and Regional Development in Southern California.* Berkeley: University of California Press, 1993.

Sears, David O., and Jack Citrin. *Tax Revolt: Something for Nothing in California*, enl. ed. Cambridge, MA: Harvard University Press, 1985.

Semega, Jessica, Melissa Kollar, John Creamer, and Abinash Mohanty. "Income and Poverty in the United States: 2018." U.S. Census Bureau, September 2019, https://www.census.gov/content/dam/Census/library/publications/2019/demo/p60-266.pdf.

Shermer, Elizabeth Tandy. "Counter-Organizing the Sunbelt: Right to Work Campaigns and Anti-Union Conservatism, 1943–1958." *Pacific Historical Review* 78, no. 1 (2009): 81–118.

Sheskin, Ira M., and Arnold Dashefsky, eds. "Jewish Population in the United States, 2014." In *American Jewish Yearbook*, 143–211. Dordrecht: Springer, 2014.

Siders, David. "Jerry Brown's Climate Warning: 'We Are Talking about Extinction.'" *Sacramento Bee*, July 21, 2015, https://www.sacbee.com/news/politics-government/capitol-alert/article27998554.html.

Sinclair, Upton. "Immediate EPIC: The Final Statement of the Plan." SSA History Archives, https://www.ssa.gov/history/epic.html.

Skelton, George. "In Blocking a Bad Single-Payer Bill, Assembly Speaker Anthony Rendon Was Not 'Cowardly,'—Quite the Opposite." *Los Angeles Times*, June 29, 2017, https://www.latimes.com/politics/la-pol-sac-skelton-anthony-rendon-single-payer-obamacare-20170629-story.html.

Skelton, George, and Douglas P. Shuit. "Sales Tax Sought for Quake Relief: Deukmejian and Legislative Leaders Agree on a Proposal for a Quarter-cent Increase for 13 Months." *Los Angeles Times*, October 31, 1989, http://articles.latimes.com/1989-10-31/news/mn-284_1_sales-tax-increase.

Skerry, Peter. *Mexican Americans: The Ambivalent Minority.* Cambridge, MA: Harvard University Press, 1995.

Skocpol, Theda. *Protecting Soldiers and Mothers: The Political Origins of Social Policy in the United States.* Cambridge, MA: Belknap Press, 1995.

Slater, Wayne. "Atty Gen Greg Abbott Says His Job Is Simple: Sue the Federal Government, Then Go Home." *Dallas Morning News*, June 6, 2012, https://www.dallasnews.com/news/politics/2012/06/07/atty-gen-greg-abbott-says-his-job-is-simple-sue-the-federal-government-then-go-home.

Smith, Daniel A. *Tax Crusaders and the Politics of Direct Democracy.* New York: Routledge, 1998.

"SOS Initiative: Costly, Mean and Wrong." *San Francisco Chronicle*, October 16, 1994.

Stanford Institute for Economic Policy Research. "California Pension Tracker," http://www.pensiontracker.org/.

Stark, John O. "The Establishment of Wisconsin's Income Tax." *Wisconsin Magazine of History* 71, no. 1 (Autumn 1987): 27–45.

Starr, Kevin. *Americans and the California Dream, 1850–1915.* New York: Oxford University Press, 1973.

Starr, Kevin. *Coast of Dreams: California on the Edge.* New York: Alfred A. Knopf, 2004.

Starr, Kevin. *Endangered Dreams: The Great Depression in California.* New York: Oxford University Press, 1996.

Starr, Kevin. *Golden Dreams: California in an Age of Abundance.* New York: Oxford University Press, 2009.

Starr, Kevin. *Inventing the Dream: California through the Progressive Era.* New York: Oxford University Press, 1986.

Stegner, Wallace. "California: The Experimental Society." *Saturday Review*, September 23, 1967, 28.

Steinbeck, John. *Travels with Charley in Search of America.* 1961; repr. New York: Penguin, 2017.

Sterba, James P. "Democratic Vote Propels Reagan to Texas Sweep." *New York Times*, May 3, 1976, A–1.

Stern, Alexandra Minna. *Eugenic Nation: Faults and Frontiers of Better Breeding in Modern America.* Berkeley: University of California Press, 2005.

Stockwell, Marvel M. "The Income Tax in California." *Bulletin National Tax Association* 31, no. 9 (June 1946): 257, 271–83.

Storper, Michael, Thomas Kemeny, Naji P. Makarem, and Taner Osman. *The Rise and Fall of Urban Economies: Lessons from San Francisco and Los Angeles.* Stanford, CA: Stanford Business Books, 2015.

Storper, Michael, and Allen J. Scott. "Rethinking Human Capital, Creativity, and Urban Growth." *Journal of Economic Geography* 9 (2009): 147–67.

Sturgeon, Timothy J. "How Silicon Valley Came to Be." In *Understanding Silicon Valley: The Anatomy of and Entrepreneurial Region*, edited by Martin Kenney, 15–47. Stanford, CA: Stanford University Press, 2000.

Suich Bass, Alexandra. "California and Texas Are Both Failing Their Neediest Citizens." *The Economist*, June 20, 2019, https://www.economist.com/special-report/2019/06/20/california-and-texas-are-both-failing-their-neediest-citizens.

Suich Bass, Alexandra. "California and Texas Have Different Visions for America's Future." *The Economist*, June 20, 2019, https://www.economist.com/technology-quarterly/2019/06/20/california-and-texas-have-different-visions-for-americas-future.

Suich Bass, Alexandra. "Many People Are Moving from California to Texas: The Cost of Living, as Well as High Taxes and Red Tape, Are Precipitating the Push." *The Economist*, June 20, 2019, https://www.economist.com/special-report/2019/06/20/many-people-are-moving-from-california-to-texas.

Suich Bass, Alexandra. "Peak Valley: Silicon Valley Will Lose Some of Its Lustre," The World in 2019. *The Economist,* https://worldin2019.economist.com/siliconvalleylosesitsshine.

Suro, Robert. "California Dreaming: The New Dynamism in Immigration Federalism and Opportunities for Inclusion on a Variegated Landscape." *Journal on Migration and Human Security* 3, no. 1 (2015): 1–25.

Suro, Roberto, Richard Fry, and Jeffrey Passel. "Hispanics and the 2004 Election: Population, Electorate, and Voters: How Latinos Voted in 2004." Washington, DC: Pew Hispanic Center (June 27, 2005), https://www.pewhispanic.org/2005/06/27/iv-how-latinos-voted-in-2004/.

Tarr, G. Alan. "Laboratories of Democracy?: Brandeis, Federalism, and Scientific Management." *Publius*, 31, no. 1 (Winter 2001): 37–46.

Tarrant, David, and María Méndez. "What Are the Gun Laws in Texas, and What's Changing Sept. 1?" *Dallas Morning News*, August 9, 2019, https://www.dallasnews.com/news/2019/08/09/what-are-the-gun-laws-in-texas-and-what-s-changing-sept-1/.

Tax Foundation. "Facts and Figures: How Does Your State Compare?" (2019). https://files.taxfoundation.org/20190715165329/Facts-Figures-2019-How-Does-Your-State-Compare.pdf.

Tax Policy Center. "Property Tax Revenue," https://www.taxpolicycenter.org/statistics/property-tax-revenue; California State Controller's Office, "Property Tax Financial Data [Fiscal Year 2017–2018]." https://propertytax.bythenumbers.sco.ca.gov/#!/year/default.

Taylor, Mac. "California's High Housing Costs: Causes and Consequences." Legislative Analyst's Office, March 17, 2015: 10–20, https://lao.ca.gov/reports/2015/finance/housing-costs/housing-costs.pdf.

Terner Center for Housing Innovation. "Curbing Runaway Rents: Assessing the Impact of a Rent Cap" (July 2019), https://ternercenter.berkeley.edu/curbing-runaway-rents.

Texas Demographic Center. "Age, Sex, and Race/Ethnicity (ASRE) Population, by Age Group for 2010–2050 in 1 year Increments," last modified 2018, https://demographics.texas.gov/Data/TPEPP/Projections/.

Texas Demographic Center. "Population Projections for the State of Texas (2010–2050)," State_of_Texas.csv (2020), https://demographics.texas.gov/Data/TPEPP/Projections/.

Texas Historical Commission. "1936 Texas Centennial Markers," n.d., http://www.thc. texas.gov. /preserve/projects-and-programs/state-historical-markers/1936-texas-centennial-markers.

"Texas Income Tax, Proposition 4 (1993)." Ballotpedia, n.d., https://ballotpedia.org/ Texas_Income_Tax,_Proposition_4_(1993).

Texas Legislative Budget Board. "Constitutional Limitations on Spending," presented to the House Appropriations Committee, January 2019, https://www.lbb.state.tx.us/ Documents/Publications/Presentation/5671_spen.pdf.

Texas Legislative Budget Board. "Summary of Legislative Budget Estimates, 2020–2021 Biennium: House" (January 2019): 56–58, http://www.lbb.state.tx.us/Documents/ Appropriations_Bills/86/LBB_Recommended_House/5492_House_LBE_Bill_ Summary.pdf.

Texas Legislative Council. "Amendments to the Texas Constitution since 1876." Austin, TX: Texas Legislative Council (May 2018), http://www.tlc.state.tx.us/docs/ amendments/Constamend1876.pdf.

Texas Legislature Online. "SB 6: 85th Texas Legislature Regular Session" (2017), https:// capitol.texas.gov/billlookup/History.aspx?LegSess=85R&Bill=SB6.

Texas Office of the Secretary of State. "Race Summary Report, 2018 General Election, November 6, 2018," https://elections.sos.state.tx.us/elchist331_state.htm.

Texas Right to Life. "Active State Laws," https://www.texasrighttolife.com/active-state-laws/.

Texas State Law Library. "Gun Laws," https://guides.sll.texas.gov/gun-laws.

Thomas, Mike W. "Texas Takes the Lead in Technology Exports." *San Antonio Business Journal*, February 11, 2014, https://www.bizjournals.com/sanantonio/blog/2014/02/ texas-takes-the-lead-in-technology-exports.html.

Thompson, Don. "California Attorney General Leads Trump Resistance into 2019." *AP News*, January 4, 2019, https://www.apnews.com/2a41bfdffd344b3a954a98bd44bd9ac9.

Thompson, Edward J., Jr. "California Agricultural Land Loss & Conservation: The Basic Facts." American Farmland Trust, 2009, https://4aa2dc132bb150caf1aa-7bb737f4349b47aa42dce777a72d5264.ssl.cf5.rackcdn.com/aft-ca-agricultural-land-loss-basic-facts_11-23-09.pdf https://www.cdfa.ca.gov/statistics/.

Thorburn, Wayne. *Red State: An Insider's Story of How the GOP Came to Dominate Texas Politics*. Austin: University of Texas Press, 2014.

Tilove, Jonathan. "Amid Trump-Koch Feud, Abbott Talks Texas v. California." *Austin American-Statesman*, August 4, 2018, https://www.statesman.com/news/20180804/ amid-trump-koch-feud-abbott-talks-texas-v-california.

Tilove, Jonathan. "Gov-elect Abbott: End Ban on Bags, Fracking, Tree Cutting." *Austin American-Statesman*, September 24, 2016, https://www.statesman.com/news/ 20160924/gov-elect-abbott-end-local-bans-on-bags-fracking-tree-cutting.de Tocqueville, Alexis. *Democracy in America*. Trans. George Lawrence, ed. J. P. Mayer. New York: Perennial Classics, 2000.

Todd, David A., and Jonathan Ogren. *The Texas Landscape Project: Nature and People*. College Station: Texas A&M Press, 2016.

Torget, Andrew J. *Seeds of Empire: Cotton, Slavery, and the Transformation of the Texas Borderlands, 1800–1850*. Chapel Hill: University of North Carolina Press, 2015.

Traynor, Roger John, and Frank M. Keesling. "The Scope and Nature of the California Income Tax." *California Law Review* 24, no. 5 (July 1936): 493–511.

"Treaty of Peace, Friendship, Limits, and Settlement between the United States of America and the United Mexican States," concluded at Guadalupe Hidalgo, February 2, 1848; ratification advised by Senate, with amendments, March 10, 1848; ratified by president, March 16, 1848; ratifications exchanged at Queretaro, May 30, 1848; proclaimed July 4, 1848, http://avalon.law.yale.edu/19th_century/guadhida.asp.

Trump, Donald J. "The Mexico City Policy." *Federal Register* 82, no. 15 (January 25, 2017): 8495, https://www.federalregister.gov/documents/2017/01/25/2017-01843/the-mexico-city-policy.

Turner, Fred. *From Counterculture to Cyberculture: Stewart Brand, the Whole Earth Network, and the Rise of Digital Utopianism.* Chicago: University of Chicago Press, 2006.

U.C. Hastings Law Library. California Ballot Measures Database, https://www.uchastings.edu/academics/library/ca-ballots/.

Uhler, Brian, and Justin Garosi. "California Losing Residents via Domestic Migration." California Legislative Analyst's Office, February 21, 2018.

University of Virginia Weldon Cooper Center, Demographics Research Group. "National Population Projections 2018," https://demographics.coopercenter.org/national-population-projections.

Ura, Alexa. "How Texas Killed Welfare: 'We Spend Our Dollars on Anything but Poor Families." *The Guardian,* November 30, 2017, https://www.theguardian.com/us-news/2017/nov/30/texas-welfare-spending-poor-families.

U.S. Advisory Commission on Intergovernmental Relations. "Significant Features of Fiscal Federalism, Vol. I: Budget Processes and Tax Systems" (1993), 34.

U.S. Archives and Records Administration, "U.S. Electoral College: Historical Election Results," https://www.archives.gov/federal-register/electoral-college/votes/votes_by_state.html.

U.S. Census Bureau. "The 15 Most Populous Cities, July 1, 2016," https://www.census.gov/content/dam/Census/newsroom/releases/2017/cb17-81-table3-most-populous.pdf.

U.S. Census Bureau. "2010 Census: Center of Population," https://www.census.gov/2010census/data/center-of-population.html.

U.S. Census Bureau. "2017 Annual Survey of State Government Finances" (ASFIN 2017), October 31, 2019, https://www.census.gov/data/tables/2017/econ/state/historical-tables.html.

U.S. Census Bureau. "2017 State Government Tax Tables," last revised June 19, 2019, https://www.census.gov/data/tables/2017/econ/stc/2017-annual.html.

U.S. Census Bureau. "2018 Annual Survey of State Tax Collections," June 11, 2019, https://www.census.gov/data/tables/2018/econ/stc/2018-annual.html.

U.S. Census Bureau. "2018 Annual Survey of Public Pensions: State and Local Tables," June 16, 2019, https://www.census.gov/data/tables/2018/econ/aspp/aspp-historical-tables.html.

U.S. Census Bureau. "American Factfinder: Demographic and Housing Estimates, 2013–2017 American Community Survey, 5-Year Estimates," https://factfinder.census.gov/faces/tableservices/jsf/pages/productview.xhtml?pid=ACS_17_5YR_DP05&prodType=table.

U.S. Census Bureau. "American Factfinder": Texas and California (2019), https://factfinder.census.gov.

U.S. Census Bureau. American Factfinder for Texas and California, 2000 and 2010.

U.S. Census Bureau. *Fifteenth Census of the United States, 1930,* Vol. II.

U.S. Census Bureau. *Fifteenth Census of the United States, 1930*, Vol. II, Table 11: "Color or Race and Nativity, by Divisions and States: 1930."

U.S. Census Bureau. "Florida Passes New York to Become the Nation's Third Most Populous State, Census Bureau Reports," December 23, 2014, https://www.census.gov/newsroom/press-releases/2014/cb14-232.html.

U.S. Census Bureau. *Fourteenth Census of the United States, 1920*, Vol. II, Table 11: "Distribution, by State of Residence, of Population Born in the Principal Foreign Countries: 1920, 1910, and 1900."

U.S. Census Bureau. *Government Finance and Employment Classification Manual* (2006), https://www2.census.gov/govs/pubs/classification/2006_classification_manual.pdf.

U.S. Census Bureau. "Measuring America: Our Changing Landscape," December 8, 2016, https://www.census.gov/content/dam/Census/library/visualizations/2016/comm/acs-rural-urban.pdf.

U.S. Census Bureau. "QuickFacts: California," July 1, 2019, https://www.census.gov/quickfacts/ca.

U.S. Census Bureau. "QuickFacts: Maryland," July 1, 2019, https://www.census.gov/quickfacts/md.

U.S. Census Bureau. "QuickFacts: Texas," July 1, 2019, https://www.census.gov/quickfacts/tx.

U.S. Census Bureau. "Statistical Abstract of the United States, 2012: Population," https://www.census.gov/library/publications/2011/compendia/statab/131ed/population.html.

U.S. Census Bureau. "Statistical Abstract of the United States, 2012: Table 77: Christian Church Adherents and Jewish Population, States," https://www2.census.gov/library/publications/2011/compendia/statab/131ed/tables/pop.pdf.

U.S. Census Bureau. "Urban/Rural and Metropolitan/Nonmetropolitan Population: 2000—State—Urban/Rural and Inside/Outside Metropolitan Area," https://factfinder.census.gov/faces/tableservices/jsf/pages/productview.xhtml?pid=DEC_00_SF1_GCTP1.ST93&prodType=table.

U.S. Census Bureau. "Voting and Registration Tables [2006–2018]," https://www.census.gov/topics/public-sector/voting/data/tables.All.html.

U.S. Department of Agriculture Food and Nutrition Service. "Supplemental Nutrition Assistance Program (SNAP): SNAP Community Characteristics," August 20, 2019, https://www.fns.usda.gov/ops/snap-community-characteristics.

U.S. Department of Commerce, Bureau of Economic Analysis. "GDP by State," July 3, 2019. https://www.bea.gov/data/gdp/gdp-state.

U.S. Department of Health and Human Services, Office of Family Assistance. "Annual Update of the HHS Poverty Guidelines," *Federal Register*, Vol. 85, no. 12: 3060, January 17, 2020, https://www.govinfo.gov/content/pkg/FR-2020-01-17/pdf/2020-00858.pdf.

U.S. Department of Health and Human Services, Office of Family Assistance. "TANF and MOE Spending and Transfers by Activity, FY 2017 (Contains National & State Pie Charts)," February 6, 2019, https://www.acf.hhs.gov/sites/default/files/ofa/fy2017_tanf_and_moe_state_piechart_508.pdf.

U.S. Department of Labor, Bureau of Labor Statistics. "Characteristics of Minimum Wage Workers, 2018," March 2019, https://www.bls.gov/opub/reports/minimum-wage/2018/pdf/home.pdf.

U.S. Department of Labor, Bureau of Labor Statistics. "Economic News Release: Union Members Summary," January 18, 2019. https://www.bls.gov/news.release/union2.nr0.htm.

U.S. Department of Labor, Bureau of Labor Statistics. "May 2018 State Occupational Employment and Wage Estimates, California and Texas," April 2, 2019 (California: https://www.bls.gov/oes/current/oes_ca.htm; Texas: https://www.bls.gov/oes/current/oes_tx.htm#00-0000).

U.S. Department of Labor, Bureau of Labor Statistics. "Quarterly Census of Employment and Wages: State Government: All States and U.S., 2018 Annual Average," last updated January 2, 2020, https://data.bls.gov/cew/apps/table_maker/v4/table_maker.htm#type =0&year=2018&qtr=A&own=2&ind=10&supp=0.

U.S. Energy Information Administration. "State Energy Consumption Estimates: 1960– 2017," June 2019, https://www.eia.gov/state/seds/archive/seds2017.pdf.

U.S. Energy Information Administration. "Texas: State Profile and Energy Estimates," n.d., https://www.eia.gov/state/?sid=TX#tabs-4.

U.S. Energy Information Administration. "U.S. Energy Facts Explained," August 28, 2019, https://www.eia.gov/energyexplained/us-energy-facts/.

U.S. Energy Information Administration. "What Is U.S. Electricity Generation by Source?" October 25, 2019, https://www.eia.gov/tools/faqs/faq.php?id=427&t=3.

U.S. Energy Information Administration, "Texas State Energy Profile," March 19, 2020, https://www.eia.gov/state/print.php?sid+TX#37.

U.S. Environmental Protection Agency. "California State Motor Vehicle Pollution Control Standards; Notice of Decision Denying a Waiver of Clean Air Act Preemption for California's 2009 and Subsequent Model Year Greenhouse Gas Emission Standards for New Motor Vehicles." *Federal Register* 73, no. 45 (March 6, 2008): 12156–69.

U.S. Environmental Protection Agency. "California State Motor Vehicle Pollution Control Standards; Notice of Decision Granting a Waiver of Clean Air Act Preemption for California's 2009 and Subsequent Model Year Greenhouse Gas Emission Standards for New Motor Vehicles." *Federal Register* 74, no. 129 (July 8, 2009): 32743–84.

U.S. Environmental Protection Agency. "EPA Administrator Pruitt: GHG Emissions Standards for Cars and Light Trucks Should Be Revised," April 2, 2018, https://www.epa.gov/newsreleases/epa-administrator-pruitt-ghg-emissions-standards-cars-and-light-trucks-should-be.

U.S. Environmental Protection Agency and National Highway Traffic Safety Administration. "2017 and Later Model Year Light-Duty Vehicle Greenhouse Gas Emissions and Corporate Average Fuel Economy Standards." *Federal Register* 77, no. 199 (October 15, 2012): 62624–3200.

U.S. Social Security Administration. "Vote Tallies for Passage of Medicare in 1965," https://www.ssa.gov/history/tally65.html.

Vander Meulen, Jacob. "West Coast Labor and the Military Aircraft Industry, 1935–1941." *Pacific Northwest Quarterly* 88, no. 2 (Spring 1997): 82–92.

Varner, Charles, and Cristobal Young. "Millionaire Migration in California: The Impact of Top Tax Rates." Working Paper, Stanford University Center on Poverty and Inequality, Stanford, CA (2012), https://inequality.stanford.edu/sites/default/files/millionaire-migration-california-impact-top-tax-rates.pdf.

Vogel, David. *California Greenin': How the Golden State Became an Environmental Leader.* Princeton, NJ: Princeton University Press, 2018.

Volanto, Keith. "The Far Right in Texas Politics During the Roosevelt Era." In *The Texas Right: The Radical Roots of Lone Star Conservatism*, edited by David O'Donald Cullen and Kyle G. Wilkison, 68–86. College Station: Texas A&M Press, 2014.

"Vote for Governor: Wilson vs. Kathleen Brown." *California Poll 93-02*: May 14 1993–May 22, 1993.

Vyse, Graham. "Democrats Win Control of Six More States. What Will They Do with It?" *Governing*, November 7, 2018, http://www.governing.com/topics/politics/gov-2018-state-legislative-race-results.

Walczak, Jared, Scott Drenkard, and Joseph Bishop-Henchman. "2019 State Business Climate Index." The Tax Foundation, September 26, 2018, https://taxfoundation.org/publications/state-business-tax-climate-index/.

Walker, Jack L. "The Diffusion of Innovation among the American States." *American Political Science Review* 63 (September 1969): 880–89.

Walsh, Mary Williams. "In Texas, Some Rare Good News about Cities with Pension Woes." *New York Times*, June 1, 2017, www.nytimes.com/2017/06/01/business/dealbook/municipal-pensions-dallas-houston-bankruptcy.html.

Walsh, Sean Collins. "After Standing Up Biz Group, Lt. Gov Dan Patrick Lobs Bombs Their Way." *Austin American-Statesman*, February 9, 2018, https://www.mystatesman.com/news/state--regional-govt--politics/after-standing-biz-group-gov-dan-patrick-lobs-bombs-their-way/q91CYJvGjAPL3zj4MJl9rM/.

Walters, Dan. "How the New Los Angeles Has Reshaped California Politics." In *The New Political Geography of California*, edited by Frederick Douzet, Thad Kousser, and Kenneth P. Miller. Berkeley, CA: Berkeley Public Policy Press, 2008, 197–212.

Walters, Dan. "Jerry Brown Honors the Principle of Subsidiarity Sometimes." *Sacramento Bee*, October 5, 2014, https://www.sacbee.com/news/politics-government/politics-columns-blogs/dan-walters/article2620620.html.

Walters, Dan. "The Politics of Slow Population Growth." *CalMatters*, December 12, 2020, https://calmatters.org/commentary/census-population-congressional-slow/.

Warner, Joel. "Reed Hastings: Netflix CEO Goes Nuclear on Public Schools." *Capital and Main*, November 1, 2018, https://capitalandmain.com/reed-hastings-the-disrupter-1101.

Weisberg, Lori, and Jonathan Horn. "Another SD Firm Moving to Texas." *San Diego Union-Tribune*, July 18, 2014, https://www.sandiegouniontribune.com/business/economy/sdut-rick-perry-omnitracs-texas-enterprise-fund-jobs-2014jul18-story.html.

Wellock, Thomas Raymond. *Critical Masses: Opposition to Nuclear Power in California, 1958–1978*. Madison: University of Wisconsin Press, 1998.

Wheeling, Kate, and Max Ufberg. "The Ocean Is Boiling: The Complete Oral History of the 1969 Santa Barbara Oil Spill." *Pacific Standard*, April 18, 2017, https://psmag.com/news/the-ocean-is-boiling-the-complete-oral-history-of-the-1969-santa-barbara-oil-spill.

White, G. Edward. *Earl Warren: A Public Life*. New York: Oxford University Press, 1982.

Whitehead, Seth. "Fracking, 10 Years Later: Its Benefits Far Outweigh Its Risks." *Washington Examiner*, August 28, 2018, https://www.washingtonexaminer.com/opinion/op-eds/fracking-ten-years-later-its-benefits-far-outweigh-its-risks.

"Why Start-ups Are Leaving Silicon Valley." *The Economist*, August 30, 2018, https://www.economist.com/leaders/2018/08/30/why-startups-are-leaving-silicon-valley.

Wiehe, Meg, et al. "Who Pays?: A Distributional Analysis of the Tax Systems in All 50 States." 6th ed. Washington, DC: Institute on Taxation and Economic Policy [ITEP], October 2018, https://itep.org/wp-content/uploads/whopays-ITEP-2018.pdf.

Wiener, Anna. "The Complicated Legacy of Stewart Brand's 'Whole Earth Catalog.'" *The New Yorker*, November 16, 2018, https://www.newyorker.com/news/letter-from-silicon-valley/the-complicated-legacy-of-stewart-brands-whole-earth-catalog.

Wildermuth, John. "Gov. Brown Clashes with Environmentalists over Fracking." *San Francisco Chronicle*, May 16, 2017, https://www.sfchronicle.com/science/article/Gov-Brown-clashes-with-environmentalists-over-11151180.php.

Wilford, John Noble. "Men Walk on Moon." *New York Times*, July 21, 1969, A–1.

Wilkerson, Isabel. *The Warmth of Other Suns: The Epic Story of America's Great Migration.* New York: Random House, 2010.

Williams, Daniel K. *Defenders of the Unborn: The Pro-life Movement before Roe v. Wade.* New York: Oxford University Press, 2016.

Williams, Daniel K. *God's Own Party: The Making of the Christian Right.* New York: Oxford University Press, 2010.

Williams, Robert F. *The Law of American State Constitutions.* New York: Oxford University Press, 2009.

Wilson, James Q. *The Amateur Democrat: Club Politics in Three Cities.* Chicago: University of Chicago Press, 1962.

Winkler, Adam. "The Secret History of Guns." *The Atlantic*, September 2011, https://www.theatlantic.com/magazine/archive/2011/09/the-secret-history-of-guns/308608/.

Winkler, Amber M., Janie Scull, and Dara Zeehandelaar. "How Strong Are U.S. Teachers Unions?: A State-by-State Comparison." Thomas B. Fordham Institute, October 2012, https://files.eric.ed.gov/fulltext/ED537563.pdf.

Witte, John F. *The Politics and Development of the Federal Income Tax.* rev. ed. Madison: University of Wisconsin Press, 1986.

Wolch, Jennifer, and Michael Dear. *Malign Neglect: Homelessness in an American City.* San Francisco: Jossey-Bass, 1993.

Womack, Brian. "Charles Schwab to Move HQ to DFW from San Francisco after TD Ameritrade Acquisition." *Dallas Business Journal*, November 25, 2019, https://www.bizjournals.com/dallas/news/2019/11/25/charles-schwab-dfw-td-ameritrade.html.

Woodard, Colin. *American Nations: A History of the Eleven Rival Regional Cultures of North America.* New York: Penguin, 2011.

The World Bank. "Population Growth (Annual %)" (2019), https://data.worldbank.org/indicator/SP.POP.GROW?contextual=default&locations=US-OE&name_desc=false.

Wright, Lawrence. "America's Future Is Texas." *The New Yorker*, June 10 & 17, 2017, https://www.newyorker.com/magazine/2017/07/10/americas-future-is-texas.

Wright, Lawrence. "The Dark Bounty of Texas Oil." *The New Yorker*, December 25, 2017, https://www.newyorker.com/magazine/2018/01/01/the-dark-bounty-of-texas-oil.

Wright, Lawrence. *God Save Texas: A Journey into the Soul of the Lone Star State.* New York: Knopf, 2018.

Wuthnow, Robert. *Rough Country: How Texas Became America's Most Powerful Bible-Belt State.* Princeton, NJ: Princeton University Press, 2014.

Xia, Rosanna. "Coastal Commission on Trump's Offshore Drilling Plan: Ain't Gonna Happen," February 8, 2018, https://www.latimes.com/local/lanow/la-me-california-offshore-drilling-20180208-story.html.

Yergin, Daniel. *The Prize: The Epic Quest for Oil, Money, and Power.* New York: Touchstone, 1992.

Young, Cristobal, Charles Varner, Ithai Z. Lurie, and Richard Prisinzano. "Millionaire Migration and Taxation of the Elite: Evidence from Administrative Data." *American Sociological Review* 81, no. 3 (2016): 421–46, http://journals.sagepub.com/doi/pdf/10.1177/0003122416639625#.

Young, Stephen. "Texas Lawmakers Leading the Anti-Abortion Effort Take a Gentler, More Tactical Approach." *Texas Observer*, May 22, 2019, https://www.dallasobserver.com/news/texas-lawmakers-arent-going-soft-on-abortion-theyre-going-tactical-11669327.

Zacchino, Narda. *California Comeback: How a "Failed State" Became a Model for the Nation*. New York: St. Martin's Press, 2016.

Zelinsky, Wilbur. *The Cultural Geography of the United States*. Edgewood Cliffs, NJ: Prentice Hall, 1973.

"Zillow Home Value Index." Zillow.com (2019), https://www.zillow.com/ca/home-values/; https://www.zillow.com/home-values/; https://www.zillow.com/tx/home-values/.

Index

For the benefit of digital users, indexed terms that span two pages (e.g., 52–53) may, on occasion, appear on only one of those pages.

Tables and figures are indicated by *t* and *f* following the page number